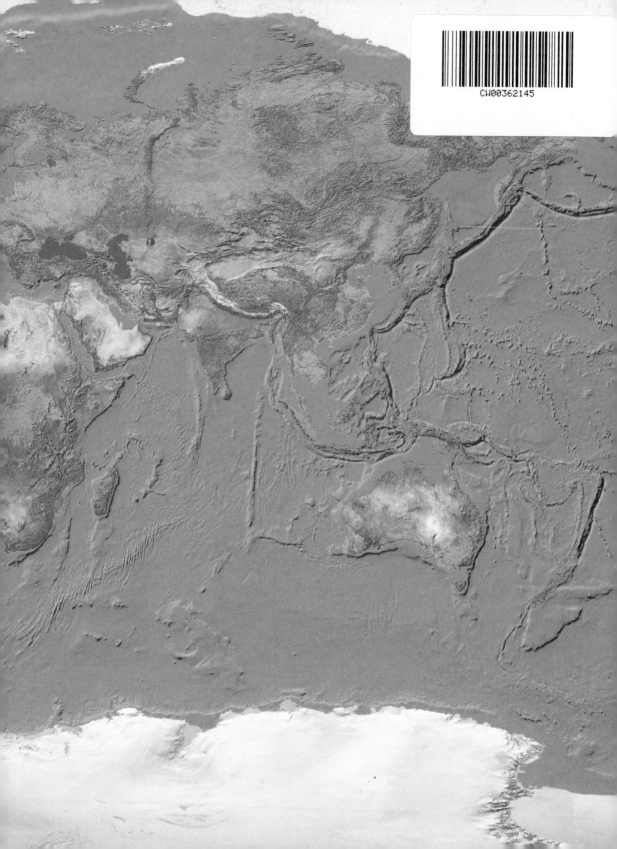

CONCISE
TWO-IN-ONE
WORLD
ATLAS

The Concise Two-in-One World Atlas
English Language Edition

Published by AND Cartographic Publishers Ltd.
Alberto House, Hogwood Lane
Finchampstead, Berks, RG40 4RF
United Kingdom

www: http://www.and.com

First edition 2000
2000 © AND Cartographic Publishers Ltd.
Finchampstead, UK
2000 © WorldSat International Inc.
Ontario, Canada

ISBN 1-84178-020-0
HRR
987654321

Cartographic production, design and layout:
AND Cartographic Publishers Ltd., Finchampstead, UK

Production of satellite imagery:
Robert Stacey, WorldSat International Inc.
Ontario, Canada; Jim Knighton
Satellite data: NOAA
Ocean floor bathymetry by NOAA courtesy of USGS
Images on pages 32, 34, 36, 38 based on
Resurs satellite imagery, provided by Satellus Ab of Kiruna, Sweden

Printed in Spain

CONCISE
TWO-IN-ONE
WORLD
ATLAS

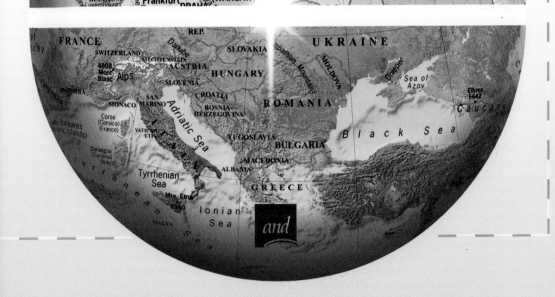

and

Contents

Key map and legend   **6**

Aspects of the World   **8-21**

Population   10

Land use and minerals   12

Energy   14

Economy   16

Defence   18

Time zones   20

Maps of the World   **22-112**

Europe

Europe   24
1:39 400 000

Scandinavia   26
1:11 300 000

Central Europe   28
1:6 750 000

Germany   30
1:5 050 000

Benelux   32
1:4 500 000

British Isles   34
1:6 750 000

France   36
1:6 750 000

Spain and Portugal   38
1:6 750 000

The Alpine States   40
1:5 050 000

Italy   42
1:6 750 000

The Balkans   44
1:6 750 000

Greece and
   Western Turkey   46
1:6 750 000

European Russia   48
1:20 300 000

Asia

Asia   50
1:64 200 000

Northwest Asia   52
1:26 900 000

Northeast Asia   54
1:26 900 000

Eastern China   56
1:22 500 000

Japan and Korea   58
1:11 300 000

Southeast Asia   60
1:22 500 000

Malaysia and Indonesia   62
1:22 500 000

Southern Asia   64
1:22 500 000

The Middle East   66
1:24 800 000

Turkey   68
1:11 300 000

The Near East 70
1:5 550 000

The Gulf States 71
1:11 300 000

Africa

Africa 72
1:58 400 000

Northeast Africa 74
1:22 500 000

Northwest Africa 76
1:22 500 000

West Africa 78
1:22 500 000

Central Africa 80
1:22 500 000

Southern Africa 82
1:22 500 000

Oceania

Oceania 84
1:79 000 000

Australia 86
1:26 900 000

New Zealand 88
1:9 000 000

North America

North America 90
1:67 600 000

Canada 92
1:26 900 000

United States 94
1:30 200 000

Northwest United States 96
1:14 000 000

Northeast United States 98
1:14 000 000

Southeast United States 100
1:14 000 000

Southwest United States 102
1:14 000 000

Central America
and the Caribbean 104
1:31 400 000

South America

South America 106
1:54 600 000

Northern South America 108
1:31 400 000

Southern South America 110
1:31 400 000

Polar Regions

Polar Regions 112
1:99 000 000

Index 113-176

How to use the index 113

Glossary 114

Index to names 115

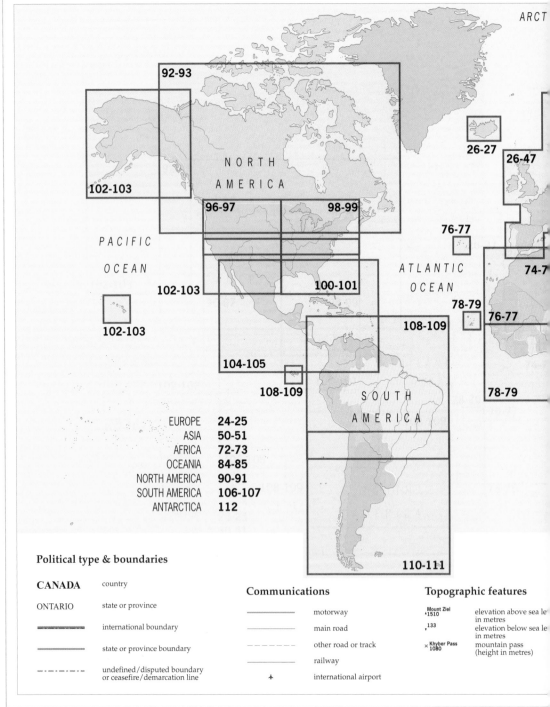

ARCT

92-93

102-103

26-27

26-47

NORTH
AMERICA

96-97

98-99

76-77

PACIFIC

OCEAN

102-103

100-101

ATLANTIC
OCEAN

74-7

102-103

78-79

76-77

104-105

108-109

108-109

SOUTH
AMERICA

78-79

EUROPE **24-25**
ASIA **50-51**
AFRICA **72-73**
OCEANIA **84-85**
NORTH AMERICA **90-91**
SOUTH AMERICA **106-107**
ANTARCTICA **112**

110-111

Political type & boundaries

CANADA   country

ONTARIO   state or province

━━━━━━━━   international boundary

───────   state or province boundary

─·──·──·─   undefined/disputed boundary
or ceasefire/demarcation line

Communications

────────   motorway

────────   main road

─ ─ ─ ─ ─   other road or track

────────   railway

✈   international airport

Topographic features

Mount Ziel
▲1510   elevation above sea le
in metres

▾133   elevation below sea le
in metres

✕ **Khyber Pass**
1080   mountain pass
(height in metres)

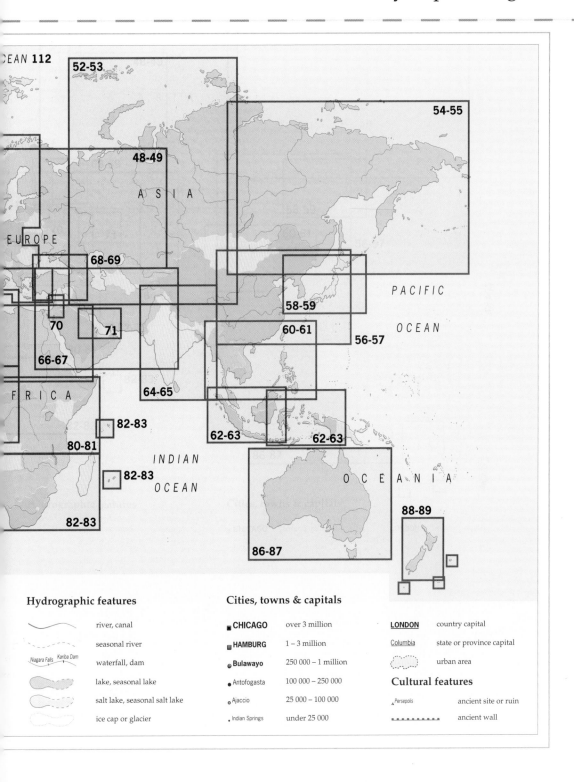

CEAN **112**

52-53

54-55

48-49

A S I A

E U R O P E

68-69

PACIFIC

OCEAN

58-59

70

71

60-61

56-57

66-67

F R I C A

64-65

82-83

62-63

62-63

80-81

INDIAN

82-83

OCEAN

O C E A N I A

88-89

82-83

86-87

Hydrographic features

	river, canal
	seasonal river
Niagara Falls Kariba Dam	waterfall, dam
	lake, seasonal lake
	salt lake, seasonal salt lake
	ice cap or glacier

Cities, towns & capitals

■ **CHICAGO**	over 3 million
▣ **HAMBURG**	1 – 3 million
● **Bulawayo**	250 000 – 1 million
• Antofagasta	100 000 – 250 000
○ Ajaccio	25 000 – 100 000
• Indian Springs	under 25 000

LONDON	country capital
Columbia	state or province capital
⬭	urban area

Cultural features

₊Persepolis	ancient site or ruin
··········	ancient wall

Aspects
of the
World

Twelve pages of informative and colourful world maps,

providing an insight into selected social and economic topics

and highlighting the dramatic contrasts which exist between

the developed and the developing world.

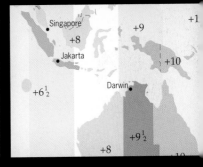

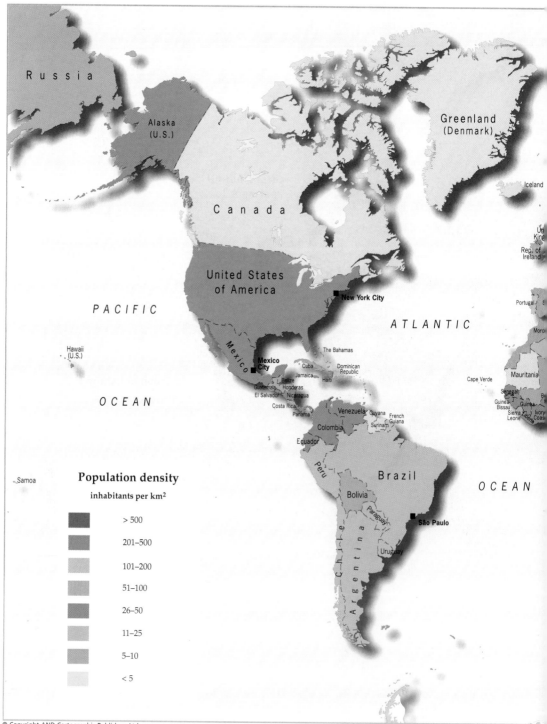

Population density
inhabitants per km²

> 500

201–500

101–200

51–100

26–50

11–25

5–10

< 5

© Copyright AND Cartographic Publishers Ltd.

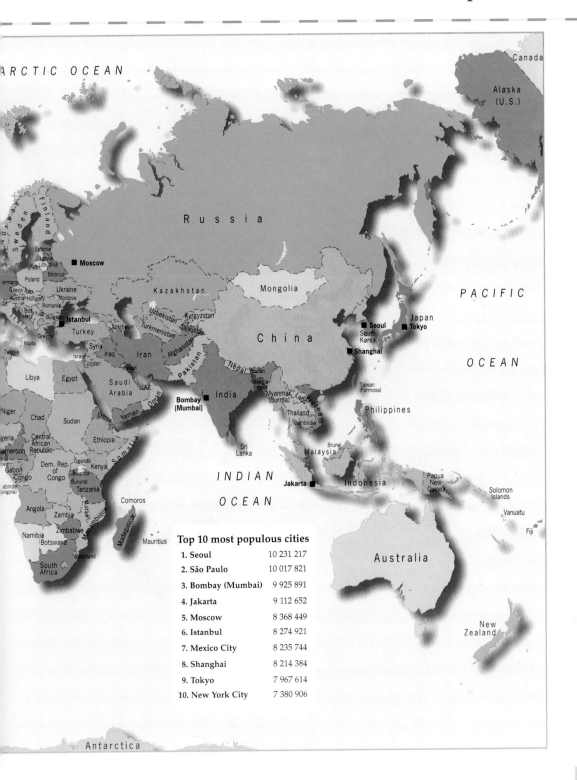

Top 10 most populous cities

1. Seoul	10 231 217
2. São Paulo	10 017 821
3. Bombay (Mumbai)	9 925 891
4. Jakarta	9 112 652
5. Moscow	8 368 449
6. Istanbul	8 274 921
7. Mexico City	8 235 744
8. Shanghai	8 214 384
9. Tokyo	7 967 614
10. New York City	7 380 906

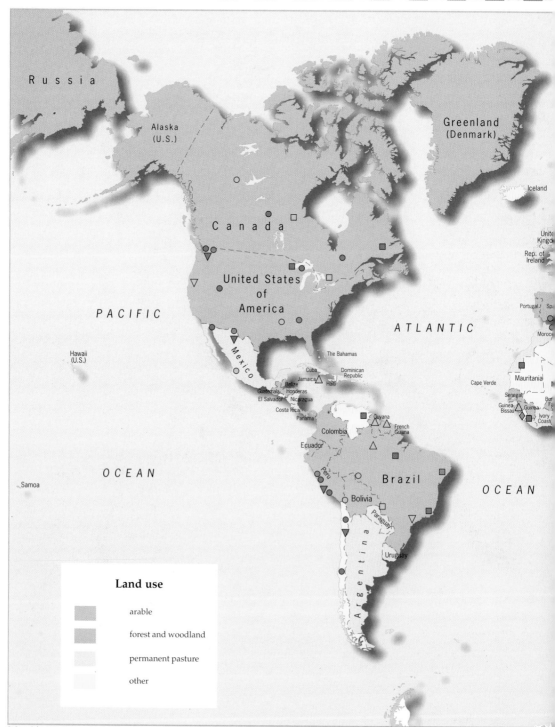

Land use

arable

forest and woodland

permanent pasture

other

© Copyright AND Cartographic Publishers Ltd.

ARCTIC OCEAN

Canada

Alaska (U.S.)

Russia

PACIFIC

OCEAN

Sweden
Finland
Estonia
Latvia
Rus. Lithuania
Poland
Belarus
Ukraine
Romania
Bulgaria
Turkey
Malta
Tunisia
Syria
Israel
Jordan
Iraq
Kuwait
Iran
Libya
Egypt
Saudi Arabia
U.A.E.
Oman
Yemen
Chad
Sudan
Eritrea
Ethiopia
Somalia
Nigeria
Cameroon
Dem. Rep. of Congo
Uganda
Rwanda
Burundi
Kenya
Tanzania
Angola
Zambia
Namibia
Swaziland
South Africa
Madagascar
Comoros
Mauritius

Kazakhstan
Mongolia
Kyrgyzstan
Turkmenistan
Azerbaijan
Afghanistan
Pakistan
India
Nepal
Bhutan
Bangladesh
Myanmar (Burma)
China
North Korea
South Korea
Japan
Taiwan (Formosa)
Thailand
Laos
Vietnam
Cambodia
Sri Lanka
Malaysia
Brunei
Philippines
Indonesia
Papua New Guinea
Solomon Islands
Vanuatu
Fiji

INDIAN

OCEAN

Australia

New Zealand

Antarctica

Mineral distribution

light metals	base metals	iron & ferro-alloys	precious metals
△ aluminium	● copper	■ iron	▽ gold
	● lead	■ chromium	▼ silver
	● mercury	■ manganese	**precious stones**
	● tin	■ nickel	◆ diamonds
	● zinc		

Russia

Alaska
(U.S.)

Canada

Greenland
(Denmark)

Iceland

PACIFIC

United States
of America ■   ■

▲   ▲

■

Mexico

The Bahamas

Cuba   Dominican
Jamaica   Republic   Haiti
Belize
Guatemala Honduras
El Salvador Nicaragua
Costa Rica
Panama

ATLANTIC

Ur
Kin

Rep. of
Ireland

Portugal

More

Mauritania

Cape Verde

Senegal

Guinea
Bissau   Guine
Sierra   Ivo
Leone   Coa

Hawaii
(U.S.)

OCEAN

Venezuela   Guyana   French
Guiana
Colombia   Surinam

Ecuador

Peru

Brazil

OCEAN

Samoa

Energy consumption
quadrillion (1 x 10^{15}) Btu

Bolivia

Paraguay

Chile

Argentina

Uruguay

> 20

10–20

1–10

0.5–1

0.1–0.5

0.05–0.1

0.01–0.05

< 0.01

▲   major oilfields

●   major gasfields

■   major coalfields

Btu = British thermal unit

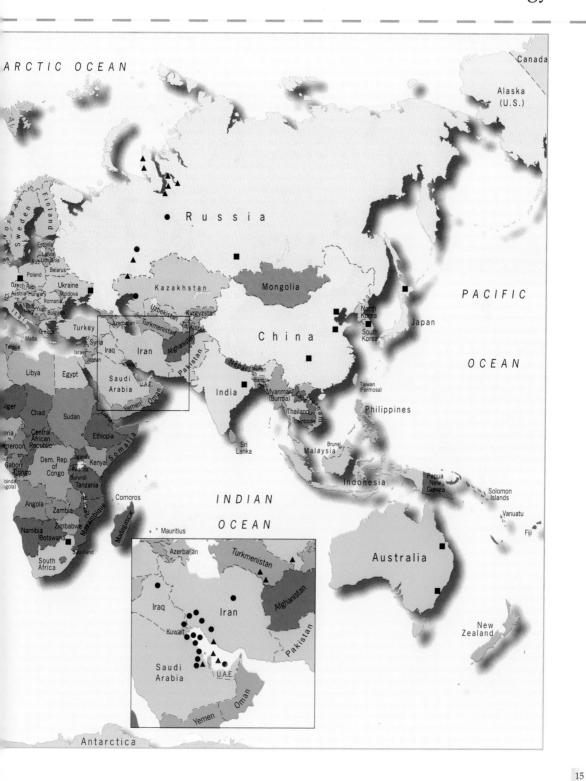

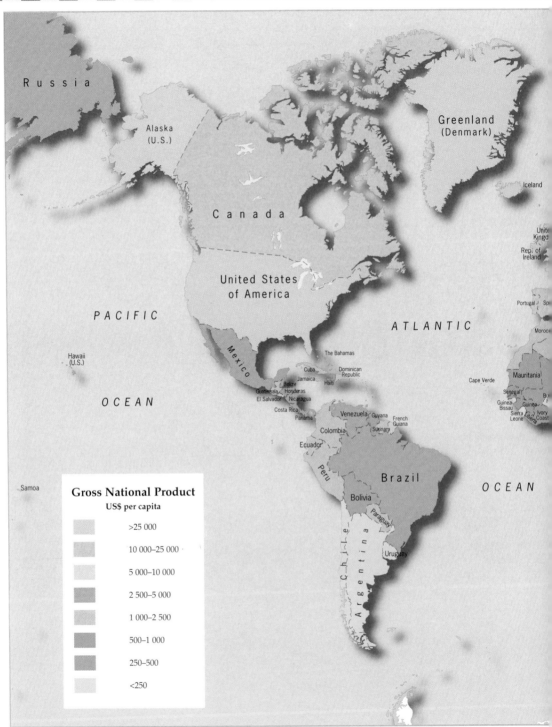

Gross National Product

US$ per capita

- >25 000
- 10 000–25 000
- 5 000–10 000
- 2 500–5 000
- 1 000–2 500
- 500–1 000
- 250–500
- <250

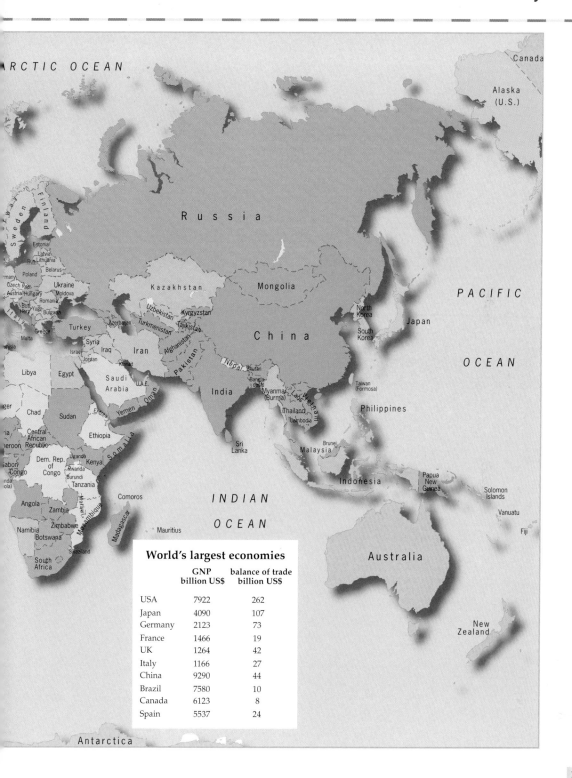

ARCTIC OCEAN

Canada

Alaska
(U.S.)

Sweden

Norway

Finland

Estonia

Latvia
Lithuania
Rus.

Belarus

Poland

Ukraine

Czech Rep.
Austria Hungary
Romania
Slovakia
Moldova
Bos-Yugo.
Herz. Bulgaria

Greece

Malta

Turkey

R u s s i a

Kazakhstan

Mongolia

North
Korea

Japan

PACIFIC

Syria
Israel
Jordan

Iraq

Iran

Azerbaijan

Uzbekistan

Turkmenistan

Kyrgyzstan

Tajikistan

Afghanistan

C h i n a

South
Korea

OCEAN

Libya

Egypt

Saudi
Arabia

U.A.E.

Oman

Pakistan

Nepal
Bhutan

Bangla-
desh

India

Myanmar
(Burma)

Laos

Vietnam

Taiwan
(Formosa)

Niger

Chad

Sudan

Eritrea

Yemen

Thailand

Cambodia

Philippines

Central
African
Republic

Cameroon

Ethiopia

Somalia

Sri
Lanka

Brunei

Malaysia

Gabon

Dem. Rep.
of
Congo

Congo

Uganda

Rwanda

Burundi

Kenya

Tanzania

Indonesia

Papua
New
Guinea

Solomon
Islands

Angola

Zambia

Malawi

Mozambique

Comoros

INDIAN

Vanuatu

Namibia

Zimbabwe

Madagascar

Mauritius

OCEAN

Fiji

Botswana

Swaziland

South
Africa

Australia

New
Zealand

World's largest economies		
	GNP billion US$	balance of trade billion US$
USA	7922	262
Japan	4090	107
Germany	2123	73
France	1466	19
UK	1264	42
Italy	1166	27
China	9290	44
Brazil	7580	10
Canada	6123	8
Spain	5537	24

Antarctica

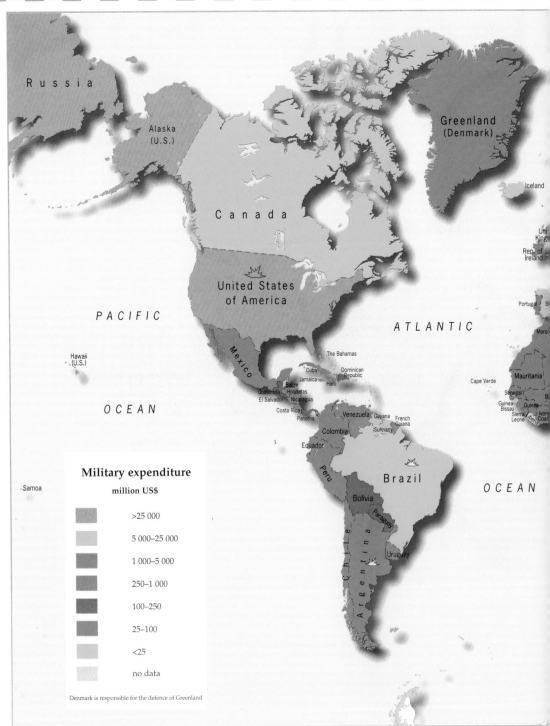

Military expenditure

million US$

	>25 000
	5 000–25 000
	1 000–5 000
	250–1 000
	100–250
	25–100
	<25
	no data

Denmark is responsible for the defence of Greenland

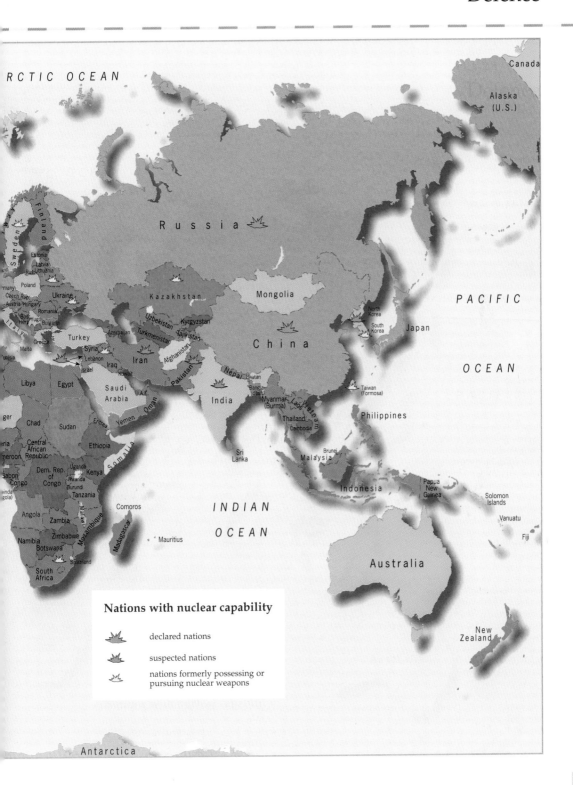

Nations with nuclear capability

declared nations

suspected nations

nations formerly possessing or
pursuing nuclear weapons

ARCTIC OCEAN

-12 -11 -10 -9 -8 -7 -6 -5 -4 -3 -2 -1

-3

GMT

-1

GMT

-9

Anchorage

-8

Edmonton

Vancouver

Winnipeg

-5

-4

-3½

Monday
Sunday

-10

-7

-6

Montreal

Chicago

New York

-1

Madr

Lisbon

San Francisco

Washington D.C.

Los Angeles

PACIFIC

Houston

ATLANTIC

GMT

International Date Line

-11

Miami

-10

Mexico City

Caracas

-1

-10

OCEAN

Bogota

GM

Dakar

-11

-9½

-5

-4

-10

Lima

-3

OCEAN

+13

La Paz

-10

Rio de Janeiro

-8½

Santiago

+12¾

Buenos
Aires

-4

© Copyright AND Cartographic Publishers Ltd.

20

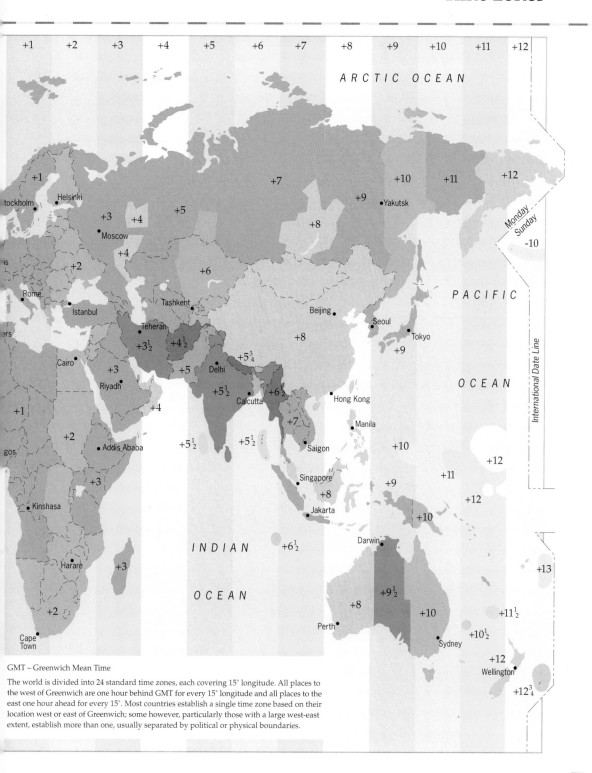

+1 +2 +3 +4 +5 +6 +7 +8 +9 +10 +11 +12

ARCTIC OCEAN

+1

tockholm • Helsinki

+3 +4 +5 +7

Moscow +9 • Yakutsk

+8 +10 +11 +12

+4

+2 +6 PACIFIC

Rome +3½ +4½ Beijing •

Istanbul Tashkent Seoul •

Teheran +5¾ Tokyo

+5 Delhi +8 +9 OCEAN

+3 +5½

Cairo Calcutta +6½ Hong Kong

Riyadh +4

+1 +5½ +5½ +7 Manila •

+2 Saigon

gos Addis Ababa +10

+3 Singapore +11 +12

+8 +9

Kinshasa Jakarta +12

+10

INDIAN +6½ Darwin •

Harare +3 +13

OCEAN +9½

+2 +8 +10 +11½

Cape Perth • +10½

Town Sydney

+12

GMT – Greenwich Mean Time Wellington

+12¾

Monday / Sunday -10

International Date Line

The world is divided into 24 standard time zones, each covering 15° longitude. All places to
the west of Greenwich are one hour behind GMT for every 15° longitude and all places to the
east one hour ahead for every 15°. Most countries establish a single time zone based on their
location west or east of Greenwich; some however, particularly those with a large west-east
extent, establish more than one, usually separated by political or physical boundaries.

Maps
of the
World

Forty-eight pairs of full colour satellite images and politically-coloured maps

covering the world. Each pair created to the same projection for easy comparison.

Each satellite image enhanced with elevation data, plus a layer of cartographic

information related directly to the detail on the accompanying map.

Scale 1 : 39 400 000

0   250   500   750   1000 km

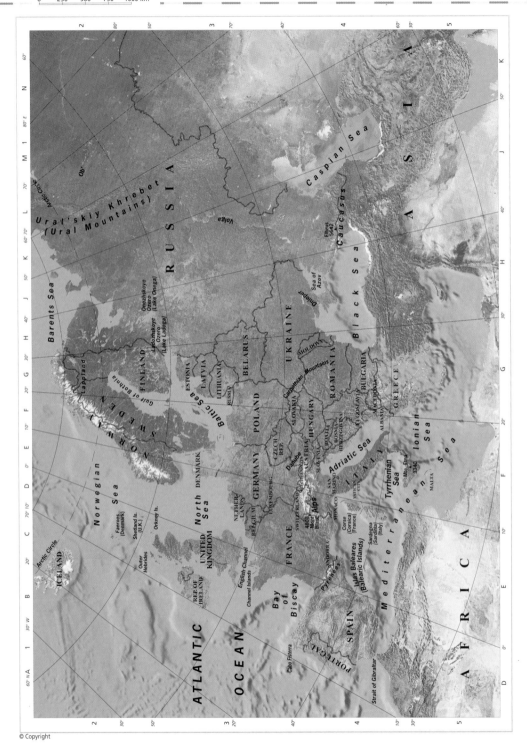

© Copyright

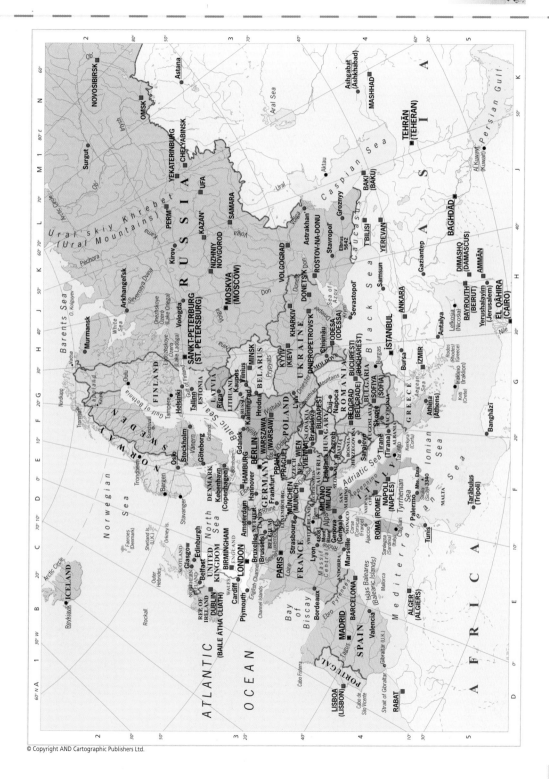

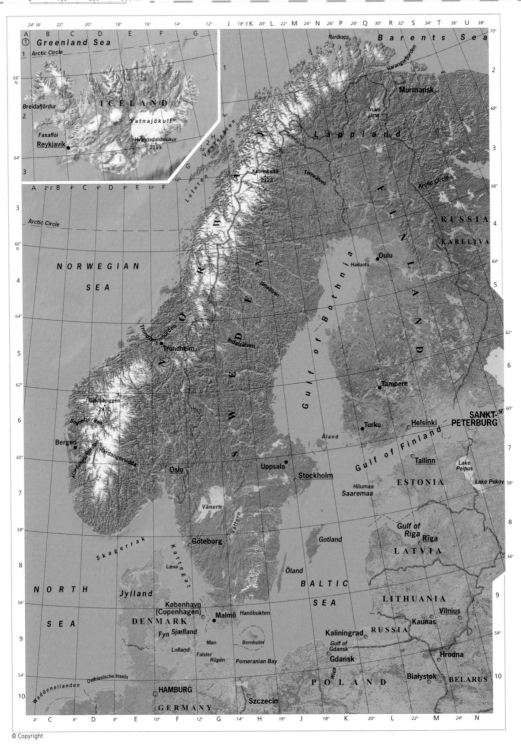

Scale 1 : 11 300 000

0   100   200   300 km

Greenland Sea

Arctic Circle

ICELAND

Vatnajökull

Breiðafjörður

Faxaflói
Reykjavik

Hvannadalshnúkur
2119

Greenland Sea

Barents Sea

Nordkapp

Varangerfjorden

Murmansk

Inari-
järvi

Lappland

Arctic Circle

RUSSIA

KARELIYA

Kebnekaise
2123

Torneälven

Oulu

Haluoto

FINLAND

NORWEGIAN

SEA

Umeälven

Gulf of Bothnia

Galdhøpiggen
2470

Indalsälven

Tampere

SANKT-
PETERBURG

Sognefjorden

Turku   Helsinki

Åland

Bergen

Hardangervidda

Hardangerfjorden

Oslo   Uppsala

Tallinn   Lake
Peipus

Trondheim

Trondheimsfjorden

Gulf of Finland

Stockholm

Hiiumaa   Lake Pskov
Saaremaa

ESTONIA

Vänern

Vättern

Gotland   Gulf of
Riga   Riga

LATVIA

Göteborg

Skagerrak

Kattegat

Öland

BALTIC

Læsø

NORTH   Jylland

SEA

Vilnius

LITHUANIA

Kaunas

København
(Copenhagen)

Malmö   Hanöbukten

RUSSIA

SEA

DENMARK

Kaliningrad

Fyn   Sjælland

Gulf of
Gdansk

Lolland   Møn

Falster   Rügen   Bornholm

Hrodna

Pomeranian Bay

Gdansk

Białystok   BELARUS

Waddeneilanden

Ostfriesische Inseln

POLAND

HAMBURG

GERMANY   Szczecin

NORWAY   SWEDEN   LOFOTEN   VESTERÅLEN

© Copyright

26

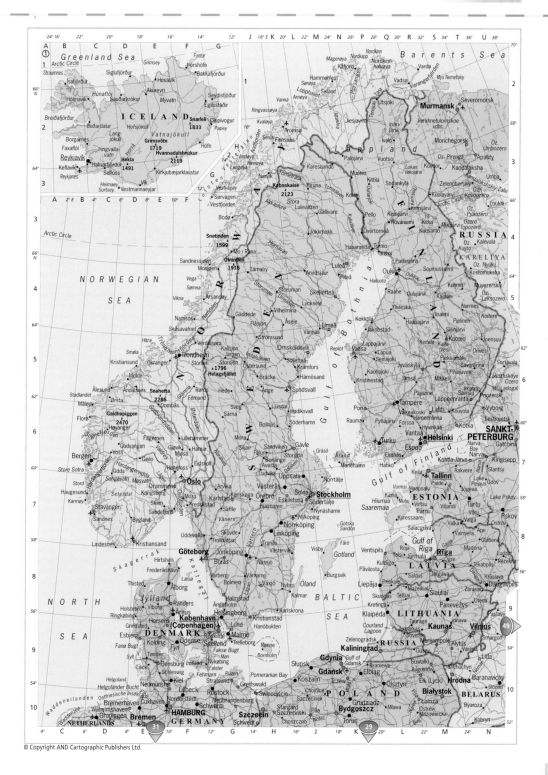

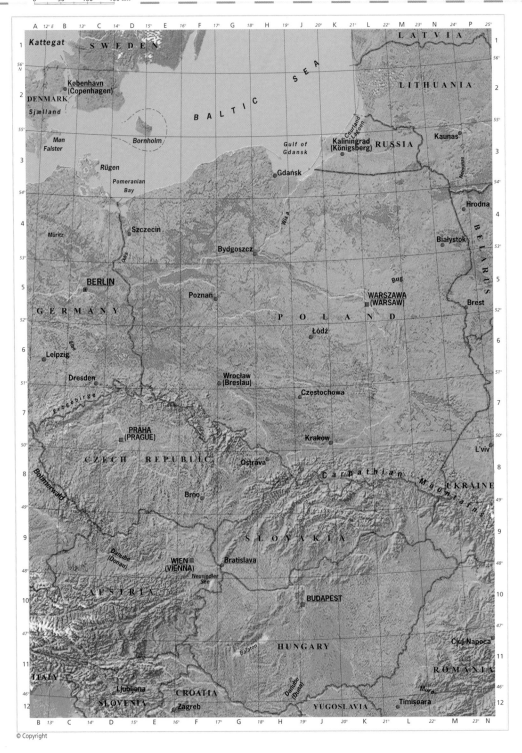

Scale 1 : 6 750 000

0   50   100   150 km

Kattegat

SWEDEN

BALTIC   SEA

København
(Copenhagen)

DENMARK

Sjælland

LATVIA

LITHUANIA

Møn
Falster

Bornholm

Rügen

Pomeranian
Bay

Courland
Lagoon

Gulf of
Gdańsk

Kaliningrad
(Königsberg)

RUSSIA

Kaunas

Gdańsk

Müritz

Szczecin

Bydgoszcz

Oder

Wisła

Hrodna

Białystok

BELARUS

BERLIN

Poznan

GERMANY

POLAND

Bug

WARSZAWA
(WARSAW)

Brest

Leipzig

Elbe

Łódź

Dresden

Wrocław
(Breslau)

Erzgebirge

Częstochowa

PRAHA
(PRAGUE)

Krakow

L'viv

CZECH   REPUBLIC

Ostrava

Carpathian   Mountains

UKRAINE

Böhmerwald

Brno

SLOVAKIA

Danube
(Donau)

WIEN
(VIENNA)

Bratislava

Neusiedler
See

AUSTRIA

BUDAPEST

Cluj-Napoca

Balaton

HUNGARY

ROMANIA

ITALY

Ljubljana

CROATIA

Danube
(Duna)

Mura

SLOVENIA

Zagreb

YUGOSLAVIA

Timişoara

© Copyright

28

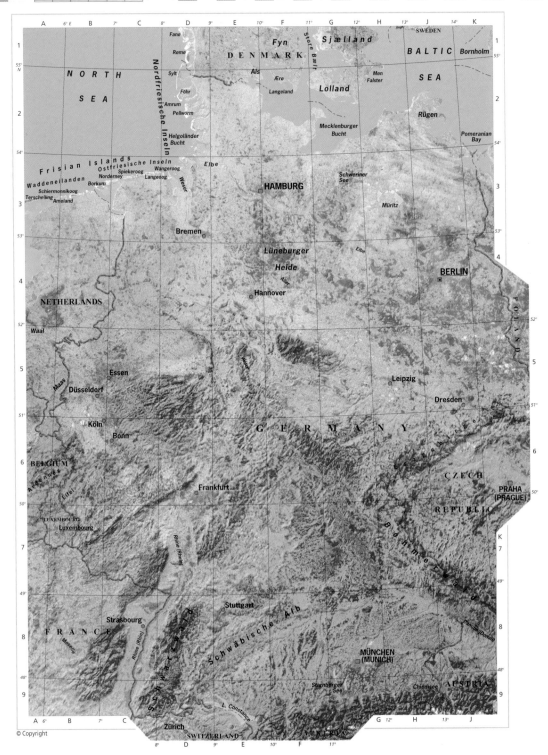

Scale 1 : 5 050 000

0   50   100   150 km

| A | 6° E | B | 7° | C | 8° | D | 9° | E | 10° | F | 11° | G | 12° | H | 13° | J | 14° | K |

NORTH SEA

Fano
Rømø
Sylt
Föhr
Amrum
Pellworm
Helgoländer Bucht

Nordfriesische Inseln

DENMARK

Als
Ærø
Langeland

Fyn

Store Bælt

Sjælland

SWEDEN

BALTIC SEA

Bornholm

Møn
Falster

Lolland

Mecklenburger Bucht

Rügen

Pomeranian Bay

Frisian Islands
Ostfriesische Inseln
Waddeneilanden
Schiermonnikoog
Terschelling
Ameland
Borkum
Norderney
Langeoog
Spiekeroog
Wangeroog

Elbe
Weser

HAMBURG

Schweriner See

Müritz

Bremen

Lüneburger Heide

Elbe

Aller

Hannover

BERLIN

NETHERLANDS

Waal

POLAND

Weser

Essen
Düsseldorf

Maas

Köln
Bonn

Leipzig

Dresden

GERMANY

BELGIUM

Ardennes

Eifel

Frankfurt

CZECH REPUBLIC

PRAHA (PRAGUE)

Erzgebirge

Böhmerwald

LUXEMBOURG
Luxembourg

Rhine (Rhein)

Rhine (Rhein)

Stuttgart

Strasbourg

Schwäbische Alb

Donau (Danube)

Schwarzwald

Mosel

FRANCE

Rhine (Rhein)

MÜNCHEN (MUNICH)

Starnberger See

Chiemsee

AUSTRIA

Zürich

L. Constance

SWITZERLAND

© Copyright

| A | 6° | B | 7° | C | | D | 8° | | 9° | E | 10° | F | 11° | G | 12° | H | 13° | J |

30

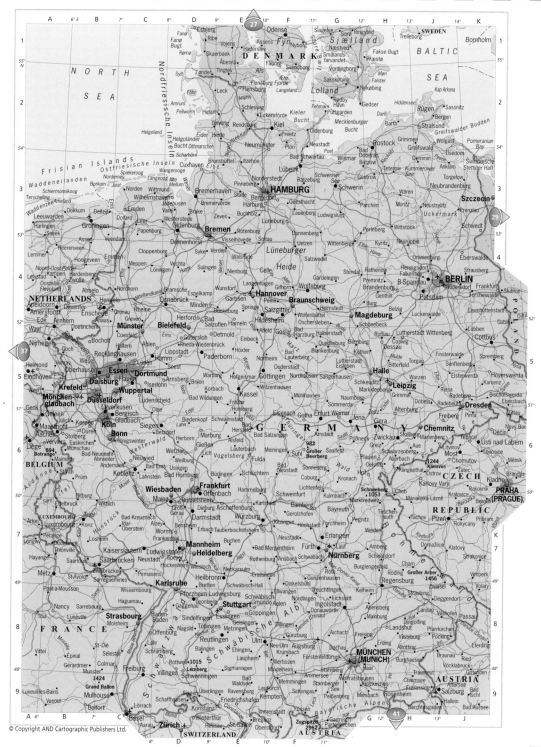

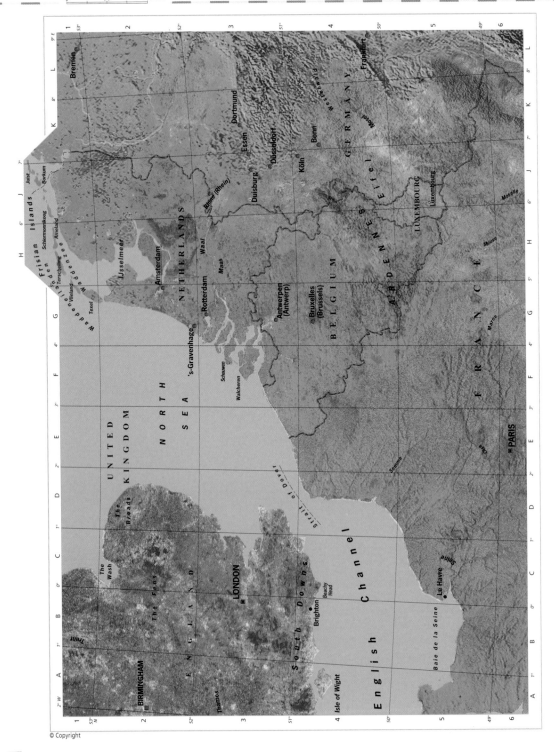

Scale 1 : 4 500 000

0   50   100 km

English Channel

NORTH SEA

UNITED KINGDOM

ENGLAND

NETHERLANDS

BELGIUM

GERMANY

FRANCE

LUXEMBOURG

ARDENNES

Eifel

Westerwald

BIRMINGHAM
LONDON
Brighton
Beachy Head
Isle of Wight
South Downs
The Wash
The Fens
The Brecks
Trent
Thames
Strait of Dover
Baie de la Seine
Le Havre
Seine
Somme
Oise
Marne
Meuse
Moselle
PARIS

Bremen
Borkum
Juist
Frisian Islands
Schiermonnikoog
Ameland
Terschelling
Texel
Waddenzee
IJsselmeer
Amsterdam
's-Gravenhage
Rotterdam
Schouwen
Walcheren
Antwerpen (Antwerp)
Bruxelles (Brussels)
Rijn (Rhein)
Waal
Maas
Duisburg
Essen
Dortmund
Düsseldorf
Köln
Bonn
Mosel
Luxembourg
Moselle
Frankfurt

© Copyright

32

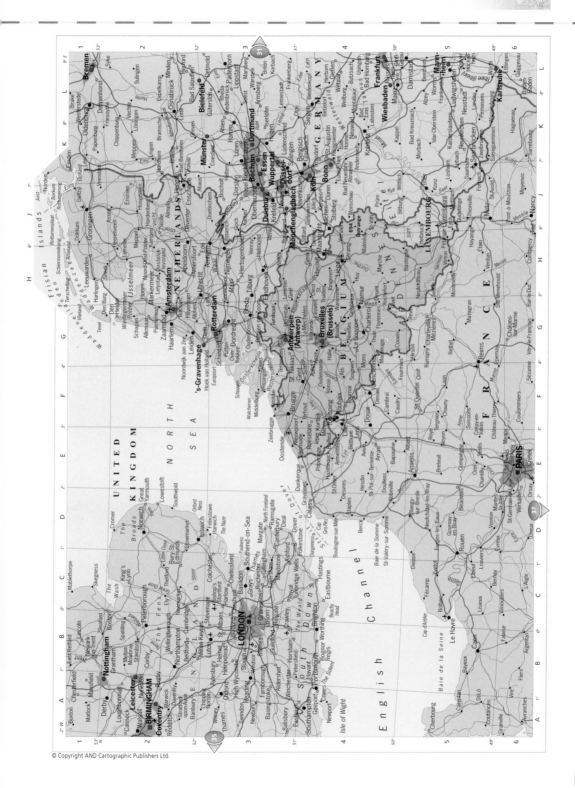

Scale 1 : 6 750 000

0   50   100   150 km

Yell
Unst
Shetland
Islands
Mainland

Fair Isle

Mainland
Orkney
Islands
Hoy

ATLANTIC

OCEAN

NORTH

Lewis
The Minch
St. Kilda
North Uist
North West Highlands
Moray Firth
Skye
Loch
Ness
Grampian Mountains
South
Uist
Barra
Rum
SEA
Sea of the
Hebrides
Coll
Ben Nevis
1343
Tiree
Mull
SCOTLAND
Colonsay
Jura
Loch
Lomond
Firth of Forth
Islay
Glasgow
Edinburgh

Malin Head
Kintyre
Arran

UNITED KINGDOM
Newcastle-
upon-Tyne

Londonderry
NORTHERN
Lough
Neagh
IRELAND
Belfast
North Channel
ISLE OF MAN
(U.K.)
Lake
District
Scafell
Pike
978
Pennines

Achill I.
IRISH
Leeds
Kingston
upon Hull

SEA
Liverpool
MANCHESTER
DUBLIN
(BAILE ÁTHA CLIATH)
Anglesey
Sheffield
The Wash
Aran
Islands
Galway Bay
REPUBLIC
1085
Snowdon
OF
Cambrian Mountains
Mouth of the Shannon
IRELAND
BIRMINGHAM
Cardigan
Bay
WALES
ENGLAND
Cork
Thames
Cardiff
Bristol
LONDON
C. Clear
Bristol
Channel
Celtic
Brighton
Strait of Dover
Sea
Isle of
Wight
Plymouth
Land's End
English Channel
ATLANTIC
Isles of
Scilly
Alderney
Seine
OCEAN
Channel
Islands
(U.K.)
Guernsey
Le Havre
Jersey
FRANCE

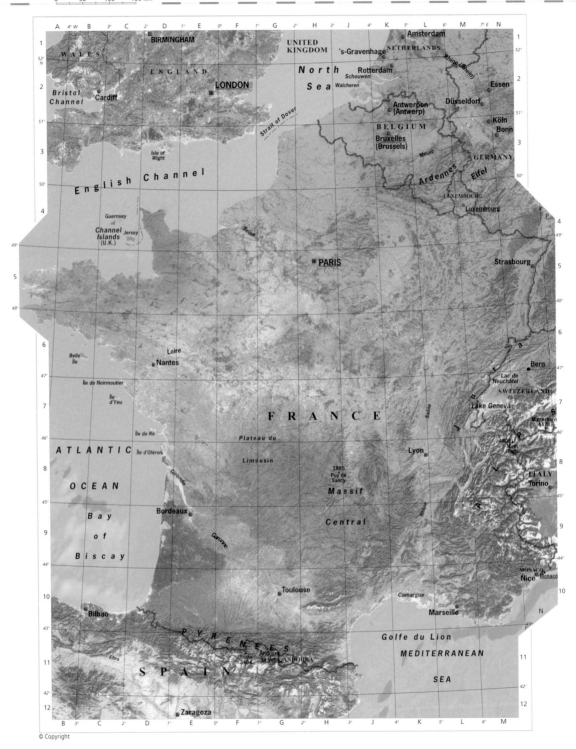

Scale 1 : 6 750 000

0   50   100   150 km

| A | 4° W | B | 3° | C | 2° | D | 1° | E | 0° | F | 1° | G | 2° | H | 3° | J | 4° | K | 5° | L | 6° | M | 7° E | N |

BIRMINGHAM

WALES

52° N

ENGLAND

LONDON

UNITED KINGDOM

North Sea

Amsterdam

's-Gravenhage   NETHERLANDS

Rotterdam
Schouwen
Walcheren

Rhine (Rhein)

Essen

Antwerpen
(Antwerp)

Düsseldorf

Köln
Bonn

BELGIUM

Bruxelles
(Brussels)

Meuse

GERMANY

Ardennes   Eifel

LUXEMBOURG

Luxembourg

P

Bristol
Channel

Cardiff

51°

Strait of Dover

Isle of
Wight

English Channel

50°

Guernsey

Channel
Islands
(U.K.)

Jersey

Seine

PARIS

Strasbourg

49°

48°

Belle
Île

Loire

Nantes

Bern

Lac de
Neuchâtel

SWITZERLAND

île de Noirmoutier

47°

Île
d'Yeu

Lake Geneva

Saône

FRANCE

ATLANTIC

Île de Ré

46°

Île d'Oléron

Plateau du

Limousin

Lyon

4806
Mont
Blanc

Matterhorn
4478

OCEAN

Gironde

1885
Puy de
Sancy

Massif

ITALY

Torino

45°

Bay

Bordeaux

Garonne

Central

Rhône

of

Biscay

44°

MONACO
Nice   Monaco

Toulouse

Camargue

N

Bilbao

Marseille

43°

PYRENEES

Ebro

Aneto
3404

Andorra
la Vella ANDORRA

Golfe du Lion

MEDITERRANEAN

SPAIN

SEA

42°

Zaragoza

| B | 3° | C | 2° | D | 1° | E | 0° | F | 1° | G | 2° | H | 3° | J | 4° | K | 5° | L | 6° | M |

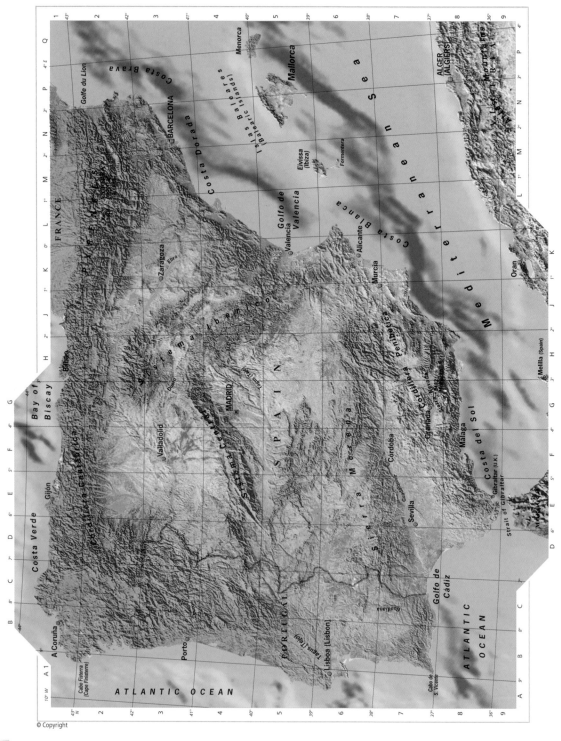

Scale 1 : 6 750 000

0   50   100   150 km

© Copyright

38

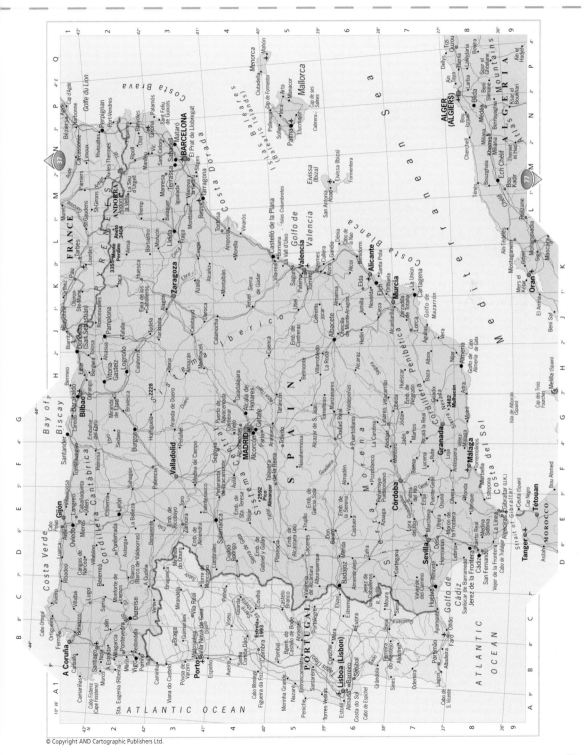

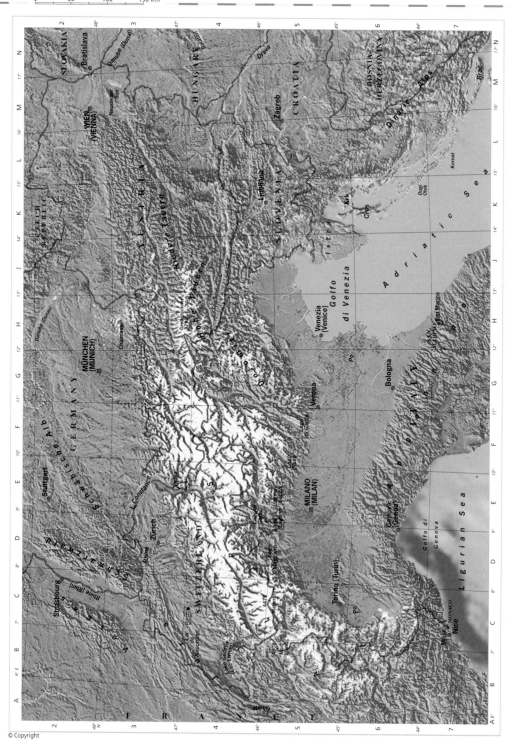

Scale 1 : 5 050 000

0   50   100   150 km

40

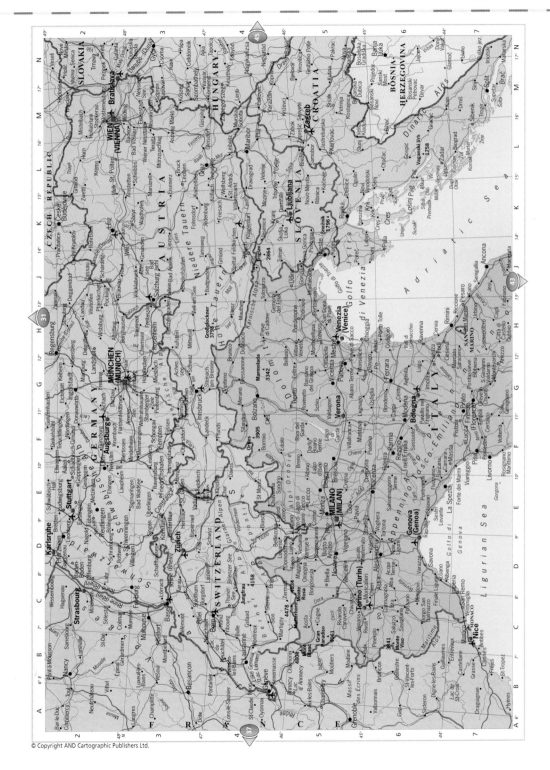

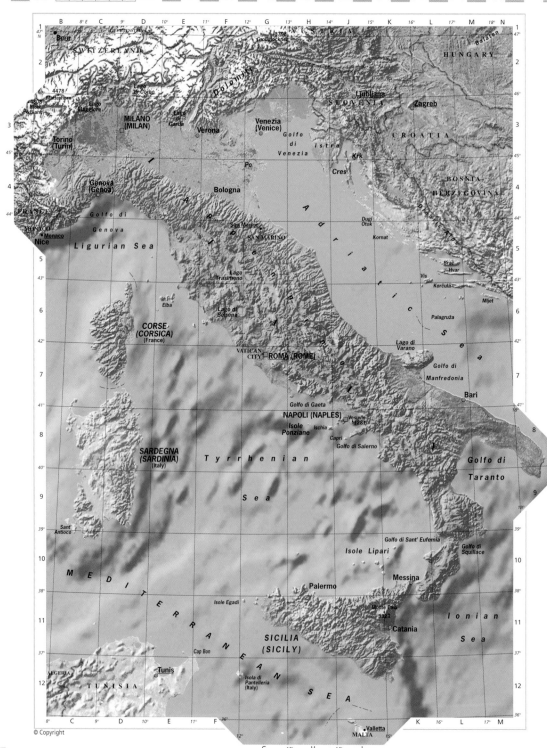

Scale 1 : 6 750 000

0   50   100   150 km

© Copyright

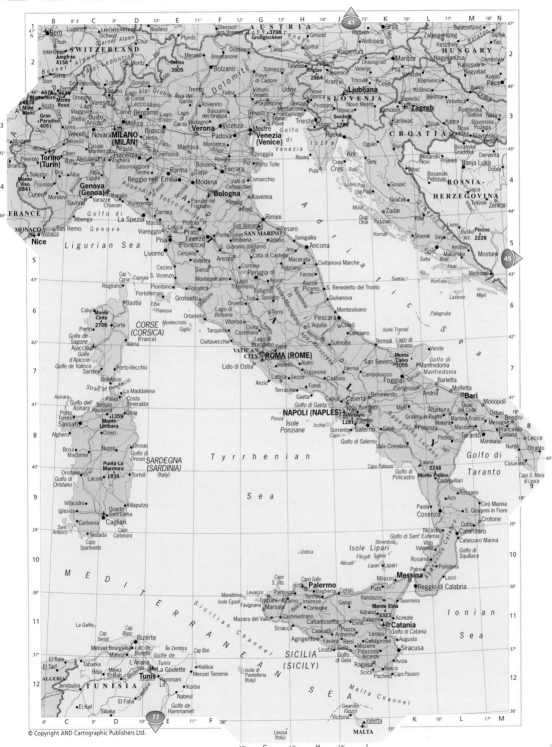

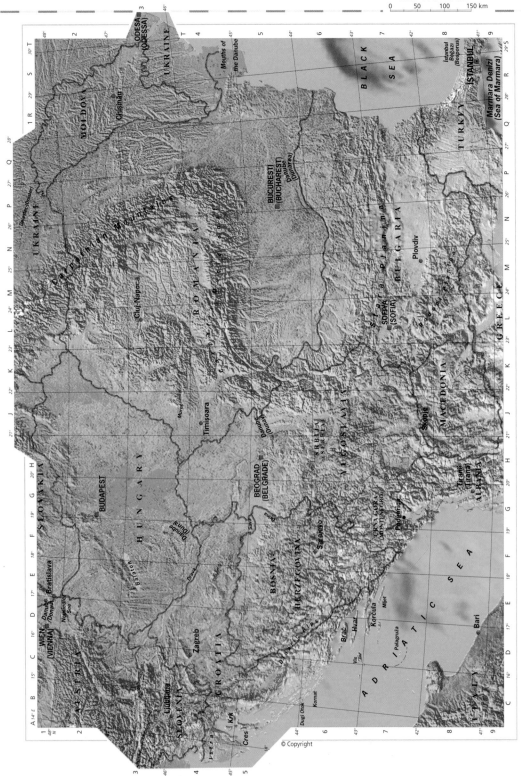

Scale 1 : 6 750 000

0   50   100   150 km

ODESA (ODESSA)
UKRAINE
MOLDOVA
Chişinău
Mouths of the Danube
BLACK SEA
İstanbul Boğazı (Bosporus)
İSTANBUL
Marmara Denizi (Sea of Marmara)
TURKEY
UKRAINE
Nistru (Dniester)
BUCUREŞTI (BUCHAREST)
Danube (Dunărea)
BULGARIA
Plovdiv
Carpathian Mountains
ROMANIA
Cluj-Napoca
Stara Planina
SOFYA (SOFIA)
GREECE
MACEDONIA
Skopje
Timişoara
Mureş
SRBIJA (SERBIA)
YUGOSLAVIA
Danube (Dunav)
Tiranë (Tirana)
ALBANIA
BEOGRAD (BELGRADE)
HUNGARY
BUDAPEST
Duna
Tisza
Sava
Dunav
Sarajevo
BOSNIA HERCEGOVINA
CRNA GORA (MONTENEGRO)
Podgorica
SLOVAKIA
Bratislava
Danube (Donau)
Neusiedler See
WIEN (VIENNA)
AUSTRIA
SLOVENIA
Ljubljana
Zagreb
CROATIA
Balaton
Drava
Krk
Cres
Dugi Otok
Kornat
Vis
Brač
Hvar
Korčula
Mljet
Palagruža
ADRIATIC SEA
IONIAN SEA
Bari
ITALY

© Copyright

44

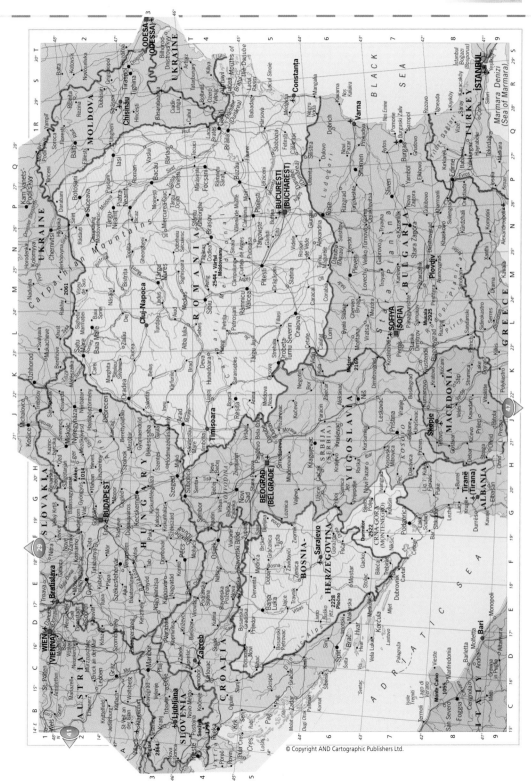

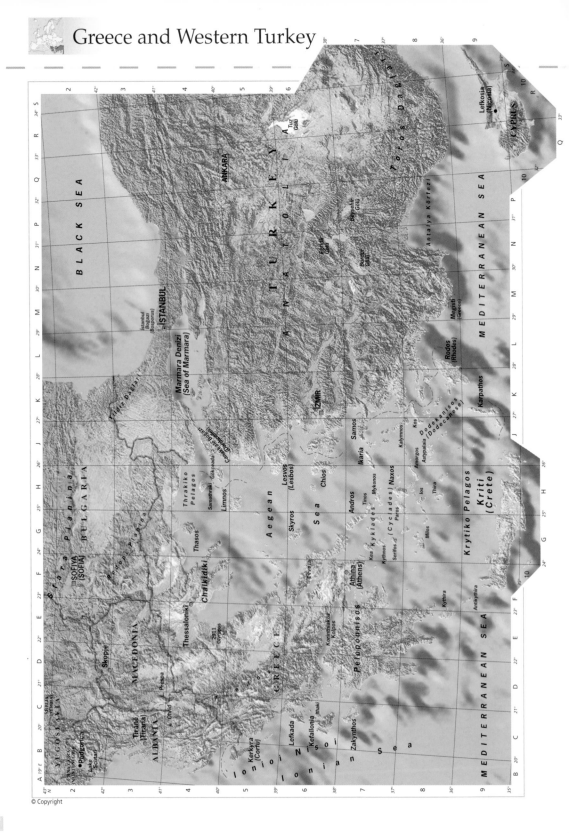

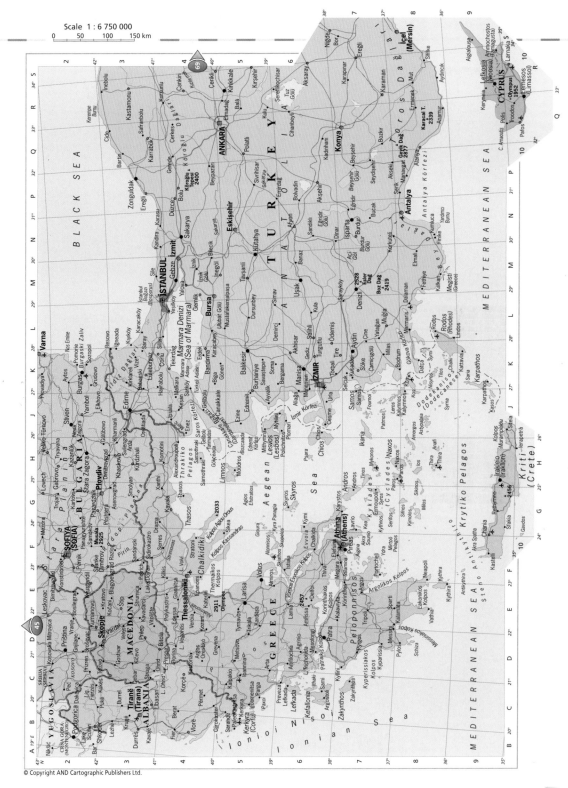

Scale 1 : 6 750 000

0   50   100   150 km

Scale 1 : 20 300 000

0   200   400   600 km

© Copyright

48

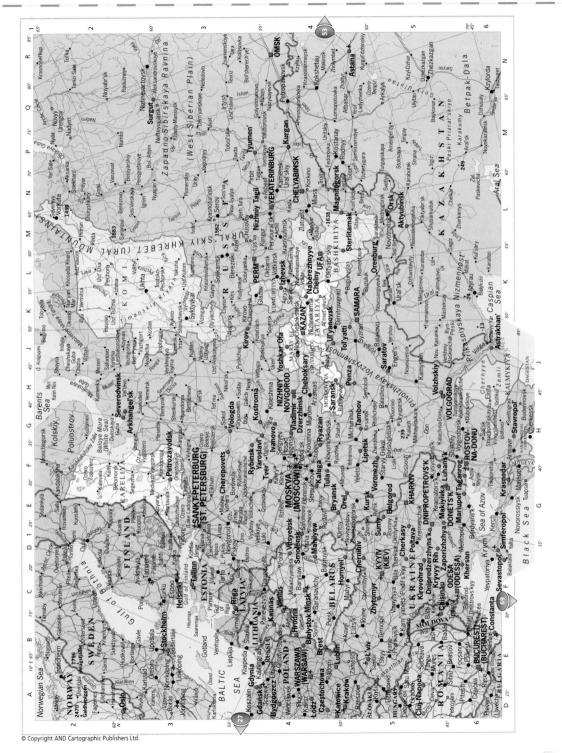

Scale 1 : 64 200 000

0   400   800   1200   1600 km

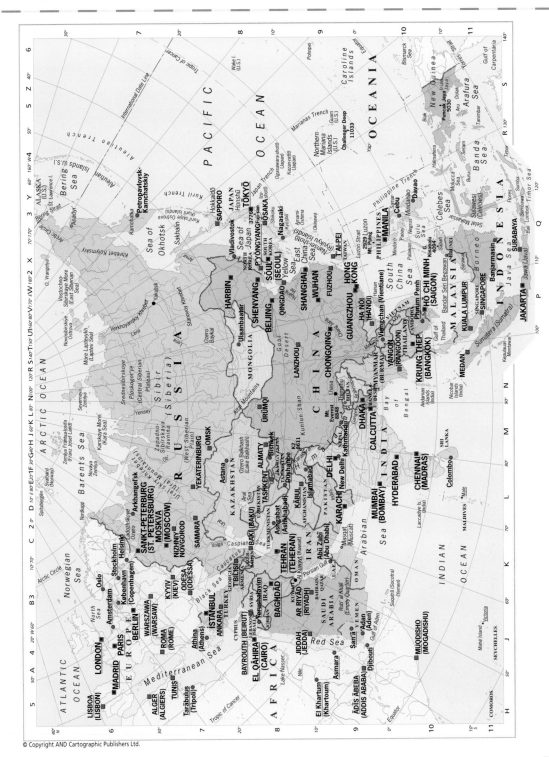

Scale 1 : 26 900 000

0   200   400   600 km

BARENTS SEA

Nordkapp

NORWAY

Murmansk

Kolskiy

Poluostrov

Arctic Circle

Beloye More
(White Sea)

Arkhangel'sk

Zemlya Frantsa-Iosifa
(Franz Josef Land)

Novaya Zemlya

**Karskoye More
(Kara Sea)**

Pechorskoye
More

Gydanskiy
Poluostrov

Obskaya Guba

Ob

Severnaya Zemlya

**More Laptevykh
(Laptev Sea)**

Poluostrov Taymyr

Lena

Arctic Circle

SAKHA

**Srednesibirskoye
Ploskogor'ye**

Yenisey

KOMI

Syktyvkar

RUSSIA
*Zapadno-Sibirskaya
Ravnina*

(West Siberian Plain)

Yeniseyskiy Kryazh

Bratskoye
Vdkhr.

Yoshkar Ola

MARIY EL

Cheboksary

UDMURTIYA

CHUVASHIYA

Izhevsk

PERM'

YEKATERINBURG

Sayany

KAZAN'

TATARIYA

UFA

BASHKIRIYA

CHELYABINSK

SAMARA

NOVOSIBIRSK

Abakan

KHAKASIYA

Kyzyl

TYVA

Ural

Gorno-
Altaysk

Prikaspiyskaya Nizmennost'

Caspian
Sea

KAZAKHSTAN

Astana

Irtysh

ALTAY

Uvs Nuur

Hangayn Nuruu

MONGOLIA

Oz.
Zaysan

Junggar
Pendi

Plato

Ustyurt

Aral Sea

Syrdarya

Ozero Balkhash

ÜRÜMQI

Altay Mountains

Zaliv Kara-
Bogaz Gol

Peski
Kyzylkum

Bishkek

ALMATY

TIEN SHAN

CHINA

Amudarya

TASHKENT

UZBEKISTAN

Ysyk-Köl

KYRGYZSTAN

Tarim

Tarim Pendi

TURKMENISTAN

Ashgabat
(Ashkhabad)

Dushanbe

TAJIKISTAN

7495 Kommunizma

KUNLUN SHAN

Hoh Xil Shan

MASHHAD

IRAN

AFGHANISTAN

Hindu Kush

PAKISTAN

URAL'SKIY MOUNTAINS

URAL'SKIY KHREBET

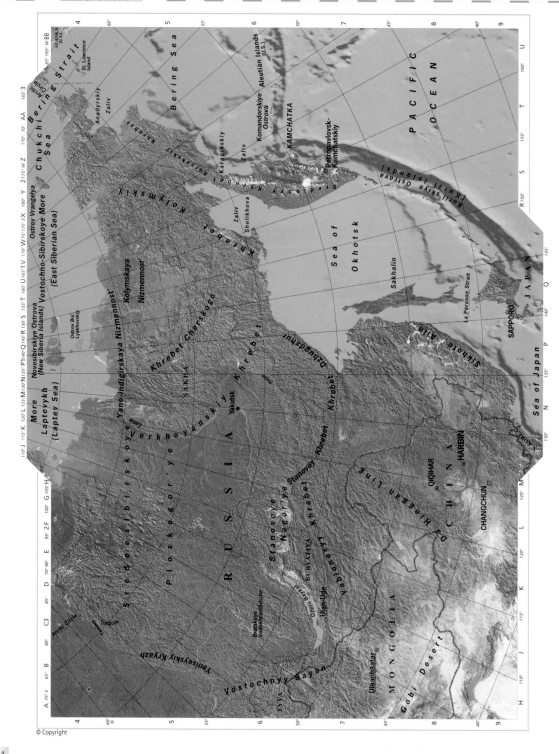

Scale 1 : 26 900 000

0   200   400   600 km

© Copyright

54

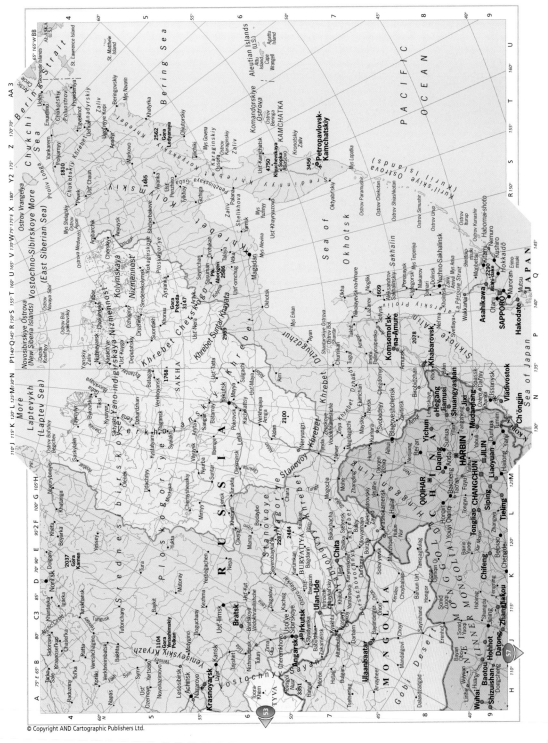

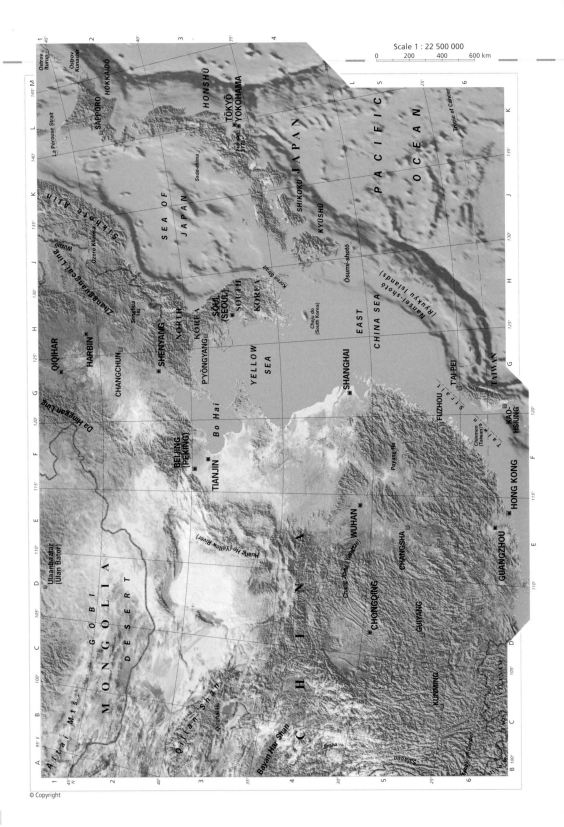

Scale 1 : 22 500 000

0   200   400   600 km

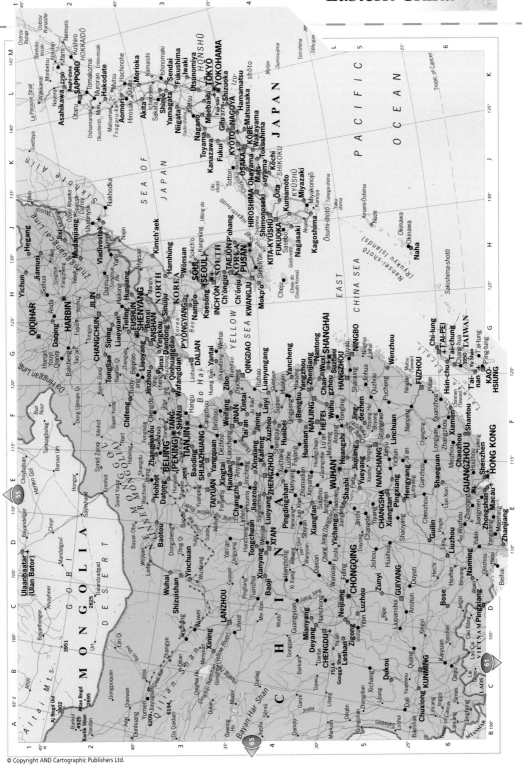

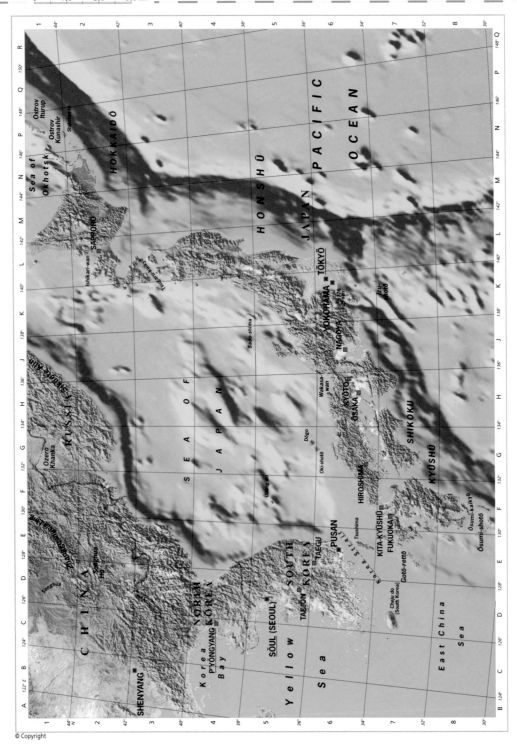

Scale   1 : 11 300 000

0   100   200   300 km

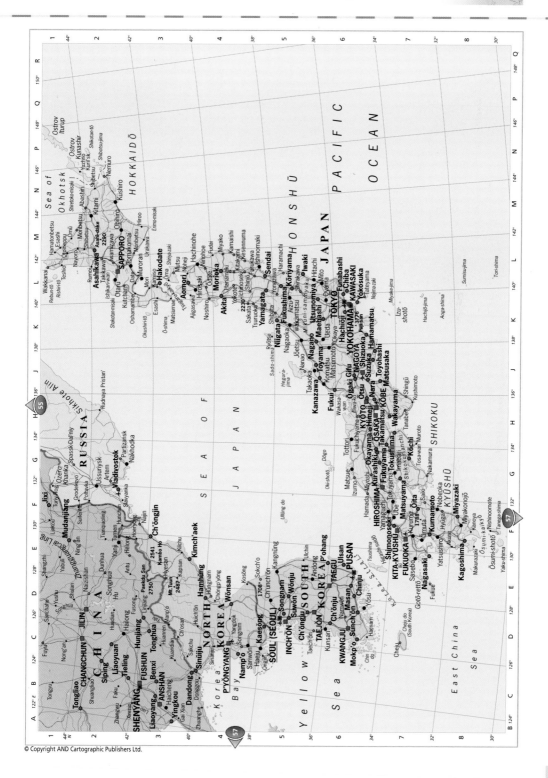

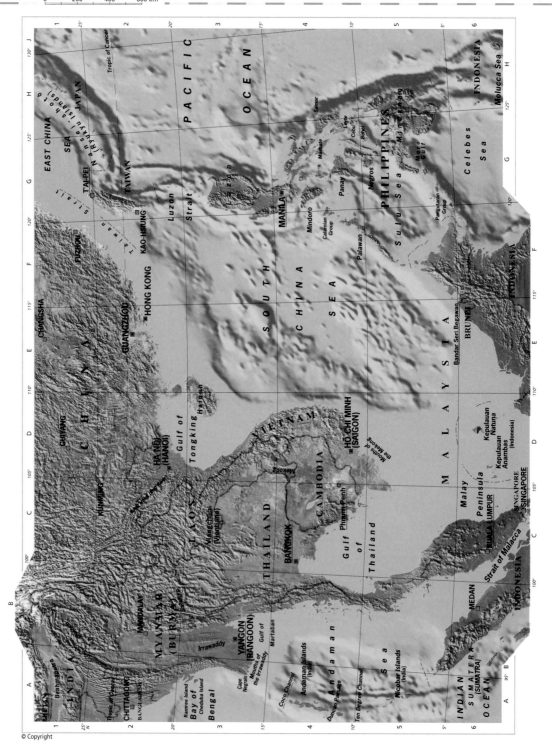

Scale 1 : 22 500 000

0   200   400   600 km

© Copyright

60

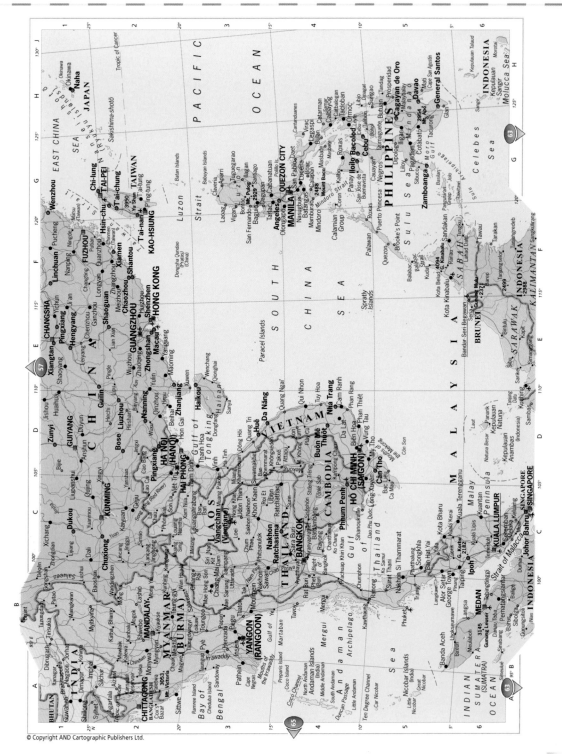

Scale 1 : 22 500 000

0   200   400   600 km

① 95° E   100°   105°   110°   115°   120°

THAILAND

South China

Malay   Sea

MALAYSIA Peninsula

MEDAN

KUALA LUMPUR   BRUNEI   Bandar Seri Begawan

4094
G. Kinabalu

Simeulue   Kepulauan
Anambas   Kepulauan
Natuna   MALAYSIA   Celebes

Nias   (Indonesia)   Sea

Equator

SINGAPORE
SINGAPORE   B O R N E O

Kepulauan   Pegunungan Schwaner   Equator
Mentawai   Bangka   Balikpapan

PALEMBANG   Selat Karimata   Sulawesi
(Celebes)

Belitung   Banjarmasin

I N D O N E S I A   Laut

I N D I A N   Java Sea   Ujung
Pandang

O C E A N   JAKARTA   JAWA (JAVA)
BANDUNG   SEMARANG   Madura
SURABAYA   Bali   Lombok   Flores Sea
Flores
Christmas   Sumbawa
Island
(Australia)

Strait of Malacca

S U M A T E R A

Pegunungan Barisan

Selat Sunda

Selat Makassar

B   100°   C   105°   D   110°   E   115°   F   120°   G

© Copyright

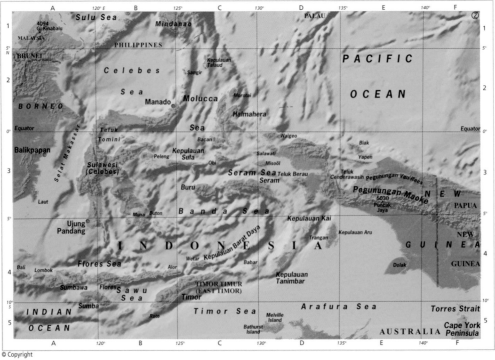

A   120° E   B   125°   C   130°   D   135°   E   140°   F

Sulu Sea   Mindanao   PALAU   ②

4094
G. Kinabalu
MALAYSIA   PHILIPPINES   P A C I F I C

BRUNEI   Celebes   Kepulauan
Talaud   O C E A N

Sea   Sangir

BORNEO   Manado   Molucca   Morotai

Halmahera

Equator   Sea   Waigeo   Equator

Teluk   Biak
Balikpapan   Tomini   Bacan   Salawati   Yapen

Peleng   Kepulauan   Obi   Misool   Teluk   pegunungan Van Rees
Sula   Cenderawasih

Sulawesi   Seram Sea   Teluk Berau   Pegunungan Maoke   NEW
(Celebes)   Buru   Seram   5030   PAPUA
Puncak
Laut   Jaya

Muna Buton   B a n d a S e a   Kepulauan Kai

Ujung   NEW
Pandang   I N D O N E S I A   Trangan   Kepulauan Aru   GUINEA

Bali Lombok   Flores Sea   Wetar Kepulauan Barat Daya   GUINEA
Alor   Babar   Dolak

Sumbawa   Flores S a w u   TIMOR TIMUR   Kepulauan
Sea   (EAST TIMOR)   Tanimbar
Sumba   Timor   Cape York
Roto   Timor Sea   Melville   Arafura Sea   Torres Strait
INDIAN   Island
OCEAN   Bathurst   AUSTRALIA   Cape York
Island   Peninsula

Selat Makassar

A   120°   B   125°   C   130°   D   135°   E   140°   F

© Copyright

62

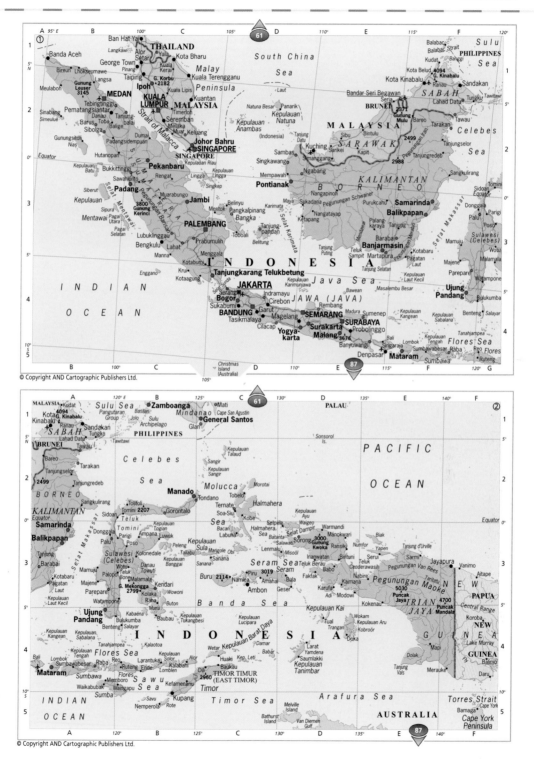

© Copyright AND Cartographic Publishers Ltd.

© Copyright AND Cartographic Publishers Ltd.

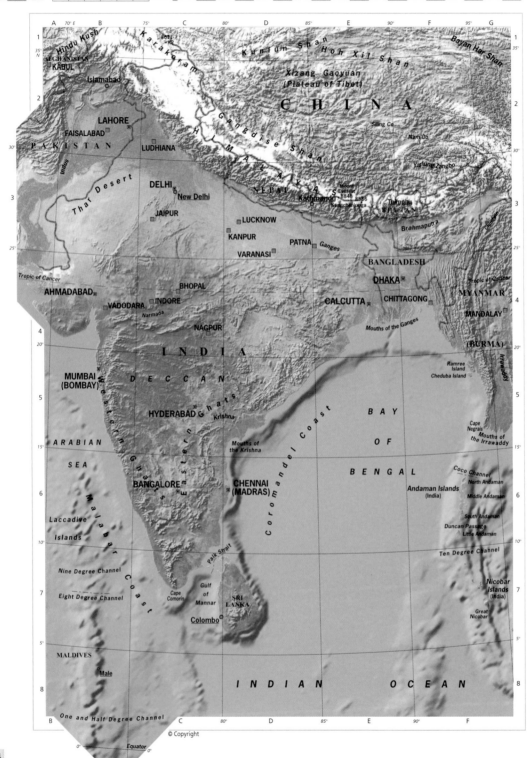

0   200   400   600 km

A 70° E   B   75°   C   80°   D   85°   E   90°   F   95°   G

1

35°
N

Hindu Kush   Karakoram   Aksai   Kunlun Shan   Hoh Xil Shan   Bayan Har Shan

AFGHANISTAN
KABUL

Islamabad

Xizang Gaoyuan
(Plateau of Tibet)

C H I N A

2

LAHORE

FAISALABAD

PAKISTAN

LUDHIANA

Gangdise Shan

H
I
M
A
L
A
Y
A
S

Siling Co

Nam Co

Yarlung Zangbo

30°

3

Indus

Thar Desert

DELHI

New Delhi

JAIPUR

NEPAL

Kathmandu   Mount
Everest
8848   8586
Kanchenjunga

Thimphu
BHUTAN

Brahmaputra

25°

LUCKNOW

KANPUR

VARANASI

PATNA   Ganges

BANGLADESH

DHAKA

Tropic of Cancer

AHMADABAD

VADODARA   INDORE

Narmada

BHOPAL

NAGPUR

CALCUTTA   CHITTAGONG

Mouths of the Ganges

MYANMAR

MANDALAY

(BURMA)

Tropic of Cancer

20°

4

20°

I N D I A

D E C C A N

Ramree
Island
Cheduba Island

Irrawaddy

5

MUMBAI
(BOMBAY)

Western Ghats

HYDERABAD   Krishna

Eastern Ghats

Mouths of
the Krishna

Coromandel Coast

B A Y

O F

B E N G A L

Cape
Negrais   Mouths of
the Irrawaddy

15°

ARABIAN

SEA

Malabar Coast

BANGALORE

CHENNAI
(MADRAS)

Coco Channel

Andaman Islands
(India)

North Andaman

Middle Andaman

6

Laccadive

Islands

South Andaman

Duncan Passage

Little Andaman

10°

Nine Degree Channel

Palk Strait

Ten Degree Channel

7

Eight Degree Channel

Cape
Comorin

Gulf
of
Mannar

SRI
LANKA

Colombo

Nicobar
Islands
(India)

Great
Nicobar

5°

5°

MALDIVES

Male

I N D I A N   O C E A N

8

One and Half Degree Channel

© Copyright

B   C   80°   D   85°   E   90°   F

0°   Equator   0°

75°

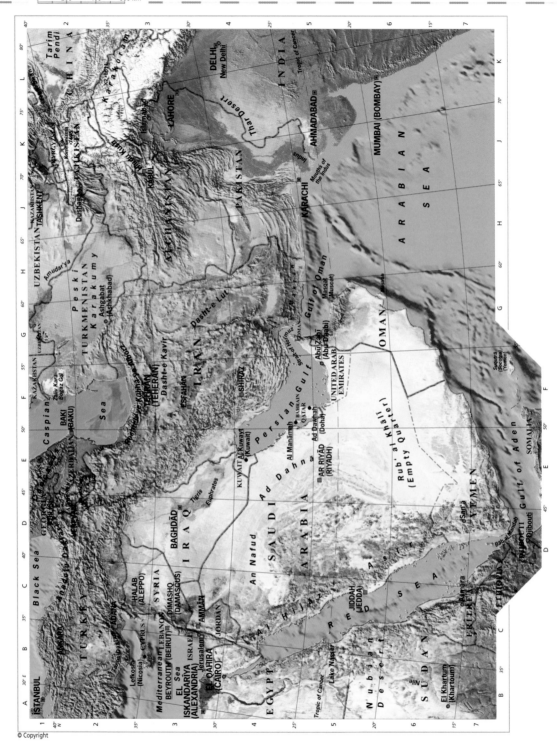

Scale 1 : 24 800 000

0   200   400   600 km

© Copyright

66

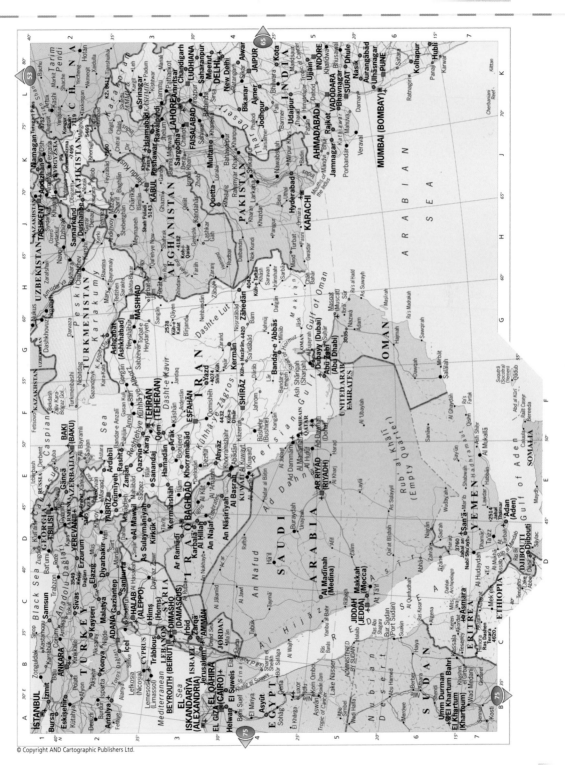

Scale 1 : 11 300 000

0   100   200   300 km

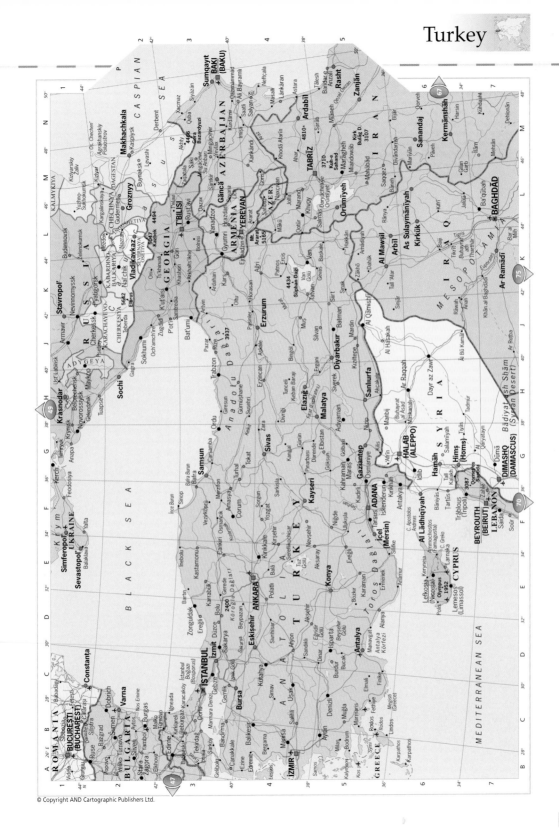

The Near East

Scale 1 : 5 550 000

0   50   100   150 km

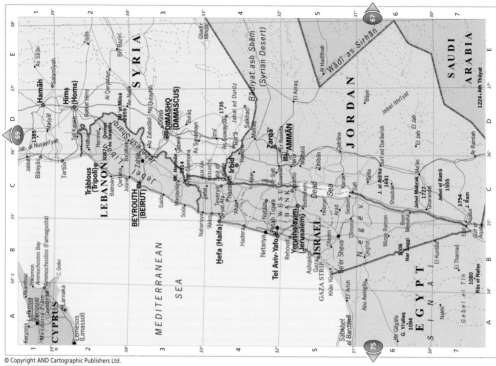

© Copyright AND Cartographic Publishers Ltd.

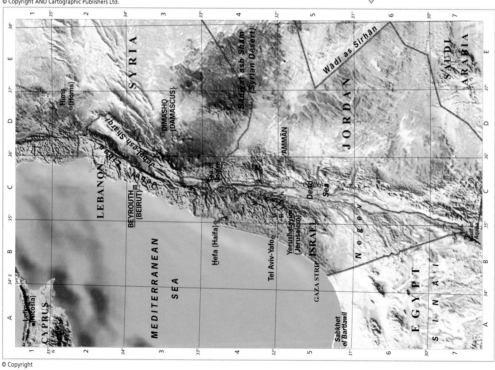

© Copyright

Scale 1 : 11 300 000

0   100   200   300 km

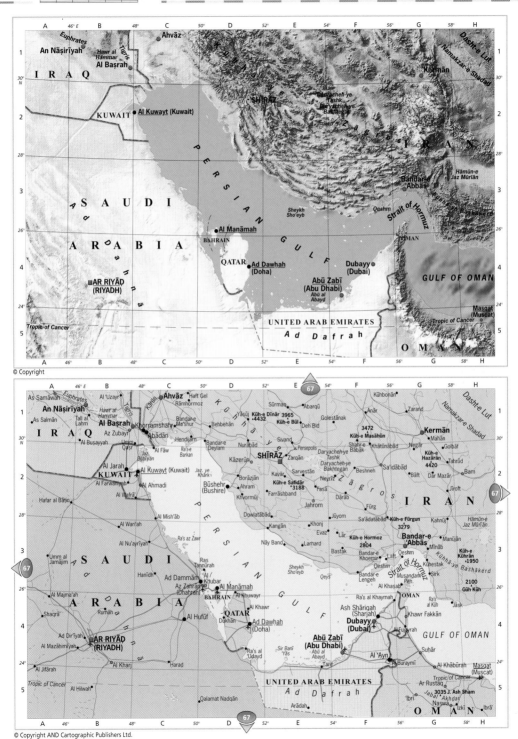

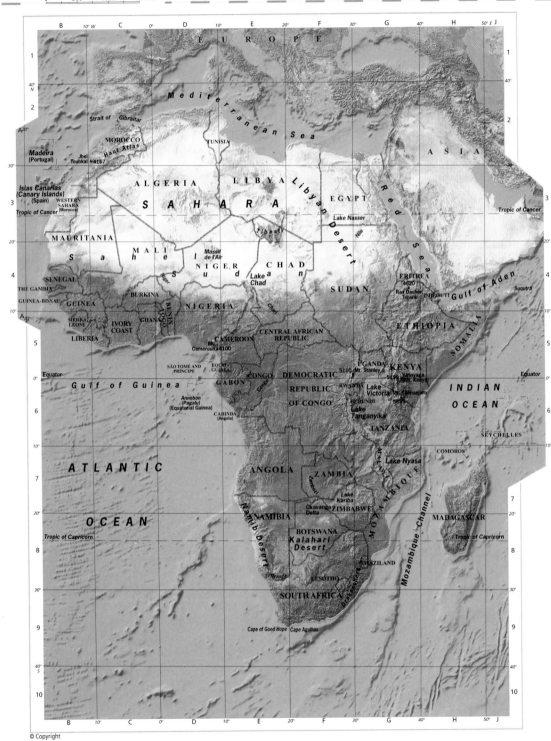

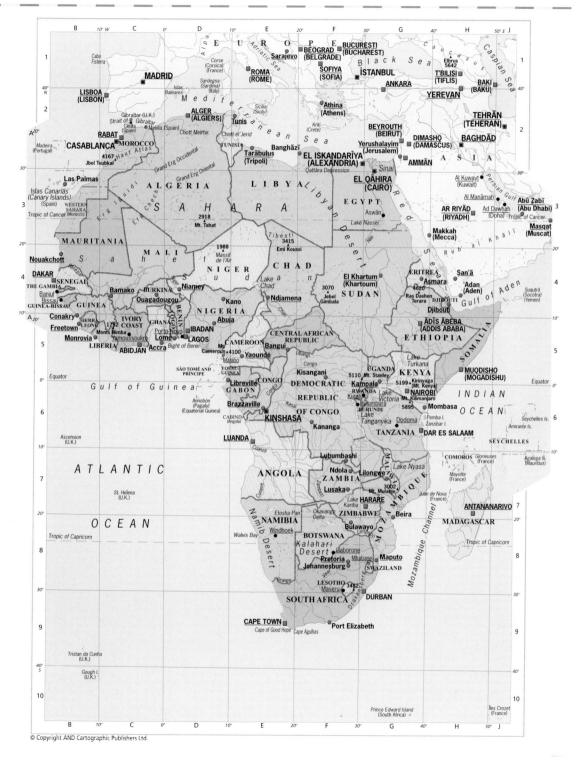

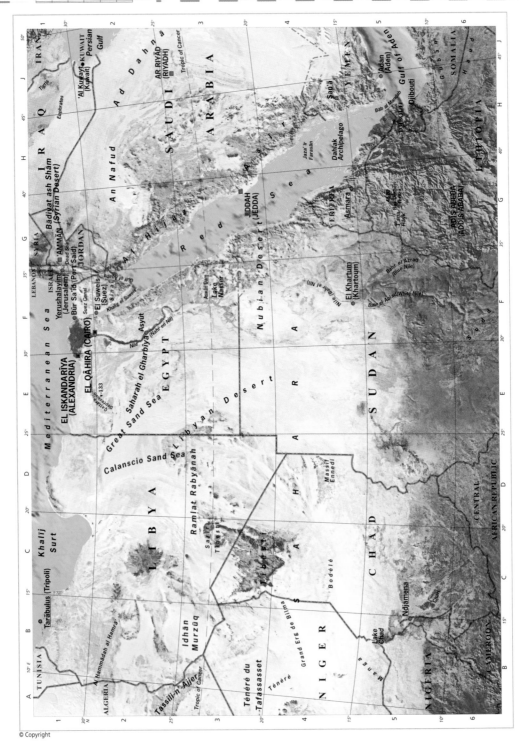

Scale 1 : 22 500 000

0   200   400   600 km

© Copyright

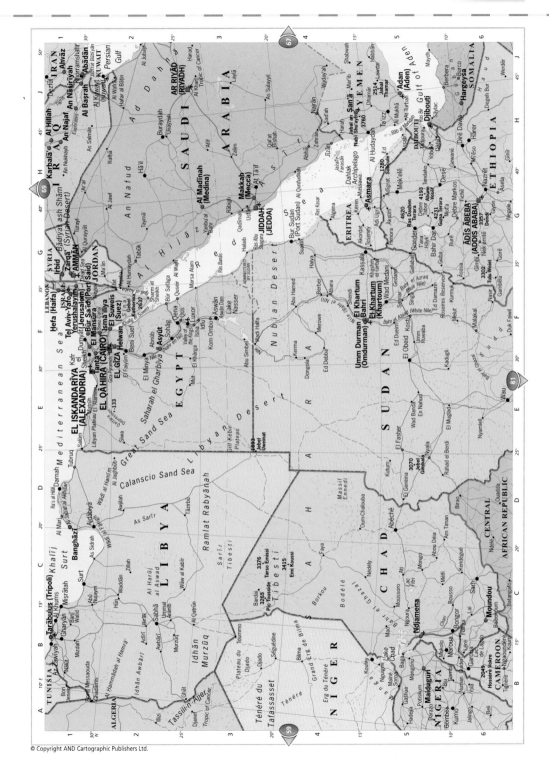

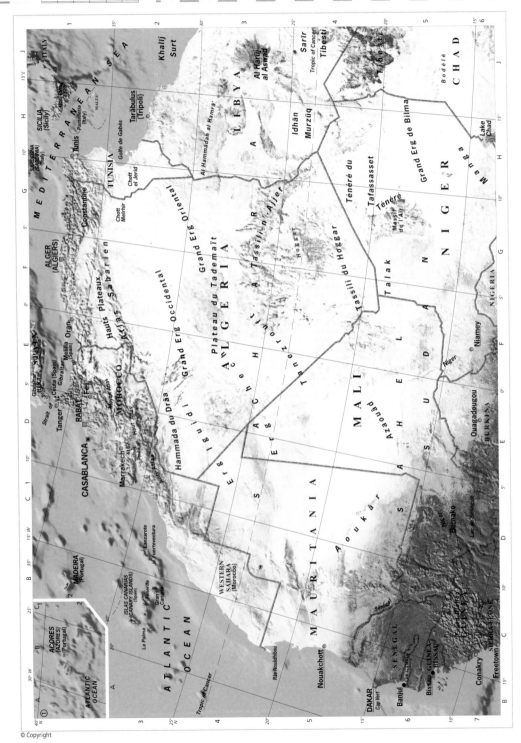

Scale 1 : 22 500 000

0   200   400   600 km

© Copyright

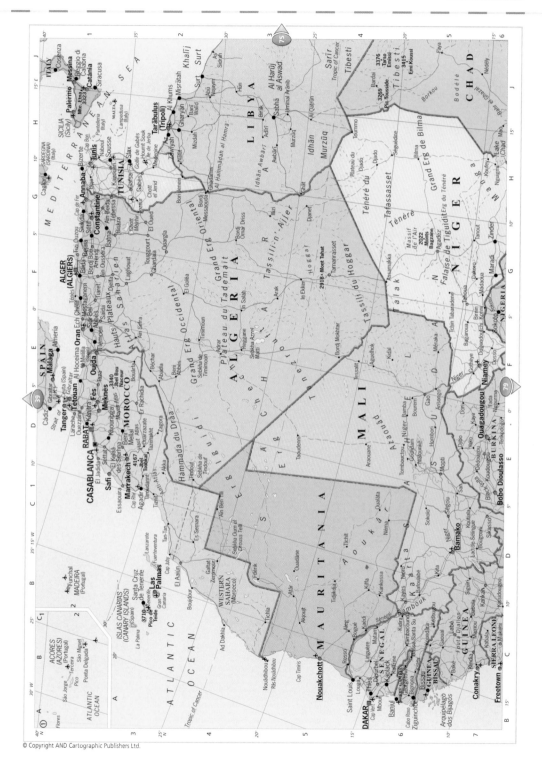

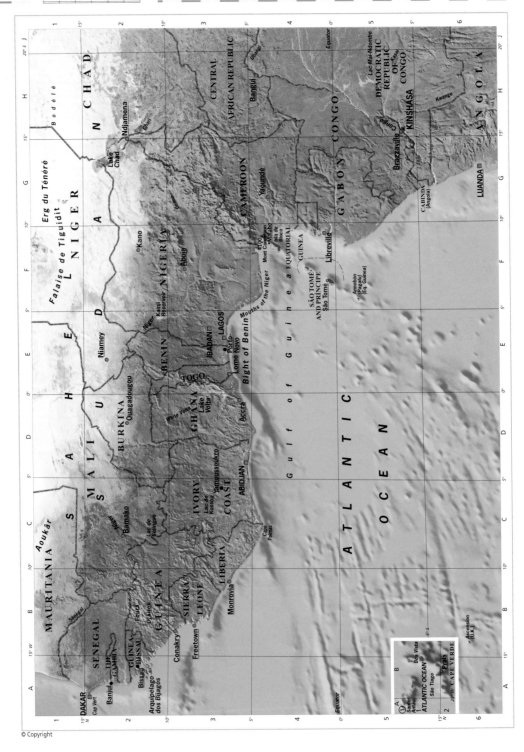

Scale 1 : 22 500 000

0   200   400   600 km

© Copyright

78

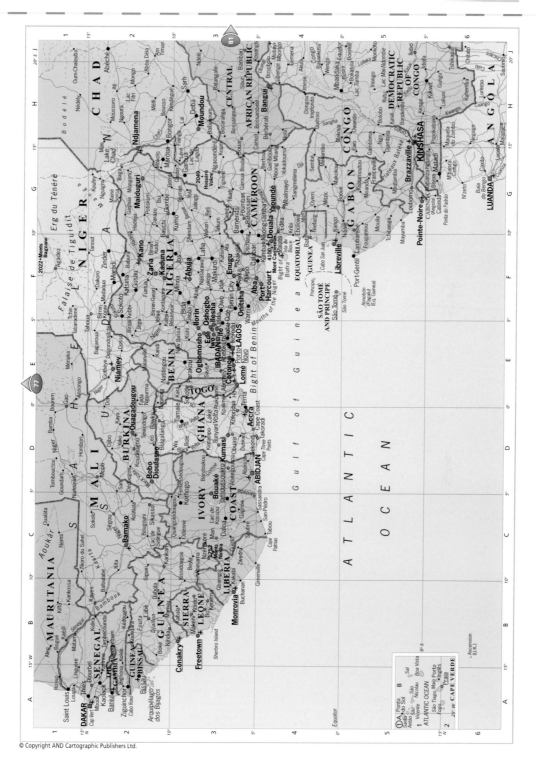

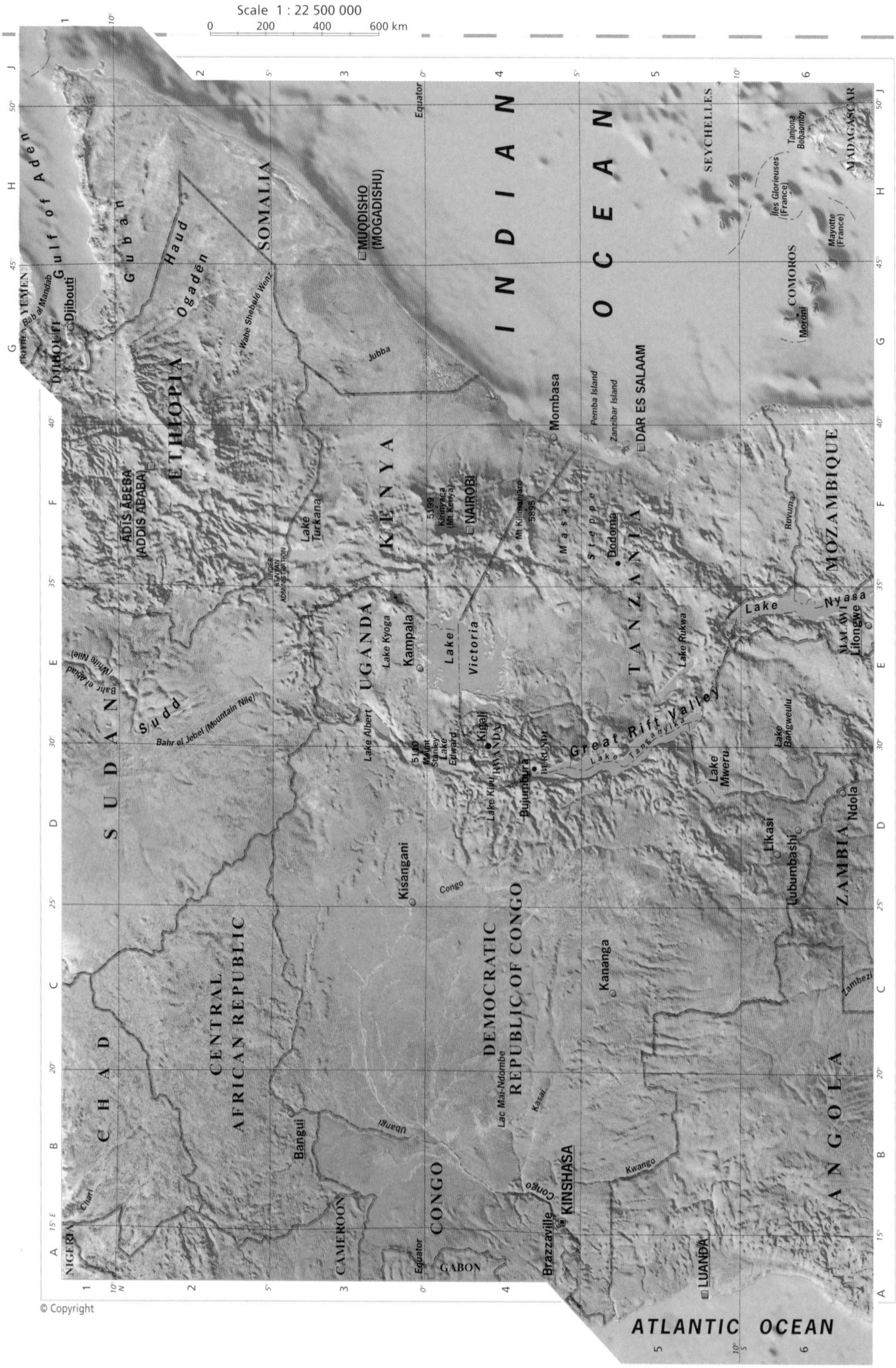

0   200   400   600 km

INDIAN OCEAN

ATLANTIC OCEAN

Gulf of Aden

YEMEN
Ras Siyan Bab al Mandab
Djibouti
DJIBOUTI
Guban
Haud
Ogaden
SOMALIA
MUQDISHO (MOGADISHU)

ETHIOPIA
ADDIS ABEBA (ADDIS ABABA)
Wabi Shebele Wenz
Jubba

SUDAN
Bahr el Abiad (White Nile)
Bahr el Jebel (Mountain Nile)
Sudd
Lake Turkana

KENYA
Kirinyaga (Mt Kenya) 5199
NAIROBI
Mt Kilimanjaro 5895
Masai
Mombasa
Pemba Island
Zanzibar Island
DAR ES SALAAM

SEYCHELLES
Îles Glorieuses (France)
Mayotte (France)
COMOROS
Moroni
Tanjona Bobaomby
MADAGASCAR

UGANDA
Lake Kyoga
Kampala
Lake Albert
Lake Edward
Lake Kivu
Lake Victoria
RWANDA
Kigali
BURUNDI
Bujumbura
Lake Tanganyika

TANZANIA
Steppe
Dodoma
Lake Rukwa
Great Rift Valley
Lake Nyasa
Lake Mweru
Lake Bangweulu
Rovuma

MOZAMBIQUE

MALAWI
Lilongwe

ZAMBIA
Likasi
Lubumbashi
Ndola
Zambezi

DEMOCRATIC REPUBLIC OF CONGO
Kisangani
Congo
Lac Mai-Ndombe
Kananga
Kasai
Ubangi
Kwango
Kwango
KINSHASA

CONGO
Brazzaville
GABON
CAMEROON
Equator

CENTRAL AFRICAN REPUBLIC
Bangui
CHAD
NIGERIA
Chari

ANGOLA
LUANDA

© Copyright

80

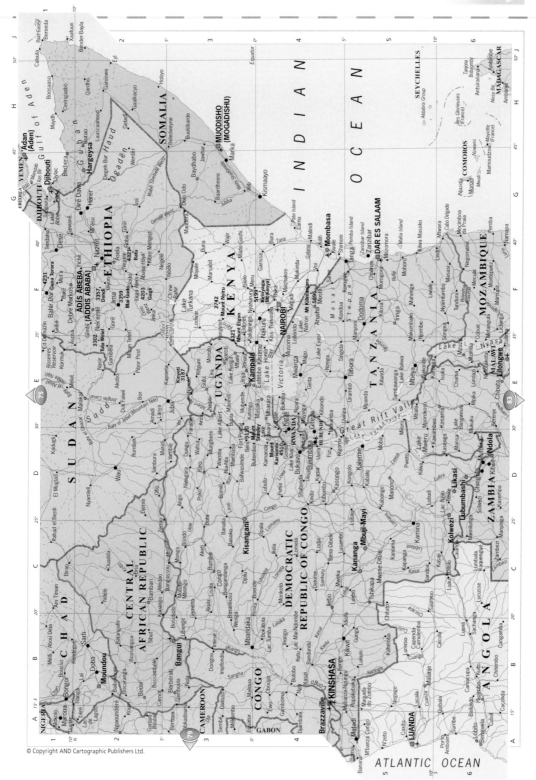

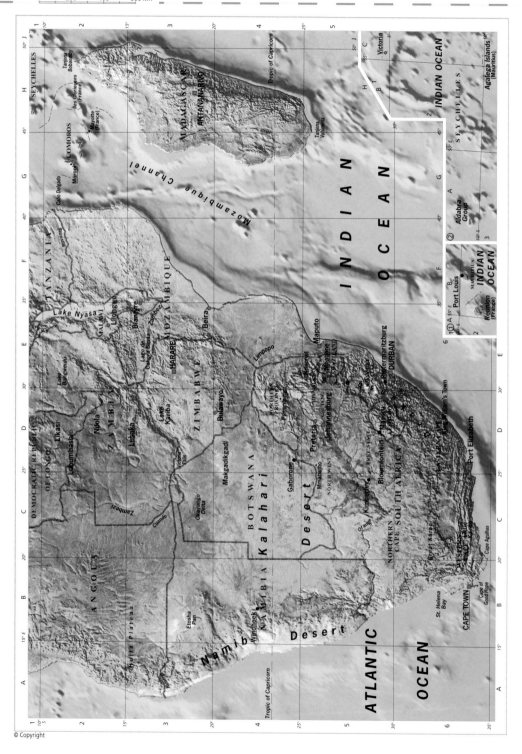

Scale 1 : 22 500 000

0   200   400   600 km

SEYCHELLES

INDIAN OCEAN

Victoria

Aldabra
Group

Agalega Islands
(Mauritius)

S E Y C H E L L E S

Port Louis

MAURITIUS

INDIAN
OCEAN

Réunion
(France)

COMOROS

Moroni

Mayotte
(France)

Îles Glorieuses
(France)

Tanjona
Bobaomby

M A D A G A S C A R

ANTANANARIVO

Tanjona
Vohimena

Tropic of Capricorn

Mozambique Channel

Cabo Delgado

TANZANIA

Ruvuma

Lake Nyasa

Lilongwe

MALAWI

Blantyre

Lago de
Cahora Bassa

HARARE

Beira

M O Z A M B I Q U E

Zambezi

Lubumbashi

Likasi

DEMOCRATIC REPUBLIC

OF CONGO

Lake
Bangweulu

Ndola

Z A M B I A

Lusaka

Lake
Kariba

Victoria
Falls

ZIMBABWE

Bulawayo

Limpopo

Maputo

ANGOLA

Bulla Plateau

Cubango

Cuando

Cuito

Zambezi

Okavango
Delta

Etosha
Pan

Windhoek

N A M I B I A

Makgadikgadi

B O T S W A N A

Kalahari
D e s e r t

Gaborone

Mmabatho

NORTH-WEST

Pretoria

GAUTENG

Johannesburg

LIMPOPO
PROVINCE

MPUMALANGA

Nelspruit

SWAZILAND

Mbabane

LESOTHO

Maseru

Pietermaritzburg

DURBAN

KWAZULU-NATAL

FREE STATE

Bloemfontein

Kimberley

Orange

NORTHERN
CAPE

S O U T H   A F R I C A

EASTERN CAPE

King William's Town

Port Elizabeth

Cape Agulhas

WESTERN CAPE

Great Karoo

CAPE TOWN

Cape of
Good Hope

St. Helena Bay

N a m i b   D e s e r t

Orange

Tropic of Capricorn

ATLANTIC

OCEAN

I N D I A N

O C E A N

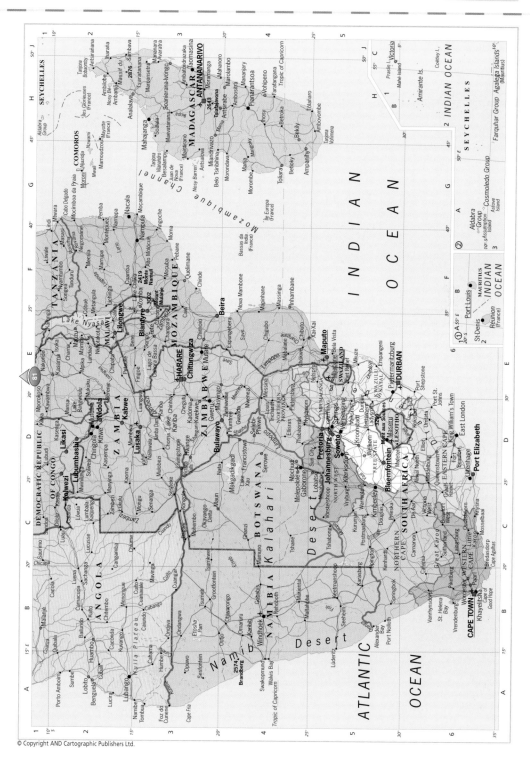

Scale 1 : 79 000 000

0   500   1000   1500   2000 km

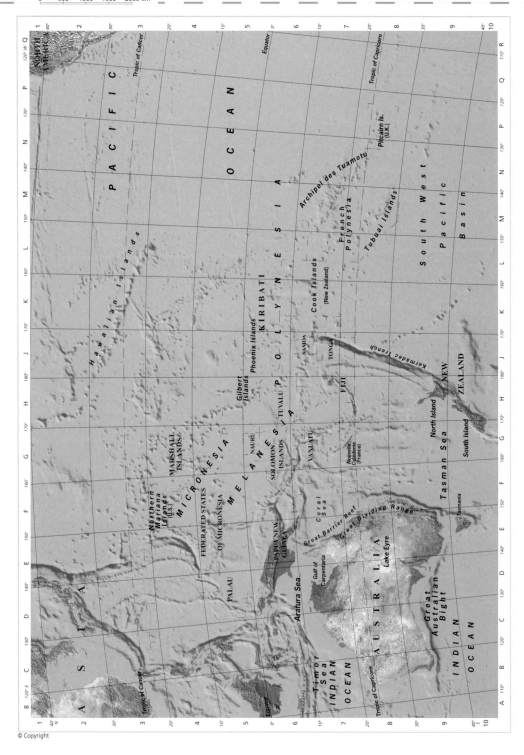

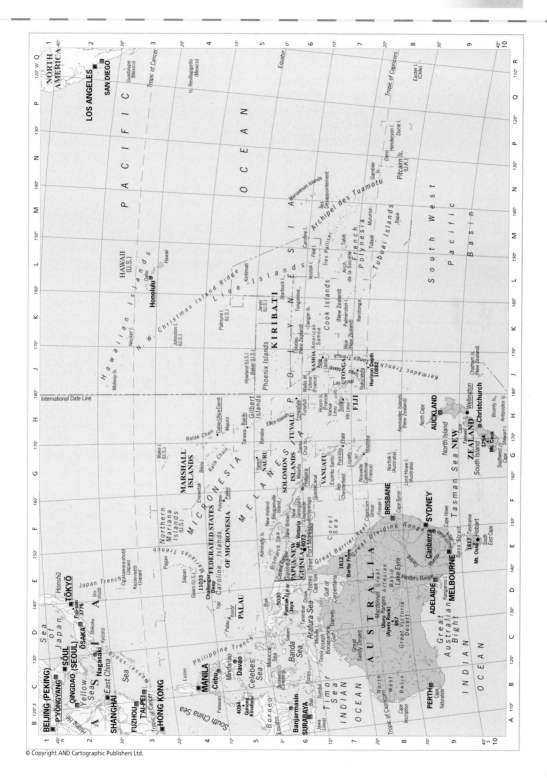

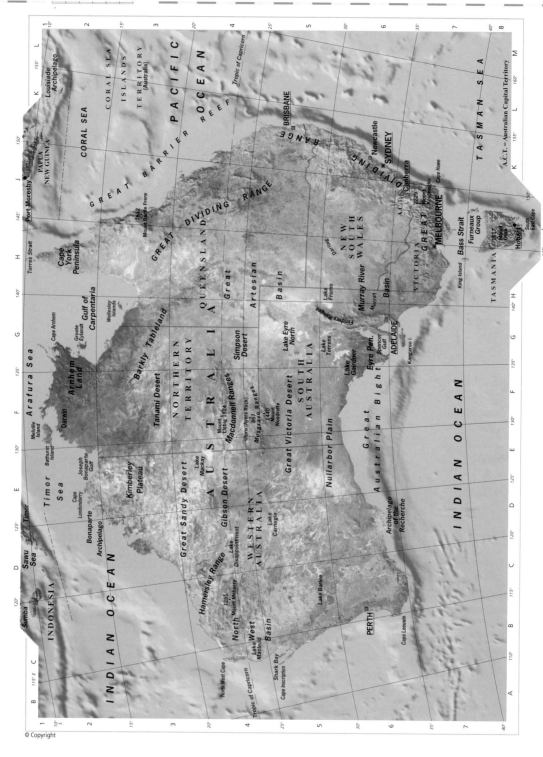

Scale 1 : 26 900 000

0   200   400   600 km

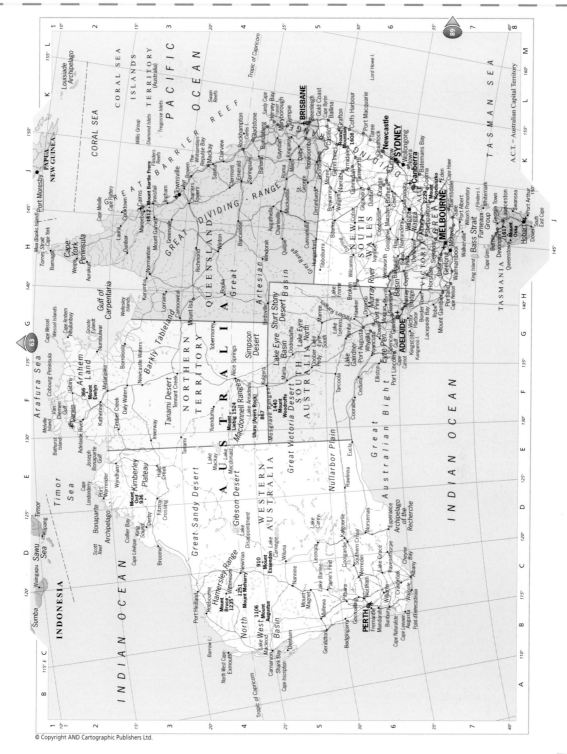

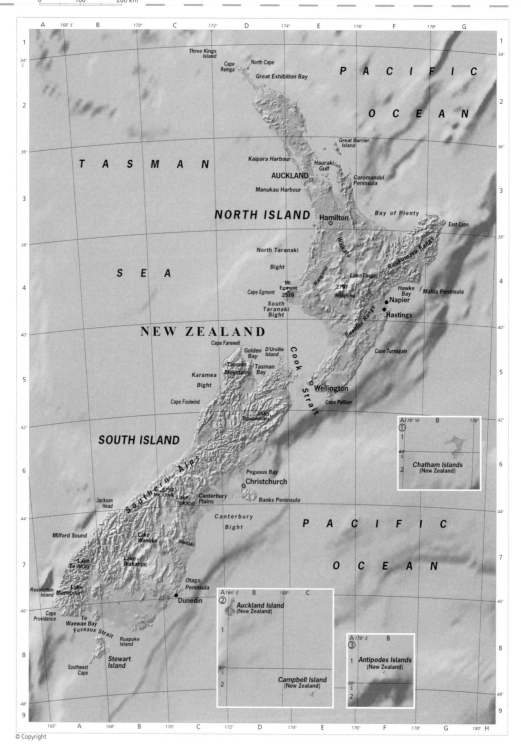

Scale 1 : 9 000 000

0   100   200 km

A 168° E   B   170°   C   172°   D   174°   E   176°   F   178°   G

Three Kings
Island

Cape
Reinga   North Cape

Great Exhibition Bay

P A C I F I C

O C E A N

Great Barrier
Island

T A S M A N

Kaipara Harbour   Hauraki
Gulf

AUCKLAND   Coromandel
Peninsula

Manukau Harbour

NORTH ISLAND   Hamilton   Bay of Plenty

East Cape

S E A   North Taranaki
Bight

Lake Taupo

Mt.
Egmont   2797
Cape Egmont   2518   Ruapehu   Hawke
Bay   Mahia Peninsula

South
Taranaki
Bight   Napier

Hastings

NEW ZEALAND

Cape Farewell

Golden   D'Urville
Bay   Island   Cape Turnagain

Tasman   Tasman
Mountains   Bay

Karamea
Bight

Cape Foulwind

2885
Tapuaenuku   **Wellington**

Cape Palliser

A 178° W   B   176°

① 1

44°
S

2

Chatham Islands
(New Zealand)

SOUTH ISLAND

Pegasus Bay

Christchurch

Jackson
Head   2794
Mt. Cook   Lake
Tekapo   Canterbury
Plains   Banks Peninsula

Milford Sound   Canterbury
Bight   **P A C I F I C**

Lake
Wanaka

Waitaki   **O C E A N**

Lake
Te Anau   Lake
Wakatipu

Resolution
Island   Lake
Manapouri   Otago
Peninsula   A 166° E   B   168°   C

② 1

Auckland Island
(New Zealand)

Dunedin

Cape
Providence   Te
Waewae Bay   2

Foveaux Strait   52°
S   Campbell Island
(New Zealand)

Ruapuke
Island   A 178° E   B

③ 1

Antipodes Islands
(New Zealand)

**Stewart
Island**

Southwest
Cape   50°
S   2

166°   A   168°   B   170°   C   172°   D   174°   E   176°   F   178°   G   180°   H

© Copyright

88

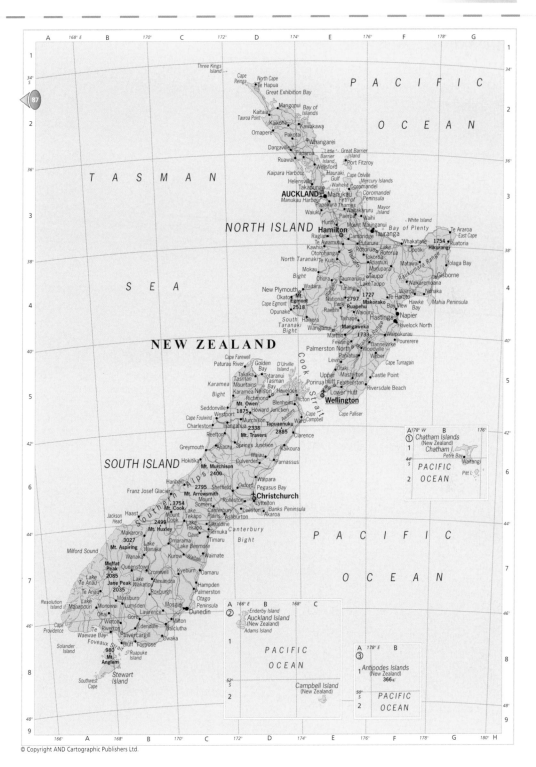

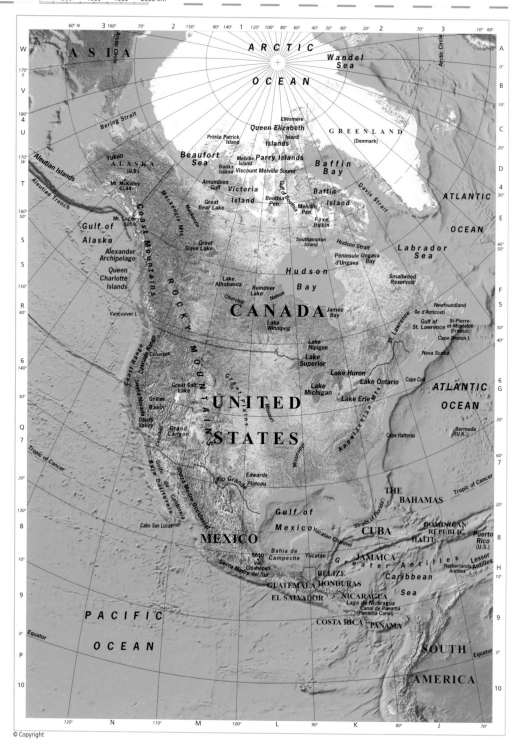

Scale 1 : 67 600 000

0   500   1000   1500   2000 km

ARCTIC OCEAN

Wandel Sea

ASIA

Arctic Circle

Bering Strait

ALASKA (U.S.)

Yukon

Beaufort Sea

Prince Patrick Island

Queen Elizabeth Islands

Ellesmere Island

GREENLAND (Denmark)

Mt. McKinley 6194

Mackenzie Mts.

Amundsen Gulf

Melville Island

Banks Island

Parry Islands

Viscount Melville Sound

Baffin Bay

Arctic Circle

ATLANTIC

Great Bear Lake

Victoria Island

Gulf of Boothia

Boothia Pen.

Melville Pen.

Baffin Island

Davis Strait

OCEAN

Mt. Logan 6059

Gulf of Alaska

Alexander Archipelago

Great Slave Lake

Foxe Basin

Southampton Island

Hudson Strait

Labrador Sea

Queen Charlotte Islands

Lake Athabasca

Reindeer Lake

Nelson

Hudson Bay

Péninsule d'Ungava

Ungava Bay

Smallwood Reservoir

Vancouver I.

Churchill

CANADA

James Bay

Newfoundland

Île d'Anticosti

St-Pierre-et-Miquelon (France)

Coast Mountains

ROCKY MOUNTAINS

Columbia

Lake Winnipeg

Lake Nipigon

St. Lawrence

Gulf of St. Lawrence

Cape Breton I.

Cascade Range

Great Salt Lake

Great Plains

Lake Superior

Lake Huron

Lake Ontario

Nova Scotia

Cape Cod

ATLANTIC

Sierra Nevada

Great Basin

UNITED

Missouri

Lake Michigan

Lake Erie

Appalachian Mts.

OCEAN

Death Valley

Grand Canyon

STATES

Cape Hatteras

Bermuda (U.K.)

Colorado

Tropic of Cancer

Edwards Plateau

Rio Grande

Mississippi

THE BAHAMAS

Tropic of Cancer

Cabo San Lucas

Golfo de California

Gulf of Mexico

Straits of Florida

CUBA

DOMINICAN REPUBLIC

Puerto Rico (U.S.)

MEXICO

Bahía de Campeche

Yucatán Channel

HAITI

Sierra Madre Occidental

5610 Citlaltépetl

Yucatán

JAMAICA

Greater Antilles

Netherlands Antilles

Lesser Antilles

BELIZE

Caribbean

Sierra Madre del Sur

GUATEMALA HONDURAS

EL SALVADOR

NICARAGUA

Sea

Lago de Nicaragua

PACIFIC

Canal de Panamá (Panama Canal)

COSTA RICA

PANAMA

Equator

OCEAN

SOUTH

AMERICA

Equator

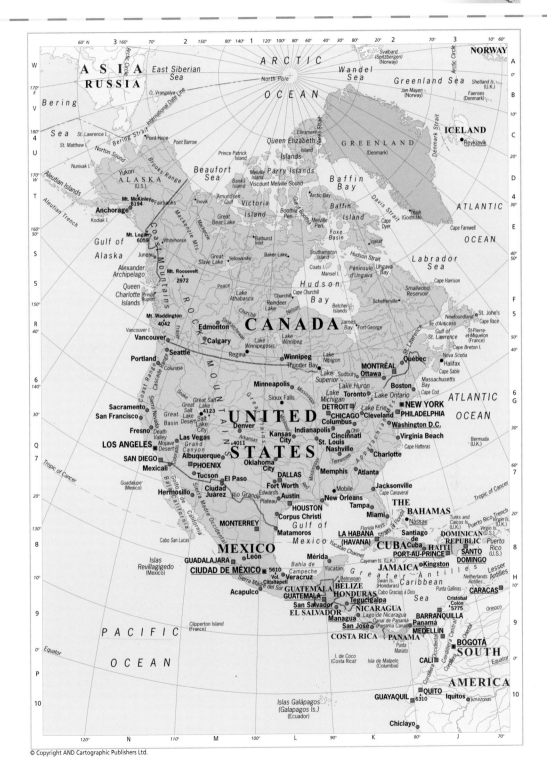

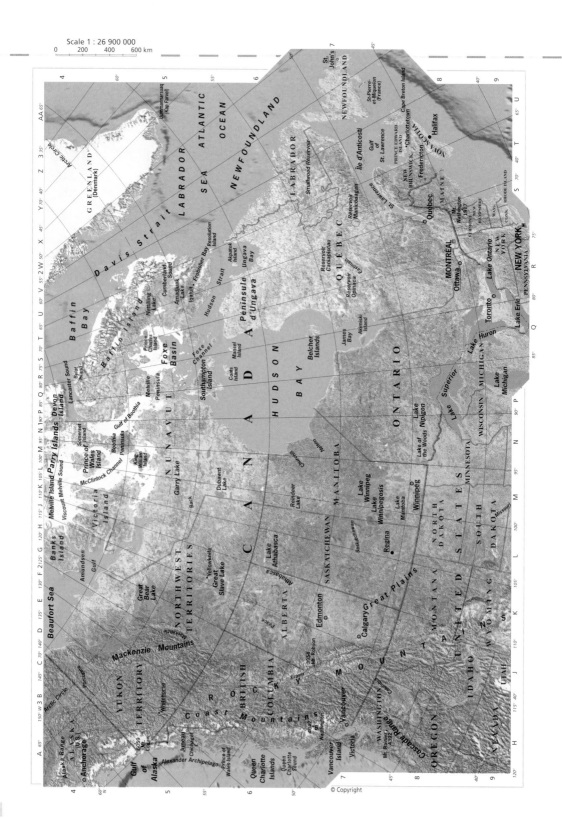

Scale 1 : 26 900 000

0   200   400   600 km

92

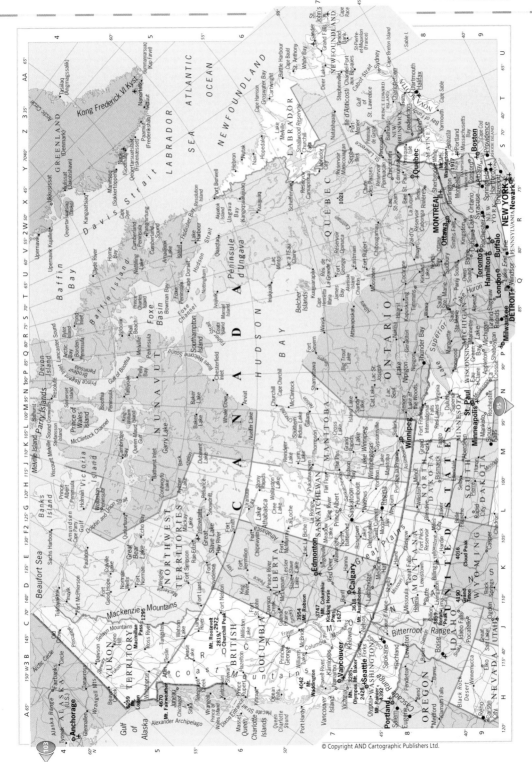

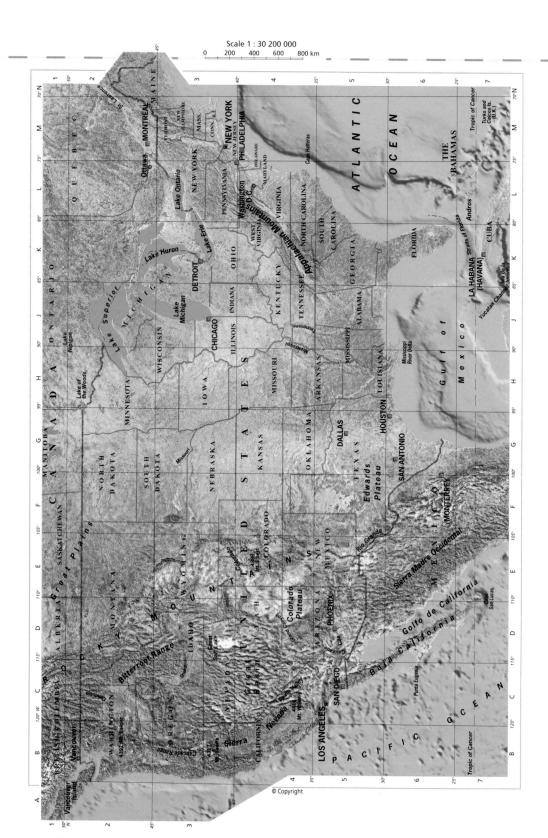

Scale 1 : 30 200 000

0 200 400 600 800 km

© Copyright

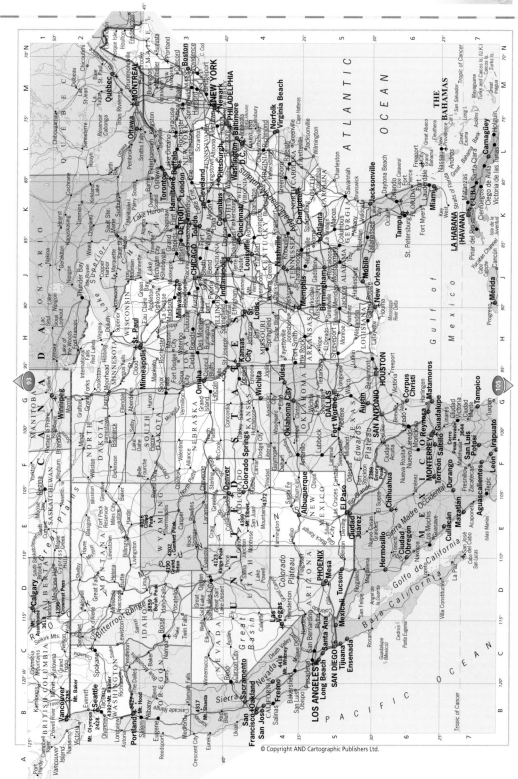

Scale 1 : 14 000 000

0   100   200   300 km

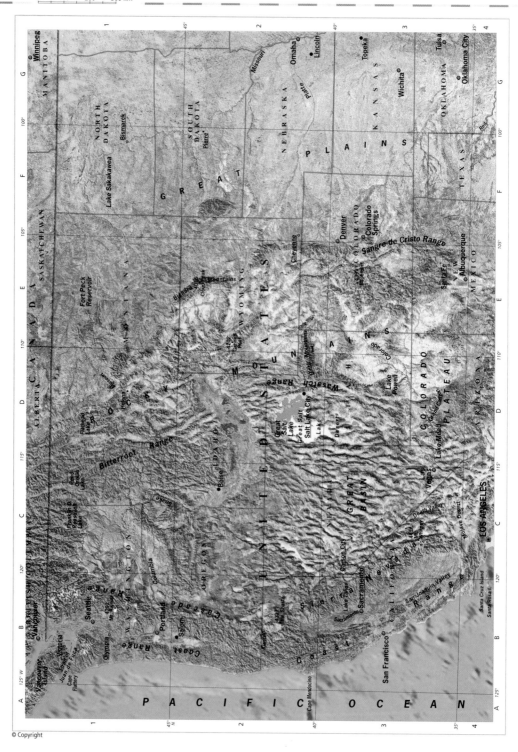

96

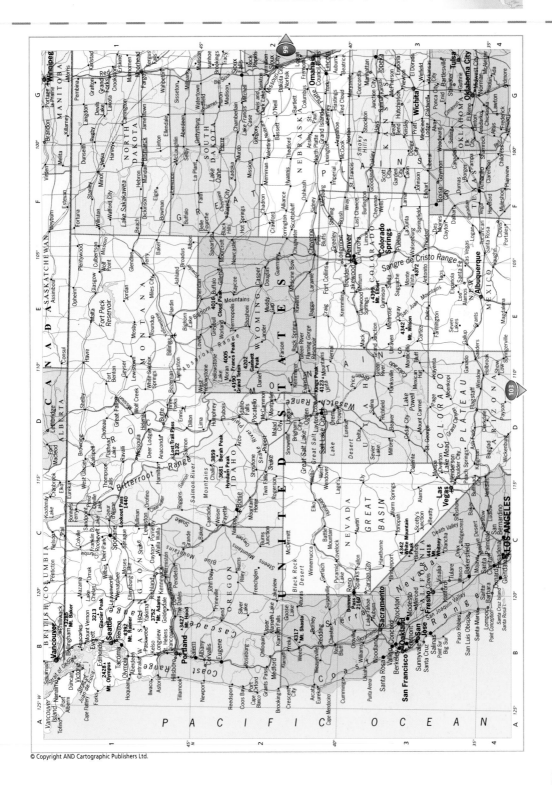

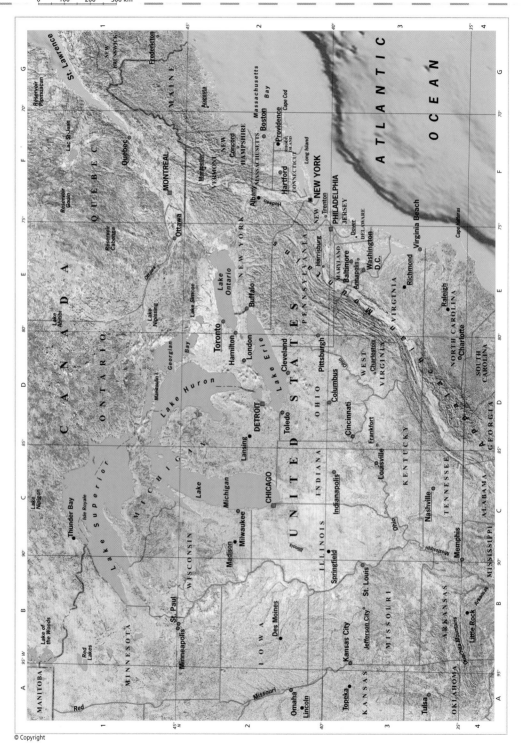

Scale 1 : 14 000 000

0   100   200   300 km

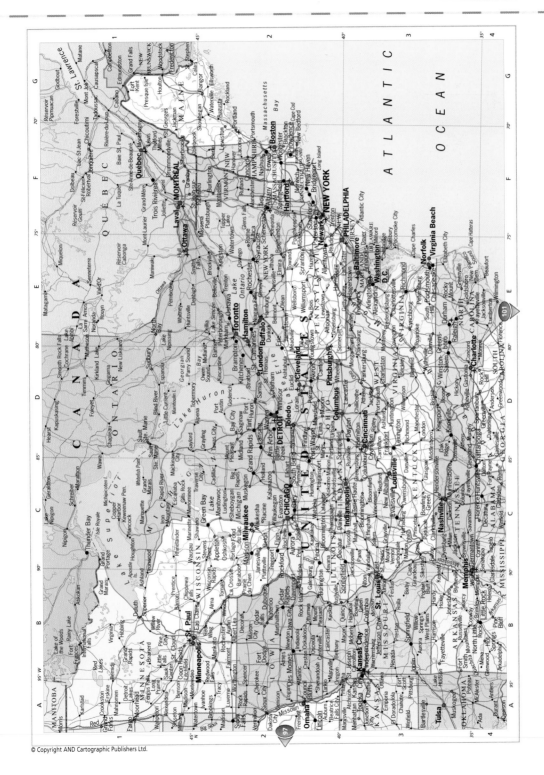

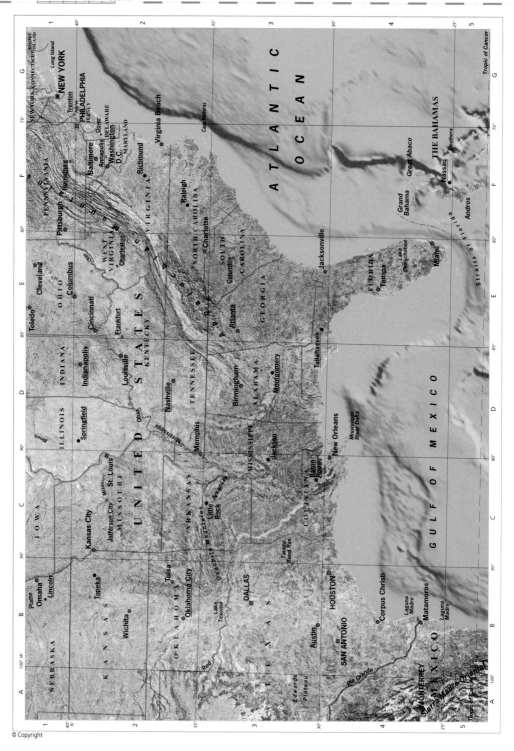

Scale 1 : 14 000 000

0   100   200   300 km

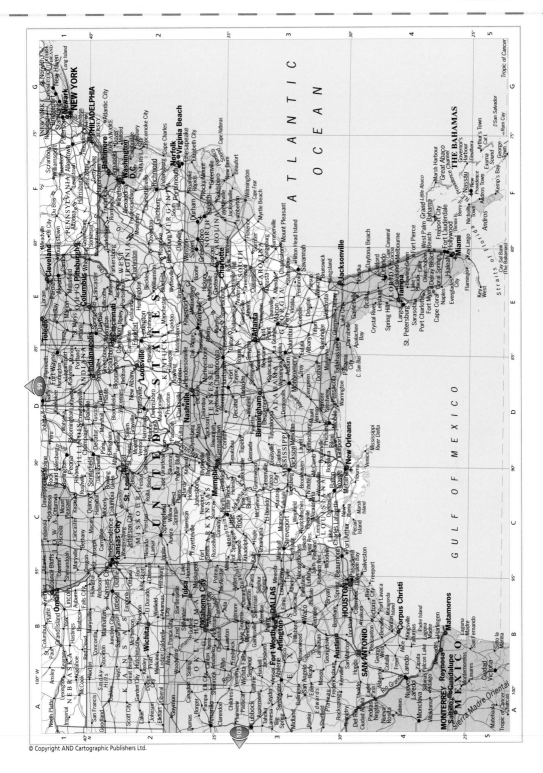

Scale 1 : 14 000 000

0   100   200   300 km

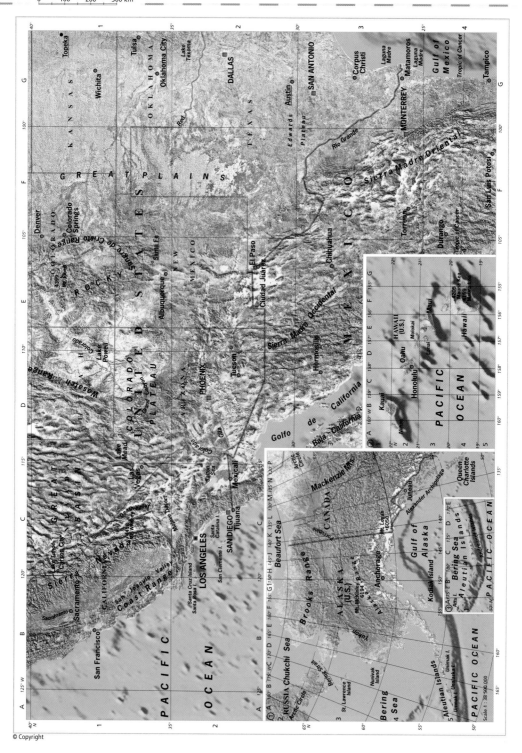

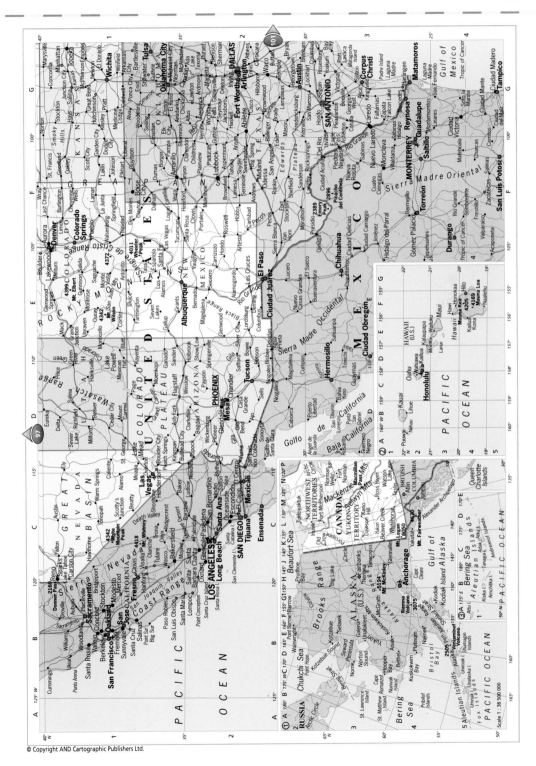

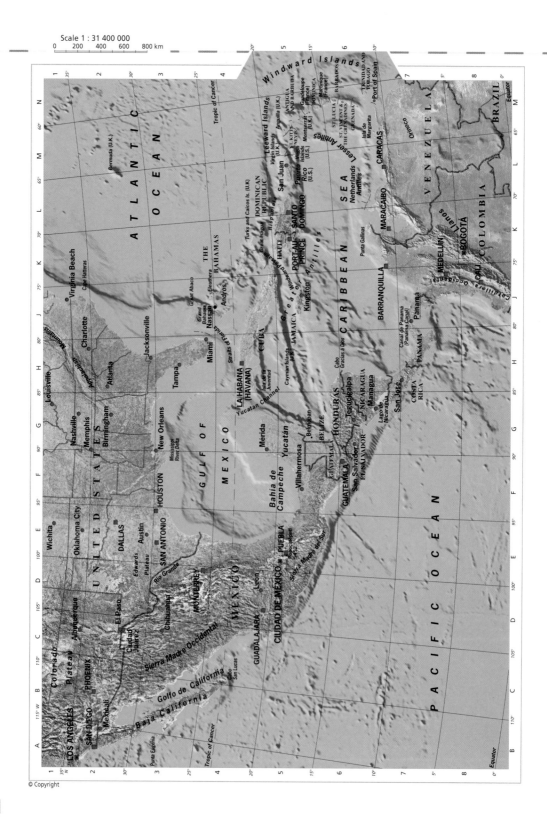

Scale 1 : 31 400 000

0   200   400   600   800 km

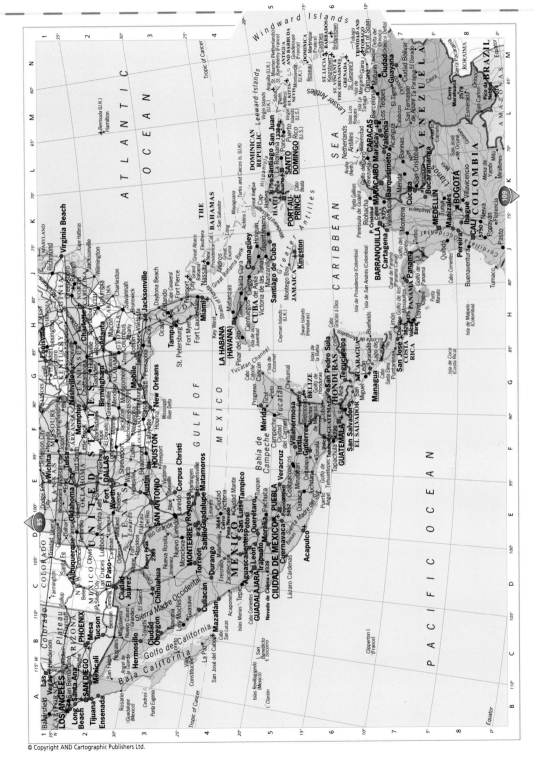

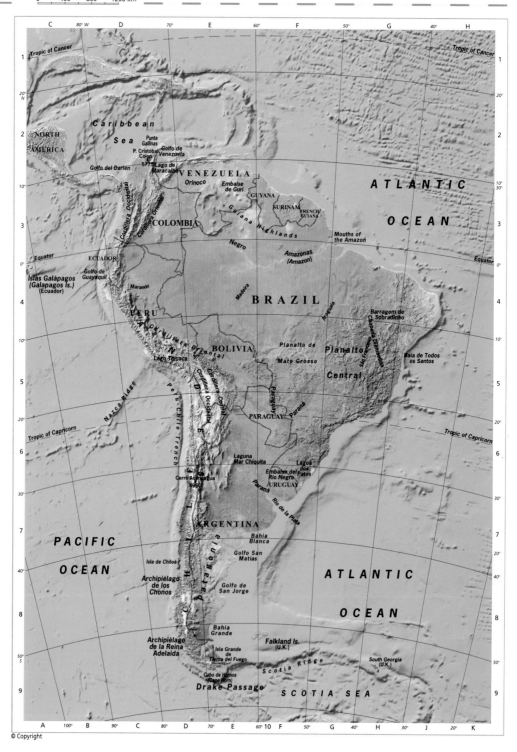

Scale 1 : 54 600 000

0   400   800   1200 km

© Copyright

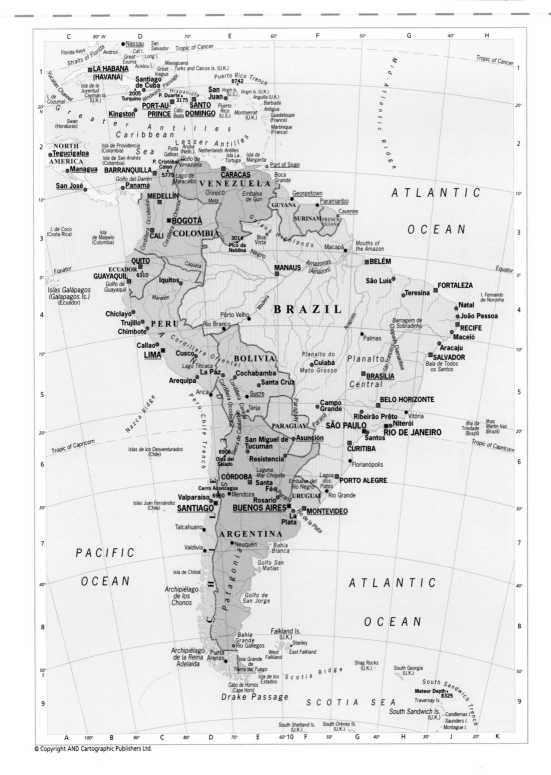

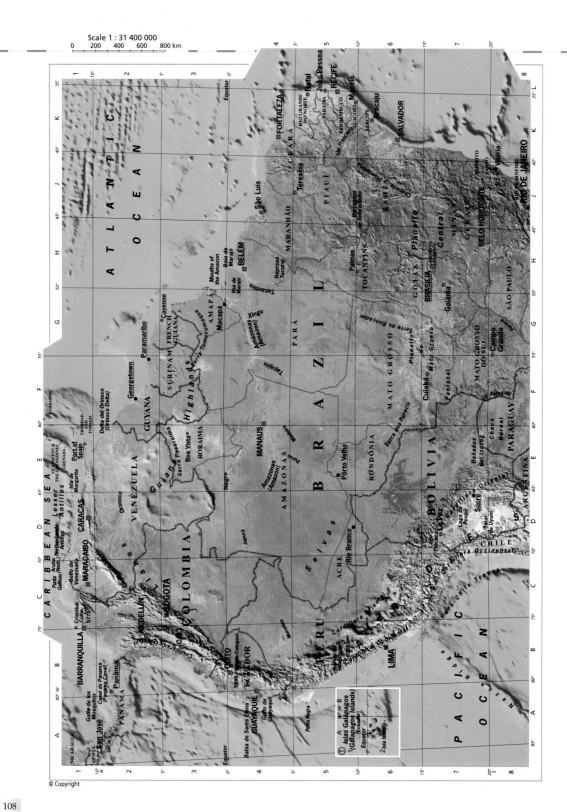

Scale 1 : 31 400 000
0   200   400   600   800 km

① Islas Galápagos
(Galápagos Islands)
(Ecuador)
1 Isabela
2 Isla Isabela

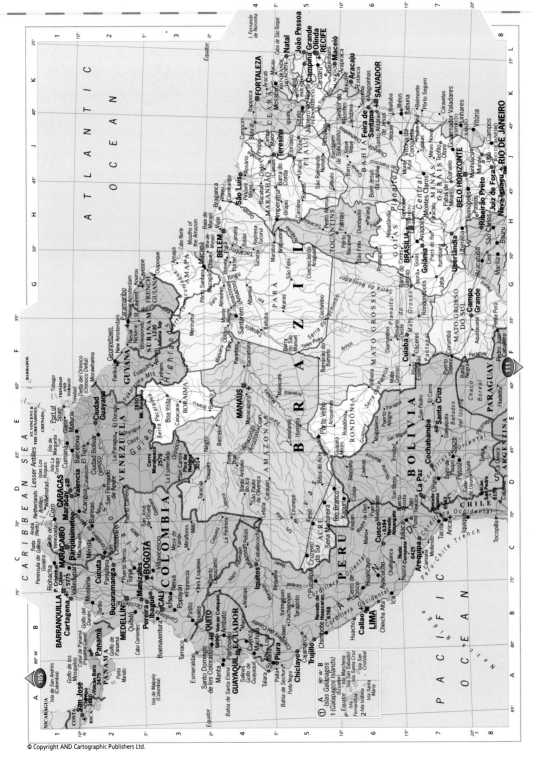

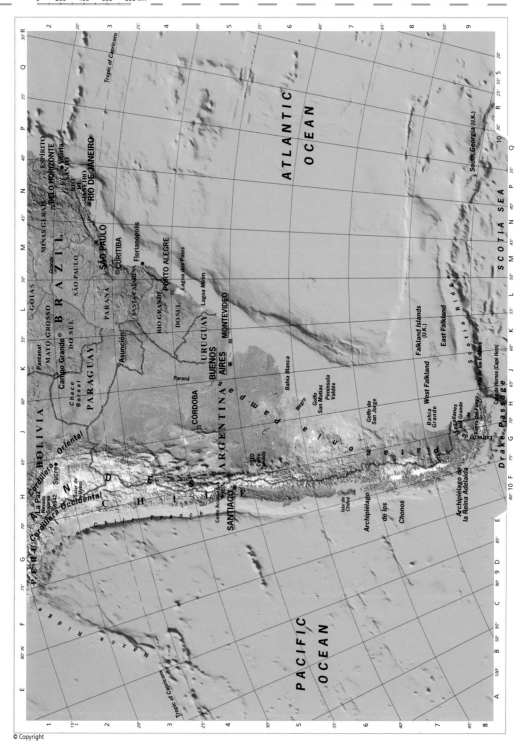

Scale 1 : 31 400 000

0   200   400   600   800 km

Tropic of Capricorn

ATLANTIC OCEAN

SCOTIA SEA

South Georgia (U.K.)

BRAZIL
ESPÍRITO SANTO
BELO HORIZONTE
Vitória
MINAS GERAIS
RIO DE JANEIRO
RIO DE JANEIRO
SÃO PAULO
SÃO PAULO
CURITIBA
PARANÁ
Florianópolis
GOIÁS
MATO GROSSO
Campo Grande
MATO GROSSO DO SUL
Pantanal
PORTO ALEGRE
RIO GRANDE
DO SUL
Lagoa dos Patos
Lagoa Mirim
SANTA CATARINA
Grande
Chaco Boreal
PARAGUAY
Asunción
URUGUAY
MONTEVIDEO
Paraná
BUENOS AIRES
Bahía Blanca

BOLIVIA
Sucre
La Paz
Nevado Sajama
Salar de Uyuni
Cordillera Oriental
Cordillera Occidental
SIERRA
CORDOBA
ARGENTINA
Río Colorado
Negro
Golfo San Matías
Península Valdés
Golfo de San Jorge
Bahía Grande

CHILE
SANTIAGO
Cerro Aconcagua
Isla de Chiloé
Archipiélago de los Chonos
Archipiélago de la Reina Adelaida
Estrecho de Magallanes
Tierra del Fuego
Isla Grande
Cabo de Hornos (Cape Horn)
Isla de los Estados

Chile Trench
Perú - Chile Trench

Nazca Ridge

Falkland Islands (U.K.)
West Falkland
East Falkland
Scotia Ridge

Drake Passage

Patagonia

PACIFIC OCEAN

Tropic of Capricorn

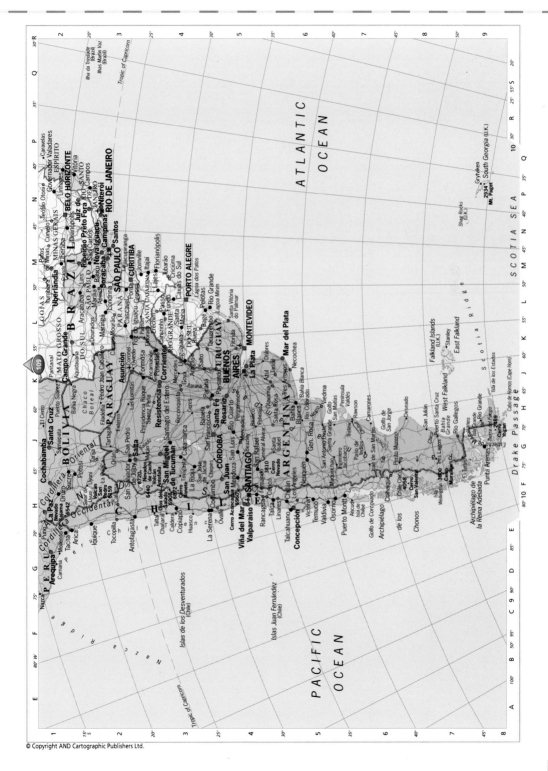

Polar Regions

Scale 1 : 99 000 000

0   500 1000 1500 2000 km

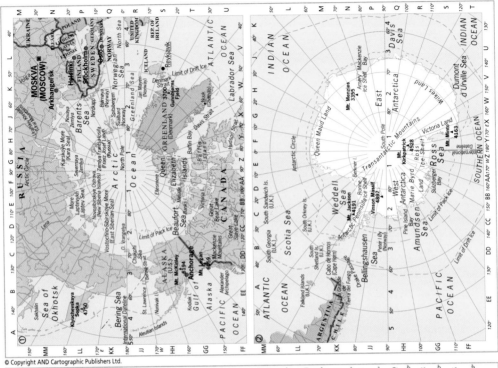

© Copyright AND Cartographic Publishers Ltd.

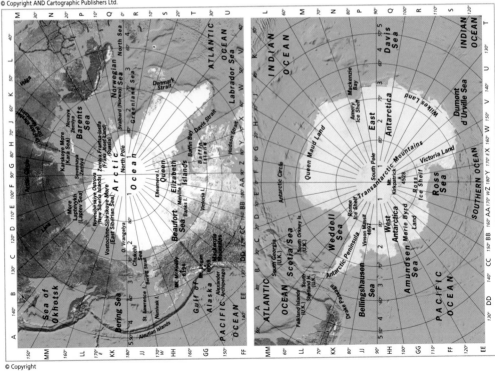

© Copyright

112

Index

How to use the index

This is an alphabetically arranged index of the places and features that can be found on the maps in this atlas. Each name is generally indexed to the largest scale map on which it appears. If that map covers a double page, the name will always be indexed by the left-hand page number.

Names composed of two or more words are alphabetised as if they were one word.

All names appear in full in the index, except for 'St.' and 'Ste.', which although abbreviated, are indexed as though spelled in full.

Where two or more places have the same name, they can be distinguished from each other by the country or province name which immediately follows the entry. These names are indexed in the alphabetical order of the country or province.

Alternative names, such as English translations, can also be found in the index and are cross-referenced to the map form by the '=' sign. In these cases the names also appear in brackets on the maps.

Settlements are indexed to the position of the symbol, all other features are indexed to the position of the name on the map.

Abbreviations used in this index are explained in the list opposite.

Finding a name on the map

Each index entry contains the name, followed by a symbol indicating the feature type (for example, settlement, river), a page reference and a grid reference:

Name	Owen Sound	●	99	D2
	Owo	●	79	F3
	Owyhee	✓	97	C2
Symbol	Oxford, New Zealand	◉	89	D6
	Oxford, U.K.	●	33	A3
	Oxnard	●	103	C2
Page reference	Oyama	●	**59**	K5
	Oyapock	✓	109	G3
	Oyem	●	79	G4
Grid reference	Oyonnax	●	41	**A4**

The grid reference locates a place or feature within a rectangle formed by the network of lines of longitude and latitude. A name can be found by referring to the red letters and numbers placed around the maps. First find the letter, which appears along the top and bottom of the map, and then the number, down the sides. The name will be found within the rectangle uniquely defined by that letter and number. A number in brackets preceding the grid reference indicates that the name is to be found within an inset map.

Abbreviations

Al.	Alabama	N.D.	North Dakota
Ariz.	Arizona	Nebr.	Nebraska
Ark.	Arkansas	Nev.	Nevada
Calif.	California	Nfld.	Newfoundland
Colo.	Colorado	N.H.	New Hampshire
Conn.	Connecticut	N. Ire.	Northern Ireland
Del.	Delaware	N. Mex.	New Mexico
Eng.	England	N.Y.	New York
Fla.	Florida	Oh.	Ohio
Ga.	Georgia	Okla.	Oklahoma
Ia.	Iowa	Oreg.	Oregon
Id.	Idaho	Orkney Is.	Orkney Islands
Ill.	Illinois	Pa.	Pennsylvania
Ind.	Indiana	S.C.	South Carolina
Kans.	Kansas	S.D.	South Dakota
Ky.	Kentucky	Shetland Is.	Shetland Islands
La.	Louisiana	Tenn.	Tennessee
Mass.	Massachusetts	Tex.	Texas
Md.	Maryland	U.K.	United Kingdom
Me.	Maine	U.S.	United States
M.G.	Mato Grosso	Ut.	Utah
Mich.	Michigan	Va.	Virginia
Minn.	Minnesota	Vt.	Vermont
Miss.	Mississippi	Wash.	Washington
Mo.	Missouri	Wis.	Wisconsin
Mont.	Montana	W. Va.	West Virginia
N.B.	New Brunswick	Wyo.	Wyoming
N.C.	North Carolina		

Symbols

✗	Continent name	✓	River, canal
Ⓐ	Country name	◖	Lake, salt lake
ⓐ	State or province name	◣	Gulf, strait, bay
■	Country capital	◢	Sea, ocean
◩	State or province capital	⊟	Cape, point
●	Settlement	⬤	Island or island group, rocky or coral reef
▲	Mountain, volcano, peak		
⛰	Mountain range	✳	Place of interest
◉	Physical region or feature	⌘	Historical or cultural region

Glossary

This is an alphabetically arranged glossary of the geographical terms used on the maps and in this index. The first column shows the map form, the second the language of origin and the third the English translation.

A

açude	Portuguese	reservoir
adası	Turkish	island
akra	Greek	peninsula
alpen	German	mountains
alpes	French	mountains
alpi	Italian	mountains
älven	Swedish	river
archipiélago	Spanish	archipelago
arquipélago	Portuguese	archipelago

B

bab	Arabic	strait
bahía	Spanish	bay
bahir, bahr	Arabic	bay, lake, river
baía	Portuguese	bay
baie	French	bay
baja	Spanish	lower
bandar	Arabic, Somalian, Malay, Persian	harbour, port
baraji	Turkish	dam
barragem	Portuguese	reservoir
ben	Gaelic	mountain
Berg(e)	German	mountain(s)
boğazı	Turkish	strait
Bucht	German	bay
buḥayrat	Arabic	lake
burnu, burun	Turkish	cape

C

cabo	Spanish	cape
canal	French, Spanish	canal, channel
canale	Italian	canal, channel
cerro	Spanish	mountain
chott	Arabic	marsh, salt lake
co	Tibetan	lake
collines	French	hills
cordillera	Spanish	range

D

dağ(ı)	Turkish	mountain
dağlar(ı)	Turkish	mountains
danau	Indonesian	lake
daryacheh	Persian	lake
dasht	Persian	desert
djebel	Arabic	mountain(s)
-do	Korean	island

E

embalse	Spanish	reservoir
erg	Arabic	sandy desert
estrecho	Spanish	strait

F

feng	Chinese	mountain
-fjördur	Icelandic	fjord
-flói	Icelandic	bay

G

Gebirge	German	range
golfe	French	bay, gulf

H

golfo	Italian, Portuguese, Spanish	bay, gulf
göl, gölü	Turkish	lake
gora	Russian	mountain
gory	Russian	mountains
gunong	Malay	mountain
gunung	Indonesian	mountain

hai	Chinese	lake, sea
hāmūn	Persian	lake, marsh
hawr	Arabic	lake
hu	Chinese	lake, reservoir

I

île(s)	French	island(s)
ilha(s)	Portuguese	island(s)
isla(s)	Spanish	island(s)

J

jabal	Arabic	mountain(s)
-järvi	Finnish	lake
jaza'ir	Arabic	islands
jazīrat	Arabic	island
jbel	Arabic	mountain
jebel	Arabic	mountain
jezero	Serbo-Croatian	lake
jezioro	Polish	lake
jiang	Chinese	river
-jima	Japanese	island
-joki	Finnish	river
-jökull	Icelandic	glacier

K

kepulauan	Indonesian	islands
khrebet	Russian	mountain range
-ko	Japanese	lake
kolpos	Greek	bay, gulf
körfezi	Turkish	bay, gulf
kryazh	Russian	ridge
küh(ha)	Persian	mountain(s)

L

lac	French	lake
lacul	Romanian	lake
lago	Italian, Portuguese, Spanish	lake
lagoa	Portuguese	lagoon
laguna	Spanish	lagoon, lake
limni	Greek	lake
ling	Chinese	mountain(s), peak
liqeni	Albanian	lake
loch, lough	Gaelic	lake

M

massif	French	mountains
-meer	Dutch	lake, sea
mont	French	mount
monte	Italian, Portuguese, Spanish	mount
montes	Portuguese, Spanish	mountains
monts	French	mountains
muntii	Romanian	mountains
mys	Russian	cape

N

nafud	Arabic	desert
nevado	Spanish	snow-capped mountain
nuruu	Mongolian	mountains

nuur	Mongolian	lake

O

ostrov(a)	Russian	island(s)
ozero	Russian	lake

P

pegunungan	Indonesian	mountains
pelagos	Greek	sea
pendi	Chinese	basin
pesky	Russian	sandy desert
pic	French	peak
pico	Portuguese, Spanish	peak
planalto	Portuguese	plateau
planina	Bulgarian	mountains
poluostrov	Russian	peninsula
puerto	Spanish	harbour, port
puncak	Indonesian	peak
punta	Italian, Spanish	point
puy	French	peak

Q

qundao	Chinese	archipelago

R

ras, rås, ra's	Arabic	cape
represa	Portuguese	dam, reservoir
-rettō	Japanese	archipelago
rio	Portuguese	river
río	Spanish	river

S

sahra	Arabic	desert
salar	Spanish	salt flat
-san	Japanese, Korean	mountain
-sanmaek	Korean	mountains
sebkha	Arabic	salt flat
sebkhet	Arabic	salt marsh
See	German	lake
serra	Portuguese	range
severnaya, severo-	Russian	northern
shan	Chinese	mountain(s)
-shima	Japanese	island
-shotō	Japanese	islands
sierra	Spanish	range

T

tanjona	Malagasy	cape
tanjung	Indonesian	cape
teluk	Indonesian	bay, gulf
ténéré	Berber	desert
-tō	Japanese	island

V

vârful	Romanian	mountain
-vesi	Finnish	lake
vodokhranilishche	Russian	reservoir
volcán	Spanish	volcano

W

wādī	Arabic	watercourse
Wald	German	forest

Z

-zaki	Japanese	cape
zaliv	Russian	bay, gulf

A

Name	Page	Grid
Aachen	33	J4
Aalen	31	F8
Aalst	33	G4
Aarau	41	D3
Aare	41	C3
Aba	79	F3
Abādān	71	C1
Abadla	77	E2
Abaji	79	F3
Abakaliki	79	F3
Abakan	53	S7
Abano Terme	41	G5
Abarqū	71	E1
Abashiri	59	N1
Ābaya Hāyk'	81	F2
Abay Wenz	75	G5
Abbeville	33	D4
Abd al Kūrī	67	F7
Abéché	75	D5
Abengourou	79	D3
Åbenrå	31	E1
Abensberg	31	G8
Abeokuta	79	E3
Aberaeron	35	H9
Aberdeen, U.K.	35	K4
Aberdeen, S.D., U.S.	97	G1
Aberdeen, Wash., U.S.	97	B1
Aberystwyth	35	H9
Abhā	75	H4
Abidjan	79	D3
Abilene	103	G2
Abiline	91	M6
Abnûb	75	F2
Aboisso	79	D3
Abomey	79	E3
Abong Mbang	79	G4
Abou Déia	75	C5
Abrantes	39	B5
Absaroka Range	97	E1
Abū al Abayḍ	71	E4
Abu Aweigîla	70	B6
Abu Dhabi = Abū Ẓabī	71	F4
Abu Hamed	75	F4
Abuja	79	F3
Ābune Yosēf	75	G5
Abū Nujaym	75	C1
Aburo	81	E3
Abu Simbel	75	F3
Abū Ẓabī	71	F4
Abv Nujaym	77	J2
Acaponeta	95	E7
Acapulco	105	E5
Acarigua	109	D2
Accra	79	D3
Achen See	41	G3
Achill Island	35	B8
Achinsk	53	S6
Achit	49	L3
Aci Göl	47	M7
A Cihanbeyli	47	Q6
Acireale	43	K11
Acklins Island	105	K4
Açores	77	(1)B2
A Coruña	39	B1
Acqui Terme	41	D6
Acre	109	C5
Acri	43	L9
Ada	29	K12
Ada	101	B3
Adak Island	103	(3)C1
Adam	67	G5
Adams Island	89	(2)B1
'Adan	67	E7
Adana	69	F5
Adda	41	E5
Ad Dafrah	71	E5
Ad Dahnā	71	B3
Ad Dakhla	77	B4
Ad Dammām	71	D3
Ad Dawḥah	71	D4
Ad Dir'īyah	71	B4
Addis Ababa = Ādīs Ābeba	81	F2
Adelaide	87	G6
Adelaide River	87	F2
Aden = Adan	67	E7
Adi	63	(2)D3
Adige	41	G5
Adīgrat	75	G5
Adīrī	75	B2
Ādīs Ābeba	81	F2
Adi Ugri	75	G5
Admiralty Islands	85	E6
Adoni	65	C5
Adour	37	F10
Adra	39	H8
Adrano	43	J11
Adrar	77	E3
Adria	41	H5
Adriatic Sea	43	H4
Adygeya	69	J1
Adz'vavom	49	L1
Aegean Sea	47	H5
A Estrada	39	B2
Afghanistan	67	H3
'Afīf	75	H3
Afikpo	79	F3
Africa	73	E5
Afrīn	69	G5
'Afula	70	C4
Afyon	47	N6
Agadez	77	G5
Agadir	77	D2
Agadyr'	53	N8
Agalega Islands	73	J7
Agartala	65	F4
Agattu Island	55	W6
Agde	37	J10
Agen	37	F9
Agios Efstratios	47	H5
Agra	65	C3
Agrakhanskiy Poluostrov	69	M2
Ağri	69	K4
Agri	43	L8
Agrigento	43	H11
Agrinio	47	D6
Agryz	49	K3
Agua Prieta	103	E2
Aguascalientes	105	D4
A Gudiña	39	C2
Aguelhok	77	F5
Águilas	39	J7
Ahar	69	M4
Ahaura	89	C6
Ahaus	33	K2
Ahlen	33	K3
Ahmadabad	65	B4
Ahmadnagar	65	B5
Ahvāz	67	E3
Aichach	31	G8
Aigina	47	F7
Aihui	55	M6
Aim	55	N5
Aïn Beïda	77	G1
'Aïn Ben Tili	77	D3
Aïn el Hadjel	39	P9
Ain Oussera	77	F1
Ainsa	39	L2
Aïn Sefra	77	E2
Ain Taya	39	P8
Aïn-Tédélès	39	L8
Aisne	33	F5
Aitape	63	(2)F3
Aiud	45	L3
Aix-en-Provence	37	L10
Aix-les-Bains	37	L8
Aizawl	65	F4
Aizu-wakamatsu	59	K5
Ajaccio	43	C7
Aj Bogd Uul	57	B2
Ajdābiyā	75	D1
Ajigasawa	59	L3
Ajka	29	G10
Ajlun	70	C4
Ajmer	65	B3
Ajo	103	D2
Akanthou	70	A1
Akaroa	89	C6
Akçakale	69	H5
Aketi	81	C3
Akhisar	47	K6
Akhty	69	M3
Akimiski Island	93	Q6
Akita	59	L4
Akjoujt	77	C5
Akka	77	D3
Akkajaure	27	J3
'Akko	70	C4
Akmeqit	67	L2
Akobo	81	E2
Akola	65	C4
Akordat	75	G4
Akpatok Island	93	T4
Akqi	53	P9
Akra Sounio	47	F7
Akra Spatha	47	F9
Akron	99	D2
Aksaray	69	E4
Akşehir	47	P6
Akseki	47	P7
Aksu	53	Q9
Aksuat	53	Q8
Āksum	75	G5
Aktau	25	K3
Aktyubinsk	49	L4
Akula	81	C3
Akune	59	F8
Akureyri	27	(1)E2
Alabama	101	D3
Alabama	101	D3
Alagoas	109	K5
Alagoinhas	109	K6
Alagón	39	J3
Al Ahmadi	71	C2
Al 'Amārah	67	E3
Alamo	97	C3
Alamogordo	103	E2
Åland	27	K6
Alanya	69	E5
Alaska	103	(1)F2
Alaska Peninsula	103	(1)E4
Alaska Range	103	(1)G3
Alatri	43	H7
Alatyr'	49	J4
Al 'Ayn	71	F4
Alba	41	D6
Albacete	39	J5
Alba Iulia	45	L3
Albania	47	B3
Albany	93	Q6
Albany, Australia	87	C6
Albany, Ga., U.S.	101	E3
Albany, Ky., U.S.	101	E2
Albany, Oreg., U.S.	97	B2
Al Başrah	67	E3
Albenga	41	D6
Albert	33	E4
Alberta	93	H6

Name	Page	Ref.
Albert Kanaal	33	G3
Albert Lea	99	B2
Albert Nile	81	E3
Albi	37	H10
Albino	41	E5
Albion	97	F1
Ålborg	27	E8
Albox	39	H7
Albufeira	39	B7
Āl Bū Kamāl	69	J6
Albuquerque	103	E1
Al Buraymī	67	G5
Alburquerque	39	D5
Albury	87	J7
Al Buşayyah	71	B1
Alcala de Henares	39	G4
Alcalá la Real	39	G7
Alcamo	43	G11
Alcañiz	39	K3
Alcantarilla	39	J7
Alcaraz	39	H6
Alcazar de San Juan	39	G5
Alcobendas	39	G4
Alcoi	39	K6
Alcorcón	39	G4
Aldabra Group	83	(2)A2
Aldan	55	M5
Aldan	55	N5
Alderney	37	C4
Aldershot	33	B3
Aleg	77	C5
Aleksandrov-Sakhalinskiy	55	Q6
Aleksandrovskiy Zavod	55	K6
Aleksandrovskoye	49	Q2
Aleksinac	45	J6
Alençon	37	F5
Aleppo = Ḥalab	69	G5
Aléria	43	D6
Alès	37	K9
Alessandria	41	D6
Ålesund	27	D5
Aleutian Islands	103	(3)B1
Aleutian Range	103	(1)F4
Aleutian Trench	51	W5
Alexander Archipelago	103	(1)K4
Alexander Bay	83	B5
Alexandra	89	B7
Alexandria = El Iskandarîya, Egypt	75	E1
Alexandria, Romania	45	N6
Alexandria, La., U.S.	101	C3
Alexandria, Minn., U.S.	99	A1
Alexandria, Va., U.S.	99	E3
Alexandroupoli	47	H4
Aleysk	53	Q7
Al Farwāniyah	71	B2
Al Fāw	71	C2
Alfeld	31	E5
Alföld	45	H2
Al-Fujayrah	71	G4
Algeciras	39	E8
Algemes	39	K5
Algena	75	G4
Alger	77	F1
Algeria	77	E3
Al Ghāṭ	71	A3
Al Ghaydah	67	F6
Alghero	43	C8
Algiers = Alger	77	F1
Algona	99	B2
Al Hadīthah	70	E5
Al Ḥammādah al Ḥamrā'	77	G3
Al Harūj al Aswad	75	C2
Al Ḥasakah	69	J5
Al Ḥijāz	75	G2
Al Ḥillah	67	D3
Al Ḥilwah	71	B5
Al Hoceima	77	E1
Al Ḥudaydah	75	H5
Al Ḥufūf	71	C4
Aliağa	47	J6
Aliakmonas	47	E4
Āli Bayramlı	69	N4
Alicante	39	K6
Alice	101	B4
Alice Springs	87	F4
Alicudi	43	J10
Aligarh	65	C3
Alindao	81	C2
Aliwal North	83	D6
Al Jabal al Akhḍar	75	D1
Al Jaghbūb	75	D2
Al Jarah	71	B2
Al Jawf	75	G2
Al Jifārah	70	A5
Al Jubayl	71	C3
Aljustrel	39	B7
Al Khābūrah	71	G5
Al Kharj	71	B4
Al Khaşab	71	G3
Al Khawr	71	D4
Al Khums	77	H2
Al Khuwayr	71	D3
Alkmaar	33	G2
Al Kūt	67	E3
Al Kuwayt	71	C2
Al Lādhiqīyah	69	F6
Allahabad	65	D3
Allakh-Yun'	55	P4
Allendale	101	E3
Allentown	99	E2
Aller = Cabañquinta	39	E1
Alliance	97	F2
Al Lith	75	H3
Alma	99	B2
Almada	39	A6
Almadén	39	F6
Al Madīnah	75	G3
Almalyk	53	M9
Al Manāmah	71	D3
Almansa	39	J6
Al Marj	75	D1
Almaty	53	P9
Al Mawşil	69	K5
Al Mazāḥimīyah	71	B4
Almazán	39	H3
Almeirim	109	G4
Almelo	33	J2
Almendralejo	39	D6
Almería	39	H8
Almiros	47	E5
Al Mish'āb	71	C2
Almonte	39	D7
Almora	65	C3
Al Mukallā	67	E7
Al Mukhā	75	H5
Al Nu'ayrīyah	71	C3
Alnwick	35	L6
Alonnisos	47	F5
Alor	63	(2)B4
Alor Setar	61	C5
Alpena	99	D1
Alphen	33	G2
Alpi Lepontine	41	D4
Alpi Orobie	41	E4
Alps	41	B5
Al Qāmishlī	69	J5
Al Qaryāt	75	B1
Al Qaryatayn	70	E2
Al Qaṭrūn	75	B3
Al Qunfudhah	75	H4
Al Qurayyāt	75	G1
Al Quṭayfah	70	D3
Als	31	E1
Alsasua	39	H2
Alsfeld	31	E6
Altaelva	27	M2
Altai Mountains	57	A1
Altamira	109	G4
Altamura	43	L8
Altanbulag	55	H6
Altay	53	R7
Altay, China	53	R8
Altay, Mongolia	57	B1
Alte Mellum	31	D3
Altenburg	31	H6
Alto Molócuè	83	F3
Alton	99	B3
Altoona	99	E2
Altötting	41	H2
Altun Shan	53	S10
Alturas	97	B2
Altus	101	B3
Al 'Ubaylah	67	F5
Al 'Uzayr	71	B1
Alva	101	B2
Al Wafrā'	71	B2
Al Wajh	75	G2
Alwar	65	C3
Al Wari'ah	71	B3
Alytus	29	P3
Alzey	31	D7
Alzira	39	K5
Amādīyah	69	K5
Amadjuak Lake	93	S4
Amahai	63	(2)C3
Amapá	109	G3
Amapá	109	G3
Amarillo	103	F1
Amasya	69	F3
Amazon = Amazonas	107	F4
Amazonas	109	D4
Amazonas	109	E4
Ambala	65	C2
Ambanjā	83	H2
Ambarchik	55	U3
Ambato	109	B4
Ambatondrazaka	83	H3
Amberg	31	G7
Ambikapur	65	D4
Ambilobe	83	H2
Ambon	63	(2)C3
Ambositra	83	H4
Ambovombe	83	H5
Amchitka Island	103	(3)B1
Amderma	53	L4
Amdo	65	F2
Ameland	33	H1
American Samoa	85	J7
Americus	101	E3
Amersfoort	33	H2
Amery Ice Shelf	112	(2)M2
Ames	99	B2
Amfilochia	47	D6
Amfissa	47	E6
Amgun'	55	P6
Amiens	33	E5
Amirante Islands	83	(2)B2
'Ammān	70	C5
Ammerland	33	K1
Ammersee	41	F2
Ammochostos	69	E6
Ammochostos Bay	70	A1
Amol	67	F2
Amorgos	47	H8
Amos	99	E1
Ampana	63	(2)B3
Ampanihy	83	G4
Amposta	39	L4
Amritsar	65	B2
Amrum	31	D2

Name	Page	Grid
Amsterdam·	33	G2
Amstetten	41	K2
Am Timan	75	D5
Amudar'ya	53	L9
Amundsen Gulf	93	G2
Amundsen Sea	112	(2)GG3
Amur	55	P6
Amursk	55	P6
Anabar	55	J2
Anaconda	97	D1
Anacortes	97	B1
Anadarko	97	G3
Anadolu Dağları	69	H3
Anadyr'	55	X4
Anadyrskiy Zaliv	55	Y3
Anafi	47	H8
'Ānah	69	J6
Analalava	83	H2
Anamur	69	E5
Anantapur	65	C6
Anapa	69	G1
Anápolis	109	H7
Anār	71	F1
Anatolia	47	M6
Anchorage	103	(1)H3
Ancona	43	H5
Ancud	111	G7
Anda	57	H1
Åndalsnes	27	D5
Andaman Islands	61	A4
Andaman Sea	61	A4
Andernach	33	K4
Anderson	101	E3
Andes	107	D5
Andfjorden	27	J2
Andizhan	53	N9
Andkhvoy	67	J2
Andoas	109	B4
Andong	59	E5
Andorra	39	L2
Andorra la Vella	39	M2
Andøya	27	H2
Andreanof Islands	103	(3)C1
Andrews	103	F2
Andria	43	L7
Andros	47	G7
Andros, *Greece*	47	G7
Andros, *The Bahamas*	101	F5
Andros Town	101	F5
Andrott	65	B6
Andújar	39	F6
Aneto	39	L2
Angarsk	55	G6
Ånge	27	H5
Angel de la Guarda	103	D3
Angeles	61	G3
Ängelholm	27	G8
Angeln	31	E2
Angers	37	E6
Anglesey	35	H8
Angmagssalik = Tasiilaq	93	Z3
Ango	81	D3
Angoche	83	F3
Angola	73	E7
Angoulême	37	F8
Anguilla	105	M5
Aniak	103	(1)F3
Anina	45	J4
Anıyaman	69	H5
Ankang	57	D4
Ankara	69	E4
Anklam	31	J3
Anna	49	H4
Annaba	77	G1
An Nabk	70	D2
An Nafud	75	G2
An Nāirīyah	67	E3
An Najaf	67	D3
Annapolis	99	E3
Annapurna	65	D3
Ann Arbor	99	D2
An Nāşirīyah	75	J1
Annecy	41	B5
Annemasse	41	B4
Anniston	101	D3
Annobón	79	F5
Annonay	37	K8
An Nukhayb	67	D3
Anqing	57	F4
Ansbach	31	F7
Anshan	59	B3
Anshun	57	D5
Ansley	97	G2
Anson	101	B3
Ansongo	77	F5
Antakya	69	G5
Antalya	47	N8
Antalya Körfezi	47	N8
Antananarivo	83	H3
Antarctica	112	(2)A1
Antarctic Peninsula	112	(2)LL3
Antequera	39	F7
Anti-Atlas	77	D3
Antibes	41	C7
Antigua	105	M5
Antigua and Barbuda	105	M5
Antikythira	47	F9
Antipodes Islands	89	(3)A1
Antlers	101	B3
Antofagasta	111	G3
Antonito	97	E3
Antrim	35	F7
Antropovo	49	H3
Antsalova	83	G3
Antsirabe	83	H3
Antsirañana	83	H2
Antu	59	E2
Antwerp = Antwerpen	33	G3
Antwerpen	33	G3
Anuradhapura	65	D7
Anxi	57	B2
Anyuysk	55	U3
Anzhero-Sudzhensk	53	R6
Anzio	43	G7
Aoga-shima	59	K7
Aomori	59	L3
Aosta	41	C5
Aoukâr	77	C5
Aoukoukar	79	C1
Apalachee Bay	101	E4
Aparri	61	G3
Apatin	45	F4
Apatity	49	F1
Ape	27	P8
Apeldoorn	33	H2
Api	65	D2
Apia	85	J7
Apostle Islands	99	B1
Apoteri	109	F3
Appalachian Mountains	101	E3
Appennino	43	G5
Appennino Abruzzese	43	H6
Appennino Calabro	43	K10
Appennino Lucano	43	K8
Appennino Tosco-Emiliano	41	D6
Appennino Umbro-Marchigiano	43	H6
Appleton	99	C2
Apure	109	D2
'Aqaba	70	C7
Aquidauana	109	F8
Ara	65	D3
Arabian Sea	67	H6
Aracaju	109	K6
Aracati	109	K4
Araçatuba	109	G8
Arad	45	J3
Arafura Sea	63	(2)D5
Araguaia	107	F4
Araguatins	109	H5
Arāk	67	E3
Arak	77	F3
Aral Sea	53	K8
Aral'sk	49	M5
Aranda de Duero	39	G3
Aran Island	35	D6
Aran Islands	35	B8
Aranjuez	39	G4
Aranyaprathet	61	C4
Araouane	77	E3
Arapahoe	97	G2
Arapiraca	109	K5
'Ar'ar	67	D3
Araras	109	G5
Ararat	69	L4
Arbīl	69	K5
Arbroath	35	K5
Arcata	97	B2
Archipelago of the Recherche	87	D6
Archipel de la Société	85	L7
Archipel des Tuamotu	85	M7
Archipiélago de la Reina Adelaida	111	F9
Archipiélago de los Chonos	111	F7
Arco	97	D2
Arctic Bay	93	P2
Arctic Ocean	112	(1)A1
Arda	47	H3
Ardabīl	69	N4
Ardahan	69	K3
Ardennes	33	G4
Ardestān	67	F3
Ardila	39	C6
Arequipa	109	C7
Arezzo	43	F5
Argenta	41	G6
Argentan	33	B6
Argentina	111	H6
Argenton-sur-Creuse	37	G7
Argolikos Kolpos	47	E7
Argos	47	E7
Argos Orestiko	47	D4
Argostoli	47	C6
Argyll	35	G5
Århus	27	F8
Ari Atoll	65	B8
Arica	109	C7
Ariège	37	G11
Arihge	39	M2
Arinos	109	F6
Aripuanã	109	E5
Ariquemes	109	E5
Arizona	103	D2
Arkadelphia	101	C3
Arkalyk	53	M7
Arkansas	101	C3
Arkansas	101	C3
Arkansas City	101	B2
Arkhalts'ikhe	69	K3
Arkhangel'sk	49	H2
Arkhipelag Nordenshel'da	53	R2
Arklow	35	F9
Arles	37	K10
Arlington, *Tex., U.S.*	101	B3
Arlington, *Va., U.S.*	99	E3
Armagh	35	F7
Armavir	69	J1
Armenia	69	K3
Armentières	33	E4

Name	Pg	Grid
Armidale	87	K6
Arnhem	33	H3
Arnhem Land	87	F2
Arno	41	F7
Arnøya	27	L1
Arnsberg	33	L3
Arnstadt	31	F6
Arquipélago dos Bijagós	79	A2
Ar Ramādī	67	D3
Ar Ramlah	70	C7
Arran	35	G6
Ar Raqqah	69	H6
Arras	33	E4
Ar Riyāḍ	67	E5
Ar Ruṭba	67	D3
Ärsandøy	27	G4
Arta, *Greece*	47	C5
Arta, *Mallorca*	39	P5
Artem	59	G2
Artesia	103	F2
Arthur's Town	101	F5
Artigas	111	K5
Artsyz	45	S4
Artux	53	P10
Artvin	69	J3
Artyk	55	Q4
Arua	81	E3
Aruba	105	K6
Arusha	81	F4
Arvayheer	57	C1
Arviat	93	N4
Arvidsjaur	27	K4
Arvika	27	G7
Aryta	55	M4
Arzamas	49	H3
Asahi-dake	59	M2
Asahikawa	59	M2
Asansol	65	E4
Asbest	49	M3
Ascension	73	B6
Aschaffenburg	31	E7
Ascoli Piceno	43	H6
Äsela	81	F2
Åsele	27	J4
Asenovgrad	47	G3
Asha	49	L3
Ashburton	89	C6
Asherton	101	B4
Asheville	99	D3
Ashford	33	C3
Ash Fork	103	D1
Ashgabat	67	G2
Ashkhabad = Ashgabat	67	G2
Ashland, *Ky., U.S.*	99	D3
Ashland, *Mont., U.S.*	97	E1
Ashland, *Wis., U.S.*	99	B1
Ashqelon	70	B5
Ash Shāriqah	71	F4
Ash Shiḥr	67	E7
Ashtabula	99	D2
Asia	51	M5
Asilah	77	D1
Asinara	43	C7
Asino	53	R6
Asīr	75	H3
Aşkale	69	J4
Asmara	75	G4
Åsosa	81	E1
Aspang Markt	41	M3
Aspermont	103	F2
As Sa'an	70	E1
Assab	75	H5
Assamakka	77	G5
Aş Şanamayn	70	D3
As Sarīr	75	D2
Assen	33	J2
Assens	31	E1
As Sidrah	75	C1
Assiniboine	93	M7
Assis	111	L3
Assisi	43	G5
As Sulaymānīyah	69	L6
As Sulayyil	67	E5
As Suwaydā'	70	D4
As Suwayh	67	G5
Astana	53	N7
Astara	67	E2
Asti	41	D6
Astorga	39	D2
Astoria	97	B1
Astrakhan'	49	J5
Astypalaia	47	J8
Asunción	111	K4
Aswân	75	F3
Aswân Dam	75	F3
Asyût	75	F2
As Zaydīyah	75	H4
Atafu	85	J6
Atakpamé	79	E3
Atâr	77	C4
Atasu	53	N8
Atbara	75	F4
Atbasar	49	N4
Atchison	101	B2
Aterno	43	H6
Ath	33	F4
Athabasca	93	J5
Athens = Athina	47	F7
Athens, *Ga., U.S.*	101	E3
Athens, *Oh., U.S.*	101	E2
Athens, *Tenn., U.S.*	101	E2
Athens, *Tex., U.S.*	101	B3
Athina	47	F7
Athlone	35	E8
Ath Thāyat	70	D7
Ati	75	C5
Atiamuri	89	F4
Atikokan	99	B1
Atka	55	S4
Atka Island	103	(3)C1
Atlanta	101	E3
Atlantic	101	B1
Atlantic City	99	F3
Atlantic Ocean	35	C2
Atlantic Ocean	73	C7
Atlas Bogd	57	B2
Atlas Mountains	39	N9
Atlasovo	55	T5
Atlas Saharien	77	E2
Atlin	93	E5
Atmore	101	D3
Aṭ Ṭā'if	67	D5
Attapu	61	D4
Attawapiskat	93	Q6
Attersee	41	J3
Attu Island	103	(3)A1
At Turbah	75	H5
Atyrau	49	K5
Aubagne	37	K5
Aube	37	K5
Auburn, *Al., U.S.*	101	D3
Auburn, *Calif., U.S.*	97	B3
Auburn, *Nebr., U.S.*	97	G2
Auch	37	F10
Auckland	89	E3
Auckland Island	89	(2)B1
Aude	37	H10
Aue	31	H6
Auerbach	31	H6
Augathella	87	J5
Augsburg	41	F2
Augusta, *Australia*	87	C6
Augusta, *Italy*	43	K11
Augusta, *Ga., U.S.*	101	E3
Augusta, *Me., U.S.*	99	G2
Augustów	29	M4
Aurangābād	65	C5
Aurillac	37	H9
Aurora, *Colo., U.S.*	97	F3
Aurora, *Ill., U.S.*	99	C2
Aurora, *Mo., U.S.*	101	C2
Aurukun	87	H2
Auschwitz = Oświęcim	29	J7
Austin, *Minn., U.S.*	99	B2
Austin, *Nev., U.S.*	97	C3
Austin, *Tex., U.S.*	101	B3
Australia	87	E4
Australian Alps	85	E9
Australian Capital Territory	87	J7
Austria	41	J3
Autun	37	K7
Auxerre	37	J6
Avallon	37	J6
Avam	55	E2
Aveiro	39	B4
Avellino	43	J8
Avesta	27	J6
Aviemore	35	J4
Avignon	37	K10
Ávila	39	F4
Avilés	39	E1
Avion	33	E4
Avola	43	K12
Avranches	37	D5
Avrig	45	M4
Awat	53	Q9
Awatere	89	D5
Awbārī	75	B2
Awjilah	75	D2
Awka	79	F3
Ax-les-Thermes	37	G11
Ayacucho	109	C6
Ayaguz	53	Q8
Ayamonte	39	C7
Ayan	55	P5
Ayanka	55	V4
Aydin	69	B5
Aydıncık	47	R8
Ayers Rock = Uluru	87	F5
Aykino	53	H5
Aylesbury	33	B3
Aylmer Lake	93	K4
Ayr, *Australia*	87	J3
Ayr, *U.K.*	35	H6
Aytos	45	Q7
Ayutthaya	61	C4
Ayvalik	47	J5
Azaila	39	K3
Azaouâd	77	E5
A'zāz	69	G5
Azerbaijan	69	M3
Azores = Açores	77	(1)B2
Azov	49	G5
Azuaga	39	E6
Azul	111	K6
Az Zabadānī	70	D3
Aẕ Ẕahrān	71	D3
Az Zāwīyah	75	B1
Az Zubayr	71	B1

B

Name	Pg	Grid
Ba'albek	70	D2
Baardheere	81	G3
Babadag	45	R5
Babaeski	47	K3
Bāb al Mandab	67	D7
Babar	63	(2)C4
Babo	63	(2)D3
Babruysk	49	E4

Name	Page	Grid
Babura	79	F2
Babushkin	55	H6
Babuyan Islands	61	G3
Bacabal	109	J4
Bacan	63	(2)C3
Bacău	45	P3
Bachu	67	L2
Bačka Palanka	45	G4
Bac Liêu	61	D5
Bacolod	61	G4
Badajoz	39	D6
Bad al Milḥ	69	K7
Bad Aussee	41	J3
Bad Bentheim	33	K2
Bad Doberan	31	G2
Bad Ems	33	K4
Baden-Baden	41	D2
Badgastein	41	J3
Badgingarra	87	C6
Bad Harzburg	31	F5
Bad Hersfeld	31	E6
Bad Homburg	31	D6
Bad Honnef	33	K4
Badin	65	A4
Bad Ischl	41	J3
Bādiyat ash Shām	70	D4
Bad Kreuznach	33	K5
Bad Lauterberg	31	F5
Bad Mergentheim	31	E7
Bad Neuenahr-Ahrweiler	33	K4
Bad Neustadt	31	F6
Bad Salzuflen	31	D4
Bad Salzungen	31	F6
Bad Schwartau	31	F3
Bad Urach	41	E2
Bad Vöslau	45	D2
Bad Waldsee	41	E3
Bad Wildungen	31	E5
Baena	39	F7
Baffin Bay	91	J2
Baffin Island	93	R2
Bafoulabé	79	B2
Bafoussam	79	G3
Bafra	69	F3
Bafra Burun	69	G3
Bāft	71	H2
Bafwasende	81	D3
Baga	75	B5
Bagani	83	C3
Bagaroua	79	E2
Bagdad	103	D2
Bagdarin	55	J6
Bagé	111	L5
Baggs	97	E2
Baghdād	103	D2
Bagheria	43	H10
Baghlān	67	J2
Bagnols-sur-Cèze	37	K9
Baguio	61	G3
Baharampur	65	E4
Bahawalpur	65	B3
Bahia	109	J6
Bahía Blanca	111	J6
Bahía Blanca	111	J6
Bahía de Campeche	105	F4
Bahía de Santa Elena	109	A4
Bahía de Sechura	109	A5
Bahía Grande	111	H9
Bahia Kino	95	D6
Bahía Negra	111	K3
Bahir Dar	75	G5
Bahraich	65	D3
Bahrain	71	D4
Baḥrat Ḥimş	70	D2
Bahr el Abiad	75	F5
Bahr el Azraq	75	F5
Bahr el Ghazal	75	C5
Bahr el Ghazal	81	D2
Bahr el Jebe	81	E2
Bahr el Nîl = Nile	75	F4
Baía de Marajó	109	H4
Baía do Bengo	79	G6
Baia Mare	45	L2
Baião	109	H4
Baia Sprie	45	L2
Baïbokoum	81	B2
Baicheng, China	53	Q9
Baicheng, China	57	G1
Baie de la Seine	33	B5
Baie de la Somme	33	D4
Baie St. Paul	99	F1
Baiji	69	K6
Baile Átha Cliath = Dublin	35	F8
Bailleul	33	E4
Bailundo	83	B2
Bainbridge	101	E3
Bairiki	85	H5
Bairin Yuoqi	57	F2
Bairin Zuoqi	57	F2
Bairnsdale	87	J7
Baja California	95	C5
Bakchar	53	Q6
Baker	85	J5
Baker, Calif., U.S.	97	C3
Baker, Mont., U.S.	97	F1
Baker, Oreg., U.S.	97	C2
Baker Lake	93	M4
Baker Lake	93	N4
Bakersfield	103	C1
Bakhta	55	D4
Baki	67	E1
Bakkafjörður	27	(1)F1
Baku = Baki	67	E1
Balâ	69	E4
Balabac	61	F5
Balabac Strait	61	F5
Balaghat	65	D4
Balaguer	39	L3
Balaklava	69	E1
Balakovo	49	J4
Balashov	49	H4
Balassagyarmat	45	G1
Balaton	45	E3
Balatonfüred	45	E3
Balclutha	89	B8
Balearic Islands = Islas Baleares	39	N5
Bāleshwar	65	E4
Baley	55	K6
Bali	63	(1)F4
Balige	63	(1)B2
Balıkesir	47	K5
Balikpapan	63	(1)F3
Balimo	63	(2)F4
Balkhash	53	N8
Ballarat	87	H7
Ballina, Australia	87	K5
Ballina, Republic of Ireland	35	C7
Ballinasloe	35	D8
Ballinger	103	G2
Balmazújváros	45	J2
Balotra	65	B3
Balranald	87	H6
Balsas	109	H5
Balsas	105	D5
Balta	45	S2
Bălţi	45	Q2
Baltic Sea	27	J8
Baltimore	99	E3
Baltiysk	29	J3
Balykshi	49	K5
Bam	67	G4
Bamaga	87	H2
Bamako	79	C2
Bamba	77	E5
Bambari	81	C2
Bamberg	31	F7
Bambouk	77	C6
Bambouk Kaarta	77	B2
Bamenda	79	G3
Bāmīān	67	J3
Banaba	85	G6
Bañados del Izozog	109	E7
Banalia	81	D3
Banana	87	K4
Banaz	47	M6
Ban Ban	61	C3
Banda	65	D3
Banda Aceh	61	B5
Bandama	79	C3
Bandar-e 'Abbās	71	G3
Bandar-e Anzalī	67	E2
Bandar-e Deylam	71	D1
Bandar-e Khoemir	71	F3
Bandar-e Lengeh	71	F3
Bandar-e Ma'shur	71	C1
Bandar Seri Begawan	63	(1)E2
Banda Sea	63	(2)C3
Bandirma	47	K4
Bandundu	81	B4
Bandung	63	(1)D4
Bāneh	69	L6
Banff	93	H6
Bangalore	65	C6
Bangassou	81	C3
Banggi	63	(1)F1
Banghāzī	75	D1
Bangka	63	(1)D3
Bangkok = Krung Thep	61	C4
Bangladesh	65	E4
Bangor, N. Ire., U.K.	35	G7
Bangor, Wales, U.K.	35	H8
Bangor, U.S.	99	G2
Bangui	81	B3
Ban Hat Yai	61	C5
Banī Walīd	77	H2
Bāniyās	69	F6
Banja Luka	45	E5
Banjarmasin	63	(1)E3
Banjul	79	A2
Ban Khemmarat	61	D3
Banks Island = Moa, Australia	87	H2
Banks Island, Canada	93	G2
Banks Peninsula	89	D6
Bannu	65	B2
Banská	29	J9
Banská Štiavnica	29	H9
Bantry	35	C10
Banyoles	39	N2
Banyuwangi	63	(1)E4
Baode	57	E3
Baoding	57	F3
Baoji	57	D4
Baoshan	61	B1
Baotou	57	E2
Baoying	57	F4
Bapaume	33	E4
Bar	45	G7
Barabai	63	(1)F3
Baraboo	99	C2
Barakaldo	39	H1
Baramula	65	B2
Baranavichy	49	E4
Barbados	109	F1
Barbastro	39	L2
Barcaldine	87	J4
Barcelona, Spain	39	N3
Barcelona, Venezuela	105	M6
Barcelos	109	E4

Name	Pg	Ref
Barco de Valdeorras =		
O Barco	39	D2
Barcs	45	E4
Bardai	75	C3
Bardejov	29	L8
Bareilly	65	C3
Barents Sea	53	E3
Bareo	63	(1)F2
Barga	65	D2
Bari	43	L7
Barikot	65	B1
Barinas	109	C2
Barisal	65	F4
Barito	63	(2)A3
Barkam	57	C4
Barkly Tableland	87	F3
Barkol	53	S9
Bârlad	45	Q3
Bar-le-Duc	33	H6
Barletta	43	L7
Barmer	65	B3
Barnaul	53	Q7
Barquisimeto	109	D1
Barra, Brazil	109	J6
Barra, U.K.	35	E4
Barracão do Barreto	109	G5
Barra do Corda	109	H5
Barra do Garças	109	G7
Barra do São Manuel	109	G5
Barragem de Sobradinho	109	J5
Barragem do Castelo de Bode	39	B5
Barranquilla	105	K6
Barreiro	39	A6
Barrie	99	E2
Barron	99	B1
Barrow	103	(1)F1
Barrow-in-Furness	35	J7
Barrow Island	87	B4
Barsi	65	C5
Barstow	103	C2
Barth	31	H2
Bartın	69	E3
Bartle Frere	85	E7
Bartlesville	101	B2
Bartlett	97	G2
Bartoszyce	29	K3
Barus	63	(1)B2
Baruun Urt	57	E1
Barysaw	49	E4
Basankusu	81	B3
Basarabeasca	45	R3
Basca	43	C2
Basel	41	C3
Bashkiriya	49	K4
Basilan	63	(2)B1
Basildon	33	C3
Basingstoke	35	L10
Başkale	69	K4
Basoko	81	C3
Bassano del Grappa	41	G5
Bassas da India	83	F4
Basse Santa Su	77	C6
Bassett	97	G2
Bass Strait	87	H7
Bastak	71	F3
Bastia	43	D6
Bastogne	33	H4
Bastrop	101	C3
Bata	79	F4
Batagay	55	N3
Batamay	55	M4
Batangas	61	G4
Batan Islands	61	G2
Batanta	63	(2)C3
Batemans Bay	87	K7
Bath	35	K10
Bathinda	65	B2
Bathurst, Australia	87	J6
Bathurst, Canada	93	T7
Bathurst Inlet	93	K3
Bathurst Island, Australia	87	E2
Bathurst Island, Canada	93	M1
Batna	77	G1
Baton Rouge	101	C3
Batroûn	70	C2
Battle Creek	99	C2
Battle Harbour	93	V6
Battle Mountain	97	C2
Batu	81	F2
Bat'umi	69	J3
Baturino	53	R6
Baubau	63	(2)B4
Bauchi	79	F2
Baukau	63	(2)C4
Bauru	111	M3
Bawean	63	(1)E4
Bawku	79	D2
Bayanaul	53	P7
Bayandelger	55	H7
Bayan Har Shan	57	B4
Bayanhongor	57	C1
Bayan Obo	57	D2
Bay City, Mich., U.S.	99	D2
Bay City, Tex., U.S.	101	B4
Bayerische Alpen	41	F3
Bayeux	33	B5
Bāyir	70	D6
Baykit	53	T5
Baykonur	53	M8
Bay of Bengal	65	E5
Bay of Biscay	37	C9
Bay of Fundy	93	T8
Bay of Islands	89	E2
Bay of Plenty	89	F3
Bayonne	37	D10
Bayramaly	67	H2
Bayreuth	31	G7
Bay View	89	F4
Baza	39	H7
Beach	97	F1
Beachy Head	33	C4
Beatrice	101	B1
Beatty	103	C1
Beaufort	101	F3
Beaufort Sea	91	Q2
Beaufort West	83	C6
Beaumont	101	C3
Beaune	37	K6
Beauvais	33	E5
Beaver	97	D3
Beaver Creek	103	(1)J3
Beawar	65	B3
Beazley	111	H5
Bečej	45	H4
Béchar	77	E2
Beckley	101	E2
Bedford	101	D2
Beenleigh	87	K5
Beer Menuha	70	C6
Be'ér Sheva'	70	B5
Beeville	101	B4
Behbehān	71	D1
Bei'an	55	M7
Beihai	61	D2
Beijing	57	F3
Beipiao	57	G2
Beira	83	E3
Beirut = Beyrouth	70	C3
Beiuș	45	K3
Béja	77	G1
Bejaïa	77	G1
Béjar	39	E4
Bekdash	67	F1
Békéscsaba	45	J3
Bekily	83	H4
Bela	67	J4
Bela Crkva	45	J5
Belarus	25	G2
Bela Vista	83	E5
Belcher Islands	93	Q5
Beledweyne	81	H3
Belém	109	H4
Belfast	35	G7
Belfort	41	B3
Belgium	33	G4
Belgorod	49	G4
Belgrade = Beograd	45	H5
Beli	79	G3
Belice	43	H11
Belinyu	63	(1)D3
Belitung	63	(1)D3
Belize	105	G5
Belize	105	G5
Bellary	65	C5
Belle Fourche	97	F2
Belle Île	37	B6
Belleville	99	E2
Bellingham	97	B1
Bellingshausen Sea	112	(2)JJ4
Bellinzona	41	E4
Belluno	41	H4
Belmont	99	E2
Belmonte, Brazil	109	K7
Belmonte, Spain	39	H5
Belmopan	105	G5
Belmullet	35	B7
Belo Horizonte	109	J7
Beloit, Kans., U.S.	101	B2
Beloit, Wis., U.S.	99	C2
Belomorsk	49	F2
Belorechensk	69	H1
Belo Tsiribihina	83	G3
Belozersk	49	G2
Belyy Yar	53	Q6
Belzig	31	H4
Bemidji	99	A1
Bena Dibele	81	C4
Benavente	39	E3
Benbecula	35	E4
Bend	97	B2
Bender-Bayla	81	J2
Bene	83	E3
Benešov	29	D8
Benevento	43	J7
Bengbu	57	F4
Bengkulu	63	(1)C3
Benguela	83	A2
Beni	81	D3
Beni Abbès	77	E2
Benidorm	39	K6
Beni Mellal	77	D2
Benin	79	F3
Benin City	79	F3
Beni Saf	39	J9
Beni Slimane	39	P8
Beni Suef	75	F2
Ben More Assynt	35	H3
Ben Nevis	35	H5
Bensheim	31	D7
Benson	103	D3
Benteng	63	(2)B4
Benue	79	G3
Benxi	57	G2
Beograd	45	H5
Bepazarı	69	D3
Berat	47	B4
Berber	75	F4
Berbera	75	H5
Berbérati	81	B3

Name	Page	Ref
Berchtesgaden	41	J3
Berck	33	D4
Berdyans'k	49	G5
Bereeda	81	J1
Berehove	45	K1
Bererreá	39	C2
Berettyóújfalu	45	J2
Bereznik	49	H2
Berezniki	49	L3
Berezovo	49	N2
Bergama	47	K5
Bergamo	41	E5
Bergara	39	H1
Bergedorf	31	F3
Bergen, Norway	27	C6
Bergen, Germany	31	J2
Bergen op Zoom	33	G3
Bergerac	37	F9
Bergisch Gladbach	31	C6
Beringovskiy	55	X4
Bering Sea	103	(1)C4
Bering Strait	103	(1)C2
Berkeley	103	B1
Berkner Island	112	(2)A2
Berlin, Germany	31	J4
Berlin, U.S.	99	F2
Bermejillo	103	F3
Bermejo	111	K4
Bermeo	39	H1
Bermuda	91	H6
Bern	41	C4
Bernay	33	C5
Bernburg	31	G5
Berner Alpen	41	C4
Berounka	31	J7
Berrouaghia	39	N8
Berry Islands	101	F4
Bertoua	79	G4
Berwick-upon-Tweed	35	L6
Besalampy	83	G3
Besançon	37	M6
Beshneh	71	F2
Bessemer	101	D3
Bestuzhevo	49	H2
Bestyakh	55	M4
Betanzos	39	B1
Bêtdâmbâng	61	C4
Bethany	99	B2
Bethel	103	(1)E3
Bethlehem, Israel	70	C5
Bethlehem, South Africa	83	D5
Béthune	33	E4
Betioky	83	G4
Betpak-Dala	53	M8
Betroka	83	H4
Betzdorf	31	C6
Bey Dağlari	47	M8
Beyla	79	C3
Beyneu	53	J8
Beypazarı	47	P4
Beyrouth	70	C3
Beyşehir	47	P7
Beyşehir Gölü	47	P7
Béziers	37	J10
Bhadrakh	65	E4
Bhagalpur	65	E3
Bhairab Bazar	65	F4
Bhakkar	65	B2
Bhamo	61	B2
Bharuch	65	B4
Bhatpara	65	E4
Bhavnagar	65	B4
Bhawanipatna	65	D5
Bhilwara	65	B3
Bhind	65	C3
Bhopal	65	C4
Bhubaneshwar	65	E4
Bhuj	65	A4
Bhusawal	65	C4
Bhutan	65	E3
Biak	63	(2)E3
Biała	29	K8
Biała Podlaska	29	N5
Białystok	29	N4
Biarritz	37	D10
Biasca	41	D4
Bibbiena	41	G7
Bicaz	45	P3
Bida	79	F3
Bidar	65	C5
Bideford	35	H10
Biedenkopf	31	D6
Biel	41	C3
Bielefeld	31	D4
Biella	41	D5
Bielsko-Biała	29	J8
Bielsk Podlaski	29	N5
Biên Hoa	61	D4
Biga	47	K4
Bighorn Lake	97	E1
Bighorn Mountains	97	E2
Bight of Bangkok	61	C4
Bight of Benin	79	E3
Bight of Biafra	79	F4
Big Lake	103	(1)H2
Bignona	77	B6
Big Rapids	99	C2
Big River	93	K6
Big Sioux	97	G2
Big Spring	103	F2
Big Sur	103	B1
Big Trout Lake	93	P6
Bihać	41	L6
Bījār	69	M6
Bijeljina	45	G5
Bijelo Polje	45	G6
Bijie	57	D5
Bikanar	65	B3
Bikin	55	N7
Bikini	85	G4
Bilaspur	65	D4
Bila Tserkva	49	F5
Bilbao	39	H1
Bileća	45	F7
Bilecik	47	M4
Bilhorod-Dnistrovs'kyy	49	F5
Billings	97	D1
Bill of Portland	35	K11
Bilma	75	B4
Biloxi	101	D3
Bimini Islands	101	F4
Binghamton	99	E2
Bingöl	69	J4
Bintulu	63	(1)E2
Bintuni	63	(2)D3
Binyang	61	D2
Binzhou	57	F3
Biograd	41	L7
Birāk	77	H3
Birao	75	D5
Bī'r Bazīrī	70	E2
Birdsville	87	G5
Bireun	63	(1)B1
Bîr Gifgâfa	70	A6
Bīrjand	67	G3
Birmingham, U.K.	35	L9
Birmingham, U.S.	101	D3
Birnin-Gwari	79	F2
Birnin Kebbi	79	E2
Birnin Konni	79	F2
Birnin Kudu	79	F2
Birobidzhan	55	N7
Biržai	29	P1
Bisbee	103	E2
Bischofshofen	41	J3
Bishkek	53	N9
Bishop	97	C3
Bishop's Stortford	33	C3
Biskra	77	G2
Bismarck	95	F2
Bismarck Sea	85	E6
Bissau	77	B6
Bistrița	45	M2
Bitburg	33	J5
Bitola	47	D3
Bitterfeld	31	H5
Bitterroot Range	97	C1
Biu	79	G2
Biwa-ko	59	H6
Bixby	99	B3
Biysk	53	R7
Bizerte	77	G1
Bjelovar	45	D4
Bjørnøya	53	B3
Black Hills	97	F2
Blackpool	35	J8
Black Range	103	E2
Black Rock Desert	97	C2
Black Sea	69	D2
Black Volta	79	D3
Blackwater	35	D9
Blagoevgrad	47	F3
Blagoveshchensk	55	M6
Blangy-sur-Bresle	33	D5
Blankenburg	31	F5
Blantyre	83	F3
Blaye-et-Sainte-Luce	37	E8
Blenheim	89	D5
Blida	77	F1
Bloemfontein	83	D5
Blois	37	G6
Bloomfield	101	D2
Bloomington, Ill., U.S.	99	C2
Bloomington, Ind., U.S.	99	C3
Bluefield	99	D3
Bluefields	105	H6
Blue Mountains	97	C2
Blue Nile = Bahr el Azraq	75	F5
Bluff, New Zealand	89	B8
Bluff, U.S.	103	E1
Blythe	103	D2
Blytheville	101	D2
Bo	79	B3
Boac	61	G4
Boa Vista, Brazil	109	E3
Boa Vista, Cape Verde Islands	79	(1)B1
Bobbili	65	D5
Bobigny	33	E6
Bobo Dioulasso	79	D2
Bôca do Acre	109	D5
Boca Grande	107	E3
Bocaranga	81	B2
Bocholt	31	B5
Bodaybo	55	J5
Bode	31	G4
Bodélé	75	C4
Bodmin	35	H11
Bodø	27	H3
Bodrum	47	K7
Boe	97	C4
Boende	81	C4
Bogalusa	101	D3
Bognor Regis	33	B4
Bogor	63	(1)D4
Bogotá	109	C3
Boguchany	55	F5
Bogué	77	C5
Bo Hai	57	F3
Bohmerwald	31	H7
Bohol	61	G5
Boiaçu	109	E4

Name		Ref
Boise	97	C2
Boise City	103	F1
Bojnürd	53	K10
Bokatola	81	B4
Boké	79	B2
Bolbec	33	C5
Bole, China	53	Q9
Bole, Ghana	79	D3
Bolechiv	29	N8
Bolesławiec	29	E6
Bolgatanga	79	D2
Bolhrad	45	R4
Bölingen	41	F4
Bolivia	109	D7
Bollène	37	K9
Bollnäs	27	J6
Bolmen	27	G8
Bolnisi	69	L3
Bolobo	79	H5
Bologna	41	G6
Bol'shaya Pyssa	49	J2
Bol'sherech'ye	49	P3
Bol'shezemel'skaya Tundra	53	J4
Bolshoy Atlym	49	N2
Bolu	69	D3
Bolvadin	47	P6
Bolzano	41	G4
Boma	79	G6
Bombay	65	B5
Bomili	81	D3
Bom Jesus da Lapa	109	J6
Bonaparte Archipelago	87	B2
Bondeno	41	G6
Bondo	81	C3
Bondoukou	79	D3
Bongandanga	81	C3
Bongor	79	H2
Bonifacio	43	D7
Bonn	31	C6
Bonners Ferry	97	C1
Bontoc	61	G3
Boone	99	D3
Boosaaso	81	H1
Boothia Peninsula	93	M2
Booué	79	G5
Bor, Sudan	81	E2
Bor, Turkey	47	S7
Bor, Yugoslavia	45	K5
Borah Peak	97	C3
Borås	27	G8
Borãzjãn	71	D2
Bordeaux	37	E9
Borden Peninsula	93	Q2
Border Town	87	H7
Bordj Bou Arréridj	77	F1
Bordj Messaouda	77	G2
Bordj Mokhtar	77	F4
Bordj Omar Driss	77	G3
Borgarnes	27	(1)C2
Borger	103	F1
Borgomanero	41	D5
Borgo San Dalmazzo	41	C6
Borgosesia	41	D5
Bori Jenein	77	H2
Borisoglebsk	49	H4
Borkou	75	C4
Borkum	31	B3
Borlänge	27	H6
Bormida	41	D6
Bormio	41	F4
Borneo	63	(1)E3
Bornholm	27	H9
Borovichi	49	F3
Borriana	39	K5
Borroloola	87	G3
Borshchovochnyy Khrebet	55	J7
Borüjerd	67	E3
Borzya	55	K6
Bosa	43	C8
Bosanska Gradiška	45	E4
Bosanski Novi	45	D4
Bosanski Petrovac	45	D5
Boşca	45	J4
Bose	61	D2
Bosilegrad	45	K7
Bosna	45	F5
Bosnia-Herzegovina	45	E5
Bosobolo	81	B3
Bosporus = İstanbul Boğazı	47	M3
Bossambélé	81	B2
Bossangoa	81	B2
Bosten Hu	53	R9
Boston, U.K.	35	M9
Boston, U.S.	99	F2
Botoşani	45	P2
Botrange	33	J4
Botswana	83	C4
Bou Ahmed	39	F9
Bouaké	79	C3
Bouar	81	B2
Bouârfa	77	E2
Bougainville Island	85	F6
Bougouni	79	C2
Bou Ismaïl	39	N8
Boujdour	77	C3
Bou Kadir	39	M8
Boulder	97	E2
Boulder City	103	D1
Boulia	87	G4
Boulogne-sur-Mer	33	H8
Bounty Islands	85	H10
Bourem	77	E5
Bourg-en-Bresse	37	L7
Bourges	37	H6
Bourke	87	J6
Bournemouth	35	L11
Bousso	75	C5
Bouzghaïa	39	M8
Bowen	87	J4
Bowie	103	E2
Bowling Green, Fla., U.S.	101	E4
Bowling Green, Ky., U.S.	101	D2
Bowling Green, Mo., U.S.	101	C2
Bowman	97	F1
Bowman Bay	93	R3
Boyang	57	F5
Boyarka	55	F2
Bozcaada	47	H5
Boz Dağ	47	M7
Bozeman	97	D1
Bozkır	47	Q7
Bra	41	C6
Brač	45	D6
Bräcke	27	H5
Brad	45	K3
Bradford	35	L8
Brady	101	B3
Braga	39	B3
Bragança, Brazil	109	H4
Bragança, Portugal	39	D3
Brahmapur	65	D5
Brahmaputra	65	F2
Brăila	45	Q4
Brainerd	99	B1
Brake	31	D3
Brampton	99	E2
Bramsche	31	D4
Branco	109	E3
Brandberg	83	A4
Brandenburg	31	H4
Braniewo	29	J3
Brasília	109	H7
Braşov	45	N4
Bratislava	29	G9
Bratsk	55	G5
Bratskoye Vodokhranilishche	55	G5
Braţul	45	R4
Braunau	41	J2
Braunschweig	31	F4
Brazil	107	F4
Brazzaville	81	B4
Brčko	45	F5
Břeclav	29	F9
Breda	33	G3
Bredasdorp	83	C6
Bredy	49	M4
Bregenz	41	E3
Breiðafjörður	27	(1)A2
Bremen	31	D3
Bremerhaven	31	D3
Bremervörde	31	E3
Brenham	101	B3
Breno	41	F5
Brescia	41	F5
Breslau = Wrocław	29	G6
Bressanone	43	F2
Bressuire	37	E7
Brest, Belarus	49	D4
Brest, France	37	A5
Breteuil	33	E5
Bretten	31	D7
Breves	109	G4
Brewarrina	87	J5
Bria	81	C2
Briançon	41	B6
Briceni	45	Q1
Bridgeport, Calif., U.S.	103	C1
Bridgeport, Conn., U.S.	99	F2
Bridgwater	35	J10
Brienzer See	41	D4
Brig	41	C4
Brigham City	97	D2
Brighton	33	B4
Brilon	31	D5
Brindisi	43	M8
Brinkley	101	C3
Brisbane	87	K5
Bristol, U.K.	35	K10
Bristol, U.S.	101	E2
Bristol Bay	103	(1)E4
Bristol Channel	35	H10
British Columbia	93	F5
Brive-la-Gaillarde	37	G8
Briviesca	39	G2
Brlik	53	N9
Brno	29	F8
Broadus	97	E1
Brockton	99	F2
Brockville	99	E2
Brodeur Peninsula	93	P2
Brodnica	29	J4
Broken Hill	87	H6
Brokopondo	109	F2
Brooke's Point	61	F5
Brookhaven	101	C3
Brookings, Oreg., U.S.	97	B2
Brookings, S.D., U.S.	97	G2
Brooks Range	103	(1)F2
Broome	87	D3
Brownfield	103	F2
Browning	97	D1
Brownsville	101	D2
Brownwood	101	B3
Bruck, Austria	41	L3
Bruck, Austria	41	M2
Bruck an der Mur	45	C2
Brugge	33	F3

Name	Pg	Grid
Bruint	65	G3
Brunei A	63	(1)E2
Brunico	41	G4
Brunsbüttel	31	E3
Brunswick	101	E3
Brush	97	F2
Brussels = Bruxelles	33	G4
Bruxelles	33	G4
Bryan	101	B3
Bryansk	49	F4
Brzeg	29	G7
Bucak	69	D5
Bucaramanga	109	C2
Buchanan	79	B3
Bucharest = București	45	P5
Buchen	31	E7
Buchholz	31	E3
Buchy	37	M5
Bückeburg	31	E4
București	45	P5
Budapest	45	G2
Budennovsk	69	L1
Büdingen	31	E6
Buenaventura, Colombia	109	B3
Buenaventura, Mexico	103	E3
Buenos Aires	111	K5
Buffalo, N.Y., U.S.	99	E2
Buffalo, S.D., U.S.	97	F1
Buffalo, Tex., U.S.	101	B3
Buffalo, Wyo., U.S.	97	E2
Buftea	45	N5
Bug	29	L5
Bugrino	53	H4
Buguruslan	49	K4
Buḩayrat al Asad	69	H5
Buḩayrat ath Tharthār	69	K6
Builth Wells	35	J9
Buir Nuur	57	F1
Bujumbura	81	D4
Bukachacha	55	K6
Bukavu	81	D4
Bukhara	67	H2
Bukittinggi	63	(1)C3
Bukoba	81	E4
Bula	63	(2)D3
Bulan	61	G4
Bulawayo	83	D4
Bulgan	55	G7
Bulgaria A	45	M7
Bulle	41	C4
Bullhead City	103	D1
Bulukumba	63	(2)B4
Bumba	81	C3
Buna	81	F3
Bunbury	87	C6
Bundaberg	87	K4
Bunia	81	E3
Buôn Mê Thuôt	61	D4
Bura	81	F4
Buranj	65	D2
Burao	81	H2
Burāq	70	D3
Buraydah	67	D4
Burco	75	J6
Burdur	69	D5
Burdur Gölü	47	N7
Burē	75	G5
Burg	31	G4
Burgas	45	Q7
Burgaski Zaliv	45	Q7
Burgdorf	41	C3
Burghausen	41	H2
Burglengenfeld	31	H7
Burgos	39	G2
Burgsvik	27	K8
Burhaniye	47	K5
Burhanpur	65	C4
Burkina A	79	D2
Burlin	49	K4
Burlington, Colo., U.S.	103	F1
Burlington, Ia., U.S.	99	B2
Burlington, Vt., U.S.	99	F2
Burma = Myanmar A	61	B2
Burney	97	B2
Burnie	87	J8
Burns	97	C2
Burns Junction	97	C2
Burqin	53	R8
Burrel	47	C3
Bursa	47	M4
Bûr Safâga	75	F2
Bûr Sa'îd	75	F1
Bur Sudan	75	G4
Buru	63	(2)C3
Burundi A	81	D4
Bururi	81	D4
Buryatiya a	55	J6
Bury St. Edmunds	33	C2
Büshehr	71	D2
Bushire = Büshehr	71	D2
Busira	81	C4
Bussum	33	H2
Busto Arsizio	41	D5
Buta	81	C3
Butare	81	D4
Butembo	81	D3
Buđardalur	27	(1)C2
Buton	63	(2)B3
Butte	97	D1
Butuan	61	H5
Bützow	31	G3
Buulobarde	81	H3
Buxton	33	A1
Buy	49	H3
Buynaksk	69	M2
Buzai Gumbad	67	K2
Buzău	45	P4
Buzuluk	49	K4
Byala Slatina	45	L6
Byaroza	27	N10
Bydgoszcz	29	H4
Bygland	27	D7
Bykovskiy	55	M2
Bylot Island	93	R2
Bytantay	55	N3
Bytom	29	H7
Bytów	29	G3

C

Name	Pg	Grid
Caballococha	109	C5
Cabanatuan	61	G3
Cabañaquinta	39	E1
Cabano	99	G1
Cabinda	79	G6
Cabinda	79	G6
Cabo Beata	105	K5
Cabo Catoche	105	G4
Cabo Corrientes, Colombia	109	B2
Cabo Corrientes, Mexico	105	C4
Cabo de Espichel	39	A6
Cabo de Gata	39	H8
Cabo de Hornos	111	H10
Cabo de la Nao	39	L6
Cabo Delgado	83	G2
Cabo de São Roque	109	K5
Cabo de São Vicente	39	A7
Cabo de Trafalgar	39	D8
Cabo Fisterra	39	A2
Cabo Frio	111	N3
Cabo Gracias á Dios	105	H6
Cabo Mondego	39	A4
Cabo Norte	109	H3
Cabo Ortegal	39	B1
Cabo Peñas	39	E1
Caborca	103	D2
Cabo Roxo	79	A2
Cabo San Juan	79	F4
Cabo San Lucas	95	D7
Cabo Santa Elena	105	J7
Cabot Strait	93	U7
Cabrera	39	N5
Čačak	45	H6
Cáceres, Brazil	109	F7
Cáceres, Spain	39	D5
Cachimbo	109	G5
Cacola	83	B2
Caconda	83	B2
Čadca	29	H8
Cadillac	99	C2
Cádiz	39	D8
Caen	33	B5
Caernarfon	35	H8
Cagayan de Oro	61	G5
Cagli	41	H7
Cagliari	43	D9
Cahama	83	A3
Cahors	37	G9
Cahul	45	R4
Caia	83	F3
Caianda	83	C2
Cairns	87	J3
Cairo	101	D2
Cairo = El Qâhira	75	F1
Cajamarca	109	B5
Calabar	79	F3
Calabozo	109	D2
Calafat	45	K6
Calahorra	39	J2
Calais	33	D4
Calama	111	H3
Calamian Group	61	F4
Calamocha	39	J4
Calanscio Sand Sea	75	D2
Calapan	61	G4
Călărași	45	Q5
Calatayud	39	J3
Calbayog	61	G4
Calcutta	65	E4
Caldwell	101	B2
Calgary	93	J6
Cali	109	B3
Calicut = Kozhikode	65	C6
Caliente	97	D3
California a	95	B4
Callao	109	B6
Caltagirone	43	J11
Caltanissetta	43	J11
Caluula	81	J1
Calvi	43	C6
Calvinia	83	B6
Camacupa	83	B2
Camagüey	105	J4
Camana	109	C7
Camargue	37	K10
Camariñas	39	A1
Camarones	111	H7
Ca Mau	61	D5
Cambodia A	61	C4
Cambrai	33	F4
Cambrian Mountains	35	H10
Cambridge, New Zealand	89	E3
Cambridge, U.K.	35	N9
Cambridge, U.S.	99	E3
Cambridge Bay	93	K3
Cameroon A	79	G3
Cametá	109	H4
Çamiçigölü	47	K7
Caminha	39	B3
Camiranga	109	H4

Camocim · ● 109 · J4
Camooweal · ● 87 · G3
Campbell Island · 89 · (2)C2
Campbellton · ● 99 · G1
Campbeltown · ● 35 · G6
Campeche · ● 105 · F5
Câmpina · ● 45 · N4
Campina Grande · ● 109 · L5
Campinas · ● 111 · M3
Campobasso · ● 43 · J7
Campo Grande · ▣ 111 · L3
Campo Maior · ● 109 · J4
Campo Mourão · ● 111 · L3
Campos · ● 111 · N3
Câmpulung · ● 45 · N4
Câmpulung Moldovenesc · ● 45 · N2
Cam Ranh · ● 61 · D4
Canada · Ⓐ 91 · M4
Canadian · ● 103 · F1
Canadian · ⊿ 103 · F1
Çanakkale · ● 47 · J4
Çanakkale Boğazı · ⊑ 47 · J4
Canal de Panamá · ⊿ 105 · J7
Canary Islands = Islas Canarias · 77 · B3
Canary Islands = Islas Canarias · 73 · A3
Canberra · ■ 87 · J7
Cancún · ● 105 · G4
Candelaro · ⊿ 45 · C8
Candlemas Island · 107 · J9
Cangamba · ● 83 · B2
Cangas de Narcea · ● 39 · D1
Cangzhou · ● 57 · F3
Canicattì · ● 43 · H11
Çankiri · ● 69 · E3
Cannanore · ● 65 · C6
Cannes · ● 41 · C7
Cannock · ● 33 · A2
Canon City · ● 103 · E1
Cantanduanes · 61 · G4
Canterbury · ● 33 · D3
Canterbury Bight · ⊑ 89 · C7
Canterbury Plains · 89 · C6
Cân Tho · ● 61 · D5
Canton · ● 101 · E1
Canutama · ● 109 · E5
Canyon · ● 103 · F1
Cao Băng · ● 61 · D2
Cap Blanc · ⊟ 43 · D11
Cap Bon · ⊟ 77 · H1
Cap Corse · ⊟ 43 · D5
Cap d'Agde · ⊟ 37 · J10
Cap d'Antifer · ⊟ 33 · C5
Cap de Fer · ⊟ 77 · G1
Cap de Formentor · ⊟ 39 · P5
Cap de la Hague · ⊟ 37 · D4

Cap de ses Salines · ⊟ 39 · P5
Cap des Trois Fourches · ⊟ 39 · H9
Cape Agulhas · ⊟ 83 · C6
Cape Andreas · ⊟ 67 · B2
Cape Apostolos Andreas · ⊟ 69 · F6
Cape Arnhem · ⊟ 87 · G2
Cape Bauld · ⊟ 93 · V6
Cape Blanco · ⊟ 97 · B2
Cape Breton Island · 93 · U7
Cape Byron · ⊟ 87 · K5
Cape Campbell · ⊟ 89 · E5
Cape Canaveral · ⊟ 101 · E4
Cape Carnot · ⊟ 87 · F6
Cape Charles · ● 99 · E3
Cape Churchill · ⊟ 93 · N5
Cape Clear · ⊟ 35 · C10
Cape Cleare · ⊟ 103 · (1)H4
Cape Coast · ● 79 · D3
Cape Cod · ⊟ 99 · G2
Cape Colville · ⊟ 89 · E3
Cape Comorin · ⊟ 65 · C7
Cape Coral · ● 101 · E4
Cape Dorset · ● 93 · R4
Cape Dyer · ⊟ 93 · U3
Cape Egmont · ⊟ 89 · D4
Cape Farewell, Greenland · ⊟ 91 · F4
Cape Farewell, New Zealand · ⊟ 89 · D5
Cape Fear · ⊟ 101 · F3
Cape Finisterre = Cabo Fisterra · ⊟ 39 · A2
Cape Flattery, Australia · ⊟ 87 · J2
Cape Flattery, U.S. · ⊟ 97 · A1
Cape Foulwind · ⊟ 89 · C5
Cape Fria · ⊟ 83 · A3
Cape Girardeau · ● 99 · C3
Cape Greko · ⊟ 69 · F6
Cape Grim · ⊟ 87 · H8
Cape Harrison · ⊟ 93 · V6
Cape Hatteras · ⊟ 101 · F2
Cape Henrietta Maria · ⊟ 93 · Q5
Cape Horn = Cabo de Hornos · ⊟ 111 · H10
Cape Howe · ⊟ 87 · K7
Cape Inscription · ⊟ 87 · B5
Cape Leeuwin · ⊟ 87 · B6
Cape Lévêque · ⊟ 87 · D3
Cape Londonderry · ⊟ 87 · E2
Cape Lookout · ⊟ 105 · J2
Cape Melville · ⊟ 87 · H2
Cape Mendocino · ⊟ 97 · A2
Cape Naturaliste · ⊟ 87 · B6
Cape Negrais · ⊟ 61 · A3
Cape Nelson · ⊟ 87 · H7
Cape of Good Hope · ⊟ 83 · B6
Cape Palliser · ⊟ 89 · E5
Cape Palmas · ⊟ 79 · C4

Cape Parry · ⊟ 93 · G2
Cape Providence · ⊟ 89 · A8
Cape Race · ⊟ 91 · G5
Cape Reinga · ⊟ 89 · D2
Cape Romanzof · ⊟ 103 · (1)D3
Cape Sable · ⊟ 93 · T8
Cape San Agustin · ⊟ 61 · H5
Cape San Blas · ⊟ 101 · D4
Cape Three Points · ⊟ 79 · D4
Cape Town · ■ 83 · B6
Cape Turnagain · ⊟ 89 · F5
Cape Verde · Ⓐ 79 · (1)B2
Cape Wessel · ⊟ 87 · G2
Cape Wrangell · ⊟ 55 · W6
Cape Wrath · ⊟ 35 · G3
Cape York · ⊟ 87 · H2
Cape York Peninsula · 87 · H2
Cap Gris-Nez · ⊟ 33 · D4
Cap-Haïtien · ● 105 · K5
Cap Juby · ⊟ 77 · C3
Cap Negro · ⊟ 39 · E9
Capo Carbonara · ⊟ 43 · D10
Capo Gallo · ⊟ 43 · H10
Capo Palinuro · ⊟ 43 · J8
Capo Passero · ⊟ 43 · K12
Capo Santa Maria di Leuca · ⊟ 43 · N9
Capo San Vito · ⊟ 43 · G10
Capo Spartivento · ⊟ 43 · C10
Capraia · ⊟ 43 · D5
Cap Rhir · ⊟ 77 · C2
Capri · 43 · J8
Cap Serrat · ⊟ 43 · D11
Cap Timiris · ⊟ 77 · B5
Capua · ● 43 · J7
Cap Vert · ⊟ 79 · A2
Caquetá · ⊿ 109 · C4
Caracal · ● 45 · M5
Caracarai · ● 109 · E3
Caracas · ■ 109 · D1
Carauari · ● 109 · D4
Caravelas · ● 109 · K7
Carazinho · ● 111 · L4
Carballo · ● 39 · B1
Carbondale · ● 101 · D2
Carbonia · ● 43 · C9
Carcassonne · ● 37 · H10
Cardiff · ⊡ 35 · J10
Cardigan Bay · ⊑ 35 · H9
Carei · ● 45 · K2
Caribbean Sea · 105 · J6
Carlisle · ● 35 · K7
Carlsbad · ● 103 · F2
Carmagnola · ● 41 · C6
Carmarthen · ● 35 · H10
Carmaux · ● 37 · H9
Carmen · 105 · B3

Carnarvon, Australia · ● 87 · B4
Carnarvon, South Africa · ● 83 · C6
Car Nicobar · 65 · F7
Carnot · ● 81 · B2
Carnsore Point · ⊟ 35 · F9
Carolina · ● 109 · H5
Caroline Island · 85 · L6
Caroline Islands · 85 · E5
Carpathian Mountains · 29 · J8
Carpatii Meridionali · 45 · J4
Carpentras · ● 37 · L9
Carpi · ● 41 · F6
Carrabelle · ● 101 · E4
Carrara · ● 41 · F6
Carrington · ● 97 · G1
Carrizozo · ● 103 · E2
Carrollton, Ky., U.S. · ● 99 · D3
Carrollton, Mo., U.S. · ● 101 · C1
Çarşamba · ● 69 · G3
Carson City · ⊡ 97 · C3
Cartagena, Colombia · ● 109 · B1
Cartagena, Spain · ● 39 · K7
Carthage · ● 101 · C3
Cartwright · ● 93 · V6
Caruarú · ● 109 · K5
Casablanca · ● 77 · D2
Casa Grande · ● 103 · D2
Casale Monferrato · ● 41 · D5
Casarano · ● 43 · N9
Cascade · ● 97 · C2
Cascade Range · 97 · B2
Cascavel · ● 111 · L3
Caserta · ● 43 · J7
Casino · ● 87 · K5
Caspe · ● 39 · K3
Casper · ● 97 · E2
Caspian Sea · 25 · J3
Cassino · ● 43 · H7
Castellane · ● 41 · B7
Castelló de la Plana · ● 39 · K5
Castelo Branco · ● 39 · C5
Castelsarrasin · ● 37 · G10
Castelvetrano · ● 43 · G11
Castlebar · ● 35 · C8
Castleford · ● 35 · L8
Castle Point · ● 89 · F5
Castres · ● 37 · H10
Castries · ■ 105 · M6
Castrovillari · ● 43 · L9
Castuera · ● 39 · E6
Catamarca · ● 111 · H4
Catania · ● 43 · K11
Catanzaro · ● 43 · L10
Catanzaro Marina · ● 43 · L10
Cataman · ● 61 · G4
Catbalogan · ● 61 · H4
Cat Island · 101 · F5
Cat Lake · ● 93 · N6

Name	Page	Grid
Cauayan	61	G5
Caucasus	69	K2
Caudry	33	F4
Caura	109	E2
Causapscal	99	G1
Cavaillon	37	L10
Cave	89	C7
Cavinas	109	D6
Cavtat	45	F7
Caxias	109	J4
Caxias do Sul	111	L4
Caxito	79	G6
Cayenne	109	J4
Cayman Islands	105	H5
Cay Sal Bank	101	E5
Ceará	109	J4
Cebu	61	G4
Cebu	61	G4
Cecina	43	E5
Cedar City	97	D3
Cedar Falls	99	B2
Cedar Rapids	99	B2
Cedros	95	C6
Ceduna	87	F6
Ceerigaabo	81	H1
Cefalù	43	J10
Cegléd	45	G2
Celebes = Sulawesi	63	(2)A3
Celebes Sea	63	(2)B2
Celje	45	C3
Celle	31	F4
Celtic Sea	35	E10
Cento	41	G6
Central African Republic	81	C2
Centralia	97	B1
Central Range	63	(2)F3
Central Siberian Plateau = Srednesibirskoye Ploskogor'ye	51	N2
Ceres, Argentina	111	J4
Ceres, Brazil	109	H7
Cerignola	43	K7
Çerkes	47	Q4
Cerritos	103	F4
Cerro Aconcagua	111	G5
Cerro Bonete	111	H4
Cerro de Pasco	109	B6
Cerro Marahuaca	109	D3
Cerro Murallón	111	G8
Cerro Nevado	111	H6
Cerro Pena Nevade	105	D4
Cerro San Valentín	111	G8
Cerro Yogan	111	H9
Certaldo	41	G7
Cervaro	43	K7
Cervia	41	H6
Cesena	41	H6
Cesano	41	J7
České Budějovice	41	K2
Český Krumlov	41	K2
Çeşme	47	J6
Cessnock	87	K6
Cetate	45	L5
Cetinje	45	F7
Ceuta	77	D1
Chachapoyas	109	B5
Chaco Boreal	111	K3
Chad	75	C5
Chadan	53	S7
Chadron	97	F2
Chāh Bahār	67	H4
Chalhuanca	109	C6
Chalki	47	K8
Chalkida	47	F6
Chalkidiki	47	F4
Challenger Deep	85	E4
Challis	97	D2
Châlons-sur-Marne	33	G6
Chalon-sur-Saône	37	K7
Chama	31	H7
Chama	83	E2
Chambal	65	C3
Chamberlain	97	G2
Chambéry	41	A5
Chamonix	41	B5
Champaign	99	C2
Champlitte	41	A3
Chañaral	111	G4
Chandigarh	65	C2
Chandler	103	D2
Chandrapur	65	C5
Changane	83	E4
Changara	83	E3
Changchun	59	C2
Changde	57	E5
Chang-hua	57	G6
Chang Jiang	57	D4
Changsha	57	E5
Changting	57	F5
Changzhi	57	E3
Changzhou	57	F4
Chania	47	G9
Channel Islands	35	K12
Channel-Port aux Basques	93	V7
Chanthaburi	61	C4
Chantilly	33	E5
Chanute	101	B2
Chao Phraya	61	C4
Chaoyang	57	G2
Chaozhou	57	F6
Chapada Diamantina	109	J6
Chapleau	99	D1
Chapra	65	C3
Chara	55	K5
Charcas	103	F4
Chardzhev	67	H2
Chari	75	C5
Chārīkār	67	J2
Charleroi	33	G4
Charleston, New Zealand	89	C5
Charleston, S.C., U.S.	101	F3
Charleston, W. Va., U.S.	101	E2
Charleville	87	J5
Charleville-Mézières	33	G5
Charlotte	101	E2
Charlottesville	101	F2
Charlottetown	93	U7
Charlton Island	93	Q6
Charsk	53	Q8
Charters Towers	87	J4
Chartres	37	G5
Chasel'ka	55	C3
Châteaubriant	37	D6
Châteaudun	37	G5
Châteauroux	37	G7
Château-Thierry	33	F5
Châtellerault	37	F7
Chatham	99	D2
Chatham Island	89	(1)B1
Chatham Islands	89	(1)B1
Châtillon-sur-Seine	37	K6
Chattanooga	95	J4
Chauk	65	F4
Chaumont	37	L5
Chauny	33	F5
Chaves	109	G4
Cheb	31	H6
Cheboksary	49	J3
Chechnya	69	L2
Cheduba Island	65	F5
Chegdomyn	55	N6
Cheju	59	D7
Cheju do	59	D7
Chélif	39	L8
Chelkar	53	K8
Chełm	29	N6
Chełmno	29	H4
Chelmsford	33	C3
Cheltenham	35	L10
Chelyabinsk	49	M3
Chemnitz	31	H6
Chengde	57	F2
Chengdu	57	C4
Chennai	65	D6
Chenzhou	57	E5
Chepes	111	H5
Cher	37	G6
Cherbourg	37	D4
Cherchell	39	N8
Cheremkhovo	55	G6
Cherepovets	49	G3
Cherkasy	49	F5
Cherkessk	69	K1
Chernihiv	49	F4
Chernivtsi	49	E5
Chernyakhovsk	29	L3
Chernyshevskiy	55	J4
Chernyye Zemli	49	J5
Cherokee	99	A2
Cherskiy	55	U3
Cherven Bryag	45	M6
Chesapeake	101	F2
Cheshskaya Guba	49	J1
Cheshunt	33	C3
Chester, U.K.	35	K8
Chester, U.S.	97	B2
Chesterfield Inlet	93	N4
Chetumal	105	G5
Ch'ew Bahir	81	F3
Cheyenne	97	F2
Cheyenne	97	F2
Cheyenne Wells	103	F1
Cheyne Bay	87	C6
Chhindwara	65	C4
Chhuka	65	E3
Chiang-Mai	61	B3
Chiang Rai	61	B3
Chiavari	41	E6
Chiavenna	41	E4
Chiba	59	L6
Chibougamau	93	S6
Chibuto	83	E4
Chicago	99	C2
Chicapa	81	C5
Chickasha	101	B3
Chiclayo	109	B5
Chico	111	H8
Chicoutimi	93	S7
Chiemsee	41	H3
Chieri	41	C5
Chiese	41	F5
Chieti	43	J6
Chifeng	57	F2
Chiganak	53	N8
Chigubo	83	E4
Chihuahua	103	E3
Chiili	53	M9
Chilas	65	B1
Childress	103	F2
Chile	107	D8
Chile Chico	111	G8
Chillán	111	G6
Chillicothe	99	D3
Chilliwack	97	B1
Chiloquin	97	B2
Chi-lung	57	G5
Chimbay	53	K9
Chimborazo	109	B5
Chimbote	109	B5
Chimec	45	J1

Name	Map	Ref
Chimoio	● 83	E3
China	Ⓐ 51	N6
Chincha Alta	● 109	B6
Chincilla de Monte-Aragón	● 39	J6
Chinde	● 83	F3
Chin do	● 59	C6
Chindwin	◹ 61	A2
Chingola	● 83	D2
Chinhoyi	● 83	E3
Chiniot	● 65	B2
Chinju	● 59	E6
Chinmen	▣ 61	F2
Chioggia	● 41	H5
Chios	● 47	J6
Chios	▣ 47	H6
Chipata	● 83	E2
Chippewa Falls	● 99	B2
Chipping Norton	● 33	A3
Chiromo	● 83	F3
Chirripo	▲ 105	H7
Chişinău	■ 45	R2
Chita	● 55	J6
Chitato	● 81	C5
Chitembo	● 83	B2
Chitradurga	● 65	C6
Chitral	● 65	B1
Chitré	● 105	H7
Chittagong	● 65	F4
Chittaurgarh	● 65	B4
Chittoor	● 65	C6
Chitungwiza	● 83	E3
Chiume	● 83	C3
Chivasso	● 41	C5
Chizha	● 49	H1
Chojnice	● 29	G4
Chokurdakh	● 55	R2
Chókwé	● 83	E4
Cholet	● 37	E6
Choma	● 83	D3
Chomutov	● 29	C7
Ch'ŏngjin	● 59	E3
Ch'ŏngju	● 59	D6
Chŏngp'yŏng	● 59	D4
Chongqing	● 51	P7
Ch'ŏnju	● 59	D5
Chornobyl'	● 49	F4
Ch'osan	● 59	C3
Chōshi	● 59	L6
Choszczno	● 29	E4
Choteau	● 97	D1
Chott el Jerid	☒ 77	G2
Chott Melrhir	☒ 77	G2
Choybalsan	● 55	J7
Choyr	● 57	D1
Christchurch	● 89	D6
Christmas Island	▣ 63	(1)D5
Chu	● 53	N9
Chubut	◹ 111	H7
Chūgoku-sanchi	◪ 57	J3
Chugwater	● 97	F2
Chukchi Sea	◻ 103	(1)C2
Chukotskiy Khrebet	◪ 55	W3
Chukotskiy Poluostrov	◉ 55	Z3
Chulucanas	● 109	A5
Chumikan	● 55	P6
Chum Phae	● 61	C3
Chumphon	● 61	B4
Ch'unch'ŏn	● 59	D5
Chundzha	● 53	P9
Chur	● 41	E4
Churchill	● 93	N5
Churchill	◹ 93	M5
Churchill Falls	● 93	U6
Churchill Peak	▲ 93	F5
Chusovoy	● 49	L3
Chute des Passes	● 93	S7
Chuvashiya	▣ 49	J3
Chuxiong	● 61	C2
Chuya	● 55	J5
Ciadîr-Lunga	● 45	R3
Ciechanów	● 29	K5
Ciego de Avila	● 105	J4
Cienfuegos	● 105	H4
Cieza	● 39	J6
Cilacap	● 63	(1)D4
Cimarron	◹ 101	B2
Cinca	◹ 39	L3
Cincinnati	● 99	D3
Çine	● 47	L7
Cintalapa	● 105	F5
Circle	● 103	(1)J2
Cirebon	● 63	(1)D4
Cirò Marina	● 43	M9
Cisco	● 101	B3
Cistierna	● 39	E2
Cittadella	● 41	G5
Città di Castello	● 41	H7
Ciucea	● 45	K3
Ciudad Acuña	● 103	F3
Ciudad Bolívar	● 109	E2
Ciudad Camargo	● 103	E3
Ciudad del Carmen	● 105	F5
Ciudad del Este	◹ 111	L4
Ciudad Delicias	● 103	E3
Ciudad del Maíz	● 103	G4
Ciudad de México	● 105	E5
Ciudad Guayana	● 109	E2
Ciudad Juárez	● 103	E2
Ciudad Madero	● 103	G4
Ciudad Mante	● 105	E4
Ciudad Obregón	● 105	C3
Ciudad Real	● 39	G6
Ciudad-Rodrigo	● 39	D4
Ciudad Victoria	● 95	G7
Ciutadella	● 39	P4
Civita Castellana	● 43	G6
Civitanova Marche	● 43	H5
Civitavecchia	● 43	F6
Clairview	● 87	J4
Clamecy	● 37	J6
Clare Island	▣ 35	B8
Clarence	● 89	D6
Clarendon	● 103	F2
Clarkdale	● 103	D2
Clarksburg	● 101	E2
Clarksdale	● 101	C3
Clarksville	● 101	D2
Claveria	● 61	G3
Clayton	● 103	F1
Clearwater	◹ 97	C1
Clermont	● 87	J4
Clermont-Ferrand	● 37	J8
Cles	● 41	F4
Cleveland, Oh., U.S.	● 99	D2
Cleveland, Tenn., U.S.	● 101	E2
Clinton	● 101	B2
Clipperton Island	▣ 105	C6
Clonmel	● 35	E9
Cloppenburg	● 31	D4
Cloud Peak	▲ 97	E2
Clovis, Calif., U.S.	● 97	C3
Clovis, N. Mex., U.S.	● 103	F2
Cluj-Napoca	● 45	L3
Cluny	● 37	K7
Clyde	◹ 35	H6
Clyde River	● 93	T2
Coalville	● 97	C2
Coari	● 109	E4
Coast Mountains	◪ 93	E5
Coast Range	◪ 97	B3
Coats Island	▣ 93	Q4
Coatzacoalcos	● 105	F5
Cobán	● 105	F5
Cobar	● 87	J6
Cobija	● 109	D6
Cobourg Peninsula	◉ 87	F2
Cobuè	● 83	E2
Coburg	● 31	F6
Cochabamba	● 109	D7
Cochin = Kochi	● 65	C7
Cochrane	● 99	D1
Coco	◹ 105	H6
Cocoa	● 101	E4
Coco Channel	◳ 61	A4
Coco Island	▣ 61	A4
Codigoro	● 41	H6
Codlea	● 45	N4
Codó	● 109	J4
Codroipo	● 41	J5
Coesfeld	● 31	C5
Coeur d'Alene	● 97	C1
Coffs Harbour	● 87	K6
Cofrents	● 39	J5
Cognac	● 37	E8
Cogne	● 41	C5
Coiba	▣ 107	C3
Coihaique	● 111	G8
Coimbatore	● 65	C6
Coimbra	● 39	B4
Colchester	● 33	C3
Colebrook	● 99	F1
Coll	▣ 35	F5
Collier Bay	◳ 87	D3
Colmar	● 41	C2
Colmenar Viejo	● 39	G4
Colombia	Ⓐ 109	C3
Colombo	■ 65	C7
Colonia Las Heras	● 111	H8
Colonsay	▣ 35	F5
Colorado	ⓐ 97	E3
Colorado, Colo., U.S.	◹ 103	E1
Colorado, Tex., U.S.	◹ 103	G2
Colorado Plateau	◉ 103	D1
Colorado Springs	● 97	F3
Columbia	◹ 97	C1
Columbia, Mo., U.S.	● 101	C2
Columbia, S.C., U.S.	▣ 101	E3
Columbia, Tenn., U.S.	● 101	D2
Columbia Mountains	◪ 93	G6
Columbus, Ga., U.S.	● 101	E3
Columbus, Ind., U.S.	● 101	D2
Columbus, Nebr., U.S.	● 97	G2
Columbus, N. Mex., U.S.	▣ 103	E2
Columbus, Oh., U.S.	▣ 101	E1
Columbus, Tex., U.S.	● 101	B4
Colville	◹ 103	(1)G2
Commentry	● 37	H7
Commercy	● 33	H6
Como	● 41	E5
Comoé	◹ 79	D3
Comoros	Ⓐ 83	G2
Compiègne	● 33	E5
Conakry	■ 79	B3
Concarneau	● 37	B6
Conceição do Araguaia	● 109	H5
Concepción, Bolivia	● 109	E7
Concepción, Chile	● 111	G6
Conchos	◹ 105	C3
Concord, Calif., U.S.	● 103	B1
Concord, N.H., U.S.	▣ 99	F2
Concord, N.C., U.S.	● 101	E2
Concordia, Argentina	● 111	K5
Concordia, U.S.	● 101	B2
Condobolin	● 87	J6
Condom	● 37	F10
Congo	Ⓐ 79	G5
Congo	◹ 73	E6
Connecticut	ⓐ 99	F2
Connemara	◉ 35	C8
Côn Son	▣ 61	D5
Constanța	● 69	C1

Name	Page	Grid
Constantine	77	G1
Consul	97	E1
Contwoyto Lake	93	J3
Conway	101	C2
Coober Pedy	87	F5
Cook Islands	85	K7
Cook Strait	89	E5
Cooktown	87	J3
Coolgardie	87	D6
Cooma	87	J7
Coon Rapids	99	B1
Coorabie	87	F6
Coos Bay	97	B2
Cootamundra	87	J6
Copenhagen = København	27	G9
Copiapó	111	G4
Copper Harbor	99	C1
Côgen	65	E2
Coquimbo	111	G4
Corabia	45	M6
Coral Sea	87	K2
Coral Sea Islands Territory	87	K2
Coral Springs	101	E4
Corbeil-Essonnes	37	H5
Corbigny	37	J6
Corby	33	B2
Cordele	101	E3
Cordillera Cantábrica	39	D2
Cordillera Central	107	E5
Cordillera del Condor	109	B5
Cordillera de Mérida	107	D3
Cordillera Occidental	107	E5
Cordillera Oriental	107	D5
Cordillera Penibética	39	G7
Cordillera Vilcabamba	109	C6
Córdoba, *Argentina*	111	J5
Córdoba, *Spain*	39	F7
Corfu = Kerkyra	47	B5
Corinth	101	D3
Cork	35	D10
Corleone	43	H11
Çorlu	47	K3
Corn Islands	107	C2
Cornwallis Island	93	M2
Coro	109	D1
Coromandel	89	E3
Coromandel Coast	65	D6
Coromandel Peninsula	89	E3
Coron	61	G4
Coronel Oviedo	111	K4
Coronel Suárez	111	J6
Corpus Christi	101	B4
Corrientes	111	K4
Corse	43	
Corsica = Corse	43	D6
Corsicana	101	B3
Corte	43	D6
Cortegana	39	D7
Cortez	103	E1
Cortona	43	F5
Coruche	39	B6
Çorum	69	F3
Corumbá	109	F7
Corvallis	97	B2
Cosenza	43	L9
Cosne-sur-Loire	37	H6
Costa Blanca	39	K7
Costa Brava	39	P3
Costa del Sol	39	F8
Costa de Mosquitos	105	H6
Costa Dorada	39	M4
Costa do Sol	39	A6
Costa Rica	105	G7
Costa Smeralda	43	D7
Costa Verde	39	D1
Coswig	31	H5
Cotabato	61	G5
Cotonou	79	E3
Cottbus	29	D6
Cotulla	101	B4
Coulommiers	33	F6
Council Bluffs	97	F2
Courland Lagoon	29	L2
Coutances	37	D4
Couvin	33	G4
Coventry	35	L9
Covilhã	39	C4
Covington, *Ga., U.S.*	101	E5
Covington, *Ky., U.S.*	101	E2
Covington, *Va., U.S.*	99	D3
Cowell	87	G6
Cowes	33	A4
Cowra	87	J6
Cox's Bazar	65	F4
Craig	97	E2
Crailsheim	31	F7
Craiova	45	L5
Cranbrook	87	C6
Crato	109	K5
Crawford	97	F2
Crawfordsville	99	C2
Crawley	33	B3
Cree Lake	93	K5
Creil	33	E5
Crema	41	E5
Cremona	41	F5
Crépy-en-Valois	33	E5
Cres	41	K6
Cres	41	K6
Crescent City	97	B2
Crest	37	L9
Creston	99	B2
Crete = Kriti	47	H10
Créteil	33	E6
Creuse	37	G7
Crewe	35	K8
Criciúma	111	M4
Cristóbal Colón	91	J8
Crna Gora	45	F7
Croatia	45	C4
Cromer	35	P9
Cromwell	89	B7
Crooked Island	105	K4
Crookston	95	G2
Cross Lake	93	M6
Crossville	99	C3
Crotone	43	M9
Crownest Pass	95	D2
Cruzeiro do Sul	109	C5
Crystal River	101	E4
Cuamba	83	F2
Cuando	83	C3
Cuangar	83	B3
Cuango	81	B5
Cuanza	81	B5
Cuatro Ciénegas	103	F3
Cuauhtémoc	103	E3
Cuba	105	H4
Cubal	81	A6
Cubali	83	A2
Cubango	83	B3
Cúcuta	109	C2
Cuddalore	65	C6
Cuddapah	65	C6
Cuenca, *Ecuador*	109	B4
Cuenca, *Spain*	39	H4
Cuernavaca	105	E5
Cuiabá	109	F7
Cuilo	81	B5
Cuito	83	B3
Cuito Cuanavale	83	B3
Culbertson	97	E1
Culiacán	105	C4
Cullera	39	K5
Culpepper	109	(1)A1
Culverden	89	D6
Cumaná	109	E1
Cumberland Peninsula	93	T3
Cumberland Sound	93	T3
Cummings	97	B3
Cumpas	103	E2
Cunene	83	A3
Cunnamulla	87	J5
Curicó	111	G5
Curitiba	111	M4
Curral Velho	79	(1)B1
Curtea de Argeş	45	M4
Curtis Island	87	K4
Curuá	109	G5
Curvelo	109	J7
Cusco	109	C6
Cutro	43	L9
Cuttack	65	E4
Cuxhaven	31	D3
Cyclades = Kyklades	47	G7
Cypress Hills	95	D2
Cyprus	69	E6
Czarnków	29	F5
Czech Republic	29	C8
Częstochowa	29	J7

D

Name	Page	Grid
Daaquam	99	F1
Dabola	79	B2
Dachau	41	G2
Daet	61	G4
Dagestan	69	M2
Dagupan	61	G3
Da Hinggan Ling	57	G1
Dahlak Archipelago	75	H4
Dahlonega	101	E3
Dahod	65	B4
Dahük	69	K5
Dakar	79	A2
Dakoro	79	F2
Dakota City	97	G2
Dakovica	45	H7
Dalandzadgad	57	C2
Dalap-Uliga-Darrit	85	H5
Da Lat	61	D4
Dalbandin	67	H4
Dalby	87	K5
Dalgān	67	G4
Dalhart	103	F1
Dalhousie	65	C2
Dali	61	C1
Dalian	57	G3
Dallas	101	B3
Daloa	79	C3
Dāltenganj	65	D4
Dalton	101	E3
Daly Waters	87	F3
Daman	65	B4
Damar	63	(2)C4
Damascus = Dimashq	70	D3
Damoh	65	C4
Danau Toba	63	(1)B2
Danau Towuti	63	(2)B3
Danba	57	C4
Dandeldhura	65	D3
Dandong	59	C3
Da Nĕng	61	D3
Dangara	67	J2
Danger Islands	85	K7
Daniel	97	D1
Dannenberg	31	G3
Dannevirke	89	F5
Dansville	99	E2

Name		Page	Grid
Danube	▨	25	F3
Danville, *Ill., U.S.*	●	101	D1
Danville, *Ky., U.S.*	●	101	E2
Danville, *Va., U.S.*	●	101	F2
Dao Phu Quôc	◩	61	C4
Dapaong	●	79	E2
Da Qaidam	●	57	B3
Daqing	●	55	M7
Dar'ä	●	70	D4
Dārāb	●	71	F2
Darabani	●	45	P1
Darazo	●	79	G2
Darbhanga	●	65	E3
Dardanelles =			
Çanakkale Boğazı	◧	47	J4
Darende	●	69	G4
Dar es Salaam	●	81	F5
Darfo Boario Terme	●	41	F5
Dargaville	●	89	D2
Darham	●	55	H7
Darjeeling	●	65	E3
Darling	▨	87	H6
Darlington	●	35	L7
Dar Mazār	●	71	G4
Darmstadt	●	31	D7
Darnah	●	75	D1
Daroca	●	39	J3
Darß	◩	31	H2
Dartmouth	●	93	U8
Daru	●	63	(2)F4
Darvaza	●	53	K9
Darwin	●	87	E2
Daryacheh-ye Bakhtegan	▨	71	E2
Daryācheh-ye Orūmīyeh	▨	69	L5
Daryācheh-ye Tashk	▨	71	E2
Dārzīn	●	71	H2
Dashkhovuz	●	53	K9
Dasht-e Kavir	⊘	67	F3
Dasht-e Lut	⊘	71	H1
Datça	●	47	K8
Date	●	59	L2
Datong	●	57	E2
Daugava	▨	49	E3
Daugavpils	●	49	E3
Davangere	●	65	C6
Davao	●	61	H5
Davenport	●	99	B2
Daventry	●	33	A2
David	●	105	H7
Davis Sea	▭	112	(2)Q3
Davis Strait	◧	93	V3
Davos	●	41	E4
Dawqah	●	67	F6
Dawson	●	93	D4
Dawson Creek	●	93	G5
Dawu	●	57	C4
Dax	●	37	D10
Daxian	●	57	D4
Dayong	●	57	E5
Dayr az Zawr	●	69	J6
Dayton, *Oh., U.S.*	●	99	D3
Dayton, *Wash., U.S.*	●	97	C1
Daytona Beach	●	101	E4
De Aar	●	83	C6
Dead Sea	▨	70	C5
Deal	●	33	D3
Deán Funes	●	111	J5
Death Valley	⊘	97	C3
Debar	●	47	C3
Dęblin	●	29	L6
Dębno	●	29	D5
Debrecen	●	45	J2
Debre Markos	●	75	G5
Debre Tabor	●	75	G5
Decatur, *Al., U.S.*	●	99	C4
Decatur, *Ill., U.S.*	●	99	C3
Decazeville	●	37	H9
Deccan	⊘	65	C5
Děčín	●	29	D7
Decize	●	37	J7
Decorah	●	99	B2
Dédougou	●	79	D2
Dee	▨	35	K4
Deer Lake	●	93	V7
Deer Lodge	●	97	D1
Deer Park	●	97	C1
Degeh Bur	●	81	G2
Deggendorf	●	41	J2
Deh Bid	●	71	E1
Dehlonān	●	67	E3
Dehra Dun	●	65	C2
Dehri	●	65	D4
Deh Shū	●	67	H3
Dej	●	45	L2
De Kalb	●	101	C3
Dekese	●	81	C4
Delaware	◪	101	F2
Delémont	●	41	C3
Delfoi	●	47	E6
Delft	●	33	G2
Delfzijl	●	33	J1
Delhi	●	65	C3
Dellys	●	39	P8
Delmenhorst	●	31	D3
Delnice	●	41	K5
Delray Beach	●	101	E4
Del Rio	●	103	F3
Delta	●	97	D3
Delta del Orinoco	◧	109	E2
Deming	●	103	E2
Demirci	●	47	L5
Demmin	●	31	J3
Democratic Republic of			
Congo	◭	81	C4
Demopolis	●	101	D3
Dem'yanskoye	●	49	N3
Denain	●	33	F4
Denau	●	67	J2
Denbigh	●	99	E1
Den Burg	●	33	G1
Dender	▨	33	F4
Dendi	▲	81	F2
Denham	●	87	B5
Den Helder	●	33	G2
Dénia	●	39	L6
Deniliquin	●	87	H7
Denison, *Ia., U.S.*	●	99	A2
Denison, *Tex., U.S.*	●	101	B3
Denizli	●	69	C5
Denmark	◭	25	E2
Denmark Strait	◧	91	D3
Denpasar	●	63	(1)E4
Denton	●	103	G2
Denver	◰	97	F3
Deogarh	●	65	D4
Deoghar	●	65	E4
Deputatskiy	●	55	P3
Dêqên	●	61	B1
Dera Ismail Khan	●	67	K3
Derbent	●	67	E1
Derby, *Australia*	●	87	D3
Derby, *U.K.*	●	35	L9
Derventa	●	45	E5
Desē	●	75	G5
Deseado	●	111	H8
Des Moines, *Ia., U.S.*	◰	95	H3
Des Moines,			
N. Mex., U.S.	●	103	F1
Desna	▨	49	F4
Dessau	●	31	H5
Desvres	●	33	D4
Detmold	●	31	D5
Detroit	●	95	K3
Detroit Lakes	●	99	A1
Deva	●	45	K4
Deventer	●	33	J2
Devils Lake	●	97	G1
Devon Island	◧	93	P1
Devonport	●	87	J8
Deyang	●	57	C4
Dezfūl	●	67	E3
Dezhou	●	57	F3
Dhahran = Az Zahrān	●	71	D3
Dhaka	◼	65	F4
Dhamār	●	75	H5
Dhanbad	●	65	E4
Dhārwād	●	65	B5
Dhībān	●	70	C5
Dhule	●	65	B4
Diamantino	●	109	F6
Diamond Islets	◩	87	K3
Dianópolis	●	109	H6
Dibbiena	●	43	F5
Dibrugarh	●	65	F3
Dickinson	●	97	F1
Dickson	●	101	D2
Dieburg	●	31	D7
Dieppe	●	33	D5
Digne-les-Bains	●	41	B6
Dijon	●	37	L6
Dikhil	●	75	H5
Diksmuide	●	33	E3
Dikson	●	53	Q3
Dili	●	63	(2)C4
Dillingen	●	31	B7
Dillon	●	97	D1
Dilolo	●	83	C2
Dimapur	●	65	F3
Dimashq	◼	70	D3
Dimitrovgrad, *Bulgaria*	●	45	N7
Dimitrovgrad, *Russia*	●	49	J4
Dimitrovgrad, *Yugoslavia*	●	45	K7
Dīmona	●	70	C5
Dinagat	◩	61	H4
Dinajpur	●	65	E3
Dinan	●	37	C5
Dinant	●	33	G4
Dinar	●	69	D4
Dinaric Alps	▰	41	L6
Dindigul	●	65	C6
Dingle Bay	◧	35	B9
Dingolfing	●	41	H2
Dingwall	●	35	H4
Dinkelsbühl	●	31	F7
Diomede Islands	◩	55	AA3
Diourbel	●	77	B6
Dipolog	●	61	G5
Dir	●	65	B1
Dirē Dawa	●	81	G2
Dirranbandi	●	87	J5
Disko = Qeqertarsuatsiaq	◩	93	V2
Distrito Federal	◼	109	H7
Dithmarschen	◿	31	D2
Dīvāndarreh	●	69	M6
Divinópolis	●	111	N3
Divriği	●	69	H4
Diyarbakır	●	69	J5
Dja	▨	79	G4
Djado	●	77	H4
Djambala	●	79	G5
Djanet	●	77	G4
Djelfa	●	77	F2
Djéma	●	81	D2
Djibo	●	79	D2
Djibouti	◭	75	H5
Djibouti	◼	75	H5
Djolu	●	81	C3
Djúpivogur	●	27	(1)F2
Dnieper	▨	49	F5
Dniester	▨	45	N1
Dniprodzerzhyns'k	●	49	F5
Dnipropetrovs'k	●	49	F5

Name	Page	Grid
Dnister = Dniester	45	N1
Dno	49	E3
Doba	81	B2
Dobbiaco	41	H4
Döbeln	31	J5
Doboj	45	F5
Dobrich	45	Q6
Dobryanka	49	L3
Dodecanese = Dodekanisos	47	J8
Dodge City	97	F3
Dodoma	81	F5
Doetinchem	33	H3
Dōgo	59	G5
Dogondoutchi	79	E2
Doha = Ad Dawḥah	71	D4
Doka	63	(2)D4
Dokkum	31	B3
Dolak	63	(2)E4
Dolbeau	99	F1
Dole	41	A3
Dolgany	55	E2
Dolinsk	55	Q7
Dollard	31	C3
Dolomiti	41	G4
Dolo Odo	81	G3
Dolores	111	K6
Dolphin and Union Strait	93	H3
Domažlice	31	H7
Dombås	27	E5
Dombóvár	45	F3
Dominica	107	E2
Dominican Republic	107	D1
Domodossola	41	D4
Domžale	41	K4
Don	25	H2
Donau = Danube	41	H2
Donauwörth	31	F8
Don Benito	39	E6
Doncaster	35	L8
Dondra Head	65	D7
Donegal	35	D7
Donegal Bay	35	D7
Donets	25	H3
Donets'k	49	G5
Dongfang	61	C6
Donggala	63	(2)A3
Donggou	59	C4
Dông Hôi	61	D3
Dongola	75	F4
Dongou	79	H4
Dongsha Qundao	61	F2
Dongsheng	57	E3
Dong Ujimqin Qi	57	F1
Donji Vakuf	41	N6
Donner Pass	97	B3
Donostia	39	J1
Dora	41	C5
Dordrecht	33	G3
Dori	79	D2
Dorsten	33	J3
Dortmund	31	C5
Dos Hermanas	39	E7
Dosso	79	E2
Dothan	101	D3
Douai	33	F4
Douala	79	F4
Douarnenez	37	A5
Doubs	41	B3
Douglas, South Africa	83	C5
Douglas, U.K.	35	H7
Douglas, Ariz., U.S.	103	E2
Douglas, Ga., U.S.	101	E3
Douglas, Wyo., U.S.	97	E2
Doullens	33	E4
Dourados	111	L3
Douro	39	B3
Dover, U.K.	33	D3
Dover, U.S.	101	F2
Dover, Australia	87	J8
Dowlatābād	71	D4
Drăgășani	45	M5
Draguignan	41	B7
Drakensberg	83	D6
Drake Passage	111	G10
Drama	47	G3
Drammen	27	F7
Drau	41	J4
Drava	45	K2
Dravograd	43	K2
Drawsko Pomorskie	29	E4
Dresden	31	J5
Dreux	33	D6
Drina	45	G5
Drobeta-Turnu Severin	45	K5
Drogheda	35	F8
Drohobych	29	N8
Drôme	37	K9
Dronne	37	F8
Drummondville	99	F1
Druzhina	55	Q3
Dschang	79	G3
Dubai = Dubayy	71	F4
Dubăsari	45	S2
Dubawnt Lake	93	L4
Dubayy	71	F4
Dubbo	87	J6
Dublin	35	F8
Dubois	97	D2
Du Bois	99	E2
Dubovskoye	49	H5
Dubrovnik	45	F7
Dubuque	99	B2
Ducie Island	85	P8
Dudelange	33	J5
Duderstadt	31	F5
Dugi Otok	45	B6
Duisburg	33	J3
Duk Faiwil	81	E2
Dukhān	71	D4
Dukou	57	C5
Dulan	57	B3
Dulce	103	E1
Dul'Durga	55	J6
Dülmen	31	C5
Dulovo	45	Q6
Duluth	99	B1
Dūmā	70	D3
Dumaguete	61	G5
Dumai	63	(1)C2
Dumas	97	F3
Ďumbier	29	J9
Dumfries	35	J6
Dümmer	31	D4
Dumont d'Urville Sea	112	(2)U3
Dumyât	75	F1
Duna = Danube	45	D1
Dunaj = Danube	29	G10
Dunărea = Danube	45	K5
Dunaújváros	45	F3
Dunav = Danube	45	J5
Dunbar	87	H3
Duncan	97	B1
Duncan Passage	61	A4
Dundalk	35	F7
Dundee, South Africa	83	E5
Dundee, U.K.	35	K5
Dunedin	89	C7
Dungarvan	35	E9
Dungeness	33	C4
Dunhua	59	E2
Dunhuang	57	A2
Dunkerque	33	E3
Dunkirk	99	E2
Dunkwa	79	D3
Dún Laoghaire	35	F8
Dunnet Head	35	J3
Dunseith	97	G1
Durance	37	L10
Durango, Mexico	103	F4
Durango, Spain	39	H1
Durant	101	B3
Durban	83	E5
Düren	33	J4
Durgapur	65	E4
Durham, U.K.	35	L7
Durham, U.S.	101	F2
Durmitor	45	G6
Durrës	47	B3
Dursunbey	47	L5
D'Urville Island	89	D5
Dushanbe	67	J2
Düsseldorf	33	J3
Duyun	57	D5
Düzce	47	P4
Dvina	25	H2
Dvinskaya Guba	49	G1
Dwarka	65	A4
Dyersburg	101	D2
Dyje	41	M2
Dzerzhinsk	49	H3
Dzhambeyty	49	K4
Dzhankoy	49	F5
Dzhardzhan	55	L3
Dzhetygara	49	M4
Dzhezkazgan	49	N5
Dzhizak	53	M9
Dzhusaly	49	M5
Działdowo	29	K4

E

Name	Page	Grid
Eagle Pass	103	F3
East Antarctica	112	(2)P2
Eastbourne	33	C4
East Cape	89	G3
East China Sea	57	H4
Easter Island	85	Q8
Eastern Cape	83	D6
Eastern Ghats	65	C6
East Falkland	111	K9
Eastleigh	33	A4
East London	83	D6
Eastmain	93	R6
Eastmain	93	S6
East Point	101	E3
East Retford	33	B1
East St. Louis	99	B3
East Siberian Sea = Vostochno-Sibirskoye More	55	U2
East Timor = Timor Timur	63	(2)C4
Eau Claire	99	B2
Ebersberg	41	G2
Eberswalde	31	J4
Eboli	43	K8
Ebolowa	79	G4
Ebro	39	K3
Ech Chélif	77	F1
Echo Bay	93	H3
Écija	39	E7
Eckernförde	31	E2
Ecuador	109	B4
Ed	75	H5
Ed Damazin	75	F5
Ed Debba	75	F4
Ed Dueim	75	F5
Ede, Netherlands	33	H2
Ede, Nigeria	79	E3
Edéa	79	G4

Name	Pg	Ref
Eden, *Australia*	87	J7
Eden, *U.S.*	103	G2
Edendale	89	B8
Eder	31	D5
Edessa	47	E4
Edinburgh	35	J6
Edirne	47	J3
Edmonds	97	B1
Edmonton	93	J6
Edmundson	95	N2
Edmundston	99	G1
Edolo	41	F4
Edremit	47	J5
Edremit Körfezi	47	H5
Edwards Plateau	103	F2
Éfaté	85	G7
Eferding	29	D9
Effingham	101	D2
Eger	45	H2
Eggenfelden	41	H2
Egilsstaðir	27	(1)F2
Eğridir	47	N7
Eğridir Gölü	47	N6
Egvekinot	55	Y3
Egypt	75	E2
Ehingen	41	E2
Eibar	39	H1
Eichstätt	41	G2
Eider	31	D2
Eidsvoll	27	F6
Eifel	33	J4
Eigg	35	F5
Eight Degree Channel	65	B7
Einbeck	31	E5
Eindhoven	33	H3
Eirunepé	109	D5
Eiseb	83	C4
Elbe	31	G4
Eisenach	31	F6
Eisenerz	41	K3
Eisenhüttenstadt	29	D5
Eisenstadt	41	M3
Eisleben	31	G5
Eivissa	39	M5
Eivissa	39	M6
Ejea de los Caballeros	39	J2
Ejin Qi	57	C2
Ejmiadzin	69	L3
Ekenäs	27	M7
Ekibastuz	53	P7
Ekimchan	55	N6
El Aaiún	77	C3
El 'Alamein	75	E1
El Amria	39	J9
El 'Arîsh	70	A5
Elat	70	B7
Elazığ	69	H4
El Azraq	70	D5
Elba	43	E6
Elbasan	47	C3
Elbeuf	33	D5
Elbistan	69	G4
Elbląg	29	J3
Elbrus	69	K2
El Cajon	103	C2
El Centro	103	C2
El Cerro	109	E7
Elch	39	K6
Elda	39	K6
Eldorado	111	L4
El Dorado, *Ark., U.S.*	101	C3
El Dorado, *Kans., U.S.*	101	B2
El Dorado, *Venezuela*	109	E2
Eldoret	81	F3
Elefsína	47	F6
Eleuthera	95	L6
El Fahs	43	D12
El Faiyûm	75	F2
El Fasher	75	E5
El Geneina	75	D5
Elgin, *U.K.*	35	J4
Elgin, *Ill., U.S.*	99	C2
Elgin, *N.D., U.S.*	97	F1
El Gîza	75	F1
El Goléa	77	F2
El Iskandarîya	75	E1
Elista	49	H5
Elizabeth City	101	F2
El Jadida	77	D2
El Jafr	70	D6
El Jafr	70	D6
Ełk	29	M4
Ełk	29	M4
El Kala	43	C12
Elk City	103	G1
El Kef	43	C12
El Kelaâ des Srarhna	77	D2
El Khârga	75	F2
Elkhart, *Ind., U.S.*	99	C2
Elkhart, *Kans., U.S.*	101	A2
El Khartum	75	F4
El Khartum Bahri	75	F4
Elkhovo	47	J2
Elko, *Canada*	97	C1
Elko, *U.S.*	97	C2
El Kuntilla	70	B7
Ellendale	95	G2
Ellensburg	97	B1
Ellesmere Island	91	K1
Ellice Islands	85	H6
Elliot	83	D6
Ellisras	83	D4
Elliston	87	F6
Ellsworth	99	G2
Ellwangen	41	F2
Elmadağ	47	R5
Elmali	47	M8
El Mansûra	75	F1
El Minya	75	F2
Elmira	99	E2
El Muglad	75	E5
El Obeid	75	F5
El Oued	77	G2
El Paso	103	E2
El Prat de Llobregat	39	N3
El Qâhira	75	F1
El Reno	101	B2
El Salvador	105	F6
Elster	31	H5
Elsterwerda	31	J5
El Sueco	103	E3
El Suweis	75	F2
El Tarf	43	C12
El Thamad	70	B7
El Tigre	109	E2
El Turbio	111	G9
Eluru	65	D5
Elvas	39	C6
Ely, *U.K.*	35	N9
Ely, *U.S.*	97	D3
Emba	49	L5
Embalse de Alcántara Uno	39	D5
Embalse de Almendra	39	D3
Embalse de Contreras	39	J5
Embalse de Gabriel y Galán	39	D4
Embalse de Garcia Sola	39	E5
Embalse de la Serena	39	E6
Embalse del Ebro	39	G1
Embalse del Río Negro	107	F7
Embalse de Negratín	39	G7
Embalse de Ricobayo	39	E3
Embalse de Santa Teresa	39	E4
Emden	31	C3
Emerald	87	J4
Emi Koussi	75	C4
Emin	53	Q8
Emirdağ	47	P5
Emmen	33	J2
Emmerich	33	J3
Emory Peak	103	F3
Empangeni	83	E5
Empoli	41	F7
Emporia	101	B2
Empty Quarter = Rub' al Khālī	67	E6
Ems	33	J1
Ems-Jade-Kanal	31	C3
Enafors	27	B2
Encarnación	111	K4
Ende	63	(2)B4
Enderby Island	89	(2)B1
Enewetak	85	F4
Enez	47	J4
Engel's	49	J4
Enggano	63	(1)C4
England	35	L9
English Channel	35	J12
Enid	101	B2
Enna	43	J11
En Nahud	75	E5
Ennis	97	D1
Enniskillen	35	E7
Enns	41	K3
Enschede	33	J2
Ensenada	103	C2
Enshi	57	D4
Entebbe	81	E3
Entrevaux	41	B7
Entroncamento	39	B5
Enugu	79	F3
Enurmino	55	Z3
Epanomi	47	E4
Épernay	37	J4
Épinal	41	B2
Epsom	33	B3
Equatorial Guinea	79	F4
Erbach	31	D7
Erciş	69	K4
Érd	45	F2
Erdek	47	K4
Erding	41	G2
Erechim	111	L4
Ereğli, *Turkey*	69	D3
Ereğli, *Turkey*	69	F5
Erenhot	57	E2
Erfurt	31	G6
Ergani	69	H4
Erg Chech	77	D4
Erg du Ténéré	77	H5
Erg Iguidi	77	D3
Erie	99	D2
Erimo-misaki	59	M3
Eritrea	75	G4
Erlangen	31	G7
Ermenek	69	E5
Ermoupoli	47	G7
Er Rachidia	77	E2
Er Rseifa	70	D4
Erskine	99	A1
Ertai	53	S8
Ertix	53	R8
Erzgebirge	31	H6
Erzin	53	S7
Erzincan	69	H4
Erzurum	69	J4
Esashi, *Japan*	59	L3
Esashi, *Japan*	59	M1
Esbjerg	27	E9
Escanaba	99	C1

Esch 33 J5
Escondido 103 C2
Eşfahān 67 F3
Eskilstuna 27 J7
Eskişehir 69 D4
Esla 39 E3
Eslamshahr 67 F2
Esler Dağ 47 M7
Esmeraldas 109 B3
Espalion 37 H9
Espanola, Canada 99 D1
Espanola, U.S. 97 E3
Espelkamp 31 D4
Esperance 87 D6
Espinho 39 B4
Espírito Santo 109 J7
Espíritu Santo 85 G7
Espoo 27 N6
Espungebera 83 E4
Essaouira 77 D2
Es Semara 77 C3
Essen 33 K3
Essequibo 109 F2
Esslingen 41 E2
Estepona 39 E8
Esteros 111 J3
Estonia 27 M7
Estoril 39 A6
Estrecho de Magallanes . . 111 G9
Estrela 39 C4
Estremoz 39 C6
Estuário do Rio
    Amazonaz 109 H3
Esztergom 45 F2
Étain 33 H5
Étampes 37 H5
Étang de Berre 37 L10
Étaples 33 D4
Etawah 65 C3
Ethiopia 73 G5
Etosha Pan 83 B3
Ettelbruck 31 B7
Eucla 87 E6
Euclid 99 D2
Eufala 101 D3
Eugene 97 B2
Euphrates = Firat 69 H4
Euphrates 67 D3
Eure 33 D6
Eureka, Calif., U.S. 97 B2
Eureka, Mont., U.S. 97 C1
Eureka, Ut., U.S. 97 D3
Europe 25 F3
Europoort 33 C3
Euskirchen 31 B6
Evanston, Ill., U.S. 99 C2
Evanston, Wyo., U.S. . . . 97 D2
Evansville 101 D2

Evaz 71 F3
Everett 97 B1
Everglades City 101 E4
Evergreen 101 D3
Évora 39 C6
Évreux 33 D5
Evvoia 47 F6
Ewo 79 G5
Exeter 35 J11
Exmouth 87 B4
Eyl 81 H2
Eyre Peninsula 87 G2
Ezine 47 J5

F

Faadippolu Atoll 65 B8
Fåborg 31 F1
Fabriano 41 H7
Fada Ngourma 79 E2
Faenza 41 G6
Faeroes 25 D1
Fǎgǎraş 45 M4
Fagernes 27 E6
Fairbanks . . . . 103 (1)H3
Fair Isle 35 L2
Fairmont 99 B2
Faisalabad 65 B2
Faith 97 F1
Faizabad 65 D3
Fakfak . . . . 63 (2)D3
Fakse Bugt 27 G9
Falaise 33 B6
Falaise de Tiguidit 77 G5
Falcon Lake 101 B4
Fǎleşti 45 Q2
Falfurrias 101 B4
Falkensee 31 J4
Falkland Islands 111 K9
Fallon 97 C3
Falls City 95 G3
Falster 31 H2
Falun 27 H6
Famagusta =
    Ammochostos 70 A1
Fangzheng 57 H1
Fano 41 J7
Fanø 31 D1
Fanø Bugt 31 D1
Faradje 81 D3
Farafangana 83 H4
Farāh 67 H3
Farah Rud 67 H3
Fargo 95 G2
Farmington 103 E1
Farnborough 33 B3
Fårö 27 K8

Faro, Brazil 109 F4
Faro, Portugal 39 C7
Farrāshband 71 E2
Farson 97 E2
Fasā 71 E2
Fǎurei 45 Q4
Favara 43 H11
Faversham 33 C3
Favignana 43 G11
Faxaflói . . . . 27 (1)B2
Faya 75 C4
Fayette 101 D3
Fayetteville, Ark., U.S. . . 101 C2
Fayetteville, N.C., U.S. . . 99 E3
Fayetteville, Tenn., U.S. . 101 D2
Fdérik 77 C4
Featherston 89 E5
Fécamp 33 C5
Federated States of
    Micronesia 85 E5
Fedorovka 49 M4
Fehmarn 31 G2
Feijó 109 C5
Feilding 89 E5
Feira de Santana 109 K6
Feistritz 41 L3
Feldbach 41 L4
Feldkirch 41 E3
Feldkirchen 41 K4
Felixstowe 33 D3
Feltre 41 G4
Femund 27 F5
Fengning 57 F2
Feng Xian 57 D4
Fenyang 57 E3
Feodosiya 69 F1
Fergana 67 K1
Fergus Falls 95 G2
Ferkessédougou 79 C3
Fermo 43 H5
Fernándópolis 111 L3
Ferrara 41 G6
Ferreira do Alentejo . . . 39 B7
Ferrol 39 B1
Fès 77 E2
Festus 99 B3
Feteşti 45 Q5
Fethiye 47 M8
Fetisovo 67 F1
Feyzābād 67 K2
Fianarantsoa 83 H4
Fianga 81 B2
Fichë 81 F2
Fidenza 41 F6
Fier 47 B4
Figueira da Foz 39 B4
Figueres 39 N2
Fiji 85 H8

Filadélfia 111 J3
Filiaşi 45 L5
Filicudi 43 J10
Finale Ligure 41 D6
Findlay 99 D2
Fingoè 83 E3
Finike 47 N8
Finland 27 P3
Finnsnes 27 K2
Finsterwalde 31 J5
Firat 69 H4
Firenze 41 G7
Firozabad 65 C3
Firozpur 65 B2
Firth of Clyde 35 G6
Firth of Forth 35 K5
Firth of Lorn 35 G5
Firth of Thames 89 E3
Fish 83 B5
Fisher Strait 93 Q4
Fishguard 35 H9
Fiskenæsset =
    Qeqertarsuatsiaat . . . 93 W4
Fitzroy Crossing 87 E3
Fivizzano 41 F6
Fizi 81 D4
Flaming Gorge
    Reservoir 97 E2
Flamingo 101 E4
Flannan Islands 35 E3
Flåsjön 27 H4
Flathead Lake 97 D1
Flensburg 31 E2
Flensburg Fjorde 31 E2
Flers 33 B6
Flinders Island 87 J7
Flinders Ranges 87 G6
Flinders Reefs 87 J3
Flin Flon 93 L6
Flint 99 D2
Flint Island 85 L7
Florac 37 J9
Florence = Firenze, Italy . 41 G7
Florence, Al., U.S. 101 D3
Florence, S.C., U.S. 101 F3
Florencia 109 B3
Florennes 33 G4
Flores, Azores . . . . 77 (1)A2
Flores, Indonesia . . . . . 63 (2)B4
Flores Sea . . . . 63 (2)A4
Floreşti 45 R2
Floriano 109 J5
Florida 101 E4
Florida 111 K5
Florida Keys 91 K7
Florina 47 D4
Florø 27 C6
Fly . . . . 63 (2)F4

Foča ... ● 45 F6
Focșani ... ● 45 Q4
Foggia ... ● 43 K7
Fogo ... 79 (1)B1
Fohnsdorf ... ● 41 K3
Föhr ... 31 D2
Foleyet ... ● 99 D1
Foligno ... ● 43 G6
Folkestone ... ● 33 D3
Follonica ... ● 43 E6
Fond du Lac ... ● 99 C2
Fondi ... ● 43 H7
Fongafale ... ■ 85 H6
Fontainebleau ... ● 37 H5
Fonte Boa ... ● 109 D4
Fontenay-le-Comte ... ● 37 E7
Fontur ... 27 (1)F1
Forbach ... ● 33 J5
Forchheim ... ● 31 G7
Forestville ... ● 99 G1
Forges-les-Eaux ... ● 33 D5
Forks ... ● 97 B1
Forlì ... ● 41 H6
Formentera ... 39 M6
Formosa, *Brazil* ... ● 109 H7
Formosa, *Paraguay* ... ● 111 K4
Forssa ... ● 27 M6
Fortaleza ... ◻ 109 K4
Fort Bayne ... ● 99 C4
Fort Beaufort ... ● 83 D6
Fort Benton ... ● 97 D1
Fort Chipewyan ... ● 93 J5
Fort Collins ... ● 97 E2
Fort Dodge ... ● 99 B2
Forte dei Marmi ... ● 41 F7
Fort Frances ... ● 99 B1
Fort George ... ● 93 R6
Fort Good Hope ... ● 93 F3
Forth ... 35 H5
Fort Kent ... ● 99 G1
Fort Lauderdale ... ● 101 E4
Fort Liard ... ● 93 G4
Fort Macleod ... ● 97 D1
Fort McMurray ... ● 93 J5
Fort McPherson ... ● 103 (1)L2
Fort Myers ... ● 101 E4
Fort Nelson ... ● 93 G5
Fort Norman ... ● 103 (1)M3
Fort Payne ... ● 101 D3
Fort Peck Reservoir ... 97 E1
Fort Pierce ... ● 101 E4
Fort Portal ... ● 81 E3
Fort Providence ... ● 93 H4
Fortrose ... ● 89 B8
Fort Rupert ... ● 93 R6
Fort St. John ... ● 93 G5
Fort Scott ... ● 101 C2
Fort Severn ... ● 93 P5

Fort Shevchenko ... ● 53 J9
Fort Simpson ... ● 93 G4
Fort Smith, *Canada* ... ● 93 J4
Fort Smith, *U.S.* ... ● 101 C2
Fort Stockton ... ● 103 F2
Fortuna ... ● 97 F1
Fort Vermilion ... ● 93 H5
Fort Wayne ... ● 101 D1
Fort William ... ● 35 G5
Fort Worth ... ● 101 B3
Fossano ... ● 41 C6
Fougamou ... ● 79 G5
Fougères ... ● 37 D5
Foula ... 35 K1
Foulness ... 33 C3
Foumban ... ● 79 G3
Fourmies ... ● 33 G4
Fournoi ... 47 J7
Fouta Djallon ... 79 B2
Foveaux Strait ... 89 A8
Foxe Basin ... 93 R3
Foxe Channel ... 93 R4
Foxe Peninsula ... 93 R4
Fox Islands ... 103 (1)D5
Foz do Cunene ... ● 83 A3
Foz do Iguaçu ... ● 111 L4
Fraga ... ● 39 L3
Francavilla Fontana ... ● 43 M8
France ... Ⓐ 37 G7
Franceville ... ● 79 G5
Francistown ... ● 83 D4
Francs Peak ... ▲ 97 E2
Frankenthal ... ● 31 D7
Frankfort ... ◻ 101 E2
Frankfurt, *Germany* ... ● 31 K4
Frankfurt, *Germany* ... ● 31 D6
Franklin D. Roosevelt
  Lake ... 97 C1
Franz Josef Glacier ... ● 89 C6
Franz Josef Land =
  Zemlya Frantsa-
  Iosifa ... 53 J2
Fraser ... 93 G6
Fraserburgh ... ● 35 L4
Fraser Island ... 87 K5
Frederick, *Md., U.S.* ... ● 99 E3
Frederick, *Okla., U.S.* ... ● 101 B3
Fredericksburg,
  Tex., U.S. ... ● 101 B3
Fredericksburg,
  Va., U.S. ... ● 99 E3
Fredericton ... ◻ 93 T7
Frederikshåb =
  Paamiut ... ● 93 X4
Frederikshavn ... ● 27 F8
Fredrikstad ... ● 27 F7
Freeport, *Ill., U.S.* ... ● 99 C2
Freeport, *Tex., U.S.* ... ● 101 B4

Freeport City ... ● 101 F4
Freer ... ● 101 B4
Free State ... ⓐ 83 D5
Freetown ... ■ 79 B3
Freiberg ... ● 31 J6
Freiburg ... ● 41 C3
Freilassing ... ● 41 H3
Freising ... ● 41 G2
Fréjus ... ● 37 M10
Fremantle ... ● 87 C6
Fremont ... ● 103 B1
Frenchglen ... ● 97 C2
French Guiana ... ⓐ 109 G3
French Polynesia ... 85 L7
Fresnillo ... ● 105 D4
Fresno ... ● 103 C1
Fribourg ... ● 41 C4
Friedrichshafen ... ● 41 E3
Friesach ... ● 41 K4
Frisian Islands ... 33 H1
Fritzlar ... ● 31 E5
Frobisher Bay ... 93 T4
Frolovo ... ● 49 H5
Frosinone ... ● 43 H7
Frýdek Místek ... ● 29 H8
Fudai ... ● 59 L4
Fuentesauco ... ● 39 E3
Fuerteventura ... 77 C3
Fuhai ... ● 53 R8
Fuji-san ... ▲ 59 K6
Fukuchiyama ... ● 59 H6
Fukue ... ● 59 E7
Fukue-jima ... 59 E7
Fukui ... ● 59 J5
Fukuoka ... ● 59 F7
Fukushima ... ● 59 L5
Fukuyama ... ● 59 G6
Fulda ... ● 31 E6
Fulda ... 31 E6
Fuling ... ● 57 D5
Fulton ... ● 101 D2
Funabashi ... ● 59 L6
Funafuti ... 85 H6
Funchal ... ● 77 B2
Funtua ... ● 79 F2
Fürg ... ● 71 F2
Furmanovo ... ● 49 J5
Furneaux Group ... 87 J8
Fürstenfeldbruck ... ● 41 G2
Fürstenwalde ... ● 31 K4
Fürth ... ● 31 F7
Furukawa ... ● 59 L4
Fushun ... ● 59 B3
Fusong ... ● 59 D2
Füssen ... ● 41 F3
Fuxhou ... ● 57 F5
Fuyang ... ● 57 F4
Fuyu ... ● 57 G1

Fuzhou ... ● 61 F1
Fyn ... 31 F1

G

Gaalkacyo ... ● 81 H2
Gabès ... ● 77 H2
Gabon ... Ⓐ 79 G5
Gaborone ... ■ 83 D4
Gabrovo ... ● 45 N7
Gacko ... ● 45 F6
Gäddede ... ● 27 H4
Gadsden ... ● 101 D3
Găești ... ● 45 N5
Gaeta ... ● 43 H7
Gafsa ... ● 77 G2
Gaggenau ... ● 41 D2
Gagnoa ... ● 79 C3
Gagra ... ● 69 J2
Gainesville, *Fla., U.S.* ... ● 101 E4
Gainesville, *Ga., U.S.* ... ● 101 E3
Gainesville, *Tex., U.S.* ... ● 101 B3
Gai Xian ... ● 59 B3
Galana ... 81 F4
Galanta ... ● 41 N2
Galapagos Islands =
  Islas Galápagos ... 109 (1)B1
Galashiels ... ● 35 K6
Galați ... ● 45 R4
Galdhøpiggen ... ▲ 27 D6
Galena ... ● 103 (1)F3
Galesburg ... ● 99 B2
Galich ... ● 49 H3
Gallabat ... ● 75 G5
Galle ... ● 65 D7
Gällivare ... ● 27 L3
Gallup ... ● 103 E1
Galtat Zemmour ... ● 77 C3
Galveston Bay ... 95 G6
Galway ... ● 35 C8
Galway Bay ... 35 C8
Gambēla ... ● 81 E2
Gambier Islands ... 85 N8
Gamboma ... ● 81 B4
Gamboula ... ● 81 B3
Ganado ... ● 103 E1
Gäncä ... ● 69 M3
Gander ... ● 93 W7
Gāndhīdhām ... ● 65 B4
Gandhinagar ... ● 65 B4
Gandia ... ● 39 K6
Ganganagar ... ● 65 B3
Gangdise Shan ... 65 D2
Ganges ... 65 E3
Gangi ... ● 43 J11
Gangtok ... ● 65 E3
Gannett Peak ... ▲ 97 E2

Name	Page	Grid
Ganzhou	57	E5
Gao	77	E5
Gaoual	77	C6
Gap	41	B6
Garanhuns	109	K5
Garbsen	31	E4
Gardelegen	31	G4
Garden City	97	F3
Gardēz	67	J3
Garissa	81	F4
Garmisch-Partenkirchen	41	G3
Garonne	37	E9
Garoowe	81	H2
Garoua	79	G3
Garoua Boulaï	79	G3
Garry Lake	93	L3
Garut	63	(1)D4
Garyarsa	65	D2
Garzē	57	B4
Gasan Kuli	67	J2
Gashua	79	G2
Gastonia	101	E2
Gatchina	49	F3
Gauja	27	N8
Gauteng	83	D5
Gavdos	47	G10
Gävle	27	J6
Gawler	87	G6
Gaya	65	E4
Gaylord	99	D1
Gayndah	87	K5
Gayny	49	K2
Gaza	70	B5
Gazandzhyk	53	K10
Gaza Strip	70	B5
Gaziantep	69	G5
Gbarnga	79	C3
Gdańsk	29	H3
Gdov	27	P7
Gdyel	39	K9
Gdynia	29	H3
Gebel el Tîh	70	A7
Gebel Katherina	75	F2
Gebel Yi'allaq	70	A6
Gebze	47	M4
Gedaref	75	G5
Gediz	47	K6
Gedser	31	G2
Geel	33	H3
Geelong	87	H7
Geesthacht	31	F3
Geilenkirchen	33	J4
Geilo	27	E6
Geislingen	41	E2
Geita	81	E4
Gejiu	61	C2
Gela	43	J11
Geladī	81	H2
Geleen	33	H4
Gelendzhik	69	H1
Gelibolu	47	J4
Gelibolu Yarimadasi	47	J4
Gembloux	33	G4
Gembu	79	G3
Gemena	81	B3
Gemlik	47	M4
Gemona del Friuli	41	J4
Genalē Wenz	81	G2
General Alvear	111	H6
General Roca	111	H6
General Santos	61	H5
Geneva	99	E2
Genève	41	B4
Genk	33	H4
Genoa = Genova	41	D6
Genova	41	D6
Gent	33	F3
Genthin	31	H4
George Town, Australia	87	J8
George Town, Malaysia	63	(1)C1
George Town, U.S.	101	F5
Georgetown, Gambia	79	B2
Georgetown, Guyana	109	F2
Georgetown, U.S.	101	B3
George West	101	B5
Georgia	69	K2
Georgia	101	E3
Georgian Bay	99	D1
Gera	31	H6
Geraldine	89	C7
Geraldton, Australia	87	B5
Geraldton, Canada	95	J2
Gérardmer	41	B2
Gerede	69	E3
Gereshk	67	H3
Gerik	61	C5
Gerlach	97	C2
Germantown	99	C3
Germany	31	E6
Gerolzhofen	31	F7
Gērzē	65	D2
Geser	63	(2)D3
Getafe	39	G4
Gettysburg	97	F2
Gevaş	69	K4
Gewanē	75	H5
Geyik Dağ	47	Q8
Geyser	97	D1
Ghadāmis	77	G2
Ghadīr Minqār	70	E3
Ghana	79	D3
Ghanzi	83	C4
Gharandal	70	C6
Ghardaïa	77	F2
Gharyān	77	H2
Ghāt	75	B2
Ghaziabad	65	C3
Ghazn	67	J3
Gheorgheni	45	N3
Ghotāru	65	B3
Giannitsa	47	E4
Gibraltar	39	E8
Gibson Desert	87	D4
Gien	37	H6
Gießen	31	D6
Gifhorn	31	F4
Gifu	59	J6
Giglio	43	E6
Gijón	39	E1
Gila	103	E2
Gila Bend	103	D2
Gilan Garb	69	L6
Gilbert Islands	85	H5
Gilbués	109	H5
Gilf Kebir Plateau	75	E3
Gilgandra	87	J6
Gilgit	67	K2
Gilgit	65	B1
Gillam	93	N5
Gillette	97	E2
Gillingham	33	C3
Gills Rock	99	C1
Gīmbī	81	F2
Gīnīr	81	G2
Gioia del Colle	43	L8
Gioura	47	F5
Giresun	69	H3
Girona	39	N3
Gironde	37	E8
Gisborne	89	G4
Gitega	81	D4
Giurgiu	45	N6
Givet	33	G4
Giyon	81	F2
Gizhiga	55	U4
Gjirokaster	47	C4
Gjøvik	27	F6
Glacier Peak	97	B1
Gladstone	87	K4
Glan	63	(2)C1
Glarner Alpen	41	D4
Glasgow, U.K.	35	H6
Glasgow, Ky., U.S.	99	C3
Glasgow, Mont., U.S.	97	E1
Glazov	53	J6
Gleisdorf	41	L3
Glendale, Ariz., U.S.	103	D2
Glendale, Calif., U.S.	103	C2
Glendive	97	F1
Glennallen	103	(1)H3
Glenn Innes	87	K5
Glens Falls	99	F2
Glenwood, Ark., U.S.	99	B4
Glenwood, N. Mex., U.S.	103	E2
Glenwood Springs	97	E3
Gliwice	29	H7
Głogów	29	F6
Glomma	27	F5
Glorieuses	73	H7
Gloucester	35	K10
Głuchołazy	29	G7
Gmünd, Austria	41	J4
Gmünd, Austria	41	L2
Gmunden	41	J3
Gniezno	29	G5
Gnjilane	47	D2
Goalpara	65	F3
Goba	81	F2
Gobabis	83	B4
Gobi Desert	57	C2
Goch	33	J3
Godbout	99	G1
Goderich	99	D2
Gödöllő	45	G2
Godthåb = Nuuk	93	W4
Goes	33	F3
Gogama	99	D1
Goiânia	109	H7
Goiás	109	G6
Goiás	109	G7
Gökçeada	47	H4
Gökova Körfezi	47	K8
Göksun	69	G5
Golan Heights	70	C3
Golbāf	71	G2
Gölbasi	69	G5
Gol'chikha	53	Q3
Gołdap	29	M3
Gold Coast	87	K5
Golden Bay	89	D5
Goldendale	97	B1
Goldsboro	99	E3
Goleniów	29	D4
Golestānak	71	F1
Golfe d'Ajaccio	43	C7
Golfe de Gabès	77	H2
Golfe de Sagone	43	C6
Golfe de Saint-Malo	37	C5
Golfe de Tunis	43	E11
Golfe de Valinco	43	C7
Golfe du Lion	37	J10
Golfo de Almería	39	H8
Golfo de Cádiz	39	C7
Golfo de California	105	B3
Golfo de Corcovado	111	F7
Golfo de Guayaquil	109	A4
Golfo de Honduras	105	G5
Golfo del Darién	109	B2
Golfo dell' Asinara	43	C7

Name	Pg	Ref
Golfo de los Mosquitos	109	A2
Golfo de Mazarrón	39	J7
Golfo de Panamá	105	J7
Golfo de San Jorge	111	H8
Golfo de Santa Clara	103	D2
Golfo de Tehuantepec	105	E5
Golfo de València	39	L5
Golfo de Venezia	41	H5
Golfo de Venezuela	109	C1
Golfo di Catania	43	K11
Golfo di Gaeta	43	H7
Golfo di Gela	43	J11
Golfo di Genova	43	C4
Golfo di Manfredonia	43	L7
Golfo di Oristano	43	C9
Golfo di Orosei	43	D8
Golfo di Policastro	43	K9
Golfo di Salerno	43	J8
Golfo di Sant'Eufemia	43	K10
Golfo di Squillace	43	L10
Golfo di Taranto	43	L8
Golfo di Trieste	41	J5
Golfo San Matías	111	J6
Goma	81	D4
Gombe	79	G2
Gombi	79	G2
Gómez Palacio	103	F3
Gonder	75	G5
Gondia	65	D4
Gönen	47	K4
Gongga Shan	57	C5
Gonghe	57	C3
Gongliu	53	Q9
Gongpoquan	57	B2
Gongshan	61	B1
Goodland	97	F3
Goolgowi	87	J6
Goomalling	87	C6
Goondiwindi	87	K5
Goose Lake	97	B2
Göppingen	41	E2
Gora Bazardyuzi	69	M3
Gora Kamen	53	S4
Gorakhpur	65	D3
Gora Ledyanaya	55	W4
Gora Pobeda	55	R4
Gora Yenashimskiy Polkan	53	S6
Goražde	45	F6
Gore	89	B8
Gorgān	67	F2
Gorgona	41	E7
Gori	69	L2
Gorinchem	33	H3
Goris	69	M4
Gorizia	41	J5
Gorki	49	N1
Gorlice	29	L8
Görlitz	29	D6
Gorna Oryakhovitsa	45	N6
Gorno-Altaysk	53	R7
Gorodets	49	H3
Gorontalo	63	(2)B2
Gory Belukha	53	R8
Gory Ulutau	49	N5
Gorzów Wielkopolski	29	E5
Goslar	31	F5
Gospić	43	K4
Gostivar	47	C3
Göteborg	27	F8
Gotha	31	F6
Gotland	27	K8
Gotō-rettō	59	E7
Gotska Sandön	27	K7
Göttingen	31	E5
Gough Island	73	B10
Goundam	77	E5
Gourdon	37	G9
Gournay-en-Bray	33	D5
Governador Valadares	109	J7
Governor's Harbour	101	F4
Goya	111	K4
Gozo = Gwardex	43	J12
Graaff-Reinet	83	C6
Gračac	41	L6
Gračanica	45	F5
Grafton, Australia	87	K5
Grafton, U.S.	97	G1
Grajaú	109	H5
Grajewo	29	M4
Gram	31	E1
Grampian Mountains	35	H5
Granada, Nicaragua	105	G6
Granada, Spain	39	G7
Gran Canaria	77	B3
Grand Bahama	101	F4
Grand Ballon	37	N6
Grand Bank	93	V7
Grand Canyon	97	D3
Grande	109	J6
Grande Prairie	93	H5
Grand Erg de Bilma	77	H5
Grand Erg Occidental	77	E3
Grand Erg Oriental	77	F3
Grand Falls, N.B., Canada	99	G1
Grand Falls, Nfld., Canada	93	V7
Grand Forks, Canada	95	C2
Grand Forks, U.S.	97	G1
Grand Island	97	G2
Grand Junction	97	E3
Grand Marais, Mich., U.S.	99	C1
Grand Marais, Minn., U.S.	99	B1
Grand-Mère	99	F1
Grândola	39	B6
Grand Portage	99	C1
Grand Rapids, Canada	93	M6
Grand Rapids, Mich., U.S.	99	C2
Grand Rapids, Minn., U.S.	99	B1
Grand Teton	97	D2
Gran Paradiso	41	C5
Grants	103	E1
Grants Pass	97	B2
Granville	37	D5
Gräsö	27	K6
Grasse	41	B7
Gravelines	33	E3
Gravesend	33	C3
Gravina in Puglia	43	L8
Grayling	99	D2
Grays	33	C3
Grayville	99	C3
Graz	41	L3
Great Abaco	101	F4
Great Artesian Basin	87	H4
Great Australian Bight	87	E6
Great Bahama Bank	105	J4
Great Barrier Island	89	E3
Great Barrier Reef	87	J2
Great Basin	97	C3
Great Bend	103	G1
Great Dividing Range	87	J4
Greater Antilles	105	J5
Great Exhibition Bay	89	D2
Great Exuma	95	L7
Great Falls	97	D1
Great Inagua	105	K4
Great Karoo	83	C6
Great Nicobar	65	F7
Great Ouse	35	N9
Great Plains	97	F2
Great Rift Valley	81	E5
Great Salt Lake	97	D2
Great Salt Lake Desert	97	D2
Great Sand Sea	75	D2
Great Sandy Desert	87	D4
Great Slave Lake	91	N3
Great Wall	57	C3
Great Yarmouth	35	P9
Greece	47	D5
Greeley	97	F2
Green	97	D3
Green Bay	99	C2
Greenland	91	G2
Greenland Sea	91	B2
Greenock	35	H6
Green River, Wyo., U.S.	97	E2
Green River, Ut., U.S.	97	D3
Greensboro	101	F2
Greensburg, Ind., U.S.	101	D2
Greensburg, Pa., U.S.	99	E2
Greenvale	87	J3
Greenville, Liberia	79	C3
Greenville, Fla., U.S.	101	E3
Greenville, Miss., U.S.	101	C3
Greenville, N.C., U.S.	99	E3
Greenville, S.C., U.S.	101	E3
Greenwood, Miss., U.S.	101	C3
Greenwood, S.C., U.S.	101	E3
Gregory	97	G2
Greifswald	31	J2
Greifswalder Bodden	31	J2
Greiz	31	H6
Grenada	109	E1
Grenoble	37	L8
Greve in Chianti	41	G7
Greven	33	K2
Grevena	47	D4
Greybull	97	E2
Greymouth	89	C6
Grey Range	87	H5
Grigoriopol	45	S2
Grimma	31	H5
Grimmen	31	J2
Grimsby	35	M8
Grimsey	27	(1)D1
Grímsvötn	27	(1)E2
Grindsted	27	E9
Grodzisk Wielkopolski	29	F5
Gronau	31	C4
Groningen	31	B3
Groote Eylandt	87	G2
Grootfontein	83	B3
Großer Arber	31	J7
Großer Beerberg	31	F6
Grosseto	43	F6
Groß-Gerau	31	D7
Großglockner	41	H3
Groswater Bay	93	V6
Groznyy	69	L2
Grudovo	47	K2
Grudziądz	29	H4
Gryazovets	49	H3
Gryfice	29	E4
Grytviken	111	P9
Gstaad	41	C4
Guadalajara, Mexico	105	D4
Guadalajara, Spain	39	G4
Guadalcanal	85	F7
Guadalquivir	39	E7
Guadalupe	105	E3
Guadalupe	105	A3
Guadeloupe	107	E2
Guadiana	39	C7
Guadix	39	G7

Name	Pg	Ref
Guajará Mirim	● 109	D6
Guam	⊠ 85	E4
Guanambi	● 109	J6
Guangshui	● 57	E4
Guangyuan	● 57	D4
Guangzhou	● 61	E2
Guantánamo	● 105	J4
Guanyun	● 57	F4
Guaporé	⊘ 109	E6
Guarda	● 39	C4
Guasave	● 95	E6
Guatemala	Ⓐ 105	F5
Guatemala	■ 105	F6
Guaviare	⊘ 109	D3
Guayaquil	● 109	B4
Guaymas	● 103	D3
Guba, *Democratic Republic of Congo*	● 81	D6
Guba, *Ethiopia*	● 75	G5
Guba Buorkhaya	⊠ 55	N2
Guban	⊘ 81	G2
Gubbio	● 41	H7
Gubin	● 29	D6
Gudbrandsdalen	⊘ 27	E6
Gudermes	● 69	M2
Gudvangen	● 27	D6
Guéret	● 37	B7
Guernsey	● 97	F2
Guernsey	⊠ 37	C4
Guerrero Negro	● 103	D3
Gugë	▲ 81	F2
Gūh Kūh	▲ 67	G4
Guiana	▲ 105	L7
Guiana Highlands	▲ 109	F3
Guider	● 79	G3
Guiglo	● 79	C3
Guildford	● 35	M10
Guilianova	● 43	H6
Guilin	● 61	E1
Guillaumes	● 41	B6
Guillestre	● 41	B6
Guimarães	● 39	B3
Guinea	Ⓐ 79	B2
Guinea-Bissau	Ⓐ 79	A2
Güines	● 105	H4
Guingamp	● 37	B5
Güiria	● 109	E1
Guiyang	● 57	D5
Gujrat	● 65	B2
Gulbarga	● 65	C5
Gulbene	● 27	P8
Gulf of Aden	⊠ 67	E7
Gulf of Alaska	⊠ 103	(1)H4
Gulf of Aqaba	⊠ 67	B4
Gulf of Boothia	⊠ 93	N2
Gulf of Bothnia	⊠ 27	K6
Gulf of Carpentaria	⊠ 87	G2
Gulf of Finland	⊠ 27	M7
Gulf of Gdansk	⊠ 29	H3
Gulf of Guinea	⊠ 79	D4
Gulf of Mannar	⊠ 65	C7
Gulf of Martaban	⊠ 61	B3
Gulf of Mexico	⊠ 105	F3
Gulf of Oman	⊠ 71	G4
Gulf of Riga	⊠ 27	M8
Gulf of St. Lawrence	⊠ 93	U7
Gulf of Thailand	⊠ 61	C4
Gulf of Tongking	⊠ 61	D3
Gulfport	● 101	D3
Gulu	● 81	E3
Gülübovo	● 47	H2
Gümüşhane	● 69	H3
Guna	● 65	C4
Guna Terara	▲ 75	G5
Gungu	● 81	B5
Gunnbjørns Fjeld	▲ 112	(1)U2
Gunnedah	● 87	K6
Gunnison	● 97	E3
Gunong Kinabalu	▲ 63	(1)F1
Guntur	● 65	D5
Gunung Kerinci	▲ 63	(1)C3
Gunung Korbu	▲ 63	(1)C2
Gunung Kwoka	▲ 63	(2)D3
Gunung Leuser	▲ 63	(1)B2
Gunung Mekongga	▲ 63	(2)B3
Gunung Mulu	▲ 63	(1)E2
Gunungsitoli	● 63	(1)B2
Günzburg	● 41	F2
Gunzenhausen	● 31	F7
Gürün	● 69	G4
Gurupi	⊘ 109	H4
Gusau	● 79	F2
Gusev	● 29	M3
Gushgy	● 67	H2
Güssing	● 41	M3
Güstrow	● 29	B4
Gütersloh	● 31	D5
Guthrie, *Okla., U.S.*	● 97	G3
Guthrie, *Tex., U.S.*	● 103	F2
Guwahati	● 65	F3
Guyana	Ⓐ 109	F2
Guymon	● 103	F1
Guyuan	● 57	D3
Guzar	● 67	J2
Gvardeysk	● 29	L3
Gwadar	● 67	H4
Gwalior	● 65	C3
Gwanda	● 83	D4
Gwardex	⊠ 43	J12
Gweru	● 83	D3
Gyangzê	● 65	E3
Gyaring Hu	⊘ 57	B4
Gyda	● 53	P3
Gydanskiy Poluostrov	⊘ 53	P3
Gympie	● 87	K5
Gyomaendrőd	● 45	H3
Gyöngyös	● 45	G2
Győr	● 45	E2
Gypsumville	● 93	M6
Gyula	● 45	J3
Gyumri	● 69	K3

H

Name	Pg	Ref
Haapajärvi	● 27	N5
Haapsalu	● 27	M7
Haar	● 41	G2
Haarlem	● 33	G2
Haast	● 89	B6
Habbān	● 67	E7
Habirag	● 57	F2
Habomai-Shoto	⊠ 55	R8
Hachijō-jima	⊠ 59	K7
Hachinohe	● 59	L3
Hachiōji	● 59	K6
Hadadong	● 53	Q9
Hadejia	● 79	G2
Hadejia	⊘ 79	F2
Hadera	● 70	B4
Haderslev	● 31	E1
Ḩaḑhramaut	⊘ 67	E6
Haeju	● 59	C4
Haenam	● 59	D6
Ḩafar al Bāţin	● 71	A2
Hafnarfjördur	● 27	(1)C2
Haft Gel	● 71	C1
Hagen	● 33	K3
Hagerstown	● 99	E3
Haguenau	● 33	K6
Haicheng	● 59	B3
Haifa = Ḩefa	● 70	B4
Haikou	● 61	E3
Ḩā'il	● 67	D4
Hailar	● 55	K7
Hailong	● 59	C2
Hailuoto	⊠ 27	N4
Hainan	⊠ 61	D3
Hai Phong	● 61	D2
Haiti	Ⓐ 105	K5
Haiya	● 75	G4
Hajdúböszörmény	● 45	J2
Hajdúhadház	● 29	L10
Hajmah	● 67	G6
Hajnówka	● 29	N5
Haka	● 65	F4
Hakkâri	● 69	K5
Hakodate	● 59	L3
Halaib	● 75	G3
Halba	● 70	D2
Halberstadt	● 31	G5
Halifax	▣ 93	U8
Hall	● 41	G3
Hall Beach	● 93	Q3
Halle	● 33	G4
Hallein	● 41	J3
Halls Creek	● 87	E3
Halmahera	⊠ 63	(2)C2
Halmahera Sea	⊠ 63	(2)C3
Halmstad	● 29	B1
Haltern	● 33	K3
Hamada	● 59	G6
Hamadān	● 67	E3
Hamāh	● 69	G6
Hamamatsu	● 59	J6
Hamar	● 27	F6
Hamatonbetsu	● 59	M1
Hamburg, *Germany*	● 31	E2
Hamburg, *U.S.*	● 99	E2
Hämeenlinna	● 27	N6
Hameln	● 31	E4
Hamersley Range	▲ 87	C4
Hamhŭng	● 59	D3
Hami	● 53	S9
Hamilton, *Bermuda*	● 105	M2
Hamilton, *Canada*	● 99	E2
Hamilton, *New Zealand*	● 89	E3
Hamilton, *Mont., U.S.*	● 97	D1
Hamilton, *Oh., U.S.*	● 99	D3
Hamirpur	● 65	D3
Hamm	● 31	C5
Hammada du Drâa	⊘ 77	D3
Hammelburg	● 31	E6
Hammerfest	● 27	M1
Hampden	● 89	C7
Hāmūn-e Jaz Mūrīān	⊘ 71	H3
Hanamaki	● 59	L4
Hancheng	● 57	E3
Hancock	● 99	C1
Handan	● 57	E3
Hanford	● 103	C1
Hangayn Nuruu	▲ 53	T8
Hangzhou	● 57	F4
Hanīdh	● 71	C3
Hanko	● 27	M7
Hanksville	● 97	D3
Hanna	● 93	K6
Hannibal	● 101	C2
Hannover	● 31	E4
Hanöbukten	⊠ 29	D2
Ha Nôi	■ 61	D2
Hanoi = Ha Nôi	■ 61	D2
Hanover	● 99	F2
Han Shui	⊘ 57	D4
Hanzhong	● 57	D4
Hāora	● 65	E4
Haparanda	● 27	N4
Hapur	● 65	C3
Ḩaraḑ, *Saudi Arabia*	● 67	E5
Ḩaraḑ, *Yemen*	● 75	H4

Name	Page	Ref
Haramachi	59	L5
Harare	83	E3
Harbin	57	H1
Harburg	31	F3
Hardangerfjorden	27	C7
Hardangervidda	27	D6
Hardenberg	33	J2
Hardin	97	E1
Hardy	101	C2
Härer	81	G2
Hargeysa	81	G2
Harihari	89	C6
Hari Rud	67	H3
Harlingen, *Netherlands*	33	H1
Harlingen, *U.S.*	101	B4
Harlow	35	N10
Harney Basin	95	B3
Härnösand	27	J5
Harrisburg, *Ill., U.S.*	99	C3
Harrisburg, *Pa., U.S.*	101	F1
Harrison	99	B3
Harrogate	35	L8
Har Saggi	70	B6
Harsin	69	M6
Hârșova	45	Q5
Hartford	99	F2
Har Us Nuur	53	S8
Harvey	97	G1
Harwich	33	D3
Harz	31	F5
Haskell	101	B3
Hassan	65	C6
Hasselt	33	H4
Hastings, *New Zealand*	89	F4
Hastings, *U.K.*	33	C4
Hastings, *U.S.*	97	G2
Hațeg	45	K4
Hatgal	55	G6
Ha Tinh	61	D3
Hattiesburg	101	D3
Hatvan	45	G2
Haud	75	H6
Haud Ogadēn	81	G2/H2
Haugesund	27	C7
Hauraki Gulf	89	E3
Haut Atlas	77	D2
Hauts Plateaux	77	E2
Havana	101	C1
Havana = La Habana	105	H4
Havelock	89	D5
Havelock North	89	F4
Haverfordwest	35	H10
Havlíčkův Brod	29	E8
Havre	97	E1
Hawaii	103	(2)E2
Hawaii	103	(2)E4
Hawaiian Islands	85	J3
Hawera	89	E4
Hawi	103	(2)F3
Hawke Bay	89	F4
Hawker	87	G6
Hawr al Ḩammar	71	B1
Hawthorne	97	C3
Hay	87	H6
Hay	93	H5
Hayange	33	J5
Hayrabolu	47	K3
Hay River	93	H4
Hays	101	B2
Hazebrouck	33	E4
Hazelton, *Canada*	93	F5
Hazelton, *U.S.*	99	E2
Hearst	99	D1
Hebron, *Canada*	93	U5
Hebron, *Israel*	70	C5
Hebron, *U.S.*	97	F1
Hecate Strait	93	E6
Hechi	61	D2
Hede	27	G5
Heerenveen	33	H2
Hefa	70	B4
Hefei	57	F4
Hegang	57	J1
Hegura-jima	59	J5
Heide	31	E2
Heidelberg	31	D7
Heilbronn	31	E7
Heimaey	27	(1)C3
Hejing	53	R9
Hekla	27	(1)D3
Helagsfjället	27	G5
Helena, *Ark., U.S.*	101	C3
Helena, *Mont., U.S.*	97	D1
Helensville	89	E3
Helgoland	31	C2
Helgoländer Bucht	31	D2
Hellin	39	J6
Helmand	67	H3
Helmond	33	H3
Helmsdale	35	J3
Helmstedt	31	G4
Helong	59	E2
Helsingborg	27	G8
Helsingør	27	G8
Helsinki	27	N6
Helwan	75	F2
Hemel Hempstead	35	M10
Henderson	97	D3
Henderson Island	85	P8
Hendersonville	99	C3
Hendijarn	71	C1
Hengelo	33	J2
Hengyang	57	E5
Hennebont	37	B6
Hennigsdorf	31	J4
Henzada	61	B3
Hepu	61	D2
Herät	67	H3
Herborn	31	D6
Hereford	35	K9
Herentals	33	G3
Herford	31	D4
Herisau	41	E3
Herlen Gol	57	E1
Herma Ness	35	M1
Hermel	70	D2
Hermiston	97	C1
Hermosillo	95	D6
Hernád	29	L9
Hervey Bay	87	K5
Hesdin	33	E4
Heshan	61	D2
Heves	29	K10
Hialeah	101	E4
Hiawatha	101	B2
Hibbing	99	B1
Hickory	99	D3
Hiddensee	31	H1
Higashi-suidō	59	E7
High Wycombe	33	B3
Hiiumaa	27	M7
Hikurangi	89	G3
Hildesheim	31	E4
Hillsboro, *Oreg., U.S.*	97	B1
Hillsboro, *Tex., U.S.*	103	G2
Hillswick	35	L1
Hilo	103	(2)F4
Hilton Head Island	101	E3
Hilversum	33	H2
Himalayas	51	L6
Himatnagar	65	B4
Himeji	59	H6
Himora	75	G5
Ḩimş	70	D2
Hîncești	45	R3
Hindu Kush	65	A1
Hinnøya	27	H2
Hiroo	59	M2
Hirosaki	59	L3
Hiroshima	59	G6
Hirson	33	G5
Hirtshals	27	E8
Hisar	65	C3
Hispaniola	107	(2)J2
Hitachi	59	L5
Hitra	27	D5
Hjälmaren	27	H7
Hlinsko	29	E8
Hlyboka	45	N1
Ho	79	E3
Hobart	87	J8
Hobbs	103	F2
Hobyo	81	H3
Hô Chi Minh	61	D4
Höchstadt	31	F7
Hockenheim	31	D7
Hódmezóvásárhely	45	H3
Hodonin	29	G9
Hoek van Holland	33	G3
Hoeryŏng	59	E2
Hof	31	G6
Hofgeismar	31	E5
Höfn	27	(1)F2
Hofsjökull	27	(1)D2
Hohe	41	H3
Hohe Dachstein	29	C10
Hohe Tauern	43	G1
Hohhot	57	F2
Hoh Xil Shan	65	E1
Hokitika	89	C6
Hokkaidō	59	N2
Holbæk	29	A2
Holbrook	103	D2
Holguín	105	J4
Holíč	41	N2
Hollabrunn	41	M2
Holland	99	C2
Hollywood	101	E4
Holman	93	H2
Hólmavik	27	(1)C2
Holstebro	27	E8
Holyhead	35	H8
Holy Island	35	L6
Holzkirchen	41	G3
Homa Bay	81	E4
Homberg	31	E5
Hombori	77	E5
Home Bay	93	T3
Homs = Ḩimş	70	D2
Homyel'	49	F4
Hondo, *N. Mex., U.S.*	103	E2
Hondo, *Tex., U.S.*	103	G3
Honduras	105	G6
Hønefoss	27	F6
Hon Gai	61	D2
Hong Kong	61	E2
Hongor	57	E1
Honiara	85	F6
Honokaa	103	(2)F3
Honolulu	103	(2)D2
Honshū	59	L5
Hoogeveen	33	J2
Hooper Bay	103	(1)D3
Hoorn	33	H2
Hoorn Islands	85	H7
Hope	101	C3
Hopedale	93	U5
Hoquiam	97	B1
Horasan	69	K3
Horizon Depth	85	D8
Horn	41	L2
Hornavan	27	J3

Name	Page	Grid
Horodenka	45	N1
Horqin Youyi Qianqi	55	L7
Horsens	27	E9
Horsham, *Australia*	87	H7
Horsham, *U.K.*	33	B3
Hortiguela	39	G2
Ḩoseynābād	71	G2
Hosséré Vokre	79	G3
Hotan	53	Q10
Hotan	53	Q10
Hot Springs	99	B4
Houghton	99	C1
Houlton	99	G1
Houma, *China*	57	E3
Houma, *U.S.*	95	H6
Houmt Souk	77	H2
Houston	95	G6
Hovd	53	S8
Hövsgöl Nuur	55	F6
Howard Junction	89	D5
Howland	85	J5
Hoxie	101	C2
Höxter	31	E5
Hoy	35	J3
Høyanger	27	D6
Hoyerswerda	31	K5
Hradeç Králové	29	E7
Hrazdan	69	L3
Hrodna	29	N4
Hsin-chu	61	G2
Huacho	109	B6
Huadian	59	D2
Huaibei	57	F4
Huaihua	57	D5
Huaiyin	57	F4
Huaki	63	(2)C4
Huallaga	109	B5
Huambo	83	B2
Huancayo	109	B6
Huang	57	F3
Huangchuan	57	F4
Huangshi	57	F4
Huang Xian	57	G3
Huanren	59	C3
Huanuco	109	B5
Huasco	111	G4
Hubli	65	C5
Huddersfield	35	L8
Hudiksvall	27	J6
Hudson	99	F2
Hudson Bay	93	L6
Hudson Bay	93	P5
Hudson Strait	93	S4
Huê	61	D3
Huelva	39	D7
Huesca	39	K2
Huéscar	39	H7
Huich'ŏn	59	D3
Huila Plateau	83	A3
Huizhou	61	E2
Hull	99	E1
Hulun Nur	55	K7
Huma	55	M6
Humaitá	109	E5
Humbe	83	A3
Humboldt	93	L6
Humboldt	97	C2
Humenné	29	L9
Humphrey	97	D2
Hūn	75	C2
Húnaflói	27	(1)C2
Hunchun	59	F2
Hunedoara	45	K4
Hungary	45	F3
Hungerford	87	H5
Hŭngnam	59	D4
Hunjiang	59	D3
Hunsrück	31	B7
Hunte	31	D4
Huntingdon	101	E2
Huntington	101	E2
Huntly	89	E3
Huntsville, *Canada*	99	E1
Huntsville, *Al., U.S.*	101	D3
Huntsville, *Tex., U.S.*	105	E2
Hunyuan	57	E3
Huron	97	G2
Húsavík	27	(1)E1
Husum	31	E2
Hutag	55	G7
Hutanopan	63	(1)B2
Hutchinson	103	G1
Huvadu Atoll	65	B8
Huy	33	H4
Hvannadalshnúkur	27	(1)E2
Hvar	45	D6
Hvar	45	D6
Hwange	83	B3
Hyannis	97	F2
Hyderabad, *India*	65	C5
Hyderabad, *Pakistan*	67	J4
Hyères	37	M10
Hyesan	59	E3
Hyndam Peak	97	D2
Hyūga	59	F7
Hyvinkää	27	N6

I

Name	Page	Grid
Ialomiţa	45	P5
Iaşi	45	Q2
Ibadan	79	E3
Ibagué	109	B3
Ibar	45	H6
Ibiza = Eivissa	39	M5
Ibiza = Eivissa	39	M6
Ibrā'	67	G5
'Ibrī	71	G5
Ica	109	B6
İçel	69	F5
Iceland	25	C1
Ichalkaranji	65	B5
Ichinoseki	59	L4
Idah	79	F3
Idaho	97	D2
Idaho Falls	97	D2
Idar-Oberstein	31	C7
Idfu	75	F3
Idhān Awbārī	77	H3
Idhan Murzūq	77	H4
Idiofa	81	C4
Idlib	69	G6
Ieper	33	E4
Ierapetra	47	H9
Ife	79	E3
Igarka	53	R4
Iglesias	43	C9
Igloolik	93	Q3
Iğneada	47	K3
Igoumenitsa	47	C5
Igrim	49	M2
Igualada	39	M3
Iguatu	109	K5
Ilharaña	83	H2
Ihosy	83	H4
Iida	59	J6
Iisalmi	27	P5
Iiulissat	93	W3
Ijebu Ode	79	E3
IJssel	33	J2
IJsselmeer	33	H2
Ikaria	47	J7
Ikela	81	C4
Iki	59	E7
Ikopa	83	H3
Ikorodu	79	E3
Ilagan	61	G3
Īlām	67	E3
Iława	29	J4
Ilbenge	55	L4
Ilebo	81	C4
Île d'Anticosti	93	U7
Île de Jerba	77	H2
Île de Noirmoutier	37	C7
Île de Ré	37	D7
Île d'Oléron	37	D8
Île d'Yeu	37	C7
Île Europa	83	G4
Ilek	49	K4
Ilek	49	K4
Îles Chesterfield	85	F7
Îles Crozet	73	J10
Îles Désappointement	85	M7
Îles d'Hyères	37	M11
Îles Glorieuses	83	H2
Ilesha	79	E3
Îles Palliser	85	M7
Île Zembra	43	E11
Ilfracombe	35	H10
Ilha da Trindade	107	H6
Ilha de Marajó	109	H4
Ilha Fernando de Noronha	109	L4
Ilhas Martin Vaz	111	Q3
Ilhéus	109	K6
Ili	53	P9
Iliamna Volcano	103	(1)G4
Iligan	61	G5
Ilkal	65	C5
Illertissen	41	F2
Illinois	95	H3
Illinois	99	C2
Illizi	77	G3
Iloilo	61	G4
Ilorin	79	E3
Ilwaco	97	B1
Ilych	49	L2
Imabari	59	G6
Imatra	27	Q6
Imeni Polinyosipenko	55	P6
Imese	81	B3
Imī	81	G2
İmişli	69	N4
Immenstadt	41	F3
Imola	41	G6
Imotski	45	E6
Imperatriz	109	H5
Imperia	41	D7
Imperial	97	F2
Impfondo	81	B3
Imphal	65	F4
Inangahua	89	C5
Inanwatan	63	(2)D3
Iñapari	109	D6
Inarijärvi	27	P2
Inca	39	N5
Ince Burun	69	F2
Inch'ŏn	59	D5
Indalsälven	27	H5
India	65	C4
Indiana	95	J3
Indianapolis	101	D2
Indian Ocean	65	D8
Indianola	99	B2
Indiga	49	J1
Indio	103	C2
Indonesia	63	(1)D3
Indore	65	C4
Indramayu	63	(1)D4
Indre	37	D6
Indus	67	K3

137

Name	Page	Ref
İnebolu	69	E3
In Ekker	77	G4
Ineu	45	J3
Ingeniero Jacobacci	111	H7
Ingham	87	J3
Ingolstadt	41	G2
Ingrãj Bãzãr	65	E3
Ingushetiya	69	L2
Inhambane	83	F4
Inner Hebrides	35	F5
Inner Mongolia = Nei Monggol	57	E2
Innisfail	87	J3
Innsbruck	41	G3
Inongo	81	B4
Inowrocław	29	H5
In Salah	77	F3
Insein	61	B3
Inta	53	K4
Interlaken	41	C4
International Falls	99	B1
Inukjuak	93	R5
Inuvik	103	(1)L2
Invercargill	89	B8
Inverness	35	H4
Inverway	87	E3
Ioannina	47	C5
Iola	101	B2
Iona	35	F5
Ionian Sea	47	B6
Ionioi Nisoi	47	B5
Ios	47	H8
Iowa	95	H3
Iowa City	99	B2
Ipatovo	49	H5
Ipiales	109	B3
Ipoh	63	(1)C2
Iporá	109	G7
İpsala	47	J4
Ipswich	35	P9
Iqaluit	93	T4
Iquique	111	G3
Iquitos	109	C4
Irakleio	47	H9
Iraklion = Irakleio	25	G4
Iran	67	F3
Īrānshahr	67	H4
Irapuato	105	D4
Iraq	67	D3
Irbid	70	C4
Irbit	49	M3
Irgiz	49	M5
Irian Jaya	63	(2)E3
Iringa	81	F5
Iriri	109	G4
Irish Sea	35	G8
Irkutsk	55	G6
Iron Mountain	99	C1
Ironwood	99	B1
Irrawaddy	65	F5
Irta	49	J2
Irtysh	49	P3
Irtyshsk	53	P7
Irvine	35	H6
Irving	103	G2
Ísafjörður	27	(1)B1
Isahaya	57	J4
Isar	41	G3
Ischia	43	H8
Ise	59	J6
Isel	41	H4
Isère	41	B5
Iserlohn	33	K3
Isernia	43	J7
Isetskoye	49	N3
Ishikari-wan	59	L2
Ishim	49	N3
Ishim	49	N4
Ishinomaki	59	L4
Isiolo	81	F3
Isiro	81	D3
Iskär	45	M6
İskenderun	69	G5
Isla Clarión	105	B5
Isla de Alborán	39	G9
Isla de Bioco	79	F4
Isla de Chiloé	111	G7
Isla de Coco	105	G7
Isla de Cozumel	105	G4
Isla de la Juventud	105	H4
Isla de los Estados	111	J9
Isla de Malpelo	109	A3
Isla de Margarita	109	E1
Isla de Providencia	105	H6
Isla de San Andrés	105	H6
Isla Fernandina	109	(1)A2
Isla Grande de Tierra del Fuego	111	H9
Isla Isabela	109	(1)A2
Isla La Tortuga	109	D1
Islamabad	65	B2
Isla Marchena	109	(1)A1
Island Lake	93	M6
Isla San Benedicto	105	B5
Isla San Cristóbal	109	(1)B2
Isla San Salvador	109	(1)A2
Isla Santa Cruz	109	(1)A2
Isla Santa María	109	(1)A2
Islas Baleares	39	N5
Islas Canarias	77	B3
Islas Canarias	73	A3
Islas Columbretes	39	L5
Islas de la Bahía	105	G5
Islas de los Desventurados	111	E4
Islas Galápagos	109	(1)B1
Islas Juan Fernández	111	E5
Islas Los Roques	109	D1
Islas Marías	105	C4
Isla Socorro	105	B5
Islas Revillagigedo	105	B5
Isla Wellington	111	F8
Islay	35	F6
Isle	37	F8
Isle of Man	35	H7
Isle of Wight	35	L11
Isle Royale	99	C1
Isles of Scilly	35	F12
Ismâ'ilîya	75	F1
Isna	75	F2
Isoka	83	E2
Isola di Pantelleria	43	G12
Isole Egadi	43	F11
Isole Lipari	43	J10
Isole Ponziane	43	H8
Isole Tremiti	43	K6
Isparta	47	N7
Ispica	43	J12
Israel	70	B5
Issoire	37	J8
Issoudun	37	H7
İstanbul	69	C3
İstanbul Boğazı	69	C3
Istiaia	47	F6
Istra	41	J5
Istres	37	K10
Itabuna	109	K6
Itacoatiara	109	F4
Itaituba	109	F4
Itajaí	111	M4
Italy	43	D3
Itanagar	65	F3
Itapipoca	109	K4
Itarsi	65	C4
Ithaca	99	E2
Ithaki	47	C6
Itumbiara	109	H7
Ituri	81	D3
Itzehoe	31	E3
Ivalo	27	P2
Ivangrad	45	G7
Ivanhoe, Australia	87	H6
Ivanhoe, U.S.	99	A2
Ivano-Frankivs'k	49	D5
Ivanovo	49	H3
Ivdel'	49	M2
Ivittuut	93	X4
Ivory Coast	79	C3
Ivosjön	29	D1
Ivrea	41	C5
Ivujivik	93	R4
Iwaki	59	L5
Iwamizawa	59	L2
Iwo	79	E3
Izhevsk	49	K3
Izhma	49	K1
Izkī	71	G5
Izmayil	45	R4
İzmir	69	B4
İzmir Körfezi	47	J6
İzmit	69	C3
İznik Gölü	69	C3
Izra'	70	D4
Izumo	59	G6
Izu-shotō	59	K6

J

Name	Page	Ref
Jabal ad Durūz	70	D4
Jabal Akhḍar	71	G5
Jabal al Nuşayrīyah	70	D1
Jabal an Nabī Shu'ayb	75	H4
Jabal Ash Sham	71	G5
Jabalpur	65	C4
Jabal Thamar	75	J5
Jabiru	87	F2
Jablah	70	C1
Jaca	39	K2
Jackman	99	F1
Jacksboro	101	B3
Jackson, Miss., U.S.	101	C3
Jackson, Oh., U.S.	101	E2
Jackson, Tenn., U.S.	101	D2
Jackson Head	89	B6
Jacksonville, Fla., U.S.	101	E3
Jacksonville, Ill., U.S.	99	B3
Jacksonville, N.C., U.S.	101	F3
Jacobabad	65	A3
Jacobina	109	J6
Jacupiranga	111	M3
Jadebusen	31	D3
Jaén	39	G7
Jaen	109	B5
Jaffna	65	D7
Jagdalpur	65	D5
Jagst	31	E7
Jahrom	71	E2
Jaipur	65	C3
Jaisalmer	65	B3
Jajce	45	E5
Jakarta	63	(1)D4
Jakobshavn = Iiulissat	93	W3
Jakobstad	27	M5
Jalālābād	65	B2
Jalandhar	65	C2
Jalgaon	65	C4
Jalingo	79	G3
Jalna	65	C5
Jalpaiguri	65	E3
Jalūlā	69	L6
Jamaica	105	H5

Name	Page	Grid
Jambi	63	(1)C3
James	97	G2
James Bay	93	Q6
Jamestown, *N.Y., U.S.*	99	E2
Jamestown, *N.D., U.S.*	97	G1
Jammu	65	B2
Jammu and Kashmir	65	C2
Jamnagar	65	B4
Jämsä	27	N6
Jamshedpur	65	E4
Janakpur	65	E3
Jandaq	67	F3
Jane Peak	89	B7
Janesville	99	C2
Jan Mayen	91	C2
Janów Lubelski	29	M7
Japan	59	L5
Japan Trench	85	E2
Japurá	109	D4
Jarash	70	C4
Jarosław	29	M7
Järpen	27	G5
Jarvis	85	K6
Jäsk	71	G4
Jasper	101	E3
Jastrebarsko	41	L5
Jászberény	45	G2
Jataí	109	G7
Jaunpur	65	D3
Java = Jawa	63	(1)E4
Java Sea	63	(1)E4
Jawa	63	(1)E4
Jawhar	81	H3
Jayapura	63	(2)F3
Jaza'ir Farasan	75	H4
Jazirat Bubiyan	71	C2
Jazirat-ye Khark	71	D2
Jbel Bou Naceur	77	E2
Jbel Toubkal	77	D2
Jebba	79	E3
Jebel el Ata'ita	70	C6
Jebel el Batra	70	C7
Jebel-esh Sharqi	70	C3
Jebel Gimbala	75	D5
Jebel Ithriyat	70	D6
Jebel Liban	70	C3
Jebel Mubrak	70	C6
Jebel Ram	70	C7
Jebel Uweinat	75	E3
Jedda = Jiddah	67	C5
Jędrzejów	29	K7
Jega	79	E2
Jēkabpils	27	N8
Jelgava	27	M8
Jena	31	G6
Jequié	109	J6
Jerez de la Frontera	39	D8
Jerez de los Caballeros	39	D6
Jericho	70	C5
Jersey	37	C4
Jerusalem = Yerushalayim	70	C5
Jesenice	45	B3
Jesenik	29	G7
Jesi	41	J7
Jesup	101	E3
Jezioro	29	D4
Jezioro Śniardwy	29	L4
Jhang Maghiana	65	B2
Jhansi	65	C3
Jhelum	65	B2
Jialing Jiang	57	D4
Jiamusi	57	J1
Ji'an	57	E5
Jiangling	57	E4
Jiangmen	57	E6
Jiaozou	57	E3
Jiayuguan	57	B3
Jiddah	67	C5
Jiesjavrre	27	N2
Jihlava	29	E8
Jilib	81	G3
Jilin	59	D2
Jima	81	F2
Jimbolia	45	H4
Jiménez	103	F3
Jinan	57	F3
Jinchang	57	C3
Jincheng	57	E3
Jingdezhen	57	F5
Jinggu	57	C6
Jinghe	53	Q9
Jinghong	57	C6
Jingmen	57	E4
Jingxi	57	D6
Jinhua	57	F5
Jining, *China*	57	E2
Jining, *China*	57	F3
Jinja	81	E3
Jinka	81	F2
Jinsha	57	C5
Jinshi	57	E5
Jinta	57	B2
Jinxi	57	G2
Jinzhou	57	G2
Jiroft	71	G2
Jishou	57	D5
Jiu	45	L4
Jiujiang	57	F5
Jixi	59	F1
Jizan	75	H4
J. J. Castelli	109	D4
João Pessoa	109	L5
Jódar	39	G7
Jodhpur	65	B3
Joensuu	49	E2
Jōetsu	59	K5
Jōgeva	27	P7
Johannesburg	83	D5
John Day	97	C2
John o' Groats	35	J3
Johnson	101	A2
Johnston Island	85	J4
Johor Bahru	63	(1)C2
Joigny	37	J5
Joinville	111	M4
Jokkmokk	27	K3
Jolfa	69	L4
Joliet	95	J3
Joliette	99	F1
Jolo	63	(2)B1
Jonava	29	P2
Jonesboro	99	B3
Jonglei Canal	81	E2
Jönköping	27	H8
Jonquière	99	F1
Joplin	101	C2
Jordan	70	D5
Jordan	97	E1
Jorhat	65	F3
Jos	79	F3
José de San Martín	111	G7
Joseph Bonaparte Gulf	87	E2
Joûnié	70	C2
Juan de Nova	83	G3
Juàzeiro do Norte	109	K5
Juba	81	E3
Jubba	81	G3
Júcar	39	J5
Juchitán	105	F5
Judenburg	41	K3
Juist	31	B3
Juiz de Fora	111	N3
Julesburg	97	F2
Juliaca	109	C7
Juliana Top	109	F3
Jülich	33	J4
Jumilla	39	J6
Junction City	101	B2
Jungfrau	41	C4
Junggar Pendi	53	R8
Jun Xian	57	E4
Jura	41	B4
Jura	35	G5
Jurbarkas	29	M2
Jurf ed Darawish	70	C6
Jürmala	27	M8
Jürmala	49	D3
Jutaí	109	D5
Ju Xian	57	F3
Jüyom	71	F2
Jylland	27	E8
Jyvädskäla	49	E2
Jyväskylä	49	E2
Jyväskylä	27	N5

K

Name	Page	Grid
K2	65	C1
Kaarta	77	C6
Kabaena	63	(2)B4
Kabala	79	B3
Kabale	81	E4
Kabalo	81	D5
Kabardino-Balkariya	69	K2
Kabongo	81	D5
Kabul	67	J3
Kabwe	83	D2
Kachikattsy	55	M4
Kachug	55	H6
Kadama	65	B6
Kadaň	29	C7
Kadınhanı	47	Q6
Kadirli	69	G5
Kadoka	97	F2
Kadoma	83	D3
Kadugli	75	E5
Kaduna	79	F2
Kaédi	77	C5
Kaesŏng	59	D5
Kaffrine	79	A2
Kåfjord	27	N1
Kafr el Sheikh	75	F1
Kafue	83	D3
Kagoshima	59	F8
Kahemba	81	B5
Kahnūj	71	G3
Kahraman Maraş	69	G5
Kaifeng	57	E4
Kaikohe	89	D2
Kaikoura	89	D6
Kailua	103	(2)D2
Kailua Kona	103	(2)E4
Kaimana	63	(2)D3
Käina	27	M7
Kainji Reservoir	79	E2
Kaipara Harbour	89	D3
Kairouan	77	H1
Kaiserslautern	31	C7
Kaitaia	89	D2
Kaiyuan	61	C2
Kajaani	27	P4
Kakamega	81	E3
Kakata	79	B3
Kakhovs'ke Vodoskhovyshche	49	F5
Kākināda	65	D5
Kalabahi	63	(2)B4
Kalabo	83	B2
Kalach	49	H4
Kalach-na-Donu	49	H5

Name	Page	Grid
Kalahari Desert	83	C4
Kalakan	55	K5
Kalamata	47	E7
Kalamazoo	99	C2
Kalaotoa	63	(2)B4
Kalaupapa	103	(2)E2
Kalavryta	47	E6
Kalemie	81	D5
Kalevala	27	R4
Kalewa	65	F4
Kalgoorlie	87	D6
Kalibo	61	G4
Kalima	81	D4
Kalimantan	63	(1)E2
Kaliningrad	29	K3
Kaliningradskiy Zaliv	29	J3
Kalispell	97	D1
Kalisz	29	H6
Kalixälven	27	M3
Kalkan	47	M8
Kallavesi	27	P5
Kallsjön	27	G5
Kalmar	27	J8
Kalmykiya	69	M1
Kalmykovo	49	K5
Kalocsa	45	F3
Kalpakio	47	C5
Kaluga	49	G4
Kalyan	65	B5
Kalymnos	47	J8
Kalymnos	47	J7
Kama	81	D4
Kama	25	K1
Kamaishi	59	L4
Kamande	81	D4
Kambo Ho	59	E3
Kamchatka	55	U6
Kamenka	49	H1
Kamen'-na-Obi	53	Q7
Kamensk-Ural'skiy	49	M3
Kamenz	29	D6
Kamet	65	C2
Kamiiso	59	L3
Kamina	81	C5
Kamloops	93	G6
Kampala	81	E3
Kampen	33	H2
Kampong Cham	61	D4
Kam"yanets'-Podil's'kyy	49	E5
Kamyshin	49	J4
Kananga	81	C5
Kanazawa	59	J5
Kanbalu	65	G4
Kanchipuram	65	C6
Kandahār	67	J3
Kandalaksha	27	S3
Kandalakshskiy Zaliv	49	F1
Kandi	79	E2
Kandira	47	N3
Kandy	65	D7
Kangaatsiaq	93	W3
Kangal	69	G4
Kangān	71	E3
Kangaroo Island	87	G7
Kangchenjunga	65	E3
Kangetet	81	F3
Kangiqsualujjuaq	93	T5
Kangmar	65	E3
Kangnüng	59	E5
Kaniama	81	C5
Kankakee	99	C2
Kankan	79	C2
Kankossa	77	C5
Kano	79	F2
Kanoya	59	F8
Kanpur	65	D3
Kansas	101	A2
Kansas	101	B2
Kansas City, Kans., U.S.	101	C2
Kansas City, Mo., U.S.	101	C2
Kansk	53	T6
Kao-Hsiung	57	G6
Kaolack	77	B6
Kaoma	83	C2
Kapanga	81	C5
Kap Arkona	29	C3
Kapchagay	53	P9
Kap Farvel = Uummannarsuaq	93	Y5
Kapit	63	(1)E2
Kapoeta	81	E3
Kaposvár	45	E3
Kapsan	59	E3
Kapuskasing	95	K2
Kapuvár	45	E2
Kara, Russia	53	M4
Kara, Togo	79	E3
Kara-Balta	53	N9
Karabutak	49	M5
Karacabey	47	L4
Karacaköy	47	L3
Karacal Tepe	47	Q8
Karachayevo-Cherkesiya	69	J2
Karachi	67	J5
Karaganda	53	N8
Karaginskiy Zaliv	55	V5
Karaj	67	F2
Karak	70	C5
Kara-Kala	67	G2
Karakol	53	P9
Karakoram	51	L6
Karaman	69	E5
Karamay	53	R8
Karamea	89	D5
Karamea Bight	89	C5
Karapınar	47	R7
Kara-Say	53	P9
Karasburg	83	B5
Kara Sea = Karskoye More	53	L3
Karasuk	53	P7
Karatobe	49	K5
Karaton	49	K5
Karbalā'	67	D3
Karcag	45	H2
Karditsa	47	D5
Kareliya	27	R4
Karepino	49	L2
Karesuando	27	M2
Kargalinskaya	69	M2
Kargasok	53	Q6
Kargopol'	49	G2
Kariba	83	D3
Kariba Dam	83	D3
Karibib	83	B4
Karimata	63	(1)D3
Karimnagar	65	C5
Karkaralinsk	53	P8
Karlik Shan	57	A2
Karlovac	45	C4
Karlovo	47	G2
Karlovy Vary	31	H6
Karlshamn	29	D1
Karlskoga	27	H7
Karlskrona	27	H8
Karlsruhe	31	D8
Karlstad, Norway	27	G7
Karlstad, U.S.	99	A1
Karlstadt	31	E7
Karmøy	27	C7
Karnafuli Reservoir	65	F4
Karnal	65	C3
Karnische Alpen	41	H4
Karonga	81	E5
Karpathos	47	K9
Karpathos	47	K9
Karrabük	69	E3
Kars	69	K3
Karshi	67	J2
Karskoye More	53	L3
Kartaly	49	M4
Karufa	63	(2)D3
Karumba	87	H3
Karvina	29	H8
Karwar	65	B6
Karystos	47	G6
Kasai	81	B4
Kasaji	83	C2
Kasama	83	E2
Kasempa	83	D2
Kasenga	83	D2
Kāshān	67	F3
Kashi	67	L2
Kasimov	49	H4
Kasli	49	M3
Kasongo	81	D4
Kasos	47	K9
Kaspiysk	69	M2
Kassala	75	G4
Kassel	31	E5
Kastamonu	69	E3
Kastelli	47	F9
Kastoria	47	D4
Kasur	65	B2
Katerini	47	E4
Katha	65	G4
Katherine	87	F2
Kathiawar	67	K5
Kathmandu	65	E3
Katihar	65	E3
Katonga	81	E3
Katowice	29	J7
Katsina	79	F2
Katsina-Ala	79	F3
Kattavia	47	K9
Kattegat	27	F8
Kauai	103	(2)B1
Kauhajoki	27	M5
Kaunas	29	N3
Kauno	29	P3
Kaunus	25	G2
Kavadarci	47	D3
Kavajë	47	B3
Kavala	47	G4
Kavār	71	E2
Kavaratti	65	B6
Kavarna	45	R6
Kawakawa	89	E2
Kawambwa	81	D5
Kawasaki	59	K6
Kawhia	89	E4
Kawthaung	61	B4
Kaya	79	D2
Kaycee	97	E2
Kayenta	103	D1
Kayes	79	B2
Kaynar	53	P8
Kayseri	69	F4
Kazach'ye	55	P2
Kazakhstan	53	L8
Kazan'	49	J3
Kazanlŭk	47	H2
Kazan-rettō	85	E3
Kazbek	69	L2
Kāzerūn	71	D2
Kazincbarcika	45	H1
Kea	47	G7
Keban Barajı	69	H4
Kebnekaise	27	K3
Kecskemet	45	G3
Kédougou	79	B2

Name	Page	Grid
Kędzierzyn-Koźle	29	H7
Keetmanshoop	83	B5
Kefallonia	47	C6
Kefamenanu	63	(2)B4
Keflavík	27	(1)B2
Keg River	93	H5
Keila	27	N7
Keitele	27	N5
Kékes	45	H2
Kelai Thiladhunmathee Atoll	65	B7
Kelheim	41	G2
Kelibia	43	F12
Kelkit	69	G3
Kelmë	29	M2
Kelowna	93	H7
Kelso	97	B1
Keluang	63	(1)C2
Kem'	49	F2
Kemerovo	53	R6
Kemi	27	N4
Kemijärvi	27	P3
Kemijärvi	27	P3
Kemmerer	97	D3
Kemp's Bay	101	F5
Kempten	41	F3
Kendari	63	(2)B3
Kendégué	79	H2
Kenema	79	B3
Kenge	81	B4
Kengtung	61	B2
Kenhardt	83	C5
Kénitra	77	D2
Kennett	101	D2
Kennewick	97	C1
Keno Hill	103	(1)K3
Kenora	95	H2
Kentucky	95	J4
Kenya	73	G5
Keokuk	99	B2
Kepulauan Anambas	63	(1)D2
Kepulauan Aru	63	(2)E4
Kepulauan Ayu	63	(2)D2
Kepulauan Banggai	63	(2)B3
Kepulauan Barat Daya	63	(2)C4
Kepulauan Batu	63	(1)B3
Kepulauan Kai	63	(2)D4
Kepulauan Kangean	63	(1)F4
Kepulauan Karimunjawa	63	(1)D4
Kepulauan Laut Kecil	63	(1)F3
Kepulauan Leti	63	(2)C4
Kepulauan Lingga	63	(1)C2
Kepulauan Lucipara	63	(2)C4
Kepulauan Mentawai	63	(1)B3
Kepulauan Natuna	63	(1)D2
Kepulauan Riau	63	(1)C2
Kepulauan Sabalana	63	(1)F4
Kepulauan Sangir	63	(2)C2
Kepulauan Solor	63	(2)B4
Kepulauan Sula	63	(2)B3
Kepulauan Talaud	63	(2)C2
Kepulauan Tanimbar	63	(2)D4
Kepulauan Tengah	63	(1)F4
Kepulauan Togian	63	(2)B3
Kepulauan Tukangbesi	63	(2)B4
Kerch	69	G1
Kerchevskiy	49	L3
Kerempe Burnu	47	R2
Keren	75	G4
Kerio	81	F3
Kerki	67	J2
Kerkyra	47	B5
Kerkyra	47	B5
Kerma	75	F4
Kermadec Islands	85	H8
Kermadec Trench	85	J9
Kermān	71	G1
Kermānshāh	67	E3
Kerpen	33	J4
Kerrville	101	B3
Kerulen	55	J7
Keryneia	69	E6
Keşan	47	J4
Kesennuma	59	L4
Keşiş Dağları	67	C2
Keszthely	45	E3
Ketapang	63	(1)D3
Kêtou	79	E3
Kętrzyn	29	L3
Keweenaw Peninsula	99	C1
Key Largo	101	E4
Key West	101	E5
Kezhma	55	G5
Khabarovsk	55	P7
Khakasiya	53	R7
Khalīg el Suweis	75	F2
Khalīj Surt	75	C1
Khamrà	55	J4
Khān al Baghdād	69	K7
Khandwa	65	C4
Khanewal	65	B2
Khanpur	65	B3
Khantau	53	N9
Khantayka	49	N2
Khanty-Mansiysk	49	N2
Khān Yūnis	70	B5
Kharagpur	65	E4
Kharan	67	J4
Khargon	65	C4
Kharkiv	49	G5
Kharmanli	47	H3
Kharnmam	65	D5
Khartoum = El Khartum	75	F4
Khāsh	67	H4
Khashm el Girba	75	G4
Khashuri	69	K3
Khaskovo	47	H3
Khatanga	55	G2
Khātūnābād	71	F1
Khatyrka	55	X4
Khawr Fakkān	71	G4
Khayelitsha	83	B6
Kherson	49	F5
Kheta	53	T3
Khilok	55	J6
Khodā Afarīn	69	M4
Khouribga	77	D2
Khrebet Cherskogo	55	P3
Khrebet Dzhagdy	55	N6
Khrebet Dzhugdzhur	55	N5
Khrebet Kolymskiy	51	U3
Khrebet Kopet Dag	67	G2
Khrebet Suntar Khayata	55	P4
Khrebet Tarbagatay	53	Q8
Khujand	67	J1
Khulna	65	E4
Khust	45	L1
Khuzdar	67	J4
Khvoy	69	L4
Khyber Pass	67	K3
Kibombo	81	D4
Kibondo	81	E4
Kibre Mengist	81	F2
Kičevo	47	C3
Kicking Horse Pass	93	H6
Kidal	77	F5
Kidira	79	B2
Kiel	31	F2
Kielce	29	K7
Kieler Bucht	31	F2
Kiev = Kyyiv	49	F4
Kiffa	77	C5
Kigali	81	E4
Kigoma	81	D4
Kıkıköy	47	L3
Kikwit	81	B5
Kilchu	59	E3
Kilifi	81	F4
Kilis	69	G5
Kiliya	45	S4
Kilkenny	35	E9
Kilkis	47	C3
Killarney	35	C9
Kilmarnock	35	H6
Kilosa	81	F5
Kilrush	35	C9
Kilwa	81	D5
Kilwa Masoko	81	F5
Kimberley	83	C5
Kimberley Plateau	87	E3
Kimch'aek	59	E3
Kimolos	47	G8
Kimry	49	G3
Kincardine	99	D2
Kindia	79	B2
Kindu	81	D4
Kineshma	49	H3
Kingaroy	87	K5
Kingisepp	27	Q7
King Island	87	H7
Kingman	103	D1
Kingscote	87	G7
Kingsland	101	E3
King's Lynn	35	N9
Kings Sound	87	D3
Kings Peak	97	D2
Kingsport	101	E2
Kingston, Canada	99	E2
Kingston, Jamaica	105	J5
Kingston upon Hull	35	M8
Kingsville	101	B4
King William Island	93	M3
King William's Town	83	D6
Kinsale	35	D10
Kinshasa	81	B4
Kinsley	101	B2
Kintampo	79	D3
Kintyre	35	G6
Kinyeti	81	E3
Kircudbright	35	H7
Kiribati	85	J6
Kirikhan	69	G5
Kırıkkale	69	E4
Kirinyaga	81	F4
Kirishi	49	F3
Kiritimati	85	L5
Kirkcaldy	35	J5
Kirkjubæjarklaustur	27	(1)E3
Kirkland Lake	99	D1
Kırklareli	47	K3
Kirkūk	69	L6
Kirkwall	35	K3
Kirov, Russia	49	F4
Kirov, Russia	49	J3
Kirovo-Chepetsk	49	K3
Kirovohrad	49	F5
Kirs	49	K3
Kirsanov	49	H4
Kırşehir	69	F4
Kiruna	27	L3
Kisangani	81	D3
Kisbér	45	E2
Kishi	79	E3

Name		Pg	Ref
Kisii	●	81	E4
Kiska Island	⊠	103	(3)B1
Kiskunfélegyháza	●	45	G3
Kiskunhalas	●	45	G3
Kismaayo	●	81	G4
Kissidougou	●	79	B3
Kisumu	●	81	E4
Kisvárda	●	45	K1
Kita	●	79	C2
Kitakami	●	59	L4
Kita-Kyūshū	●	59	F7
Kita-Kyūshū	⊠	57	H4
Kitami	●	59	M2
Kitchener	●	99	D2
Kitgum	●	81	E3
Kitimat	●	93	F6
Kittilä	●	27	N3
Kitunda	●	81	E5
Kitwe	●	83	D2
Kitzingen	●	31	F7
Kizel	●	49	L3
Kızılırmak	◪	69	F3
Kizil'skoye	●	49	L4
Kızıltepe	●	69	J5
Kizlyar	●	69	M2
Kizlyarskiy Zaliv	⊵	69	M1
Kladno	●	29	D7
Klagenfurt	●	41	K4
Klaipėda	●	27	L9
Klamath	◪	97	B2
Klamath Falls	●	97	B2
Klarälven	◪	27	G6
Klatovy	●	31	J7
Klerksdorp	●	83	D5
Klin	●	49	G3
Klingenthal	●	31	H6
Klínovec	▲	31	H6
Klintsy	●	49	F4
Kłodzko	●	29	F7
Klosterneuburg	●	41	M2
Klosters	●	41	E4
Kluczbork	●	29	H7
Klyuchevskaya Sopka	▲	55	U5
Knin	●	45	D5
Knittelfeld	●	45	B2
Knokke-Heist	●	33	F3
Knoxville	●	99	D3
Knysna	●	83	C6
Kōbe	●	59	H6
Kobe	●	63	(2)C2
København	■	27	G9
Koblenz	●	31	C6
Kobroör	⊠	63	(2)E4
Kočani	●	47	E3
Kočevje	●	45	B4
Ko Chang	⊠	61	C4
Kochi	●	65	C7
Kōchi	●	59	G7
Kodiak	●	103	(1)G4
Kodiak Island	⊠	103	(1)G4
Köflach	●	45	C2
Kōfu	●	59	K6
Køge	●	29	B2
Køge Bugt	⊵	29	B2
Kohat	●	65	B2
Kohima	●	65	F3
Koh-i-Qaisir	▲	67	H3
Kohtla-Järve	●	27	P7
Koidu	●	79	B3
Koitere	◪	27	R5
Kokenau	●	63	(2)E3
Kokkola	●	27	M5
Kokomo	●	101	D1
Kokshetau	●	49	N4
Kokstad	●	83	D6
Kolaka	●	63	(2)B3
Kolar	●	65	C6
Kolari	●	27	M3
Kolašin	●	45	G7
Kolda	●	79	B2
Kolding	●	27	E9
Kolhapur	●	65	B5
Kolin	●	29	E7
Köln	●	31	B6
Kołobrzeg	●	29	E3
Kolomna	●	49	G3
Kolomyya	●	45	N1
Kolonedale	●	63	(2)B3
Kolosovka	●	49	P3
Kolpashevo	●	53	Q6
Kolpos Agiou Orous	⊵	47	F4
Kolpos Kassandras	⊵	47	F4
Kolpos Murampelou	⊵	47	H9
Kolskiy Poluostrov	⊘	49	G1
Kolva	◪	49	L2
Kolwezi	●	83	D2
Kolyma	◪	55	R4
Kolymskaya Nizmennost'	⊘	55	S3
Komandorskiye Ostrova	⊠	55	V5
Komárno	●	45	F2
Komatsu	●	59	J5
Komi	●	49	K2
Komló	●	45	F3
Kom Ombo	●	75	F3
Komotini	●	47	H3
Komsomol'sk-na-Amure	●	55	P6
Konārka	●	65	E5
Kondoa	●	81	F4
Kondopoga	●	49	F2
Kondūz	●	67	J2
Kong Frederik VI Kyst	⊘	93	Y4
Kongola	●	83	C3
Kongolo	●	81	D5
Kongsberg	●	27	E7
Kongur Shan	▲	53	N10
Königsberg = Kaliningrad	●	29	K3
Königswinter	●	31	C6
Konin	●	29	H5
Köniz	●	41	C4
Konstanz	●	41	E3
Kontagora	●	79	F2
Kon Tum	●	61	D4
Konya	●	69	E5
Konz	●	31	B7
Koper	●	41	J5
Koprivnica	●	45	D3
Korba	●	43	E12
Korbach	●	31	D5
Korçë	●	47	C4
Korčula	⊠	45	D7
Korea Bay	⊵	59	B4
Korea Strait	⊵	59	E6
Korhogo	●	79	C3
Korinthiakos Kolpos	⊵	47	E6
Korinthos	●	47	E7
Kōriyama	●	59	L5
Korkino	●	49	M4
Korla	●	53	R9
Korliki	●	55	C4
Kornat	⊠	45	C6
Koroba	●	63	(2)F4
Köroğlu Dağları	▲	47	Q4
Köroğlu Tepesi	▲	47	P4
Korogwe	●	81	F5
Koror	■	85	D5
Kortrijk	●	33	F4
Koryakskiy Khrebet	▲	55	V4
Kos	●	47	K8
Kos	⊠	47	K8
Ko Samui	⊠	61	C5
Kościerzyna	●	29	H3
Kosh Agach	●	53	R8
Košice	●	29	L9
Koslan	●	49	J2
Kosŏng	●	59	E4
Kosovo	⊞	47	C2
Kosovska Mitrovica	●	47	C2
Kostajnica	●	41	M5
Kostanay	●	49	M4
Kosti	●	75	F5
Kostinbrod	●	45	L7
Kostomuksha	●	27	R4
Kostroma	●	49	H3
Kostrzyn	●	29	D5
Koszalin	●	29	F3
Kőszeg	●	45	D2
Kota	●	65	C3
Kotaagung	●	63	(1)C4
Kotabaru	●	63	(1)F3
Kota Belud	●	63	(1)F1
Kota Bharu	●	63	(1)C1
Kotabumi	●	63	(1)C3
Kota Kinabalu	●	63	(1)F1
Kotapinang	●	63	(1)B2
Kotel'nich	●	49	J3
Köthen	●	31	G5
Kotido	●	81	E3
Kotka	●	27	P6
Kotlas	●	49	J2
Kotov'sk	●	49	E5
Kottagudem	●	65	D5
Kotto	◪	81	C2
Kotuy	◪	55	G3
Kotzebue	●	103	(1)E2
Kotzebue Sound	⊵	103	(1)D2
Kouango	●	79	H3
Koudougou	●	79	D2
Koufey	●	79	G2
Koulamoutou	●	79	G5
Koum	●	79	G3
Koundâra	●	79	B2
Koupéla	●	77	C6
Kourou	●	109	G2
Koutiala	●	79	C2
Kovdor	●	27	R3
Kovel'	●	49	D4
Kovrov	●	49	H3
Koykuk	●	103	(1)E3
Koynas	●	49	J2
Kozani	●	47	D4
Kozhikode	●	65	C6
Kpalimé	●	79	E3
Kragujevac	●	45	H5
Kraków	●	29	J7
Kraljevo	●	45	H6
Kramators'k	●	49	G5
Kramfors	●	27	J5
Kranj	●	45	B3
Krasino	●	53	J3
Kräslava	●	27	P9
Kraśnik	●	29	M7
Krasnoarmeysk	●	49	N4
Krasnodar	●	49	G5
Krasnokamensk	●	55	K6
Krasnosel'kup	●	55	C3
Krasnotur'insk	●	49	M3
Krasnoufimsk	●	49	L3
Krasnovishersk	●	49	L2
Krasnoyarsk	●	55	E5
Krasnoyarskoye Vodokhranilishche	◪	53	S6
Krasnystaw	●	29	N7
Krasnyy Chikoy	●	55	H6
Krasnyy Yar	●	49	J5
Kratovo	●	47	E2
Krefeld	●	33	J3
Kremenchuk	●	49	F5
Kremmling	●	97	E2
Krems	●	41	L2
Kretinga	●	29	L2

Name	Page	Grid
Krishna	65	C5
Kristiansand	27	E7
Kristianstad	27	H8
Kristiansund	27	D5
Kristinestad	27	L5
Kriti	47	H10
Križevci	45	D3
Krk	41	K5
Krk	41	K5
Kronach	31	G6
Krŏng Kaôh Kŏng	61	C4
Kronotskiy Zaliv	55	U6
Kroonstad	83	D5
Kroper	43	H3
Krosno	29	L8
Krugë	47	B3
Krui	63	(1)C4
Krumbach	41	F2
Krung Thep	61	C4
Kruševac	45	J6
Krym'	69	E1
Krymsk	69	H1
Krynica	29	L8
Krytiko Pelagos	47	G9
Kryvyy Rih	49	F5
Krzna	29	N5
Ksar el Boukhari	39	N9
Kuala Kerai	63	(1)C1
Kuala Lipis	63	(1)C2
Kuala Lumpur	63	(1)C2
Kuala Terengganu	63	(1)C1
Kuandian	59	C3
Kuantan	63	(1)C2
Kuçadasi	47	K7
Kučevo	45	J5
Kuching	63	(1)E2
Kudat	63	(1)F1
Kudymkar	49	K3
Kufstein	41	H3
Kūhbonān	71	G1
Kūhdasht	69	M7
Kūh-e Bül	71	E1
Kūh-e Dīnār	71	D1
Kūh-e Fürgun	71	G3
Kūh-e Hazārān	71	G2
Kūh-e Hormoz	71	F3
Kūh-e Kalat	67	G3
Kūh-e Kührān	71	H3
Kūh-e Masāhūn	71	F1
Kūh-e Safidār	71	E2
Kuh-e Sahand	69	M5
Kühestak	71	G3
Kūh-e Taftān	67	H4
Kühhā-ye Bashākerd	71	G3
Kühhā-ye Zāgros	71	D1
Kuhmo	27	Q4
Kuito	83	B2
Kukës	45	H7
Kula	45	K6
Kulandy	53	K8
Kuldīga	27	L8
Kulgera	87	F5
Kulmbach	31	G6
Külob	67	J2
Kul'sary	49	K5
Kulunda	53	P7
Kumamoto	59	F7
Kumanovo	45	J7
Kumara	55	M6
Kumasi	79	D3
Kumba	79	F4
Kumbakonam	65	C6
Kumertau	49	L4
Kumluca	47	N8
Kummerower See	31	H3
Kumo	79	G3
Kumta	65	B6
Kunene	83	A3
Kungrad	53	K9
Kungur	49	L3
Kunhing	61	B2
Kunlun Shan	65	D1
Kunming	57	C6
Kunsan	59	D6
Kuolayarvi	27	Q3
Kuopio	49	E2
Kupang	87	B2
Kuqa	53	Q9
Kura	67	C2
Kurashiki	59	G6
Kurchum	53	Q8
Kürdämir	69	N3
Kurduvadi	65	C5
Kürdzhali	47	H3
Kure	59	G6
Kuressaare	27	M7
Kurgal'dzhinskiy	53	N7
Kurgan	49	N3
Kuril Islands =		
Kuril'skiye Ostrova	55	S7
Kuril'skiye Ostrova	55	S7
Kuril Trench	51	V5
Kurmuk	75	F5
Kurnool	65	C5
Kurow	89	C7
Kuršėnai	29	M1
Kursk	49	G4
Kuršumlija	45	J6
Kuruman	83	C5
Kurume	59	F7
Kurumkan	55	J6
Kushimoto	59	H7
Kushiro	59	N2
Kuskokwim Bay	103	(1)E4
Kuskokwim Mountains	103	(1)F3
Kütahya	69	C4
K'ut'aisi	69	K2
Kutchan	59	L2
Kutina	45	D4
Kutno	29	J5
Kutu	79	H5
Kutum	75	D5
Kuujjuaq	93	T5
Kuujjuarapik	93	R5
Kuusamo	49	E1
Kuvango	83	B2
Kuwait	71	B2
Kuwait = Al Kuwayt	71	C2
Kuybyshev	53	P6
Kuygan	53	N8
Kuytun	53	R9
Kuznetsk	49	J4
Kuzomen'	49	G1
Kvaløya	27	J2
Kwale	81	F4
Kwangju	59	D6
Kwango	81	B5
Kwazulu Natal	83	E5
Kwekwe	83	D3
Kwilu	79	H5
Kyakhta	55	H6
Kyancutta	87	G6
Kyeburn	89	C7
Kyklades	47	G7
Kyle of Lochalsh	35	G4
Kyll	33	J4
Kyllini	47	D7
Kymi	47	G6
Kyōto	59	H6
Kyparissia	47	D7
Kyperissiakos Kolpos	47	C7
Kyra Panagia	47	G5
Kyrgyzstan	53	N9
Kyritz	31	H4
Kyshtovka	53	P6
Kystatyam	55	L3
Kythira	47	E8
Kythira	47	F8
Kythnos	47	G7
Kyūshū-sanchi	59	F7
Kyustendil	47	E2
Kyusyur	55	M2
Kyyiv	49	F4
Kyzyl	53	S7
Kyzylorda	49	N6
Kzyl-Dzhar	49	N5
Kzyltu	53	N7

L

Name	Page	Grid
Laascaanood	81	H2
La Bañeza	39	E2
Labé	79	B2
Labin	41	K5
Labrador	93	U6
Labrador City	93	T6
Labrador Sea	93	V4
Lábrea	109	E5
Labuha	63	(2)C3
Laç	45	G8
Lac à l'Eau Claire	93	R5
La Carolina	39	G6
Laccadive Islands	65	B6
Lac d'Annecy	41	B5
Lac de Bizerte	43	D11
Lac de Kossou	79	C3
Lac de Lagdo	79	G3
Lac de Neuchâtel	41	B4
Lac de Retenue de la		
Lufira	81	D6
Lac de St-Croix	41	B7
Lac des Bois	93	G3
Lac de Sélingue	79	C2
Lacepede Bay	87	G7
Lac Fitri	75	C5
La Charité-sur-Loire	37	J6
Lac La Biche	93	J6
Lac Léman =		
Lake Geneva	41	B4
Lac Mai-Ndombe	81	B4
Lac Minto	93	R5
Lac Nzilo	81	D6
Laconi	43	D9
Laconia	99	F2
La Crosse	99	B2
Lac St-Jean	99	F1
Lac St. Joseph	93	N6
Lac Seul	93	N6
Lac Tumba	81	B4
Lacul Brateş	45	Q4
Lacul Razim	45	R5
Lacul Sinoie	45	R5
Ladozhskoye Ozero	49	F2
Ladysmith	83	D5
Ladyzhenka	49	N4
La Esmeralda	109	D3
Læsø	27	F8
Lafayette, *Ind., U.S.*	99	C2
Lafayette, *La., U.S.*	101	C3
Lafia	79	F3
La Flèche	37	E6
Laft	71	F3
Lagan	27	G8
Lågen	27	E6
Lage's	97	D2
Laghouat	77	F2
Lagoa dos Patos	111	L5
Lagoa Mirim	111	L5
Lago de Cahora Bassa	83	E3
Lago de Maracaibo	109	C2
Lago de Nicaragua	105	G6

Name	Page	Grid
Lago de Poopó	109	D7
Lago di Bolsena	43	F6
Lago di Bracciano	43	G6
Lago di Como	41	E4
Lago di Garda	41	F5
Lago di Lecco	41	E5
Lago di Lugano	41	E5
Lago d'Iseo	41	E5
Lago di Varano	43	K7
Lago Maggiore	41	D5
Lagos, *Nigeria*	79	E3
Lagos, *Portugal*	39	B7
Lago Titicaca	109	D7
Lago Trasimeno	43	G5
La Goulette	43	E12
La Grande	97	C1
La Grange	101	E3
Laguna Madre	101	B4
Laguna Mar Chiquita	107	E7
La Habana	105	H4
Lahad Datu	61	F5
Lahat	63	(1)C3
Lahn	33	L4
Lahnstein	33	K4
Lahore	65	B2
Lahr	41	C2
Lahti	27	N6
Laï	81	B2
Lai Chau	61	C2
L'Aigle	33	C6
Laingsburg	83	C6
Lajes	111	L4
La Junta	97	F3
Lake Abbe	81	G1
Lake Abitibi	99	E1
Lake Albert	81	D3
Lake Amadeus	87	F4
Lake Athabasca	93	K5
Lake Balkhash =		
Ozero Balkhash	51	L5
Lake Bangweulu	83	E2
Lake Barlee	87	C5
Lake Benmore	89	C7
Lake Carey	87	D5
Lake Carnegie	87	D5
Lake Chad	75	B5
Lake Charles	101	C3
Lake Chelan	97	B1
Lake Chilwa	83	F3
Lake City	101	E3
Lake Constance	41	E3
Lake Diefenbaker	93	K6
Lake Disappointment	87	D4
Lake District	35	J7
Lake Dojran	47	E3
Lake Edward	81	D4
Lake Erie	99	D2
Lake Eyasi	81	E4
Lake Eyre	85	D8
Lake Eyre Basin	87	G5
Lake Eyre North	87	G5
Lake Eyre South	87	G5
Lake Francis Case	97	G2
Lake Frome	87	H6
Lake Gairdner	87	G6
Lake Geneva	41	B4
Lake Grace	87	C6
Lake Harbour	93	T4
Lake Hudson	101	B2
Lake Huron	99	D1
Lake Kariba	83	D3
Lake Kivu	81	D4
Lake Kyoga	81	E3
Lake Ladoga =		
Ladozhskoye Ozero	49	F2
Lakeland	101	E4
Lake Macdonald	87	E4
Lake Mackay	87	E4
Lake Macleod	87	B4
Lake Manapouri	89	A7
Lake Manitoba	93	M6
Lake Mead	97	D3
Lake Melville	93	U6
Lake Michigan	99	C2
Lake Murray	63	(2)F4
Lake Mweru	81	D5
Lake Nasser	75	F3
Lake Natron	81	F4
Lake Nipigon	93	P6/7
Lake Nipissing	99	E1
Lake Nyasa	83	E2
Lake Oahe	97	F2
Lake of the Woods	99	B1
Lake Ohrid	47	C4
Lake Okeechobee	101	E4
Lake Onega =		
Onezhskoye Ozero	25	H1
Lake Ontario	99	E2
Lake Peipus	27	P7
Lake Placid	101	E4
Lake Powell	97	D3
Lake Prespa	47	D4
Lake Pskov	27	P7
Lake Rotorua	89	F4
Lake Rukwa	81	E5
Lake Sakakawea	97	F1
Lake Scutari	45	G7
Lake Simcoe	99	E2
Lake Superior	99	C1
Lake Tahoe	97	B3
Lake Tanganyika	81	D5
Lake Taupo	89	E4
Lake Te Anau	89	A7
Lake Tekapo	89	C6
Lake Tekapo	89	C6
Lake Texoma	101	B3
Lake Torrens	87	G6
Lake Turkana	81	F3
Lake Victoria	81	E4
Lakeview	97	B2
Lake Volta	79	D3
Lake Waikaremoana	89	F4
Lake Wakatipu	89	B7
Lake Wanaka	89	B7
Lake Winnipeg	93	M6
Lake Winnipegosis	93	L6
Lakewood	97	E3
Lake Xau	83	C4
Lakhdaria	39	P8
Lakin	101	A2
Lakonikos Kolpos	47	E8
Lakota	97	G1
Lalín	39	B2
La Línea	39	E8
Lalitpur	65	C4
La Loche	93	K5
La Louvière	33	G4
La Maddalena	43	D7
Lamar	103	F1
Lamard	71	E3
Lambaréné	79	G5
Lamesa	103	F2
Lamia	47	E6
Lamone	41	G6
Lampang	61	B3
Lampasas	103	G2
Lampedusa	43	H1
Lamu	81	G4
Lanai	103	(2)D3
Lancang	61	B2
Lancaster, *U.K.*	35	K7
Lancaster, *Mo., U.S.*	99	B2
Lancaster, *Pa., U.S.*	99	E2
Lancaster Sound	93	Q2
Lanciano	43	J6
Landau, *Germany*	33	L5
Landau, *Germany*	41	H2
Landeck	41	F3
Lander	97	E2
Landerneau	37	A5
Land's End	35	F11
Landshut	41	H2
Landskrona	29	B2
Langarüd	69	N5
Langdon	97	G1
Langeland	31	F2
Langenhagen	31	E4
Langeoog	31	C3
Langjökull	27	(1)C2
Langkawi	61	B5
Langon	37	E9
Langøya	27	H2
Langreo	39	E1
Langres	41	A3
Langsa	61	B6
Langtry	103	F3
Länkäran	69	N4
Lannion	37	B5
Lansing	99	D2
Lanya	81	E2
Lanzarote	77	C3
Lanzhou	57	C3
Laoag	61	G3
Lao Cai	61	C2
Laon	33	F5
Laos	61	C3
La Palma	105	J7
La Palma	77	B3
La Paragua	109	E2
La Paz, *Bolivia*	109	D7
La Paz, *Mexico*	105	B4
La Pedrera	109	D4
La Pérouse Strait	57	L1
La Pesca	101	B5
La Pine	97	B2
La Plant	97	F1
La Plata	111	K5
Lappajärvi	27	M5
Lappeenranta	27	Q6
Lappland	27	M2
Laptev Sea =		
More Laptevykh	55	L1
Lapua	27	M5
Łapy	29	M5
La Quiaca	111	H3
L'Aquila	43	H6
Lār	71	F3
Larache	77	D1
Laramie	97	E2
Larantuka	63	(2)B4
Larat	63	(2)D4
Larba	39	P8
Laredo, *Spain*	39	G1
Laredo, *U.S.*	103	G3
Largo	101	E4
L'Ariana	43	E12
La Rioja	111	H4
Larisa	47	E5
Larkana	67	J4
Larnaka	70	A2
Larne	35	G7
La Rochelle	37	D7
La Roche-sur-Yon	37	D7
La Roda	39	H5
La Romana	105	L5
La Ronge	93	K5
La Sarre	99	E1
Las Cruces	103	E2
La Serena	111	G4
La Seu d'Urgell	39	M2
La Seyne-sur-Mer	37	L10
Lashio	61	B2

Name	Pg.	Grid
Lashkar Gāh	67	H3
Las Lomitas	111	J3
Las Palmas	77	B3
La Spezia	41	E6
Last Chance	97	F3
Lastovo	45	D7
Las Vegas, Nev., U.S.	97	C3
Las Vegas, N. Mex., U.S.	103	E1
La Teste	37	D9
Latina	43	G7
La Tuque	99	F1
Latur	65	C5
Latvia	27	M8
Lauenburg	31	F3
Lauf	31	G7
Lau Group	85	J7
Launceston, Australia	87	J8
Launceston, U.K.	35	H11
La Union	39	K7
Laupheim	41	E2
Laura	87	H3
Laurel	101	D3
Lauria	43	K8
Lausanne	41	B4
Laut, Indonesia	63	(1)F3
Laut, Malaysia	63	(1)D2
Lauterbach	31	E6
Lava	29	L3
Laval, Canada	99	F1
Laval, France	37	E5
La Vall d'Uixo	39	K5
Lavant	41	K4
Lavrio	47	G7
Lawdar	75	J5
Lawrence	89	B7
Lawton	101	B3
Laya	49	L1
Laylā	75	J3
Layton	97	D2
Lazarev	55	Q6
Lázaro Cárdenas	105	D5
Leavenworth	97	B1
Lebach	33	J5
Lebanon	70	C3
Lębork	29	G3
Lebrija	39	D8
Lecce	43	N8
Lecco	41	E5
Leck	31	D2
Le Creusot	37	K7
Łęczyca	29	J5
Leeds	35	L8
Leer	31	K1
Leesburg	101	E4
Leeston	89	D6
Leesville	101	C3
Leeuwarden	33	H1
Leeward Islands	105	M5
Lefkada	47	C6
Lefkada	47	C6
Lefkosia	47	R9
Legaspi	61	G4
Legionowo	29	K5
Legnago	41	G5
Legnica	29	F6
Leh	65	C2
Le Havre	33	C5
Leiah	65	B2
Leibnitz	41	K4
Leicester	33	A2
Leiden	33	G2
Leie	33	F4
Leine	31	E4
Leipzig	31	H5
Leiyang	57	E5
Lek	33	G3
Lelystad	33	H2
Le Mans	37	F6
Lemberg	31	D8
Lemesos	47	Q10
Lemmer	33	H2
Lemmon	97	F1
Lena	39	E1
Lena	55	L4
Leninsk-Kuznetskiy	53	R7
Lenmalu	63	(2)D3
Lenne	33	K3
Lennestadt	33	L3
Lens	33	E4
Lensk	55	K4
Lenti	41	M4
Lentini	43	J11
Léo	79	D2
Leoben	41	L3
León, Mexico	105	D4
León, Nicaragua	105	G6
León, Spain	39	E2
Leonberg	41	E2
Leonora	87	D5
Lepsy	53	P8
Le Puy	37	J8
Léré	79	G3
Leros	47	J7
Lerwick	35	L1
Lesbos = Lesvos	47	H5
Leshan	57	C5
Leshukonskoye	49	J2
Leskovac	45	J7
Lesosibirsk	53	S6
Lesotho	83	D5
Les Sables-d'Olonne	37	D7
Les Sept Îles	37	B5
Lesser Antilles	105	L6
Lesser Slave Lake	93	J5
Lesvos	47	H5
Leszno	29	F6
Lethbridge	97	D1
Lethem	109	F3
Leticia	109	D4
Letterkenny	35	E7
Leutkirch	41	F3
Leuven	33	G4
Levanzo	43	G10
Levashi	69	M2
Leverkusen	33	J3
Levice	29	H9
Levin	89	E5
Lévis	99	F1
Levski	45	N6
Lewis	35	F3
Lewis and Clark Lake	97	G2
Lewiston, Id., U.S.	97	C1
Lewiston, Me., U.S.	99	F2
Lewistown, Mont., U.S.	97	E1
Lewistown, Pa., U.S.	99	E2
Lexington, Ky., U.S.	99	D3
Lexington, Nebr., U.S.	97	G2
Leyte	61	G4
Lezhë	45	G8
Lhasa	65	F3
Lhazà	65	E3
Lhokseumawe	61	B5
Lian Xian	61	E2
Liaocheng	57	F3
Liao He	59	B3
Liaoyang	59	B3
Liaoyuan	59	C2
Liard River	93	F5
Libenge	81	B3
Liberal	101	A2
Liberec	29	E7
Liberia	79	B3
Libjo	61	H4
Libourne	37	E9
Libreville	79	F4
Libya	75	C2
Libyan Desert	75	D2
Libyan Plateau	75	E1
Licata	43	H11
Lich	31	D6
Lichinga	83	F2
Lichtenfels	31	G6
Lida	27	N10
Lido di Ostia	43	G7
Lidzbark Warmiński	29	K3
Liechtenstein	41	E3
Liège	33	H4
Lienz	41	H4
Liepāja	29	L1
Liezen	41	K3
Ligurian Sea	41	D7
Lihue	103	B2
Lijiang	61	C1
Likasi	81	D6
Lille	33	F4
Lillehammer	27	F6
Lilongwe	83	E2
Liloy	61	G5
Lima, Peru	109	B6
Lima, Mont., U.S.	97	D2
Lima, Oh., U.S.	99	D2
Limassol = Lemesos	47	Q10
Limerick	35	D9
Limni Trichonida	47	D6
Limni Vegoritis	47	D4
Limni Volvi	47	F4
Limnos	47	H5
Limoges	37	G8
Limon	97	F3
Limón	105	H7
Limoux	37	H10
Limpopo	83	D4
Linares, Chile	111	G6
Linares, Mexico	103	G4
Linares, Spain	39	G6
Lincang	61	C2
Linchuan	57	F5
Lincoln, U.K.	33	B1
Lincoln, U.S.	97	G2
Lindesnes	27	D8
Lindi	81	F6
Lindi	81	D3
Lindos	47	L8
Line Islands	85	L5
Linfen	57	E3
Lingen	33	K2
Lingga	63	(1)C3
Linguère	79	A1
Linhal	57	G5
Linhares	109	J7
Linhe	57	D2
Linjiang	59	D3
Linköping	27	H7
Linkou	59	F1
Linosa	43	G13
Lins	111	M3
Linton	97	F1
Linxia	57	C3
Linyi	57	F3
Linz	41	K2
Lipari	43	J10
Lipari	43	J10
Lipetsk	49	G4
Lipno	29	J5
Lippe	33	L3
Lippstadt	33	L3
Liqeni i Fierzës	45	H7
Lira	81	E3
Lisala	81	C3
Lisboa	39	A6
Lisbon = Lisboa	39	A6

Name	Page	Grid
Lisburn	35	G7
Lisieux	33	C5
Liski	49	G4
Litang	57	C5
Litani	109	G3
Litchfield	99	B1
Lithgow	87	K6
Lithuania	27	L9
Little Abaco	101	F4
Little Andaman	65	F6
Little Barrier Island	89	E3
Little Current	99	D1
Little Falls	99	B1
Little Karoo	83	C6
Little Minch	35	E4
Little Nicobar	65	F7
Little Ouse	33	C2
Little Rock	101	C3
Litvinov	31	J6
Liupanshui	57	C5
Liuzhou	57	D6
Liverpool	35	K8
Livingston	97	D1
Livingstone	83	D3
Livno	45	E6
Livorno	41	F7
Liwale	81	F5
Lizard Point	35	G12
Ljubljana	41	K4
Ljusdal	27	C2
Llanos	109	C2
Lleida	39	L3
Llucmajor	39	N5
Loano	41	D6
Lobatse	83	D5
Lobito	83	A2
Locarno	41	D4
Lochinver	35	G3
Loch Lomond	35	H5
Loch Ness	35	H4
Lockhart	101	B4
Locri	43	L10
Lodève	37	J10
Lodi	41	E5
Lodja	81	C4
Lodwar	81	F3
Łódź	29	J6
Loei	61	C3
Lofoten	27	G3
Logan, Ia., U.S.	99	A2
Logan, N. Mex., U.S.	103	F1
Logan, Ut., U.S.	97	D2
Logansport	99	C2
Logroño	39	H2
Loikaw	61	C3
Loir	37	F6
Loire	37	D6
Loja, Ecuador	109	B4
Loja, Spain	39	F7
Lokan tekojärvi	27	P3
Lokoja	79	F3
Lolland	31	G2
Lollondo	81	F4
Lom	45	L6
Lomami	81	C4
Lomas de Zamora	111	K5
Lomblen	63	(2)B4
Lombok	63	(1)F4
Lomé	79	E3
Lomela	81	C4
Lomela	81	C4
Lommel	33	H3
Lomonosovka	49	N4
Lompoc	103	B2
Łomża	29	M4
London, Canada	99	D2
London, U.K.	33	B3
London, U.S.	101	E2
Londonderry	35	E6
Londrina	111	L3
Long Bay	105	J2
Long Beach	103	C2
Longford	35	E8
Long Island	99	F2
Longmont	97	E2
Long Prairie	99	B1
Longview, Tex., U.S.	101	C3
Longview, Wash., U.S.	97	B1
Longwy	33	H5
Long Xuyên	61	D4
Longyan	61	F1
Löningen	33	K2
Lons-le-Saunier	41	A4
Lookout Pass	97	C1
Loop Head	35	B9
Lopez	61	G4
Lop Nur	53	S9
Lopphavet	27	L1
Loptyuga	49	J2
Lora del Rio	39	E7
Lorain	99	D2
Loralai	65	A2
Lorca	39	J7
Lord Howe Island	87	L6
Lordsburg	103	E2
Loreto	105	B3
Lorient	37	B6
Lörrach	41	C3
Lorraine	87	G3
Los Alamos	103	E1
Los Angeles, Chile	111	G6
Los Angeles, U.S.	103	C2
Losheim	33	J5
Lošinj	41	K6
Los Mochis	105	C3
Los Teques	109	D1
Lost Trail Pass	97	D1
Lotte	33	K2
Louang Namtha	61	C2
Louangphrabang	61	C3
Loubomo	79	G5
Loudéac	37	C5
Louga	79	A1
Loughborough	33	A2
Lough Corrib	35	C8
Lough Derg	35	D8
Lough Foyle	35	E6
Lough Mask	35	C8
Lough Neagh	35	F7
Lough Ree	35	E8
Louisiade Archipelago	87	K2
Louisiana	101	C3
Louis Trichardt	83	D4
Louisville, Ga., U.S.	101	E3
Louisville, Ky., U.S.	101	D2
Louisville, Miss., U.S.	101	D3
Loukhi	27	S3
Lourdes	37	E10
Louth	87	J6
Louviers	33	D5
Lovech	45	M6
Lovell	97	E2
Lovelock	97	C2
Lovosice	31	K6
Lowa	81	D4
Lowell	99	F2
Lower Hutt	89	E5
Lower Lough Erne	35	E7
Lowestoft	33	D2
Loyalty Islands	85	G8
Loyno	49	K3
Loznica	45	G5
Lu'an	57	F4
Luanda	81	A5
Luangwa	83	E3
Luangwa	83	E2
Luarca	39	D1
Luau	83	C2
Lubango	83	A2
Lubao	81	D5
Lübben	31	J5
Lubbock	103	F2
Lübeck	31	F3
Lubilash	81	C5
Lubin	29	F6
Lublin	29	M6
Lubliniec	29	H7
Luboń	29	F5
Lubudi	81	D5
Lubuklinggau	63	(1)C3
Lubumbashi	81	D6
Lubutu	81	D4
Lucala	81	B5
Lucca	41	F7
Lucena, Philippines	61	G4
Lucena, Spain	39	F7
Lucero	103	E2
Lucira	83	A2
Luckenwalde	31	J4
Lucknow	65	D3
Lucusse	83	C2
Lüdenscheid	33	K3
Lüderitz	83	B5
Ludhiana	65	C2
Ludington	99	C2
Ludlow	103	C2
Ludogori	45	P6
Luduş	45	M3
Ludvika	27	H6
Ludwigsburg	41	E2
Ludwigshafen	33	L5
Ludwigslust	31	G3
Ludza	27	P8
Luebo	81	C5
Luena	83	B2
Lufeng	61	F2
Lufira	81	D6
Lufkin	101	C3
Luga	49	E3
Lugano	41	D4
Lugenda	83	F2
Lugo	41	G6
Lugoj	45	J4
Lugovoy	53	N9
Luhans'k	49	G5
Luilaka	81	B4
Luino	41	D4
Łuków	29	M6
Lukulu	83	C2
Lukuni	81	B5
Luleå	27	M4
Lüleburgaz	47	K3
Lulua	81	D5
Lumbala Kaquengue	83	C2
Lumberton	101	F3
Lumbrales	39	D4
Lumsden	89	B7
Lund	29	C2
Lundazi	83	E2
Lüneburg	31	F3
Lüneburger Heide	31	F4
Lünen	33	K3
Lunéville	41	B2
Lungau	41	J3
Luntai	53	Q9
Luohe	57	E4
Luoyang	57	E4
Luremo	81	B5
Lurio	83	F2
Lusaka	83	D3
Lusambo	81	C5
Lushui	57	B5

Lüshun 57 G3
Lutherstadt Wittenberg . . 31 H5
Luton 33 B3
Luts'k 49 E4
Luverne 99 A2
Luvua 81 D5
Luwuk . . . . 63 (2)B3
Luxembourg [A] 33 H5
Luxembourg 33 J5
Luxeuil-les-Bains 41 B3
Luxor 75 F2
Luza 49 J2
Luzern 41 D3
Luzhou 57 D5
Luznice 41 K1
Luzon 61 G3
Luzon Strait 61 G2
L'viv 29 N8
Lyapin 49 M2
Lynchburg 99 E3
Lynn Lake 93 L5
Lyon 37 K8
Lys 33 E4
Lys'va 49 L3
Lysychans'k 49 G5
Lyttelton 89 D6

M

Ma'ān 70 C6
Maastricht 33 H4
Mabalane 83 E4
Mabanza-Ngungu 79 G6
Mablethorpe 33 C1
Macapá 109 G3
Macas 109 B4
Macau, Brazil 109 K5
Macau, China 61 E2
Macdonnell Ranges 87 F4
Macedonia [A] 47 C3
Maceió 109 K5
Macerata 41 J7
Machakos 81 F4
Machala 109 B4
Macheng 57 F4
Machilipatnam 65 D5
Machiques 109 C1
Mack 103 E1
Mackay 87 J4
Mackay Lake 93 J4
Mackenzie 93 G4
Mackenzie Bay 93 D3
Mackenzie Mountains . . 93 E3
Mackinaw City 99 D1
Macmillan Pass 93 F4
Macomer 43 C8
Macon, Ga., U.S. 101 E3

Macon, Mo., U.S. 101 C2
Mâcon 37 K7
Mādabā 70 C5
Madagascar [A] 83 H3
Madaoua 79 F2
Madeira 109 E5
Madeira 77 B2
Madikeri 65 C6
Madison 99 C2
Madison, Minn., U.S. . . . 99 A1
Madison, S.D., U.S. 97 G2
Madiun . . . . 63 (1)E4
Mado Gashi 81 F3
Madoi 57 B4
Madona 27 P8
Madras = Chennai 65 D6
Madre de Dios 109 C6
Madrid 39 G4
Madura . . . . 63 (1)E4
Madurai 65 C6
Maebashi 59 K5
Mae Hong Son 61 B3
Mae Sariang 61 B3
Maevatanana 83 H3
Mafeteng 83 D5
Mafia Island 81 G5
Mafraq 70 D4
Magadan 55 S5
Magadi 81 F4
Magdagachi 55 M6
Magdalena 109 C2
Magdalena, Bolivia 109 E6
Magdalena, Mexico 103 D2
Magdalena, U.S. 103 E2
Magdeburg 31 G4
Magelang . . . . 63 (1)E4
Magerøya 27 N1
Magnitogorsk 49 L4
Magu 81 E4
Magwe 61 A2
Mahābād 69 L5
Mahajanga 83 H3
Mahanoro 83 H3
Mahasamund 65 D4
Mahbubnagar 65 D5
Mahé Island . . . . 83 (2)C1
Mahenge 81 F5
Mahesāna 65 B4
Mahia Peninsula 89 F4
Mahilyow 49 F4
Mahnomen 99 A1
Mahón 39 Q5
Mahuva 67 K5
Maicao 109 C1
Maidstone 33 C3
Maiduguri 79 G2
Mai Gudo 81 F2
Maímédy 31 B6

Main 31 E7
Mainburg 41 G2
Main-Donau-Kanal 31 G7
Maine 99 G1
Maïné Soroa 79 G2
Maingkwan 61 B1
Mainland,
  Orkney Is., U.K. 35 J2
Mainland,
  Shetland Is., U.K. 35 L1
Maintirano 83 G3
Mainz 31 D6
Maio . . . . 79 (1)B1
Majene . . . . 63 (2)A3
Majuro 85 H5
Makamba 81 D4
Makarora 89 B7
Makarov 55 Q7
Makarska 45 E6
Makat 49 K5
Makgadikgadi 83 C4
Makhachkala 69 M2
Makindu 81 F4
Makinsk 49 P4
Makiyivka 49 G5
Makkah 75 G3
Makó 45 H3
Makokou 79 G4
Makorako 89 F4
Makoua 79 H4
Makran 67 G4
Mākū 69 L4
Makumbako 81 E5
Makurazaki 59 F8
Makurdi 79 F3
Makūyeh 71 E2
Malabar Coast 65 B6
Malabo 79 F4
Malack 29 F9
Malad City 97 D2
Maladzyechna 49 E4
Málaga 39 F8
Malaita 85 G6
Malakal 81 E2
Malamala . . . . 63 (2)B3
Malang . . . . 63 (1)E4
Malanje 81 B5
Malanville 79 E2
Malaryta 29 P6
Malatya 69 H4
Malawi [A] 83 E2
Malaya Vishera 49 F3
Malaybalay 61 H5
Malay Peninsula 61 C6
Malaysia [A] . . . . 63 (1)C2
Malbork 29 J3
Maldives [A] 65 B8

Male 65 B8
Male Atoll 65 B8
Mali [A] 77 E5
Malindi 81 G4
Malin Head 35 E6
Malkara 47 J4
Mallaig 35 G4
Mallawi 75 F2
Mallorca 39 P5
Malmédy 33 J4
Malmö 29 C2
Maløy 27 C6
Malozemel'skaya Tundra . 49 K1
Malta [A] 43 J13
Malta 97 E1
Malta Channel 43 J12
Maltahöhe 83 B4
Malvern 99 B4
Malý Dunaj 41 N2
Mama 55 J5
Mambasa 81 D3
Mamburao 61 G4
Mamonovo 29 J3
Mamoré 109 D6
Mamou 79 B2
Mamoudzou 83 H2
Mamuju . . . . 63 (2)A3
Ma'mūl 67 G6
Mamuno 83 C4
Man 79 C3
Manacapuru 109 E4
Manacor 39 P5
Manado . . . . 63 (2)B2
Managua 105 G6
Manali 65 C2
Mananara Avaratra 83 H3
Mananjary 83 H4
Manaus 109 E4
Manavgat 47 P8
Manbij 69 G5
Manchester, U.K. 35 K8
Manchester, Ky., U.S. . . . 99 D3
Manchester, Vt., U.S. . . . 99 F2
Mand 67 H4
Mandalay 61 B2
Mandalgovĭ 57 D1
Mandan 97 F1
Mandera 81 G3
Manding 77 D6
Mandla 65 D4
Mandsaur 65 C4
Mandurah 87 C6
Manduria 43 M8
Mandvi 65 A4
Mandya 65 C6
Manfredonia 43 K7
Manga 79 G2
Mangalia 45 R6

Name	Page	Grid
Mangalore	65	B6
Mangaweka	89	F4
Mangnai	53	S10
Mangoky	83	G4
Mangole	63	(2)C3
Mangonui	89	D2
Manhattan	101	B2
Manhuaçu	109	J8
Mania	83	H3
Manicoré	109	E5
Maniitsoq	93	W3
Manila	61	G4
Manisa	47	K6
Manitoba	93	M6
Manitoulin Island	99	D1
Manitowoc	99	C2
Maniwaki	99	E1
Manizales	109	B2
Manja	83	G4
Mankato	99	B2
Manlleu	39	N3
Manna	63	(1)C3
Mannheim	33	L5
Manokwari	63	(2)D3
Manono	81	D5
Manosque	37	L10
Manp'o	59	D3
Manresa	39	M3
Mansa	83	D2
Mansel Island	93	Q4
Mansfield, U.K.	33	A1
Mansfield, U.S.	99	D2
Manta	109	A4
Mantes-la-Jolie	33	D5
Mantova	41	F5
Manturovo	49	H3
Manú	109	C6
Manüjän	71	G3
Manukau	89	E3
Manukau Harbour	89	E3
Manyinga	83	C2
Manyoni	81	E5
Manzanares	39	G5
Manzanillo	105	J4
Manzhouli	55	K7
Mao	75	C5
Maoming	61	E2
Mapi	63	(2)E4
Mapinhane	83	F4
Maple Creek	95	E2
Mapuera	109	E4
Maputo	83	E5
Maquela do Zombo	81	B5
Maquinchao	111	H7
Maraba	109	H5
Maracaibo	109	C1
Maracay	109	D1
Maradi	79	F2
Marägheh	69	M5
Marand	69	L4
Maranhão	109	H5
Marañón	109	B4
Mărăşeşti	45	Q4
Marathon, Canada	99	C1
Marathon, U.S.	103	F2
Marbella	39	F8
Marche	33	H4
Marchena	39	E7
Mardan	65	B2
Mar del Plata	111	K6
Mardin	69	J5
Mareeba	87	J3
Marettimo	43	F11
Margate	33	D3
Marghita	45	K2
Marianas Trench	85	E4
Marianna	101	D3
Máriánská Lázně	31	H7
Mariazell	41	L3
Mar'ib	75	J4
Maribor	41	L4
Maridi	81	D2
Marie Byrd Land	112	(2)FF2
Mariehamn	27	K6
Marienberg	31	J6
Mariental	83	B4
Marietta	101	B3
Mariinsk	53	R6
Marijampolė	29	N3
Marília	111	M3
Marín	39	B2
Marinette	99	C1
Maringá	111	L3
Marion, Ill., U.S.	99	C3
Marion, Ind., U.S.	99	C2
Marion, Oh., U.S.	99	D2
Maritime Alps	41	C6
Mariupol'	49	G5
Marīvān	69	M6
Mariy El	49	J3
Marjayoûn	70	C3
Marka	81	G3
Markam	57	B5
Markaryd	29	C1
Markermeer	33	H2
Markham	99	E2
Markit	53	P10
Markkleeberg	31	H5
Markovo	55	W4
Marktredwitz	31	H7
Marla	87	F5
Marmande	37	F9
Marmara Adası	47	K4
Marmara Denizi	47	L4
Marmaris	47	L8
Marmolada	41	G4
Marne	33	F5
Maroansetra	83	H3
Marolambo	83	H4
Maroni	109	G3
Maroua	79	G2
Marquesas Islands	85	M6
Marquette	99	C1
Marrakech	77	D2
Marree	87	G5
Marrupa	83	F2
Marsa Alam	75	F2
Marsabit	81	F3
Marsala	43	G11
Marsberg	33	L3
Marsden	87	J6
Marseille	37	L10
Marshall, Ill., U.S.	101	D2
Marshall, Tex., U.S.	101	C3
Marshall Islands	85	G4
Marshalltown	99	B2
Marsh Harbour	101	F4
Marsh Island	101	D3
Martapura	63	(1)E3
Martigny	41	C4
Martigues	37	L10
Martin	29	H8
Martina Franca	43	M8
Martinique	105	M6
Marton	89	E5
Martos	39	G7
Mary	67	H2
Maryborough	87	K5
Maryland	99	E3
Marysville	101	B2
Maryville	99	B2
Masai Steppe	81	F4
Masaka	81	E4
Masalembu Besar	63	(1)E4
Masallı	69	N4
Masan	59	E6
Masasi	81	F6
Masbate	61	G4
Masbate	61	G4
Maseru	83	D5
Mashhad	67	G2
Masindi	81	E3
Maşīrah	67	G5
Maskanah	69	H5
Mason	101	B3
Mason City	99	B2
Masqaṭ	71	H5
Massa	41	F6
Massachusetts	99	F2
Massachusetts Bay	99	G2
Massafra	43	M8
Massawa	75	G4
Massena	99	F2
Masset	93	E6
Massif Central	37	H8
Massif de l'Aïr	77	G5
Massif des Écrins	41	B5
Massif du Tsaratanana	83	H2
Massif Ennedi	75	D4
Massinga	83	F4
Masteksay	49	K5
Masterton	89	E5
Mastung	67	J4
Masvingo	83	E4
Maşyāf	70	D1
Matadi	81	A5
Matagami	99	E1
Matagorda Island	101	B4
Matam	79	B1
Matamoros	103	G3
Matane	99	G1
Matanzas	95	K7
Matara	65	D7
Mataram	63	(1)F4
Mataranka	87	F3
Mataró	39	N3
Matawai	89	F4
Matehuala	103	F4
Matera	43	L8
Mátészalka	45	K2
Mateur	43	D11
Matheson	99	D1
Mathura	65	C3
Mati	61	H5
Matlock	33	A1
Mato Grosso	109	F6
Mato Grosso	109	F6
Mato Grosso do Sul	109	F7
Matosinhos	39	B3
Matrûh	75	E1
Matsu	57	G5
Matsue	59	G6
Matsumae	59	L3
Matsumoto	59	J5
Matsusaka	59	J6
Matsuyama	59	G7
Matterhorn	41	C5
Maturín	109	E2
Maubeuge	33	F4
Maui	103	(2)F3
Maun	83	C3
Maun	41	K6
Mauna Kea	103	(2)F4
Mauna Loa	103	(2)F4
Mauritania	77	C5
Mauritius	83	(1)B2
Mauron	37	C5
Mauthen	41	H4
Mawlaik	65	A2
Maya	63	(1)D3
Mayaguana	105	K4
Maydh	81	H1

Name	Page	Grid
Mayenne	37	E5
Maykop	69	J1
Mayor Island	89	F3
Mayotte	83	H2
Mayskiy	55	M6
Mayya	55	N4
Mazagão	109	G4
Mazagran	37	K4
Mazama	97	B1
Mazamet	37	H10
Mazara del Vallo	43	G11
Mazār-e Sharīf	67	J2
Mazatlán	105	C4
Mažeikiai	29	M1
Mazomora	81	F5
Mazyr	49	E4
Mazzarino	43	J11
Mbabane	83	E5
Mbala	81	E5
Mbale	81	E3
Mbalmayo	79	G4
Mbandaka	81	B3
M'banza Congo	81	A5
Mbarara	81	E4
Mbeya	81	E5
Mbomou	81	C3
Mbour	79	A2
Mbuji-Mayi	81	C5
McAlester	101	B3
McBride	93	G6
McCammon	97	D2
McClintock	93	N5
McClintock Channel	93	L2
McComb	101	C3
McCook	97	F2
McDermitt	97	C2
McGehee	101	C3
McGrath	103	(1)F3
McLaughlin	97	F1
McLennan	93	H5
McPherson	101	B2
Meadow Lake	93	K6
Meadville	99	D2
Meaux	33	E6
Mecca = Makkah	75	G3
Mechelen	33	G3
Mecklenburger Bucht	31	G2
Mecula	83	F2
Medak	65	C5
Medan	63	(1)B2
Médéa	39	N8
Medellín	109	B2
Medenine	77	H2
Medford	97	B2
Medgidia	45	R5
Mediaş	45	M3
Medicine Bow	97	E2
Medicine Hat	93	J7
Medicine Lodge	101	B2
Medina = Al Madīnah	75	G3
Medinaceli	39	H3
Medina de Campo	39	F3
Medina Sidonia	39	E8
Mediterranean Sea	25	E4
Mednogorsk	49	L4
Medvezh'vyegorsk	49	F2
Meeker	97	E2
Meerut	65	C3
Megara	47	F6
Megisti	47	M8
Mehrān	69	M7
Meiktila	61	B2
Meiningen	31	F6
Meizhou	61	F2
Mejez El Bab	43	D12
Mékambo	79	G4
Mek'elē	75	G5
Meknès	77	D2
Mekong	61	D4
Melaka	63	(1)C2
Melanesia	85	F5
Melbourne, Australia	87	H7
Melbourne, U.S.	101	E4
Melchor de Mencos	105	G5
Mélfi	75	C5
Melfi	43	K8
Melilla	39	H9
Melita	97	F1
Melitopol'	49	G5
Melk	41	L2
Melkosopochnik	53	N8
Mělník	31	K6
Melo	111	L5
Melton Mowbray	33	B2
Melun	37	H5
Melut	75	F5
Melville Island, Australia	87	F2
Melville Island, Canada	91	N2
Melville Peninsula	93	P3
Memboro	63	(2)A4
Memmingen	41	F3
Mempawah	63	(1)D2
Memphis	99	C3
Mena	101	C3
Ménaka	77	F5
Mendawai	63	(1)E3
Mende	37	J9
Mendoza	111	H5
Menemen	47	K6
Menen	33	F4
Menggala	63	(1)D3
Menominee	99	C1
Menongue	83	B2
Menorca	39	Q4
Mentok	63	(1)D3
Menyuan	57	C3
Menzel Bourguiba	43	D11
Menzel Temime	43	E12
Meppel	33	J2
Meppen	33	K2
Merano	41	G4
Merauke	63	(2)F4
Mercato Saraceno	41	H7
Merced	97	B3
Mercedes, Argentina	111	H5
Mercedes, Argentina	111	K4
Mercedes, U.S.	101	B4
Mercedes, Uruguay	111	K5
Mercury Islands	89	E3
Mergenevo	49	K5
Mergui	61	B4
Mergui Archipelago	61	B4
Mérida, Mexico	105	G4
Mérida, Spain	39	D6
Mérida, Venezuela	105	K7
Meridian	101	D3
Merinha Grande	39	B5
Meriruma	109	G3
Meriş	47	J3
Merowe	75	F4
Merredin	87	C6
Merriman	97	F2
Mers el Kébir	39	K9
Mersey	35	J8
Mersin = İcel	47	S8
Merthyr Tydfil	35	J10
Meru	81	F3
Merzifon	69	F3
Mesa	103	D2
Mesa de Yambi	109	C3
Mesagne	43	M8
Mesōaria Plain	70	A1
Mesolongi	47	D6
Mesopotamia	69	K6
Messina, Italy	43	K10
Messina, South Africa	83	D4
Messini	47	E7
Messiniakos Kolpos	47	D8
Mestre	41	H5
Meta	109	C2
Metairie	101	C4
Metán	111	J4
Metangula	83	E2
Meteor Depth	107	J9
Metković	45	E6
Metsovo	47	D5
Mettlach	33	J5
Metz	33	J5
Metzingen	41	E2
Meulaboh	61	B6
Meuse	33	G4
Mexicali	103	C2
Mexican Hat	103	E1
Mexico	105	D4
Meymaneh	67	H2
Mezdra	45	L6
Mezen'	49	H1
Mezenskaya Guba	49	H1
Mezőkövesd	45	H2
Mezőtúr	45	H2
Miami	101	E4
Miandowāb	69	M5
Miandrivazo	83	H3
Mīāneh	69	M5
Mianwali	65	B2
Mianyang	57	C4
Miass	49	M4
Michalovce	29	L9
Michigan	99	C1
Michipicoten Island	99	C1
Michurinsk	49	H4
Micronesia	85	F4
Mid-Atlantic Ridge	107	G1
Middelburg, Netherlands	33	F3
Middelburg, South Africa	83	D6
Middelkerke	33	E3
Middle Andaman	61	A4
Middlesboro	99	D3
Middlesbrough	35	L7
Middletown	99	F2
Midland, Canada	99	E2
Midland, Mich., U.S.	99	D2
Midland, Tex., U.S.	103	F2
Midway Islands	85	J3
Midwest City	101	B2
Midzor	45	K6
Miechów	29	K7
Mielec	29	L7
Miercurea-Ciuc	45	N3
Mieres	39	E1
Miesbach	41	G3
Mī'ēso	81	G2
Miging	65	F3
Mikhaylovka	49	H4
Mikhaylovskiy	53	P7
Mikkeli	27	P6
Mikuni-sammyaku	59	K5
Miladhunmadulu Atoll	65	B7
Milan = Milano, Italy	41	E5
Milan, U.S.	101	D2
Milano	41	E5
Milas	47	K7
Milazzo	43	K10
Miles	87	K5
Miles City	97	E1
Milford, Del., U.S.	99	E3
Milford, Ut., U.S.	97	D3
Milford Sound	89	A7
Miliana	39	N8
Millau	37	J9
Millbank	97	G1
Millerovo	49	H5

Name	Page	Grid
Miloro	81	E5
Milos	47	G8
Milton	89	B8
Milton Keynes	33	B2
Milwaukee	99	C2
Mimizan-Plage	37	D9
Mīnāb	71	G3
Minas Gerais	109	H7
Minas Novas	109	J7
Minatitlán	105	F5
Mindanao	61	G5
Mindelheim	41	F2
Mindelo	79	(1)B1
Minden	33	L2
Mindoro	61	G4
Mindoro Strait	61	G4
Mineola	101	B3
Minfeng	53	Q10
Mingäçevir	69	M3
Mingäçevir Su Anbarı	69	M3
Mingulay	35	D5
Minicoy	65	B7
Minna	79	F3
Minneapolis	99	B2
Minnesota	99	A1
Miño	39	C2
Minot	97	F1
Minsk	49	E4
Minturn	97	E3
Minusinsk	53	S7
Min Xian	57	C4
Min'yar	49	L3
Miquelon	99	E1
Miraflores	109	C3
Miranda de Ebro	39	H2
Miranda do Douro	39	D3
Mirandela	39	C3
Mirbāt	67	F6
Mirnyy	55	J4
Mirpur Khas	65	A3
Mirtoö Pelagos	47	F7
Mirzapur	65	D3
Miskolc	45	H1
Misoöl	63	(2)D3
Mişrātah	75	C1
Mission	101	C3
Mississippi	101	C3
Mississippi	101	D2
Mississippi River Delta	101	D4
Missoula	97	D1
Missouri	99	B3
Missouri	97	F1
Mistelbach	41	M2
Mitchell	97	C2
Mithymna	47	J5
Mito	59	L5
Mits'iwa	67	C6
Mittellandkanal	33	K2
Mittersill	41	H3
Mitú	109	C3
Mitzic	79	G4
Miyake-jima	59	K6
Miyako	59	L4
Miyakonojō	59	F8
Miyazaki	59	F8
Miyoshi	59	G6
Mīzan Teferī	81	F2
Mizdah	77	H2
Mizen Head	35	B10
Mizil	45	P4
Mizpe Ramon	70	B6
Mjøsa	27	F6
Mkuze	83	E5
Mladá Boleslav	29	D7
Mladenovac	45	H5
Mława	29	K4
Mljet	45	E7
Mmabatho	83	D5
Moa	87	H2
Moanda	79	G5
Moapa	97	D3
Moba	81	D5
Mobayi-Mbongo	81	C3
Moberly	99	B3
Mobile	101	D3
Moçambique	83	G3
Mochudi	83	D4
Mocímboa da Praia	83	G2
Mocuba	83	F3
Modane	41	B5
Modena	41	F6
Modesto	97	B3
Mödling	41	M2
Modowi	63	(2)D3
Modriča	45	F5
Moenkopi	103	D1
Moffat	35	J6
Moffat Peak	89	B7
Mogadishu = Muqdisho	81	H3
Mogocha	55	K6
Mogok	61	B2
Mohács	45	F4
Mohammadia	39	L9
Mohe	55	L6
Mohembo	83	C3
Mohoro	81	F5
Mohyliv-Podil's'kyy	45	Q1
Moincêr	65	D2
Moineşti	45	P3
Mo i Rana	27	H3
Mojave	103	C1
Mojave Desert	103	C2
Mokau	89	E4
Mokolo	79	G2
Mokp'o	59	D6
Mola di Bari	43	M7
Molat	41	K6
Molde	27	D5
Moldova	45	R2
Moldova	45	P2
Moldova Nouă	45	J5
Molepolole	83	C4
Molfetta	43	L7
Molina de Aragón	39	J4
Moline	99	B2
Mollendo	109	C7
Molokai	103	(2)D2
Molopo	83	C5
Molsheim	41	C2
Molucca Sea	63	(2)C2
Moma	83	F3
Mombasa	81	G4
Møn	31	H2
Monaco	41	C7
Monaco	41	C7
Monbetsu, Japan	59	M1
Monbetsu, Japan	59	M2
Moncalieri	41	C5
Monchegorsk	27	S3
Mönchengladbach	33	J3
Monclova	103	F3
Mondovi	41	C6
Monfalcone	41	J5
Monforte de Lemos	39	C2
Monfredónia	43	K7
Monga	81	C3
Mongo	75	C5
Mongolia	57	B2
Mongonu	79	G2
Mongu	83	C3
Mong Yai	61	B2
Mong Yu	61	B2
Monkoto	81	C4
Mono Lake	97	C3
Monopoli	43	M8
Monor	29	J10
Monowai	89	A7
Monroe, La., U.S.	101	C3
Monroe, N.C., U.S.	101	E3
Monroe, Wash., U.S.	97	B1
Monrovia	79	B3
Mons	33	F4
Monschau	33	J4
Monselice	41	G5
Montabaur	33	K4
Montague Island	107	J9
Montalbán	39	K4
Montana	97	E1
Montana	45	L6
Montargis	37	H6
Montauban	37	G10
Mont aux Sources	83	D5
Montbard	37	K6
Montbéliard	41	B3
Mont Blanc	41	B5
Montblanc	39	M3
Mont Cameroun	79	F4
Montceau-les-Mines	37	K7
Mont-de-Marsan	37	E10
Monte Alegre	109	G4
Monte Azul	109	J7
Montebelluna	41	H5
Monte Calvo	43	K7
Monte Cinto	43	C6
Montecristo	43	E6
Monte Etna	43	J11
Montego Bay	105	J5
Montélimar	37	K9
Monte Limbara	43	D8
Montemorelos	101	B4
Monte Namuli	83	F3
Montenegro = Crna Gora	45	F7
Monte Perdino	39	L2
Monte Pollino	43	L9
Montepuez	83	F2
Montepulciano	43	F5
Montereau-faut-Yonne	37	H5
Monterey	99	E3
Montería	109	B2
Monte Rosa	41	C5
Monterrey	103	F3
Montes Claros	109	J7
Montesilvano Marina	43	J6
Montevarchi	41	G7
Montevideo, U.S.	99	A1
Montevideo, Uruguay	111	K5
Monte Viso	41	C6
Monte Vista	103	E1
Montgomery	101	D3
Monticello	97	E3
Mont Joli	99	G1
Mont-Laurier	99	E1
Montluçon	37	H7
Montmagny	99	F1
Montmedy	33	H5
Mont Mézenc	37	K9
Montoro	39	F6
Mont Pelat	37	M9
Montpelier, Id., U.S.	97	D2
Montpelier, Vt., U.S.	99	F2
Montpellier	37	J10
Montréal	99	F1
Montreux	41	B4
Montrose	97	E3
Monts Bagzane	77	G5
Montserrat	105	M5
Monts Nimba	79	C3
Mont Tahat	77	G4
Monywa	61	A2
Monza	41	E5
Monzón	39	L3

Place	Page	Grid
Moorcroft	97	F2
Moorhead	99	A1
Moosburg	41	G1
Moosonee	93	Q6
Mopti	77	E6
Mór	45	F2
Móra	39	B6
Moradabad	65	C3
Moramanga	83	H3
Moran	97	D2
Morava	29	G8
Moravské Budějovice	41	L1
Morawhanna	109	L1
Moray Firth	35	J4
Morbach	33	K5
Mordoviya	49	H4
Moree	87	J5
More Laptevykh	55	L1
Morelia	105	D5
Morella	39	K4
Morgan	87	G6
Morgantown	99	D3
Mori	59	L2
Morioka	59	L4
Morkoka	55	J4
Morlaix	37	B5
Morocco	73	C2
Morogoro	81	F5
Moro Gulf	61	G5
Morombe	83	G4
Mörön	55	G7
Morondava	83	G4
Morón de la Frontera	39	E7
Moroni	83	G2
Morotai	63	(2)C2
Moroto	81	E3
Morris	97	G1
Morristown	101	E2
Mors	27	E8
Morwell	87	J7
Mosby	97	D1
Moscow = Moskva	49	G3
Mosel	33	K4
Moselle	33	G6
Moses Lake	97	C1
Mosgiel	89	C7
Moshi	81	F4
Mosjøen	27	F4
Moskva	49	G3
Mosonmagyaróvár	41	N3
Moss	27	F7
Mossburn	89	B7
Mosselbaai	83	C6
Mossoró	109	K5
Most	31	J6
Mostaganem	39	L9
Mostar	45	E6
Møsvatn	27	E7
Mot'a	75	G5
Motherwell	35	J6
Motril	39	G8
Motygino	53	S6
Moudros	47	H5
Mouila	79	G5
Moulins	37	J7
Moulmein	61	B3
Moundou	75	C6
Mount Adams	97	B1
Mountain Nile = Bahr el Jebel	81	E2
Mount Anglem	89	A8
Mount Apo	61	H5
Mount Ararat	69	L4
Mount Arrowsmith	89	C6
Mount Aspiring	89	B7
Mount Assiniboine	93	H6
Mount Augustus	87	C4
Mount Baco	61	G3
Mount Baker	97	B1
Mount Bartle Frere	87	J3
Mount Bruce	87	C4
Mount Cameroun	73	D5
Mount Carmel	97	D3
Mount Columbia	93	H6
Mount Cook	89	C6
Mount Cook	89	C6
Mount Egmont	89	E4
Mount Elbert	97	E3
Mount Elgon	81	E3
Mount Essendon	87	D4
Mount Evelyn	87	F2
Mount Everest	65	E3
Mount Fairweather	93	D5
Mount Gambier	87	H7
Mount Garnet	87	J3
Mount Hermon	70	C4
Mount Hood	97	B1
Mount Huxley	89	B7
Mount Isa	87	G4
Mount Jackson	112	(2)MM2
Mount Karisimbi	81	D4
Mount Kenya = Kirinyaga	81	F4
Mount Kilimanjaro	81	F4
Mount Kirkpatrick	112	(2)AA1
Mount Kosciuszko	87	J7
Mount Liebig	87	F4
Mount Logan	93	C4
Mount Magnet	87	C5
Mount Maunganui	89	F3
Mount McKinley	103	(1)G3
Mount Meharry	87	C4
Mount Menzies	112	(2)L2
Mount Minto	112	(2)Y2
Mount Mulanje	83	F3
Mount Murchison	89	C6
Mount Nyiru	81	F3
Mount Olympus	97	B1
Mount Ord	87	E3
Mount Ossa	87	J8
Mount Owen	89	D5
Mount Paget	111	P9
Mount Pleasant, Ia., U.S.	99	B2
Mount Pleasant, Mich., U.S.	99	D2
Mount Pleasant, S.C., U.S.	101	F3
Mount Pulog	61	G3
Mount Rainier	97	B1
Mount Robson	93	H6
Mount Roosevelt	93	F5
Mount Roraima	109	E2
Mount Shasta	97	B2
Mount Somers	89	C6
Mount Stanley	81	D3
Mount Tahat	73	D3
Mount Travers	89	D6
Mount Tuun	59	D3
Mount Vernon, Al., U.S.	101	D3
Mount Vernon, Ill., U.S.	99	C3
Mount Vernon, Wash., U.S.	97	B1
Mount Victoria, Myanmar	61	A2
Mount Victoria, Papua New Guinea	85	E6
Mount Waddington	93	F6
Mount Washington	93	S8
Mount Whitney	97	C3
Mount Wilson	97	E3
Mount Woodroffe	87	F5
Moura	39	C6
Moussoro	75	C5
Moutamba	79	G5
Mouth of the Shannon	35	B9
Mouths of the Amazon	107	G3
Mouths of the Danube	45	S4
Mouths of the Ganges	65	E4
Mouths of the Indus	67	J5
Mouths of the Irrawaddy	61	A3
Mouths of the Krishna	65	D5
Mouths of the Mekong	61	D5
Mouths of the Niger	79	F4
Moûtiers	41	B5
Moyale	81	F3
Moyen Atlas	77	D2
Moyenvic	33	J6
Moyynty	53	N8
Mozambique	83	E3
Mozambique Channel	83	F4
Mozdok	69	L2
Mozirje	41	K4
Mpanda	81	E5
Mpika	83	E2
Mporokoso	81	E5
Mpumalanga	83	D5
Mrągowo	29	L4
Mtsensk	49	G4
Mtwara	81	G6
Muang Khammouan	61	C3
Muang Không	61	D4
Muang Khôngxédôn	61	D3
Muang Pakxan	61	C3
Muang Sing	61	C2
Muar	63	(1)C2
Muarabungo	63	(1)C3
Mubende	81	E3
Muckadilla	87	J5
Mudanjiang	59	E1
Muddy Gap	97	E2
Mufulira	83	D2
Muğla	47	L7
Mühldorf	41	H2
Mühlhausen	31	F5
Muhu	27	M7
Mukacheve	29	M9
Mukuku	83	D2
Mulaku Atoll	65	B8
Mulde	31	H5
Muleshoe	103	F2
Mulhacén	39	G7
Mulhouse	41	C3
Mull	35	G5
Mullewa	87	C5
Müllheim	41	C3
Mullingar	35	E8
Mulobezi	83	D3
Multan	67	K3
Mumbai	65	B5
Mumbwa	83	D2
Muna	63	(2)B4
München	41	G2
Mungbere	81	D3
Munich = München	41	G2
Munster, France	41	C2
Münster, Germany	33	K3
Muojärvi	27	Q4
Muonio	27	M3
Muqdisho	81	H3
Mur	41	L4
Murat	69	K4
Murchison	89	D5
Murcia	39	J7
Murdo	97	F2
Mureş	45	J3
Muret	37	G10
Murfreesboro	101	D2
Murghob	67	K2
Muriaé	109	J8

Name	Page	Ref
Müritz	31	H3
Murmansk	27	S2
Murom	49	H3
Muroran	59	L2
Muros	39	A2
Muroto	59	H7
Murphy	101	E2
Murray	87	H6
Murray Bridge	87	G7
Murray River Basin	87	H6
Murska Sobota	41	M4
Murter	41	L7
Murupara	89	F4
Mururoa	85	M8
Murwara	65	D4
Murzūq	77	H3
Mürzzuschlag	41	L3
Muş	69	J4
Musala	47	F2
Musandam Peninsula	71	G3
Muscat = Masqaţ	71	H5
Musgrave Ranges	87	E5
Muskegon	99	C2
Muskogee	101	B2
Musoma	81	E4
Mustafakemalpaşa	47	L4
Mut, *Egypt*	75	E2
Mut, *Turkey*	47	R8
Mutare	83	E3
Mutoray	53	U5
Mutsu	59	L3
Muyezerskiy	27	R5
Muyinga	81	E4
Muynak	53	K9
Muzaffarpur	65	E3
Mwali	83	G2
Mwanza	81	E4
Mweka	81	C4
Mwene-Ditu	81	C5
Mwenezi	83	E4
Mwenezi	83	E4
Mwinilunga	83	C2
Myanmar	61	B2
Myingyan	61	B2
Myitkyina	61	B1
Myjava	41	N2
Mykolayiv	29	N8
Mykonos	47	H7
Mymensingh	65	F4
Mynbulak	53	L9
Myōjin	57	K4
Myrtle Beach	101	F3
Mys Alevina	55	S5
Mys Enkan	55	P5
Mys Govena	55	V5
Mys Kanin Nos	49	H1
Mys Lopatka	55	T6
Mys Navarin	55	X4
Mys Nemetskiy	27	S2
Mysore	65	C6
Mys Shelagskiy	55	V2
Mys Terpeniya	55	Q7
Mys Yuzhnyy	55	T5
Mys Zhelaniya	53	M2
My Tho	61	D4
Mytilini	47	J5
Mývatn	27	(1)E2
Mzimba	83	E2
Mzuzu	83	E2

N

Name	Page	Ref
Naalehu	103	(2)F4
Naberezhnyye Chelny	49	K3
Nabeul	43	E12
Nabire	63	(2)E3
Nablus	70	C4
Nacala	83	G2
Náchod	29	F7
Nacogdoches	101	C3
Nadiad	65	B4
Nadvirna	45	M1
Nadym	49	P1
Nadym	49	P2
Næstved	31	G1
Nagano	59	K5
Nagaoka	59	K5
Nagaon	65	F3
Nagasaki	59	E7
Nagaur	65	B3
Nagercoil	65	C7
Nagold	31	D8
Nagorsk	49	K3
Nagoya	59	J6
Nagpur	65	C4
Naggu	65	F2
Nagyatád	41	N4
Nagykanizsa	41	N4
Naha	57	H5
Nahr en Nile = Nile	75	F2
Naiman Qi	57	G2
Nain	93	U5
Nairn	35	J4
Nairobi	81	F4
Naivasha	81	F4
Naizishan	59	D2
Najibabad	65	C3
Najin	59	F2
Najrān	75	H4
Nakamura	59	G7
Nakhl	70	A7
Nakhodka	59	G2
Nakhon Ratchasima	61	C3
Nakhon Sawan	61	B3
Nakhon Si Thammarat	61	B5
Nakina	93	P6
Naknek	103	(1)F4
Nakonde	81	E5
Nakuru	81	F4
Nal'chik	69	K2
Nālūt	77	H2
Namagan	53	N9
Namakzar-e Shadad	71	G1
Namapa	83	F2
Nam Co	65	F2
Namdalen	27	G4
Nam Dinh	61	D2
Namib Desert	83	A4
Namibe	83	A3
Namibia	83	B4
Namlea	63	(2)C3
Nampa	97	C2
Nam Ping	61	B3
Namp'o	59	C4
Nampula	83	F3
Namsos	27	F4
Namur	33	G4
Namwala	83	D3
Namwŏn	59	D6
Nan	61	C3
Nanaimo	97	B1
Nanao	59	J5
Nanchang	57	F5
Nanchong	57	D4
Nancy	41	B2
Nanda Devi	65	C2
Nänded	65	C5
Nandurbar	65	B4
Nangapinoh	63	(1)E3
Nangatayap	63	(1)E3
Nang Xian	65	F3
Nanjing	57	F4
Nannine	87	C5
Nanning	61	D2
Nanortalik	93	X4
Nanping	57	F5
Nanton	95	D1
Nantong	57	G4
Nanyang	57	E4
Napalkovo	53	N3
Napas	55	C4
Napier	89	F4
Naples = Napoli	43	J8
Naples	101	E4
Napo	109	C4
Napoli	43	J8
Nara	59	H6
Narbonne	37	H10
Nardò	43	N8
Nares Strait	91	J2
Narev	29	N5
Narew	29	L5
Narmada	65	C4
Narnaul	65	C3
Narrabri	87	J6
Narrandera	87	J6
Nart	57	F2
Narva	27	Q7
Narva	27	P7
Narva Bay	27	P7
Narvik	27	J2
Nar'yan Mar	49	K1
Năsăud	45	M2
Nashua	99	F2
Nashville	101	D2
Našice	45	F4
Nasik	65	B4
Nasir	81	E2
Nassarawa	79	F3
Nassau	101	F4
Nässjö	27	H8
Nasugbu	61	G4
Naswá	71	G5
Nata	83	D4
Natal	109	K5
Natashquan	93	U6
Natchez	101	C3
Natchitoches	101	C3
National Park	89	E4
Natitingou	79	E2
Natuna Besar	63	(1)D2
Naumburg	31	G5
Na'ūr	70	C5
Nauru	85	G6
Nautonwa	65	D3
Navahermosa	39	F5
Navoi	53	M9
Navojoa	95	E6
Navsari	65	B4
Nawabshah	67	J4
Naxçivan	69	L4
Naxos	47	H7
Naxos	47	H7
Näy Band, *Iran*	67	G3
Näy Band, *Iran*	71	E3
Nayoro	59	M1
Nazaré	39	A5
Nazareth	70	C4
Nazarovo	53	S6
Nazca	109	C6
Nazca Ridge	111	E3
Naze	57	H5
Nazino	53	P6
Nazran'	69	L2
Nazrēt	81	F2
Nazwá	67	G5
Nazyvayevsk	49	P3
Ndélé	81	C2
Ndjamena	75	B5

Name	Pg	Grid		Name	Pg	Grid		Name	Pg	Grid		Name	Pg	Grid
Ndjolé	79	G5		Nettilling Lake	93	S3		Newmarket	33	C2		Nikopol'	49	F5
Ndola	83	D2		Neubrandenburg	31	J3		New Mexico	103	E2		Nikšić	45	F7
Neapoli	47	F8		Neuchâtel	41	B3		Newnan	101	E3		Nile	75	F3
Nebbi	81	E3		Neuenhagen	31	J4		New Orleans	101	D4		Nîmes	37	K10
Nebitdag	67	F2		Neufchâteau, Belgium	33	H5		New Plymouth	89	E4		Nimule	81	E3
Nebraska	97	G2		Neufchâteau, France	37	L5		Newport, Eng., U.K.	33	A4		Nine Degree Channel	65	B7
Neckar	31	D7		Neufchâtel-en-Bray	33	D5		Newport, Wales, U.K.	35	K10		Ning'an	59	E1
Neckar	31	D8		Neumünster	31	F2		Newport, Oreg., U.S.	97	B2		Ningbo	57	G5
Neckarsulm	31	E7		Neunkirchen	41	M3		New Providence	101	F5		Ningde	57	F5
Necker Island	85	K3		Neuquén	111	H6		Newquay	35	G11		Ninghai	57	G5
Necochea	111	K6		Neuruppin	31	H4		New Siberia Islands =				Ninohoe	59	L3
Nédély	75	C4		Neusiedler	29	F10		Novosibirskiye				Niobrara	97	F2
Needles	103	D2		Neusiedler See	41	M3		Ostrova	55	P1		Nioro	77	D5
Nefedovo	49	P3		Neuss	33	J3		New South Wales	87	H6		Nioro du Sahel	79	C1
Neftçala	69	N4		Neustadt, Germany	33	L5		Newton, Ia., U.S.	99	B2		Niort	37	E7
Neftekamsk	49	K3		Neustadt, Germany	31	F2		Newton, Kans., U.S.	101	B2		Nipigon	99	C1
Nefteyugansk	49	P2		Neustadt, Germany	31	F7		New York	99	E2		Niquelândia	109	H6
Negage	81	B5		Neustrelitz	31	J3		New York	99	F2		Nirmal	65	C5
Negār	71	G2		Neu-Ulm	31	F8		New Zealand	89	B5		Niš	45	J6
Negēlē	81	F2		Neuwied	33	K4		Neya	49	H3		Niscemi	43	J11
Negele	81	F2		Nevada	97	C3		Neyrīz	71	F2		Nishinoomote	59	F8
Negev	70	B6		Nevada	99	B3		Neyshābūr	67	G2		Nisyros	47	K8
Negomane	83	F2		Nevado Auzangate	109	C6		Ngabang	63	(1)D2		Niterói	111	N3
Negombo	65	C7		Nevado de Colima	105	D5		Ngaoundéré	79	G3		Nitra	29	H9
Negotin	45	K5		Nevado de Huascaran	109	B5		Ngara	81	E4		Nitsa	49	M3
Negro, Argentina	111	J7		Nevado de Illampu	109	D7		Ngo	79	H5		Niue	85	K7
Negro, Brazil	109	E4		Nevado Sajama	109	D7		Ngoura	75	C5		Nivelles	33	G4
Negros	61	G5		Nevados de Cachi	111	H4		Nguigmi	79	G2		Nizamabad	65	C5
Negru Vodă	45	R6		Never	55	L6		Nha Trang	61	D4		Nizhnekamsk	49	K3
Nehbandān	67	G3		Nevers	37	J7		Nhulunbuy	87	G2		Nizhnekamskoye		
Neijiang	57	C5		Nevėžis	27	M9		Niafounké	77	E5		Vodokhranilishche	49	K3
Nei Monggol	57	E2		Nevinnomyssk	69	J1		Niagara Falls	99	E2		Nizhneudinsk	55	F5
Neiva	109	B3		Nevşehir	69	F4		Niamey	79	E2		Nizhnevartovsk	49	Q2
Neixiang	57	E4		New Amsterdam	109	F2		Niangara	81	D3		Nizhneyansk	55	P2
Nek'emtë	81	F2		Newark	99	F2		Nia-Nia	81	D3		Nizhniy Novgorod	49	H3
Nellore	65	C6		Newark-on-Trent	33	B1		Nias	63	(1)B2		Nizhniy Tagil	49	M3
Nel'ma	55	P7		New Bedford	99	F2		Nicaragua	105	G6		Nizip	69	G5
Nelson	93	N5		New Bern	101	F2		Nicastro	43	L10		Njazidja	83	G2
Nelson, Canada	97	C1		New Britain	85	F6		Nice	41	C7		Njombe	81	E5
Nelson, New Zealand	89	D5		New Brunswick	93	T7		Nicholls Town	101	F4		Njombe	81	E5
Nelspruit	83	E5		Newbury	33	A3		Nicobar Islands	61	A5		Nkhotakota	83	E2
Nëma	77	D5		New Bussa	79	E3		Nicosia = Lefkosia	47	R9		Nkongsamba	79	F4
Neman	29	M2		Newcastle, Australia	87	K6		Niedere Tauern	41	J3		Nobeoka	59	F7
Nëman	27	N10		Newcastle, U.S.	97	F2		Niefang	79	G4		Nogales, Mexico	103	D2
Nemperola	63	(2)B5		Newcastle-upon-Tyne	35	L6		Nienburg	31	E4		Nogales, U.S.	103	D2
Nemunas	29	P3		Newcastle Waters	87	F3		Nieuw Amsterdam	109	F2		Nogat	29	J3
Nemuro	59	N2		New Delhi	65	C3		Nieuw Nickerie	109	F2		Nogent-le-Rotrou	37	F5
Nen	55	L7		Newfoundland	93	V7		Nieuwpoort	33	E3		Noginsk	49	G3
Nenana	103	(1)H3		Newfoundland	93	V5		Niğde	47	S7		Nogliki	55	Q6
Nene	33	B2		New Georgia Island	85	F6		Niger	77	G5		Noheji	59	L3
Nenjiang	55	M7		New Guinea	51	S10		Niger	79	E2		Noia	39	B2
Nepa	55	H5		New Hampshire	99	F2		Nigeria	79	F2		Nojima-zaki	59	K6
Nepal	65	D3		New Haven	99	F2		Niigata	59	K5		Nok Kundi	67	H4
Nepalganj	65	D3		New Iberia	101	C3		Niihau	103	(2)A2		Nola, Central African		
Neryungri	55	L5		New Ireland	85	F6		Nijar	39	H8		Republic	81	B3
Netanya	70	B4		New Jersey	99	F2		Nijmegen	33	H3		Nola, Italy	43	J8
Netherlands	33	H2		New Liskeard	99	E1		Nikolayevsk-na-Amure	55	Q6		Nome	103	(1)D3
Netherlands Antilles	105	L6		Newman	87	C4		Nikol'sk	49	J3		Nong'an	59	C1

153

Name		
Nong Khai	61	C3
Noord-Oost-Polder	33	H2
Noordwijk aan Zee	33	G2
Norak	67	J2
Noranda	99	E1
Norden	31	C3
Norderney	31	C3
Norderstedt	31	F3
Nordfriesische Inseln	31	C2
Nordhausen	31	F5
Nordhorn	33	K2
Nordkapp	27	N1
Nordkinn	27	P1
Nordkinnhalvøya	27	P1
Nördlingen	31	F8
Nord-Ostsee-Kanal	31	E2
Nordvik	53	W3
Norfolk, Nebr., U.S.	97	G2
Norfolk, Va., U.S.	99	E3
Norfolk Island	85	G8
Noril'sk	53	R4
Norman	101	B2
Normanton	87	H3
Norman Wells	93	F3
Norrköping	27	J7
Norrtälje	27	K7
Norseman	87	D6
Norsk	55	N6
Northam	87	C6
North America	91	M5
Northampton	33	B2
North Andaman	61	A4
North Battleford	93	K6
North Bay	99	E1
North Cape	89	D2
North Carolina	101	F2
North Channel	35	G6
North Dakota	97	F1
Northeast Providence Channel	101	F4
Northeim	31	F5
Northern Cape	83	C5
Northern Ireland	35	E7
Northern Mariana Islands	85	E4
Northern Province	83	D4
Northern Territory	87	F4
North Foreland	33	D3
North Island	89	D3
North Korea	59	C4
North Little Rock	101	C3
North Platte	97	F2
North Platte	95	F3
North Ronaldsay	35	K2
North Sea	35	N4
North Taranaki Bight	89	D4
North Uist	35	E4
North West	83	C5
North West Basin	87	C4
North West Cape	87	B4
North West Christmas Island Ridge	85	K4
North West Highlands	35	G4
Northwest Territories	93	G4
Norton	101	B2
Norton Sound	103	(1)E3
Norway	27	F5
Norwegian Sea	27	B4
Norwich, U.K.	33	D2
Norwich, U.S.	99	F2
Nos Emine	45	Q7
Noshiro	59	K3
Nos Kaliakra	45	R6
Noşratābād	67	G4
Nosy Barren	83	G3
Nosy Bé	83	H2
Notios Evvoïkos Kolpos	47	F6
Nottingham	33	A2
Nottingham Island	93	R4
Nouâdhibou	77	B4
Nouakchott	77	B5
Nouméa	85	G8
Nouvelle Calédonie	85	G8
Nova Gorica	41	J5
Nova Gradiška	45	E4
Nova Iguaçu	111	N3
Nova Mambone	83	F4
Novara	41	D5
Nova Scotia	93	T8
Novaya Kasanka	49	J5
Novaya Lyalya	49	M3
Novaya Zemlya	53	J3
Nova Zagora	45	P7
Novelda	39	K6
Nové Město	29	F8
Nové Mesto	29	G9
Nové Zámky	29	H10
Novgorod	49	F3
Novi Bečej	45	H4
Novi Ligure	41	D6
Novi Pazar, Bulgaria	45	Q6
Novi Pazar, Yugoslavia	45	H6
Novi Sad	45	G4
Novi Vinodolski	41	K5
Novoalekseyevka	49	L4
Novocheboksarsk	49	J3
Novokazalinsk	49	M5
Novokutznetsk	53	R7
Novo Mesto	41	L5
Novomoskovsk	49	G4
Novonazimovo	55	E5
Novorossiysk	69	G1
Novorybnoye	55	H2
Novoselivka	45	S2
Novosergiyevka	49	K4
Novosibirsk	53	Q6
Novosibirskiye Ostrova	55	P1
Novotroitsk	49	L4
Novouzensk	49	J4
Novozybkov	49	F4
Nový Bor	31	K6
Novyy Port	53	N4
Novyy Urengoy	53	P4
Novyy Uzen'	53	J9
Nowra	87	K6
Nowy Sącz	29	K8
Nowy Targ	29	K8
Noyon	33	E5
Ntem	79	G4
Nu	65	G2
Nubian Desert	75	F3
Nudo Coropuna	109	C7
Nueltin Lake	93	M4
Nueva Rosita	103	F3
Nuevo Casas Grandes	103	E2
Nuevo Laredo	103	G3
Nuhaka	89	F4
Nuku'alofa	85	J8
Nukunonu	85	J6
Nukus	53	K9
Nullarbor Plain	87	E6
Numan	79	G3
Numazu	59	K6
Numbulwar	87	G2
Numfor	63	(2)E3
Numto	49	P2
Nunavut	93	M3
Nuneaton	33	A2
Nunivak Island	103	(1)D3
Nuoro	43	D8
Nurābād	71	D1
Nurmes	27	Q5
Nürnberg	31	G7
Nutak	93	U5
Nuuk	93	W4
Nyagan'	49	N2
Nyahururu	81	F3
Nyala	75	D5
Nyamlell	81	D2
Nyamtumbo	81	F6
Nyandoma	49	H2
Nyborg	31	F1
Nybro	27	H8
Nyda	53	N4
Nyima	65	E2
Nyingchi	65	F3
Nyírbátor	45	K2
Nyíregyháza	29	L10
Nykøbing	31	G2
Nyköping	27	J7
Nylstroom	83	D4
Nynäshamn	27	J7
Nyon	41	B4
Nysa	29	G7
Nysa	29	D6
Nyukhcha	49	J2
Nyurba	55	K4
Nzega	81	E4
Nzérékoré	79	C3
N'zeto	81	A5
Nzwami	83	G2

O

Name		
Oahu	103	(2)D2
Oakland	97	B3
Oakley	101	A2
Oak Ridge	99	D3
Oamaru	89	C7
Oaxaca	105	E5
Ob'	49	N2
Oban	35	G5
O Barco	39	D2
Oberhausen	33	J3
Oberstdorf	41	F3
Obi	63	(2)C3
Obidos	109	F4
Obigarm	67	K2
Obihiro	59	M2
Obninsk	49	G3
Obo	81	D2
Obskaya Guba	53	N4
Obuasi	79	D3
Ob'yachevo	49	J2
Ocala	101	E4
Ocean Falls	93	F6
Oceania	85	G7
Oceanside	103	C2
Och'amch'ire	69	J2
Ōdate	59	L3
Odda	27	D6
Odemira	39	B7
Ödemiş	47	L6
Odense	31	F1
Oder = Odra	29	F6
Odesa	49	F5
Odessa = Odesa, Ukraine	49	F5
Odessa, U.S.	103	F2
Odienné	79	C3
Odorheiu Secuiesc	45	N3
Odra	29	F6
Oelsnitz	31	H6
Oeno	85	N8
Oestev	111	H7
Ofaqim	70	B5
Offenbach	31	D6
Offenburg	41	C2
Ōgaki	59	J6
Ogasawara-shotō	51	T7
Ogbomosho	79	E3
Ogden	97	D2

Name	Pg	Ref
Oglio	41	E5
Ogre	27	N8
Ogulin	41	L5
Ohai	89	A7
Ohio	99	D2
Ohio	99	C3
Ohrid	47	C3
Ohura	89	E4
Oiapoque	109	G3
Oil City	99	E2
Ōita	59	F7
Ojinaga	103	F3
Ojos del Salado	111	H4
Oka	55	G6
Okato	89	D4
Okavango Delta	83	C3
Okaya	59	K5
Okayama	59	G6
Okha	55	Q6
Okhansk	49	L3
Okhotsk	55	Q5
Okhtyrka	49	F4
Okinawa	57	H5
Okinawa	57	H5
Oki-shotō	59	G5
Oklahoma	101	B2
Oklahoma City	101	B2
Okranger	27	E5
Oksino	49	K1
Oktinden	27	H4
Oktyabr'sk	49	L5
Oktyabr'skiy	49	K4
Okushiri-tō	59	K2
Olancha	97	C3
Öland	27	J8
Olathe	101	C2
Olavarría	111	J6
Olbia	43	D8
Old Crow	103	(1)K2
Oldenburg, *Germany*	31	D3
Oldenburg, *Germany*	31	F2
Old Head of Kinsale	35	D10
Olean	99	E2
Olekma	55	L5
Olekminsk	55	L4
Olenek	55	J3
Olenëk	55	L2
Olhão	39	C7
Olib	41	K6
Olinda	109	L5
Olonets	49	F2
Olongapo	61	G4
Oloron-Ste-Marie	37	E10
Olot	39	N2
Olovyannaya	55	K6
Olpe	31	K3
Olsztyn	29	K4
Olt	45	M6

Name	Pg	Ref
Oltenița	45	P5
Oltu	69	K3
Olvera	39	E8
Olympia	97	B1
Olympos	47	E4
Olympus	47	Q10
Olyutorskiy	55	W4
Oma	65	D2
Omagh	35	E7
Omaha	97	G2
Omak	97	C1
Oman	67	G5
Omapere	89	D2
Omarama	89	B7
Omaruru	83	B4
Ombrone	43	F6
Omdurman =		
Umm Durman	75	F4
Omegna	41	D5
Omolon	55	T3
Omo Wenz	81	F2
Omsk	53	N6
Ōmū	59	M1
Ōmuta	59	F7
Ondangwa	83	B3
Ondjiva	83	B3
Ondo	79	E3
One and a Half Degree		
Channel	65	B8
Onega	49	G2
O'Neill	97	G2
Oneonta	99	F2
Onești	45	P3
Onezhskoye Ozero	49	F2
Ongjin	59	C5
Ongole	65	D5
Onguday	53	R7
Oni	69	K2
Onitsha	79	F3
Onon	55	J7
Onon	55	J7
Ontario	93	N6
Onyx	103	C1
Oodnadatta	87	G5
Oostelijk-Flevoland	33	H2
Oostende	33	E3
Oosterschelde	33	E3
Opala	81	C4
Opava	29	G8
Opelika	101	D3
Opelousas	101	C3
Opheim	97	E1
Opole	29	G7
Opotiki	89	F4
Opunake	89	D4
Opuwo	83	B3
Oradea	45	J2
Oran	39	K9

Name	Pg	Ref
Orán	111	J3
Orange	83	C5
Orange, *Australia*	87	J6
Orange, *France*	37	K9
Orangeburg	101	E3
Oranienburg	31	J4
Orbetello	43	F6
Orco	41	C5
Ordu	69	G3
Örebro	27	H7
Oregon	97	B2
Oregon	99	A3
Orel	49	G4
Orem	97	D2
Orenburg	49	L4
Orestiada	47	J3
Orford Ness	33	D2
Orihuela	39	K6
Orillia	99	E2
Orinoco	109	D2
Orinoco Delta =		
Delta del Orinoco	109	E2
Oristano	43	C9
Orivesi	27	Q5
Orkney Islands	35	K3
Orlando	101	E4
Orléans	37	G6
Ormara	67	H4
Ormoc	61	G4
Örnsköldsvik	27	K5
Orofino	97	C1
Oroqen Zizhiqi	55	L6
Orosei	43	D8
Orotukan	55	S4
Oroville	97	B3
Orroroo	87	G6
Orsha	49	F4
Orsk	49	L4
Orşova	45	K5
Ørsta	27	D5
Orthez	37	E10
Ortigueira	39	C1
Ortles	41	F4
Orūmīyeh	69	L5
Oruro	109	D7
Orvieto	43	G6
Ōsaka	59	H6
Osăm	45	M6
Osceola	99	B2
Oschersleben	31	G4
Osh	53	N9
Oshamambe	59	L2
Oshawa	99	E2
Oshkosh, *Nebr., U.S.*	97	F2
Oshkosh, *Wis., U.S.*	99	C2
Oshogbo	79	E3
Osijek	45	F4
Oskaloosa	99	B2

Name	Pg	Ref
Oslo	27	F7
Oslofjorden	27	F7
Osmancık	69	F3
Osmaniye	69	G5
Osnabrück	33	L2
Osorno	111	G7
Ossora	55	U5
Ostashkov	49	F3
Østerdalen	27	F6
Östersund	27	H5
Ostfriesische Inseln	31	C3
Ostiglia	41	G5
Ostrava	29	H8
Ostrołęka	29	L4
Ostrov, *Czech Republic*	31	H6
Ostrov, *Russia*	49	E3
Ostrova Medvezh'I	55	T2
Ostrova Vrangelya	91	V4
Ostrov Ayon	55	V2
Ostrov Belyy	53	N3
Ostrov Beringa	55	V6
Ostrov Bol'shevik	53	V2
Ostrov Bol'shoy		
Begichev	55	J2
Ostrov Bol'shoy		
Lyakhovskiy	55	Q2
Ostrov Bol'shoy		
Shantar	55	P6
Ostrov Chechen'	69	M2
Ostrov Iturup	59	P1
Ostrov Karaginskiy	55	U5
Ostrov Kolguyev	53	H4
Ostrov Komsomolets	53	T1
Ostrov Kotel'nyy	55	P1
Ostrov Kunashir	59	P1
Ostrov Novaya Sibir'	55	S2
Ostrov Oktyabr'skoy	53	S2
Ostrov Onekotan	55	S7
Ostrov Paramushir	55	T6
Ostrov Shiashkotan	55	S7
Ostrov Simushir	55	S7
Ostrov Urup	55	S7
Ostrov Ushakova	53	Q1
Ostrov Vaygach	53	K3
Ostrov Vise	53	P2
Ostrov Vosrozhdeniya	53	K9
Ostrov Vrangelya	55	W2
Ostrowiec Świętokrzyski	29	L7
Ostrów Mazowiecka	29	L5
Ostrów Wielkopolski	29	G6
Ostuni	43	M8
Ōsumi-shotō	59	F8
Osuna	39	E7
Oswego	99	E2
Oświęcim	29	J7
Otago Peninsula	89	C7
Otaki	89	E5
Otaru	59	L2

Name	Pg	Ref
Oti	79	E3
Otjiwarongo	83	B4
Otočac	41	L6
Otog Qi	57	D3
Otoineppu	59	M1
Otorohanga	89	E4
Otranto	43	N8
Ōtsu	59	H6
Ottawa	99	E1
Ottawa, *Canada*	99	E1
Ottawa, *U.S.*	101	B2
Ottumwa	99	B2
Ouachita Mountains	101	C3
Ouadâne	77	C4
Ouadda	81	C2
Ouagadougou	79	D2
Oualàta	77	D5
Ouargla	77	G2
Ouarzazate	77	D2
Oudenaarde	33	F4
Oudenbosch	33	G3
Oudtshoorn	83	C6
Oued Medjerda	43	D12
Oued Meliane	43	D12
Ouésso	79	H4
Ouezzane	77	D2
Oujda	77	E2
Oulu	27	N4
Oulujärvi	27	P4
Oulujoki	27	P4
Oulx	41	B5
Oum-Chalouba	75	D4
Ounarjoki	27	N3
Our	33	J4
Ouray	97	E3
Ourense	39	C2
Ourthe	33	H4
Outer Hebrides	35	D4
Outjo	83	B4
Out Skerries	35	M1
Ouyen	87	H7
Ovalle	111	G5
Overflakkee	33	G3
Overton	97	D3
Övertorneå	27	M3
Oviedo	39	E1
Owaka	89	B8
Owando	79	H5
Owensboro	99	C3
Owen Sound	99	D2
Owo	79	F3
Owyhee	97	C2
Oxford, *New Zealand*	89	D6
Oxford, *U.K.*	33	A3
Oxnard	103	C2
Oyama	59	K5
Oyapock	109	G3
Oyem	79	G4
Oyonnax	41	A4
Ózd	29	K9
Ozero Alakol'	53	Q8
Ozero Balkhash	53	N8
Ozero Baykal	55	H6
Ozero Beloye	49	G2
Ozero Chany	53	P7
Ozero Il'men'	49	F3
Ozero Inder	53	J8
Ozero Khanka	59	G1
Ozero Kovdozero	27	S3
Ozero Kuyto	27	R4
Ozero Leksozero	27	R5
Ozero Nyuk	27	R4
Ozero Pirenga	27	R3
Ozero Pyaozero	27	R3
Ozero Taymyr	53	U3
Ozero Tengiz	49	N4
Ozero Topozero	27	R4
Ozero Umbozero	27	T3
Ozero Vygozero	49	G2
Ozero Yalpug	45	R4
Ozero Zaysan	53	Q8
Ozhogino	55	R3
Ozieri	43	C8

P

Name	Pg	Ref
Paamiut	93	X4
Paarl	83	B6
Pabianice	29	J6
Pachino	43	K12
Pachuca	105	E4
Pacific Ocean	85	M3
Packwood	97	B1
Padang	63	(1)C3
Padangsidempuan	63	(1)B2
Paderborn	31	D5
Padova	41	G5
Padre Island	101	B4
Paducah, *Ky., U.S.*	99	C3
Paducah, *Tex., U.S.*	103	F2
Padum	65	C2
Paekdu San	59	D3
Paeroa	89	E3
Pafos	47	Q10
Pag	41	L6
Pag	41	K6
Pagadian	61	G5
Pagai Selatan	63	(1)B3
Pagai Utara	63	(1)B3
Pagalu = Annobón	79	F5
Pagan	85	E4
Pagatan	63	(1)F3
Page	103	D1
Pagri	65	E3
Pahiatua	89	E5
Paide	27	N7
Päijänne	27	N6
Paisley	35	H6
Paita	109	A5
Pakaraima Mountains	109	E2
Pakistan	67	J4
Pakokku	61	D3
Pakotai	89	D2
Pakrac	41	N5
Paks	45	F3
Pakxé	61	D3
Palagónia	43	J11
Palagruža	43	L6
Palamós	39	P3
Palana	55	U5
Palangkaraya	63	(1)E3
Palanpur	65	B4
Palatka	101	E4
Palau	85	D5
Palau	43	D7
Palau	85	D5
Palawan	61	F5
Palazzolo Arceide	43	J11
Palembang	63	(1)C3
Palencia	39	F2
Paleokastritsa	47	B5
Palermo	43	H10
Palestine	101	B3
Paletwa	61	A2
Pali	65	B3
Palikir	85	F5
Palk Strait	65	C7
Palma	39	N5
Palma del Rio	39	E7
Palmas	111	L4
Palmas	109	H6
Palmdale	103	C2
Palmerston	89	C7
Palmerston Island	85	K7
Palmerston North	89	E5
Palm Harbor	101	E4
Palmi	43	K10
Palmyra Island	85	K5
Palojärvi	27	M2
Palopo	63	(2)B3
Palu	63	(2)A3
Paluostrov Taymyr	53	R3
Pamiers	37	G10
Pamlico Sound	101	F2
Pampa	103	F1
Pampas	111	J6
Pamplona, *Colombia*	105	K7
Pamplona, *Spain*	39	J2
Pana	99	C3
Panagyurishte	45	M7
Panaji	65	B5
Panama	105	H7
Panamá	109	B2
Panama Canal =		
Canal de Panamá	105	J7
Panama City	101	D3
Panarik	63	(1)D2
Panay	61	G4
Pančevo	45	H5
Panevėžys	29	P2
Pangkalpinang	63	(1)D3
Pangnirtung	93	T3
Pangutaran Group	61	G5
Panjgur	67	H4
Pantanal	109	F7
Pantelleria	77	H1
Paola	43	L9
Pápa	45	E2
Papakura	89	E3
Paparoa	89	E3
Papa Stour	35	L1
Papenburg	31	C3
Papey	27	(1)F2
Papua New Guinea	85	E6
Papun	61	B3
Pará	109	G5
Para	109	H7
Paracatu	109	H7
Paracel Islands	61	E3
Paraćin	45	J6
Paragua	109	E6
Paraguay	111	J3
Paraguay	107	F6
Paraíba	109	K5
Parakou	79	E3
Paramaribo	109	F2
Paraná	111	L3
Paranã	109	H6
Paraná	111	J5
Paranã	109	H6
Paraná	111	K4
Paray-le Monial	37	K7
Parchim	31	G3
Pardo	109	H7
Pardubice	29	E7
Parepare	63	(2)A3
Parga	47	C5
Parigi	63	(2)B3
Parika	109	F2
Parintins	109	F4
Paris, *France*	37	H5
Paris, *U.S.*	101	B3
Parkersburg	99	D3
Parla	39	G4
Parma	41	F6
Parma, *Italy*	41	F6
Parma, *U.S.*	99	D2
Parnassus	89	D6
Pärnu	27	N7
Pärnu	27	N7
Paros	47	H7

Name	Page	Ref
Paros	47	H7
Parry Islands	93	L1
Parry Sound	99	D2
Parthenay	37	E7
Partinico	43	H10
Partizansk	59	G2
Paru	109	G4
Paryang	65	D2
Pasadena, *Calif., U.S.*	103	C2
Pasadena, *Tex., U.S.*	101	B4
Paşcani	45	P2
Pasinler	69	J3
Pašman	41	L7
Pasni	67	H4
Paso de Indios	111	H7
Paso Robles	103	B1
Passau	31	J8
Passo Fundo	111	L4
Passos	109	H8
Pastavy	27	P9
Pasto	109	B3
Patagonia	111	G8
Patan, *India*	65	C2
Patan, *Nepal*	65	E3
Pate Island	81	G4
Paterna	39	K5
Paterno	43	J11
Paterson	99	F2
Pathankot	65	C2
Pathein	61	A3
Patiala	65	C2
Patmos	47	J7
Patna	65	E3
Patnos	69	K4
Patos de Minas	109	H7
Patra	47	D6
Patraikis Kolpos	47	D6
Patti	43	J10
Paturau River	89	D5
Pau	39	K1
Paulo Afonso	109	K5
Pāveh	69	M6
Pavia	41	E5
Pāvilosta	27	L8
Pavlodar	53	P7
Pavullo nel Frignano	41	F6
Paxoi	47	C5
Payette	97	C1
Payne's Find	87	C5
Paysandu	111	K5
Payson	103	D2
Pazar	69	J3
Pazardzhik	45	M7
Peace	93	H5
Peace River	93	H5
Peach Springs	103	D1
Pebane	83	F3
Pebas	109	C5
Peć	45	H7
Pecan Island	101	C4
Pechora	49	L1
Pechorskoye More	53	J4
Pecos	103	F2
Pecos	103	F2
Pécs	45	F3
Pedra Azul	109	J7
Pedra Lume	79	(1)B1
Pedro Afonso	109	H5
Pedro Juan Caballero	111	K3
Peene	31	J3
Pegasus Bay	89	D6
Pegnitz	31	G7
Pegu	61	B3
Pegunungan Barisan	63	(1)B2
Pegunungan Iran	63	(1)F2
Pegunungan Maoke	63	(2)E3
Pegunungan Meratus	63	(1)F3
Pegunungan Schwaner	63	(1)E3
Pegunungan Van Rees	63	(2)E3
Pehuajó	111	J6
Peine	31	F4
Peißenberg	41	G3
Pekalongan	63	(1)D4
Pekanbaru	63	(1)C2
Peking = Beijing	57	F3
Peleng	63	(2)B3
Pelhřimov	29	E8
Pello	27	N3
Pellworm	31	D2
Pelly Bay	93	P3
Peloponnisos	47	D7
Pelotas	111	L5
Pelym	49	M2
Pematangsiantar	63	(1)B2
Pemba	83	G2
Pemba Island	81	F5
Pembina	97	G1
Pembroke, *Canada*	99	E1
Pembroke, *U.K.*	35	H10
Pembroke, *U.S.*	101	E3
Peñafiel	39	F3
Peñaranda de Bracamonte	39	E4
Peñarroya-Pueblonuevo	39	E6
Pendleton	97	C1
Pend Oreille Lake	97	C1
Peniche	39	A5
Peninsula de Guajira	105	K6
Península Valdés	111	J7
Péninsule de Gaspé	93	T7
Péninsule d'Ungava	93	R4
Pennines	35	K7
Pennsylvania	99	E2
Penrith	35	K7
Pensacola	105	G2
Penticton	97	C1
Penza	49	J4
Penzance	35	G11
Penzhinskaya Guba	55	U4
Peoria	99	C2
Peregrebnoye	49	N2
Pereira	109	B3
Pergamino	111	J5
Périgueux	37	F8
Perito Moreno	111	G8
Perleberg	31	G3
Perm'	49	L3
Përmet	47	C4
Pernambuco	109	K5
Pernik	45	L7
Perpignan	37	H11
Perry	101	E3
Persepolis	71	E2
Persian Gulf	71	C2
Perth, *Australia*	87	C6
Perth, *U.K.*	35	J5
Pertuis Breton	37	D7
Peru	109	C6
Peru	99	C2
Peru-Chile Trench	107	D5
Perugia	43	G5
Pervoural'sk	49	L3
Pesaro	41	H7
Pescara	43	J6
Peshawar	65	B2
Peshtera	47	G2
Peski Karakumy	67	G2
Peski Kyzylkum	53	L9
Peski Priaral'skiye Karakumy	53	L8
Pessac	37	E9
Petah Tiqwa	70	B4
Petalioi	47	G7
Pétange	33	H5
Petauke	83	E2
Peterborough, *Canada*	99	E2
Peterborough, *U.K.*	35	M9
Peterhead	35	L4
Peter I Øy	112	(2)JJ3
Petersburg	99	E3
Petersfield	33	B3
Petershagen	31	D4
Peto	105	G4
Petre Bay	89	(1)B1
Petrich	47	F3
Petrila	45	L4
Petrinja	41	M5
Petrolina	109	J5
Petropavlovsk	49	N4
Petropavlovsk-Kamchatskiy	55	T6
Petroşani	45	L4
Petrovsk-Zabaykal'skiy	55	H6
Petrozavodsk	49	F2
Petrun	49	M1
Pevek	55	W3
Pfaffenhofen	31	G8
Pfarrkirchen	31	H8
Pforzheim	31	D8
Pfunds	41	F4
Phalodi	65	B3
Phan Rang	61	D4
Phan Thiêt	61	D4
Phatthalung	61	C5
Phet Buri	61	B4
Philadelphia	101	F2
Philippines	61	G5
Philippine Trench	51	R8
Phitsanulok	61	C3
Phnom Penh	61	C4
Phoenix	103	D2
Phoenix Islands	85	J6
Phôngsali	61	C2
Phuket	61	B5
Piacenza	41	E5
Piadena	41	F5
Pianosa	43	E6
Piatra-Neamţ	45	P3
Piauí	109	J5
Piazza Armerina	43	J11
Pibor Post	81	E2
Picacho del Centinela	103	F3
Pico	77	(1)B2
Pico Almanzor	39	E4
Pico Cristóbal Colón	105	K6
Pico da Bandeira	111	N3
Pico da Neblina	109	D3
Pico de Teide	77	B3
Pico Duarte	105	K5
Picos	109	J5
Picton	89	D5
Pic Tousside	75	C3
Piedras Negras	103	F3
Pieksämäki	27	P5
Pielinen	27	Q5
Pierre	97	F2
Piers do Rio	109	H7
Piešťany	29	G9
Pietermaritzburg	83	E5
Pietersburg	83	D4
Piet Retief	83	E5
Pieve di Cadore	41	H4
Pihlájavesi	27	P6
Pik Aborigen	55	R4
Piketberg	83	B6
Pik Kommunizma	67	K2
Pik Pobedy	53	P9
Piła	29	F4
Pilcomayo	109	E8
Pilibhit	65	C3
Pimba	87	G6
Pinang	61	B5

Pınarbası	● 69	G4	Plateau of Tibet =			Polykastro	● 47	E4
Pinar del Río	● 105	H4	Xizang Gaoyuan	⊘ 65	D2	Polynesia	⌘ 85	J6
Pindaré Mirim	● 109	H4	Platinum	● 103	(1)E4	Pombal	● 39	B5
Pindos	▲ 47	D5	Plato Ustyurt	⊘ 53	J9	Pomeranian Bay	⊵ 29	C3
Pine Bluff	● 99	B4	Platte	◪ 101	B1	Pomeroy	● 97	C1
Pine Bluffs	● 97	F2	Platteville	● 99	B2	Pomorie	● 45	Q7
Pine City	● 99	B1	Plattsburgh	● 99	F2	Pompei	● 43	J8
Pinega	◪ 49	H2	Plauen	● 31	H6	Ponca City	● 101	B2
Pine Island Bay	⊵ 112	(2)GG3	Plây Cu	● 61	D4	Ponce	● 105	L5
Pineland	● 101	C3	Pleasanton	● 103	G3	Pondicherry	● 65	C6
Pinerolo	● 41	C6	Plentywood	● 97	F1	Pond Inlet	● 93	R2
Pineville	● 101	C3	Plesetsk	● 49	H2	Ponferrada	● 39	D2
Pingdingshan	● 57	E4	Pleven	● 45	M6	Pons	● 37	E8
Pingle	● 61	E2	Płock	● 29	J5	Ponta Delgada	● 77	(1)B2
Pingliang	● 57	D3	Pločno	▲ 45	E6	Ponta do Podrão	⊠ 79	G6
P'ing-tung	● 61	G2	Ploiești	● 45	P5	Ponta do Sol	● 79	(1)B1
Pingxiang, *China*	● 61	D2	Plomari	● 47	J6	Ponta Grossa	● 111	L4
Pingxiang, *China*	● 61	E1	Plön	● 31	F2	Pont-à-Mousson	● 37	M5
Pinhel	● 39	C4	Plovdiv	● 45	M7	Pontarlier	● 37	M7
Pinneberg	● 31	E3	Plungė	● 29	L2	Pontassieve	● 41	G7
Pinsk	● 49	E4	Plymouth, *U.K.*	● 35	H11	Pontedera	● 41	F7
Piombino	● 43	E6	Plymouth, *U.S.*	● 99	C2	Pontevedra	● 39	B2
Pioneer	● 103	D2	Plzeň	● 29	C8	Pontianak	● 63	(1)D3
Pionerskiy	● 49	M2	Pocatello	● 97	D2	Pontoise	● 33	E5
Piotrków Trybunalski	● 29	J6	Pochinok	● 49	F4	Pontremoli	● 41	E6
Piove di Sacco	● 41	H5	Pocking	● 41	J2	Ponza	⌘ 43	G8
Pireas	● 47	F7	Pocomoke City	● 99	E3	Poole	● 35	L11
Pirin	▲ 47	F3	Podgorica	⊡ 45	G7	Popayán	● 105	J8
Piripiri	● 109	J4	Podol'sk	● 49	G3	Poperinge	● 33	E4
Pirmasens	● 31	C7	Podravska Slatina	● 45	E4	Popigay	● 53	W3
Pirna	● 31	J6	Poel	◪ 31	G2	Poplar Bluff	● 99	B3
Piru	● 63	(2)C3	P'ohang	● 59	E5	Poplarville	● 101	D3
Pisa	● 41	F7	Pohnpei	⌘ 85	F5	Popocatépetl	▲ 105	E5
Pisa	◪ 29	L4	Point Arena	⊵ 95	B4	Popokabaka	● 79	H6
Písek	● 29	D8	Point Barrow	⊵ 103	(1)F1	Poprad	● 29	K8
Pīshīn	● 67	H4	Point Conception	⊵ 103	B2	Porangatu	● 109	H6
Pisticci	● 43	L8	Point d'Entrecasteaux	⊵ 87	B6	Porbandar	● 67	J5
Pistoia	● 41	F7	Pointe-Noire	● 79	G5	Porcupine	◪ 103	(1)K2
Pitcairn Islands	⌘ 85	P8	Point Hope	⊵ 103	(1)D2	Pordenone	● 41	H5
Piteå	● 27	L4	Point Sur	⊵ 97	B3	Poreč	● 41	J5
Pitești	● 45	M5	Poitiers	● 37	F7	Pori	● 27	L6
Pithara	● 87	C6	Pokhara	● 65	D3	Porirua	● 89	E5
Pithiviers	● 37	H5	Poko	● 81	D3	Poronaysk	● 55	Q7
Pitlyar	● 49	N1	Pokrovsk	● 55	M4	Porozina	● 41	K5
Pitt Island	⌘ 89	(1)B2	Poland	⊞ 29	G6	Porriño	● 39	B2
Pittsburg	● 101	C2	Polar Bluff	● 105	F1	Porsangen	⊵ 27	N1
Pittsburgh	● 99	D2	Polatlı	● 47	Q5	Portage	● 99	C2
Piura	● 109	A4	Polatsk	● 49	E3	Portage la Prairie	● 97	G1
Placerville	● 103	B1	Polichnitos	● 47	J5	Port Alberni	● 97	B1
Plainview	● 103	F2	Polillo Islands	⌘ 61	G4	Port Albert	● 87	J7
Planalto Central	⊘ 109	H6	Polis	● 47	Q9	Portalegre	● 39	C5
Planalto do Mato			Polistena	● 43	L10	Portales	● 103	F2
Grosso	⊘ 109	G6	Pollachi	● 65	C6	Port Arthur, *Australia*	● 87	J8
Plasencia	◪ 39	D5	Pollença	● 39	P5	Port Arthur, *U.S.*	● 101	C4
Plateau Batéké	⊘ 79	G5	Poltava	● 49	F5	Port Augusta	● 87	G6
Plateau du Djado	⊘ 77	H4	Poltavka	● 59	F1	Port-au-Prince	■ 105	K5
Plateau du Limousin	⊘ 37	F8	Poluostrov Yamal	⊘ 53	M3	Port Austin	● 99	D2
Plateau du Tademaït	⊘ 77	F3	Polyarnyy	● 55	X3	Port Burwell	● 93	U4

Port Charlotte	● 101 E4
Portel	● 109 G4
Port Elizabeth	● 83 D6
Port Ellen	● 35 F6
Port Fitzroy	● 89 E3
Port-Gentil	● 79 F5
Port Harcourt	● 79 F4
Port Hardy	● 93 F6
Port Hedland	● 87 C4
Port Huron	● 99 D2
Portimão	● 39 B7
Portland, *Australia*	● 87 H7
Portland, *Ind., U.S.*	● 99 D2
Portland, *Me., U.S.*	● 99 F2
Portland, *Oreg., U.S.*	● 97 B1
Port Laoise	● 35 E8
Port Lavaca	● 101 B4
Port Lincoln	● 87 G6
Port Louis	■ 83 (1)B2
Port Macquarie	● 87 K6
Port-Menier	● 93 U7
Port Moresby	● 87 J1
Port Nolloth	● 83 B5
Porto, *Corsica*	● 43 C6
Porto, *Portugal*	● 39 B3
Porto Alegre	▣ 111 L5
Porto Amboim	● 83 A2
Portocheli	● 47 F7
Pôrto Esperidião	● 109 F7
Portoferraio	● 43 E6
Port of Spain	● 109 F1
Portogruaro	● 41 H5
Porto Inglês	● 79 (1)B1
Pôrto Nacional	● 109 H6
Porto-Novo	■ 79 E3
Port Orford	● 97 B2
Pôrto Santana	● 109 G3
Pôrto Seguro	● 109 K7
Porto Tolle	● 41 H6
Porto-Vecchio	● 43 D7
Pôrto Velho	▣ 109 E5
Portoviejo	● 109 A4
Port Pire	● 87 G6
Portree	● 35 F4
Port Said = Bûr Sa'îd	● 75 F1
Port St. Johns	● 83 D6
Port Shepstone	● 83 E6
Portsmouth, *U.K.*	● 33 A4
Portsmouth, *N.H., U.S.*	● 99 F2
Portsmouth, *Oh., U.S.*	● 99 D3
Portsmouth, *Va., U.S.*	● 99 E3
Port Sudan = Bur Sudan	● 75 G4
Port Talbot	● 35 J10
Portugal	⊞ 39 B5
Port-Vendres	■ 37 J11
Port-Vila	■ 85 G7
Port Warrender	● 87 E2

Name	Page	Grid
Posadas	111	K4
Poso	63	(2)B3
Pößneck	31	G6
Postmasburg	83	C5
Postojna	41	K5
Potapovo	53	R4
Poteau	101	C2
Potenza	43	K8
P'ot'i	69	J2
Potiskum	79	G2
Potosi	109	D7
Potsdam	31	J4
Pottuvil	65	D7
Poughkeepsie	99	F2
Pourerere	89	F5
Póvoa de Varzim	39	B3
Povorino	49	H4
Powder	97	E1
Powell River	93	G7
Poyang Hu	57	F5
Požarevac	45	J5
Poznań	29	F5
Pozoblanco	39	F6
Prabumulih	63	(1)C3
Prachatice	29	D8
Prachuap Khiri Khan	61	B4
Præstø	31	H1
Prague = Praha	29	D7
Praha	29	D7
Praia	79	(1)B2
Prairie du Chien	99	B2
Praslin Island	83	(2)B1
Pratas =		
Dongsha Qundao	61	F2
Prato	41	G7
Pratt	97	G3
Preetz	31	F2
Premnitz	31	H4
Premuda	41	K6
Prentice	99	B1
Prenzlau	29	C4
Preparis Island	61	A4
Přerov	29	G8
Preševo	45	J7
Presidencia Roque		
Sáenz Peña	111	J4
Presidio	103	F3
Presnogorkovka	49	N4
Prešov	29	L9
Presque Isle	99	G1
Preston, U.K.	35	K8
Preston, U.S.	99	B3
Pretoria	83	D5
Preveza	47	C6
Pribilof Islands	103	(1)D4
Priboj	45	G6
Příbram	29	D8
Price	97	D3
Prichard	101	D3
Priekule	27	L8
Prienai	29	N3
Prieska	83	C5
Prievidza	29	H9
Prijedor	45	D5
Prijepolje	45	G6
Prikaspiyskaya		
Nizmennost'	49	K5
Prilep	47	D3
Prince Albert	93	K6
Prince Albert Peninsula	93	H2
Prince Charles Island	93	R3
Prince Edward Island	93	U7
Prince Edward Island	73	G10
Prince George	93	G6
Prince of Wales Island,		
Canada	93	L2
Prince of Wales Island,		
U.S.	93	E5
Prince Patrick Island	91	Q2
Prince Regent Inlet	93	N2
Prince Rupert	93	E6
Princeton	99	C3
Príncipe	79	F4
Prineville	97	B2
Priozersk	27	R6
Priština	45	J7
Privas	37	K9
Privolzhskaya		
Vozvyshennost	49	H4
Prizren	45	H7
Probolinggo	63	(1)E4
Progreso	105	G4
Prokop'yevsk	53	R7
Proliv Longa	55	X2
Proliv Vil'kitskogo	53	U2
Propriano	43	C7
Prosna	29	G6
Prosperidad	61	H5
Prostojov	29	G8
Provadiya	45	Q6
Providence	99	F2
Providencia	55	Z4
Provins	37	J5
Provo	97	D2
Prudhoe Bay	103	(1)H1
Prüm	33	J4
Pruszków	29	K5
Prut	45	R4
Prvić	41	K6
Prypyats'	25	G2
Psara	47	H6
Psebay	69	J1
Pskov	49	E3
Ptuj	41	L4
Pucallpa	109	C5
Pucheng	57	F5
Púchov	29	H8
Pucioasa	45	N4
Puck	29	H3
Pudasjärvi	27	P4
Puebla	105	E5
Pueblo	97	F3
Puente-Genil	39	F7
Puerto Acosta	109	D7
Puerto Alegre	109	E6
Puerto Angel	105	E5
Puerto Berrío	109	C2
Puerto Carreño	105	L7
Puerto de Navacerrada	39	G4
Puerto Leguizamo	109	C4
Puerto Libertad	103	D3
Puertollano	39	F6
Puerto Maldonado	109	D6
Puerto Montt	111	G7
Puerto Princesa	61	F5
Puerto Real	39	D8
Puerto Rico	105	L5
Puerto Rico Trench	107	E1
Puerto Santa Cruz	111	H9
Puerto Suárez	109	F7
Pukatawagen	93	L5
Pukë	45	G7
Pula	41	J6
Puławy	29	M6
Pullman	97	C1
Puncak Jaya	63	(2)E3
Puncak Mandala	63	(2)F3
Pune	65	B5
Punia	81	D4
Puno	109	C7
Punta Arena	97	B3
Punta Arenas	111	G9
Punta Eugenia	105	A3
Punta Gallinas	105	K6
Punta La Marmora	43	D8
Punta Mariato	105	H7
Punta Negra	109	A5
Puntarenas	105	H6
Punta San Gabriel	103	D3
Puqi	57	E5
Puri	65	E5
Purukcahu	63	(1)E3
Purus	109	E5
Pusan	59	E6
Putao	61	B1
Putaruru	89	E3
Putian	57	F5
Puttalami	65	C7
Putten	33	G3
Puttgarden	31	G2
Putumayo	109	C4
Puuwai	103	(2)A2
Puy de Dôme	37	H8
Puy de Sancy	37	H8

Q

Name	Page	Grid
Qādub	67	F7
Qalamat Nadqān	71	D5
Qalāt	67	J3
Qal'at Bīshah	67	D5
Qal'eh-ye Now	67	H3
Qamdo	57	B4
Qardho	81	H2
Qartaba	70	C2
Qaṭanā	70	D3
Qatar	71	D4
Qaṭrāna	70	D5
Qattâra Depression	75	E2
Qāyen	67	G3
Qazax	69	L3
Qazimämmäd	69	N3
Qazvīn	67	E2
Qena	75	F2
Qeqertarsuatsiaat	93	W4
Qeqertarsuatsiaq	93	V2
Qeshm	71	G3
Qeshm	71	F3
Qeys	71	E3
Qezel Owzan	69	N5
Qezi'ot	70	B6
Qianshanlaoba	53	Q8
Qiaowan	57	B2
Qiemo	53	R10
Qilian	57	C3
Qilian Shan	57	B3
Qingdao	57	G3
Qinghai Hu	57	B3
Qinghai Nanshan	57	B3
Qingjiang	57	F4
Qingyang	57	D3
Qinhuangdao	57	F3
Qinzhou	61	D2
Qionghai	61	E3
Qiqihar	55	L7
Qira	53	Q10
Qiryat Ata	70	C4
Qiryat Shemona	70	C3
Qishn	67	F6
Qolleh-ye Damāvand	67	F2

Name	Page	Grid
Qom	67	F3
Qomishēh	67	F3
Qornet es Saouda	70	D2
Qorveh	69	M6
Qotūr	69	L4
Quang Ngai'	61	D3
Quangolodougou	79	C3
Quang Tri	61	D3
Quanzhou	61	F2
Quaqtaq	93	T4
Quarto Sant'Elena	43	D9
Quba	69	N3
Québec	99	F1
Quedlinburg	31	G5
Queen Charlotte Islands	93	E6
Queen Charlotte Sound	93	E6
Queen Elizabeth Islands	91	M2
Queen Maud Gulf	93	L3
Queen Maud Land	112	(2)F2
Queensland	87	G4
Queenstown, *New Zealand*	89	B7
Queenstown, *South Africa*	83	D6
Quelimane	83	F3
Querétaro	105	D4
Quetta	67	J3
Quezon	61	F5
Quezon City	61	G4
Quibala	83	A2
Quibdó	105	J7
Quilpie	87	H5
Quimper	37	A5
Quimperlé	37	B6
Quincy	99	B3
Qui Nhon	61	D4
Quito	109	B4
Qujing	61	C1
Qumaryan	65	F1
Qurlurtuuq	93	H3
Qus	75	F2
Quseir	75	F2
Quzhou	57	F5

R

Name	Page	Grid
Raab	41	L3
Raahe	27	N4
Raas Caseyr	81	J1
Rab	41	K6
Rab	41	K6
Raba	63	(2)A4
Rába	45	E2
Rabat	77	D2
Rābigh	67	C5
Rabka	29	K8
Racine	99	C2
Ráckeve	45	F2
Rădăuți	45	N2
Radbuza	31	H7
Radeberg	31	J5
Radebeul	31	J5
Radom	29	L6
Radomsko	29	J6
Radstadt	29	C10
Raduznny	53	P5
Radviliškis	29	N2
Rae-Edzo	93	H4
Raetihi	89	E4
Rafaela	111	J4
Rafḥā	67	D4
Raglan	89	E3
Ragusa	43	J12
Raha	63	(2)B3
Rahad el Berdi	75	D5
Rahimyar Khan	67	K4
Rainy River	99	B1
Raipur	65	D4
Rajahmundry	65	D5
Rajapalaiyam	65	C7
Rajgarh	65	C3
Rajkot	67	K5
Raj Nangaon	65	D4
Rajshahi	65	E4
Rakhiv	45	M1
Rakovník	29	C7
Rakvere	27	P7
Raleigh	101	F2
Ralik Chain	85	G5
Rambouillet	37	G5
Rameswaram	65	C7
Rāmhormoz	71	C1
Ramlat Rabyānah	75	C3
Râmnicu Sărat	45	Q4
Râmnicu Vâlcea	45	M4
Ramree Island	61	A3
Ramsgate	35	P10
Ramtha	70	D4
Ranau	63	(1)F1
Rancagua	111	G5
Ranchi	65	E4
Randazzo	43	J11
Randers	27	F8
Rangoon = Yangon	61	B3
Rankin	103	F2
Ranong	61	B5
Ransiki	63	(2)D3
Rānya	69	L5
Rapa	85	M8
Rapalla	43	D4
Rapallo	41	E6
Raperswil	41	D3
Rapid City	97	F2
Rapid River	99	C1
Rarotonga	85	K8
Rās Abu Shagara	75	G3
Ra's al Ḥadd	67	G5
Ra's al Hilāl	75	D1
Ra's al Khaymah	71	F4
Ra's al Kūh	71	G4
Ra's al 'Udayd	71	D4
Ra's az Zawr	71	C3
Rās Banās	75	G3
Ras Bir	75	H5
Ras Dashen Terara	75	G5
Ra's-e Barkan	71	C2
Rās el Nafas	70	B7
Ra's Fartak	67	F6
Rasht	69	N5
Raška	45	H6
Ras Kasar	75	G4
Ra's Madrakah	67	G6
Rās Nouâdhibou	77	B4
Ras Tannūrah	71	D3
Ratak Chain	85	H4
Ratangarh	67	K4
Rat Buri	61	B4
Rathenow	31	H4
Rathlin Island	35	F6
Ratlam	65	C4
Ratnagiri	67	K6
Ratta	55	C4
Ratzeburg	31	F3
Raukumara Range	89	F4
Rauma	27	L6
Rāut	45	R2
Ravalli	97	D1
Ravenna	41	H6
Ravensburg	41	E3
Ravensthorpe	87	D6
Ravnina	67	H2
Rāwah	69	J6
Rawalpindi	67	K3
Rawicz	29	F6
Rawlinna	87	E6
Rawlins	97	E2
Rawson	111	J7
Rayong	61	C4
Razgrad	45	P6
Razlog	45	L8
Reading, *U.K.*	35	M10
Reading, *U.S.*	99	E2
Realicó	111	J6
Rechytsa	49	F4
Recife	109	L5
Recklinghausen	33	K3
Recknitz	31	H3
Reconquista	111	K4
Red, *Canada/U.S.*	97	G1
Red, *U.S.*	101	H7
Red Cloud	101	B1
Red Deer	93	J6
Redding	97	B2
Redditch	33	A2
Redfield	97	G2
Red Lakes	95	H2
Redon	37	C6
Redondela	39	B2
Red River = Song Hông	61	C2
Red Sea	75	G3
Red Wing	99	B2
Redwood Falls	99	A2
Reedsport	97	B2
Reefton	89	C6
Regensburg	31	H7
Reggane	77	F3
Reggio di Calabria	43	K10
Reggio nell'Emilia	41	F6
Regina	95	F1
Rehoboth	83	B4
Rehovot	70	B5
Reigate	35	M10
Reims	33	G5
Reindeer Lake	93	L5
Reinosa	39	F1
Reisi	43	J11
Reliance	93	K4
Rembang	63	(1)E4
Rendsburg	31	E2
Rengat	63	(1)C3
Renmark	87	H6
Rennes	37	D5
Reno	97	C3
Renton	97	B1
Reo	63	(2)B4
Replot	27	L5
Represa Tucuruí	109	H4
Republic of Ireland	35	D8
Repulse Bay	87	J4
Requena	109	C5
Réservoir Cabonga	99	E1
Réservoir Caniapiscau	93	T6
Réservoir de La Grande 2	93	R6
Réservoir Gouin	99	F1
Réservoir Manicouagan	93	T6
Réservoir Opinaca	93	R6
Réservoir Pipmuacan	99	G1
Reshteh-ye Kūhhā-ye Alborz	67	F2
Resistencia	111	K4
Reşița	45	J4
Resolute	93	N2
Resolution Island, *Canada*	93	U4
Resolution Island, *New Zealand*	89	A7
Resovo	47	K3
Rethel	33	G5
Rethymno	47	G9

Name	Page	Ref
Réunion	83	(1)B2
Reus	39	M3
Reutlingen	31	E8
Revin	33	G5
Revúca	29	K9
Rewa	65	D4
Reykjanes	27	(1)B3
Reykjavík	27	(1)C2
Reynosa	101	B4
Rezé	37	D6
Rēzekne	27	P8
Rezina	45	R2
Rezovo	45	R8
Rheda-Wiedenbrück	31	D5
Rhein = Rhine	41	C2
Rheine	33	K2
Rhin = Rhine	41	C2
Rhine	41	C2
Rhinelander	99	C1
Rho	41	E5
Rhode Island	99	F2
Rhodes = Rodos	47	L8
Rhône	37	K9
Ribadeo	39	C1
Ribas do Rio Pardo	111	L3
Ribe	27	E9
Ribeirão Prêto	111	M3
Ribeiria = Santa Eugenia	39	A2
Riberalta	109	D6
Ribnica	43	J3
Rîbniţa	45	S2
Riccione	41	H7
Richfield	97	D3
Richland	97	C1
Richmond, Australia	87	H4
Richmond, New Zealand	89	D5
Richmond, Ky., U.S.	99	D3
Richmond, Va., U.S.	99	E3
Ridgecrest	103	C1
Ried	41	J2
Riesa	31	J5
Rīga	27	N8
Riggins	97	C1
Rijeka	41	K5
Riley	97	C2
Rimavská Sobota	29	K9
Rimini	41	H6
Ringkøbing	27	E8
Ringsted	31	G1
Ringvassøya	27	J1
Rio Branco	109	D5
Río Colorado	111	J6
Río Cuarto	111	J5
Rio de Janeiro	111	N3
Rio de Janeiro	111	N3
Río de la Plata	111	K6
Río Gallegos	111	H9
Rio Grande	103	E2
Río Grande, Argentina	111	H9
Río Grande, Mexico	103	F4
Rio Grande	111	L5
Rio Grande do Norte	109	K5
Rio Grande do Sul	111	L4
Ríohacha	105	K6
Riom	37	J8
Ripley	99	D3
Ripoll	39	N2
Rishiri-tō	55	Q7
Rivadavia	111	G4
Riva del Garda	41	F5
Rivarolo Canavese	41	C5
Rivera	111	K5
Riversdale Beach	89	E5
Riverton	89	A8
Rivesaltes	37	H11
Rivière-du-Loup	99	G1
Rivne	49	E4
Rivoli	41	C5
Riwoqê	65	G2
Riyadh = Ar Riyāḍ	71	B4
Rize	69	J3
Rizhao	57	F3
Roanne	37	K7
Roanoke	99	D3
Roanoke Rapids	101	F2
Robe	87	G7
Robertval	99	F1
Roccastrada	43	F6
Rochefort, Belgium	33	H4
Rochefort, France	37	E8
Rochelle	99	C2
Rochester, Minn., U.S.	99	B2
Rochester, N.Y., U.S.	99	E2
Rockall	25	C2
Rockford	99	C2
Rockhampton	87	K4
Rock Hill	99	D4
Rock Island	99	B2
Rock Rapids	99	A2
Rock Springs	97	E2
Rocksprings	103	F3
Rocky Mount	99	E3
Rocky Mountains	93	F5
Rødby Havn	31	G2
Rodez	37	H9
Roding	31	H7
Rodopi Planina	45	M7
Rodos	47	L8
Rodos	47	L8
Roebourne	87	C4
Roermond	33	J3
Roeselare	33	F4
Roes Welcome Sound	93	P4
Rogerson	97	D2
Rogliano	43	D6
Rohrbach	41	K2
Roi Et	61	C3
Roja	27	M8
Rolla	99	B3
Rolleston	89	D6
Roma, Australia	87	J5
Roma, Italy	43	G7
Roman	45	P3
Romania	45	L4
Romans-sur-Isère	37	L8
Rome = Roma	43	G7
Rome, Ga., U.S.	101	D3
Rome, N.Y., U.S.	99	E2
Romney	99	E3
Romny	49	F4
Romorantin-Lanthenay	37	G6
Rona	35	G2
Roncesvalles	39	J2
Ronda	39	E8
Rondônia	109	E6
Rondônia	109	E6
Rondonópolis	109	G7
Rønne	29	D2
Ronne Ice Shelf	112	(2)MM2
Ronse	33	F4
Roraima	109	E3
Røros	27	F5
Rosário	109	J4
Rosario, Argentina	111	J5
Rosario, Mexico	95	D6
Rosário Oeste	109	F6
Rosarito	95	C6
Rosarno	43	K10
Roscommon	35	D8
Roseau	105	M5
Roseburg	97	B2
Roseires Reservoir	75	F5
Rosenburg	103	G3
Rosenheim	41	H3
Rosetown	93	K6
Rosignano Solvay	41	F7
Roşiori de Vede	45	N5
Roskilde	27	G9
Roslavl'	49	F4
Rossano	43	L9
Ross Ice Shelf	112	(2)Z1
Roßlau	31	H5
Rosso	77	B5
Rossosh'	49	G4
Ross River	93	E4
Ross Sea	112	(2)AA2
Rostock	31	H2
Rostov-na-Donu	49	G5
Roswell	103	F2
Rote	63	(2)B5
Rotenburg	31	E3
Roth	31	G7
Rothenburg	31	F7
Rotorua	89	F4
Rotterdam	37	K2
Rottumeroog	33	J1
Rottumerplaat	33	J1
Rottweil	41	D2
Roubaix	33	F4
Rouen	33	D5
Round Mountain	87	K6
Roundup	97	E1
Rousay	35	J2
Rouyn	99	E1
Rovaniemi	27	N3
Rovereto	41	G5
Rovigo	41	G5
Rovinj	41	J5
Rovuma	81	F6
Roxas	61	G4
Roxburgh	89	B7
Royal Tunbridge Wells	33	C3
Royan	37	D8
Rozdil'na	45	T3
Rtishchevo	49	H4
Ruahine Range	89	E5
Ruapehu	89	E4
Ruapuke Island	89	B8
Ruarkela	65	D4
Ruatoria	89	G3
Ruawai	89	D3
Rub' al Khālī	67	E6
Rubtsovsk	53	Q7
Rudbar	67	H3
Rüdersdorf	31	J4
Rudnaya Pristan'	59	H2
Rudnyy	49	M4
Ruffec	37	F7
Rufiji	81	F5
Rugby	33	A2
Rügen	29	C3
Ruhnu	27	M8
Ruhr	33	K3
Rum	35	F5
Rumäh	71	B4
Rumbek	81	D2
Rumigny	33	G5
Rumoi	55	L2
Ruoqiang	53	R10
Ruo Shui	57	C2
Rupert	97	D2
Ruse	45	N6
Rushville, Ill., U.S.	99	B2
Rushville, Ind., U.S.	99	C3
Russellville	101	C2
Rüsselsheim	31	D7
Russia	27	L9
Russia	51	M3
Rust'avi	69	L3
Rutana	81	D4

Name		Page	Grid
Rute	●	39	F7
Ruteng	●	63	(2)B4
Rutland	●	99	F2
Rutog	●	65	C2
Ruvuma	◪	81	F6
Ruzayevka	●	49	H4
Ružomberok	●	29	J8
Rwanda	Ⓐ	81	D4
Ryazan'	●	49	G4
Ryazhsk	●	49	H4
Rybinsk	●	49	G3
Rybinskoye Vodokhranilishche	◪	49	G3
Rybnik	●	29	H7
Ryl'sk	●	49	F4
Ryn-Peski	⊘	49	J5
Ryōtsu	●	59	K4
Ryukyu Islands = Nansei-shotō	▨	57	H5
Rzeszów	●	29	M7
Rzhev	●	49	F3

S

Name		Page	Grid
Sa'ādatābād	●	71	F2
Saale	◪	31	G6
Saalfeld	●	31	G6
Saar	◪	33	J5
Saarbrücken	●	33	J5
Saaremaa	▨	27	L7
Saarlouis	●	33	J5
Saatli	●	69	N4
Saba	▨	105	M5
Sabadell	●	39	N3
Sabah	▨	63	(1)F1
Sabhā	●	77	H3
Sabinas	●	103	F3
Sabinas Hidalgo	●	103	F3
Sabine Lake	◪	101	C3
Sabkhet el Bardawîl	◪	70	A5
Sable Island	▨	93	V8
Sabôr	◪	39	D3
Sabzevār	●	67	G2
Sachanga	●	83	B2
Sachs Harbour	●	93	G2
Sacramento	◪	97	B3
Sacramento	▣	97	B3
Şad'ah	●	67	D6
Sadiya	●	65	G3
Sado	◪	39	B6
Sado-shima	▨	59	J4
Säffle	●	27	G7
Safford	●	103	E2
Safi, Jordan	●	70	C5
Safi, Morocco	●	77	D2
Safonovo, Russia	●	49	F3
Safonovo, Russia	●	49	J1

Name		Page	Grid
Safranbolu	●	47	Q3
Sagami-nada	▱	59	K6
Sagar	●	65	C4
Saginaw	●	99	D2
Sagiz	●	49	K5
Saguache	●	97	E3
Sagunt	●	39	K5
Sahagún	●	39	E2
Sahara	⊘	73	C3
Saharah el Gharbîya	⊘	75	E2
Saharanpur	●	65	C3
Saharsa	●	65	E3
Şahbuz	●	69	L4
Sahel	⊘	73	C4
Sahiwal	●	67	K3
Sahuaripa	●	103	E3
Saïda, Algeria	●	77	F2
Saïda, Lebanon	●	70	C3
Sa'idābād	●	71	F2
Saidpur	●	65	E3
Saigon = Hô Chi Minh	●	61	D4
Saihan Toroi	●	57	C2
Saiki	●	59	F7
Saimaa	◪	27	P6
St. Albans	●	33	B3
St-Amand-Montrond	●	37	H7
St. Andrä	●	41	K4
St. Andrews	●	35	K5
St. Anthony	●	93	V6
St. Augustin	●	33	K4
St. Austell	●	35	H11
St-Avold	●	33	J5
St. Barthélémy	▨	105	M5
St-Brieuc	●	37	C5
St. Catharines	●	95	L3
St-Chamond	●	37	K8
St-Claude	●	37	L7
St. Cloud	●	99	B1
St. David's	●	35	G10
St-Denis, France	●	33	E6
St-Denis, Réunion	●	83	(1)B2
St-Dié	●	41	B2
St-Dizier	●	37	K5
Ste-Anne-de-Beaupré	●	99	F1
Ste-Menehould	●	33	G5
St-Étienne	●	37	K8
St-Félicien	●	99	F1
St. Francis	◪	97	F3
St. Gallen	●	41	E3
St-Gaudens	●	37	F10
St. George, Australia	●	87	J5
St. George, U.S.	●	97	D3
St. Georges	●	99	F1
St. George's	■	105	M6
St. George's Channel	▱	35	F10
St-Germain-en-Laye	●	33	E6
St-Girons	●	37	G11
St. Helena	▨	73	C7

Name		Page	Grid
St. Helena Bay	▱	83	B6
St. Helens, U.K.	●	35	K8
St. Helens, U.S.	●	97	B1
St. Helier	●	37	C4
St-Jean-d'Angely	●	37	E8
St-Jean-sur-Richelieu	●	99	F1
St. John	◪	93	T7
St. John's	□	93	W7
St. Joseph	●	99	B3
St. Kilda	▨	35	D4
St. Kitts-Nevis	Ⓐ	105	M5
St. Laurent	●	109	G2
St. Lawrence	▱	99	G1
St. Lawrence Island	▨	103	(1)C3
St-Lô	●	33	A5
St. Louis, Senegal	●	77	B5
St. Louis, U.S.	●	99	B3
St. Lucia	Ⓐ	105	M6
St. Maarten	▨	105	M5
St-Malo	●	37	D5
St. Marys	●	99	D2
St. Matthew Island	▨	103	(1)C3
St. Moritz	●	41	E4
St-Nazaire	●	37	C6
St. Niklaas	●	33	G3
St-Omer	●	33	E4
St. Paul	●	97	G2
St. Paul	□	99	B2
St. Peter-Port	●	37	C4
St. Petersburg = Sankt-Peterburg	●	49	F3
St. Petersburg	●	101	E4
St-Pierre-et-Miquelon	▨	93	V7
St-Pol-sur-Ternoise	●	33	E4
St. Pölten	●	41	L2
St-Quentin	●	33	F5
St. Stephen	●	99	G1
St. Thomas	●	99	D2
St-Tropez	●	41	B7
St. Truiden	●	33	H4
St-Valéry-sur-Somme	●	33	D4
St. Veit an der Glan	●	45	B3
St. Vincent and the Grenadines	Ⓐ	105	M6
St-Vincent-les-Forts	●	41	B6
St-Vith	●	33	J4
Saipan	▨	85	E4
Sakarya	●	47	N4
Sakarya	◪	47	N4
Sakata	●	59	K4
Sakchu	●	59	C3
Sakha	◩	55	N3
Sakhalin	▨	55	Q6
Sakhon Nakhon	●	61	C3
Şäki	●	69	M3
Sakishima-shotō	●	57	H6
Sakskøbing	●	31	G2
Sal	●	79	(1)B1

Name		Page	Grid
Šal'a	●	29	G9
Salacgrīva	●	27	N8
Sala Consilina	●	43	K8
Salado	◪	111	J4
Salālah	●	67	F6
Salamanca	●	39	E4
Salamina	●	47	F7
Salamīyah	●	70	E1
Salar de Uyuni	◪	111	H3
Salawati	▨	63	(2)D3
Salayar	▨	63	(2)B4
Saldus	●	27	M8
Sale	●	87	J7
Salekhard	●	53	M4
Salem	□	97	B2
Salem, India	●	65	C6
Salem, U.S.	●	99	C3
Salerno	●	43	J8
Salgótarján	●	29	J9
Salida	●	97	E3
Salihli	●	47	L6
Salima	●	83	E2
Salina	▨	43	J10
Salina, Kans., U.S.	●	97	G3
Salina, Ut., U.S.	●	97	D3
Salinas, Brazil	●	109	J7
Salinas, Ecuador	●	109	A4
Salinas, Mexico	●	103	F4
Salinas, U.S.	●	103	B1
Salisbury, U.K.	●	33	A3
Salisbury, U.S.	●	99	E3
Şalkhad	●	70	D4
Salmās	●	69	L4
Salmon	●	97	D1
Salmon	◪	97	C1/D1
Salmon River Mountains	▲	97	C1
Salon-de-Provence	●	37	L10
Salonta	●	45	J3
Sal'sk	●	49	H5
Salsomaggiore Terme	●	41	E6
Salt	●	70	C4
Salta	●	111	H3
Saltillo	●	103	F3
Salt Lake City	□	97	D2
Salto	●	111	K5
Salton Sea	◪	103	C2
Salūm	●	75	E1
Saluzzo	●	41	C6
Salvador	●	109	K6
Salvadore	●	107	H5
Salween	◪	61	B2
Salyan	●	69	N4
Salzach	◪	41	H2
Salzburg	●	41	J3
Salzgitter	●	31	F4
Salzwedel	●	31	G4
Samaipata	●	109	E7
Samar	▨	61	H4

Name	Pg	Ref
Samara	49	K4
Samarinda	63	(1)F3
Samarkand	67	J2
Sambalpur	65	D4
Sambas	63	(1)D2
Sambava	83	J2
Sambre	33	F4
Same	81	F4
Sami	47	C6
Sämkir	69	M3
Samoa	85	J7
Samobor	41	L5
Samoded	49	H2
Samokov	45	L7
Samos	47	J7
Samos	47	J7
Samothraki	47	H4
Samothraki	47	H4
Sam Rayburn Reservoir	101	C3
Samsang	65	D2
Samsø	27	F9
Samsun	69	G3
Samtredia	69	K2
Samut Songkhram	61	B4
San	79	D2
San	29	L7
Şan'ä	75	H4
Sanaga	79	G4
Sanana	63	(2)C3
Sanana	63	(2)C3
Sanandaj	69	M6
San Angelo	103	F2
San Antonia Abad	39	M6
San Antonio	105	E3
San Antonio-Oeste	111	H7
Sanäw	67	F6
San Benedetto del Tronto	43	H6
San Bernardino	103	C2
San Borja	109	D6
San Carlos	109	D3
Sanchahe	59	C1
San Clemente Island	103	C2
San Cristóbal	109	C2
Sandakan	63	(1)F1
Sandanski	47	F3
Sanday	35	K2
Sandefjord	27	F7
Sanders	103	E1
Sanderson	103	F2
San Diego	103	C2
Sandıklı	47	N6
Sandnes	27	C7
Sandnessjøen	27	G4
Sandoa	81	C5
San Donà di Piave	41	H5
Sandoway	65	F5
Sandpoint	97	C1
Sandviken	27	J6
Sandy Cape	87	K4
Sandy Lake	93	N6
San Felipe	95	D5
San Fernando, Chile	111	G5
San Fernando, Mexico	101	B5
San Fernando, Philippines	61	G3
San Fernando, Spain	39	D8
San Fernando de Apure	109	D2
Sanford	101	E4
San Francis	101	A2
San Francisco, Argentina	111	J5
San Francisco, U.S.	97	B3
Sangän	67	H3
Sangar	55	M4
Sangha	79	H4
San Gimignano	41	G7
San Giovanni in Fiore	43	L9
San Giovanni Valdarno	41	G7
Sangir	63	(2)C2
Sangkulirang	63	(1)F2
Sangli	65	B5
Sangmélima	79	G4
Sangre de Cristo Range	103	E1
Sangsang	65	E3
San Joaquin Valley	97	B3
San Jose	97	B3
San José	105	H7
San Jose de Buenavista	61	G4
San Jose de Jáchal	111	H5
San José del Cabo	105	C4
San José de Ocuné	109	C3
San Juan, Argentina	111	H5
San Juan, Costa Rica	105	H6
San Juan, Puerto Rico	105	L5
San Juan Mountains	97	E3
San Julián	111	H8
Sankt-Peterburg	49	F3
Sankuru	81	C4
Sanlıurfa	69	H5
San Lorenzo	103	D3
Sanlúcar de Barrameda	39	D8
San Luis	111	H5
San Luis Obispo	103	B1
San Luis Potosí	105	D4
San Luis Rio Colorado	103	D2
San Marcos	101	B4
San Marino	41	H7
San Marino	41	H7
Sanmenxia	57	E4
San Miguel	105	G6
San Miguel	109	E7
San Miguel de Tucumán	111	H4
San Nicolas de los Arroyos	111	J5
Sânnicolau Mare	45	H3
Sanok	29	M8
San Pablo	61	G4
San-Pédro	79	C4
San Pedro, Argentina	111	J3
San Pedro, Bolivia	109	E7
San Pedro Sula	105	G5
San Pietro	43	C9
San Rafael	111	H5
San Remo	41	C7
San Salvador	101	G5
San Salvador	105	G6
San Salvador de Jujuy	111	H3
San Sebastián = Donostia	39	J1
Sansepolcro	41	H7
San Severo	43	K7
Sanski Most	41	M6
Sant'Antioco	43	C9
Santa Ana, El Salvador	105	G6
Santa Ana, U.S.	103	C2
Santa Barbara	103	C2
Santa Catalina Island	103	C2
Santa Catarina	111	L4
Santa Clara	95	K7
Santa Clarita	103	C2
Santa Comba Dão	39	B4
Santa Cruz, Bolivia	109	E7
Santa Cruz, U.S.	103	B1
Santa Cruz de Tenerife	77	B3
Santa Cruz Island	103	B2
Santa Cruz Islands	85	G7
Santa Eugenia	39	A2
Santa Fé	111	J5
Santa Fe	97	E3
Santa Isabel	111	H6
Santa Maria, Brazil	111	L4
Santa Maria, U.S.	103	B2
Santander	39	G1
Santarém, Brazil	109	G4
Santarém, Spain	39	B5
Santa Rosa, Argentina	111	J6
Santa Rosa, Calif., U.S.	97	B3
Santa Rosa, N. Mex., U.S.	103	F2
Santa Rosa Island	103	B2
Santa Vitória do Palmar	111	L5
Sant Celoni	39	N3
Sant Feliu de Guixols	39	P3
Santiago	111	G5
Santiago, Dominican Republic	105	K5
Santiago, Philippines	61	G3
Santiago, Spain	39	B2
Santiago de Cuba	105	J5
Santiago del Estero	111	J4
Santo Antão	79	(1)A1
Santo Antônio de Jesus	109	K6
Santo Antônio do Içá	109	D4
Santo Domingo	105	L5
Santo Domingo de los Colorados	109	B4
Santos	111	M3
San Vincenzo	43	E5
Sanya	61	D3
Sao Bernardo do Campo	109	E4
São Carlos	111	M3
São Félix, M.G., Brazil	109	G6
São Félix, Pará, Brazil	109	G5
São Filipe	79	(1)B2
São Francisco	109	J6
São Jorge	77	(1)B2
São Luís	109	J4
São Miguel	77	(1)B2
Saône	37	K7
São Nicolau	79	(1)B1
São Paulo	111	L3
São Paulo	111	M3
São Paulo de Olivença	109	D4
São Raimundo Nonato	109	J5
São Tiago	79	(1)B1
São Tomé	79	F4
São Tomé	79	F4
São Tomé and Príncipe	79	F4
São Vicente	79	(1)A1
Sapporo	59	L2
Saqqez	69	M5
Saräb	69	M5
Sara Buri	61	C4
Sarajevo	45	F6
Sarakhs	67	H2
Saraktash	49	L4
Saramati	65	G3
Saran	53	N8
Saranpul	49	M2
Saransk	49	J4
Sarapul	49	K3
Sarasota	101	E4
Saratov	49	J4
Saravan	67	H4
Sarawak	63	(1)E2
Saray	47	K3
Sarayköy	47	L7
Sarbāz	67	H4
Sardegna	43	E8
Sardinia = Sardegna	43	E8
Sargodha	67	K3
Sarh	79	H3
Sārī	67	F2
Saria	47	K9
Sarikei	63	(1)E2
Sarina	87	J4
Sarīr Tibesti	75	C3
Sariwŏn	59	C4
Sark	37	C4
Sarkand	53	P8

Şarkışla . . . 69 G4
Şarköy . . . 47 K4
Sarmi . . . 63 (2)E3
Särna . . . 27 G4
Sarnia . . . 99 D2
Saronno . . . 41 E5
Saros Körfezi . . . 47 J4
Sárospatak . . . 29 L9
Sarre . . . 37 M5
Sarrebourg . . . 37 N5
Sarria . . . 39 C2
Sartène . . . 43 C7
Sárvár . . . 41 M3
Sarvestān . . . 71 E2
Saryozek . . . 53 P9
Saryshagan . . . 53 N8
Sarzana . . . 41 E6
Sasebo . . . 59 E7
Saskatchewan . . . 93 K6
Saskatchewan . . . 93 L6
Saskatoon . . . 93 K6
Saskylakh . . . 53 W3
Sassandra . . . 79 C4
Sassari . . . 43 C8
Sassnitz . . . 31 J2
Sassuolo . . . 41 F6
Satara . . . 65 B5
Satna . . . 65 D4
Satu Mare . . . 45 K2
Satun . . . 63 (1)B1
Saudi Arabia . . . 67 D4
Sauk Center . . . 99 B1
Sault Ste. Marie, *Canada* . . . 99 D1
Sault Ste. Marie, *U.S.* . . . 99 D1
Saumlakki . . . 63 (2)D4
Saumur . . . 37 E6
Saunders Island . . . 107 J9
Saurimo . . . 81 C5
Sauðárkrókur . . . 27 (1)D2
Sava . . . 41 L5
Savannah, *Ga., U.S.* . . . 101 E3
Savannah, *Tenn., U.S.* . . . 101 D2
Savannakhet . . . 61 C3
Savaştepe . . . 47 K5
Savè . . . 79 E3
Save . . . 83 E4
Savigliano . . . 41 C6
Savona . . . 41 D6
Savonlinna . . . 27 Q6
Savu . . . 63 (2)B5
Sawahlunto . . . 63 (1)C3
Sawqirah . . . 67 G6
Sawu Sea . . . 63 (2)B4
Sāylac . . . 75 H5
Saynshand . . . 57 E2
Say'ün . . . 67 E6
Say-Utes . . . 53 J9
Scafell Pike . . . 35 J7

Scarborough . . . 35 M7
Schaffhausen . . . 41 D3
Schagen . . . 33 G2
Schärding . . . 41 J2
Scharhörn . . . 31 D3
Schefferville . . . 93 T6
Scheibbs . . . 41 L3
Schelde . . . 33 F3
Schenectady . . . 99 F2
Schiedam . . . 33 G3
Schiermonnikoog . . . 33 H1
Schio . . . 41 G5
Schiza . . . 47 D8
Schkeuditz . . . 31 H5
Schleswig . . . 31 E2
Schlüchtern . . . 31 E6
Schneeberg . . . 31 G6
Schönebeck . . . 31 G4
Schongau . . . 41 F3
Schouwen . . . 33 F3
Schramberg . . . 41 D2
Schreiber . . . 99 C1
Schwabach . . . 31 G7
Schwäbische Alb . . . 41 E2
Schwäbisch-Gmünd . . . 41 E2
Schwäbisch-Hall . . . 31 E7
Schwalmstadt . . . 31 E6
Schwandorf . . . 31 H7
Schwarzenberg . . . 31 H6
Schwarzwald . . . 41 D2
Schwaz . . . 41 G3
Schwedt . . . 29 D4
Schweinfurt . . . 31 F6
Schwenningen . . . 41 D2
Schwerin . . . 31 G3
Schweriner See . . . 31 G3
Schwyz . . . 41 D3
Sciacca . . . 43 H11
Scicli . . . 43 J12
Scotia Ridge . . . 111 K9
Scotia Sea . . . 112 (2)A4
Scotland . . . 35 H5
Scott City . . . 97 F3
Scott Reef . . . 87 D2
Scottsbluff . . . 97 F2
Scotty's Junction . . . 103 C1
Scranton . . . 99 F2
Scunthorpe . . . 35 M8
Sea of Azov . . . 49 G5
Sea of Galilee . . . 70 C4
Sea of Japan . . . 59 G3
Sea of Marmara =
  Marmara Denizi . . . 47 L4
Sea of Okhotsk . . . 55 Q5
Sea of the Hebrides . . . 35 E4
Searcy . . . 99 B3
Seattle . . . 97 B1
Sebeş . . . 45 L4

Sebkha Azzel Matti . . . 77 F3
Sebkha de Timimoun . . . 77 E3
Sebkha de Tindouf . . . 77 D3
Sebkha Oum el Drouss
  Telli . . . 77 C4
Secchia . . . 41 F6
Sécure . . . 109 D7
Sedan . . . 33 G5
Sedano . . . 39 G2
Seddonville . . . 89 C5
Sedom . . . 70 C5
Seeheim . . . 83 B5
Segezha . . . 49 F2
Ségou . . . 79 C2
Segovia . . . 39 F4
Segré . . . 37 E6
Séguédine . . . 77 H4
Segura . . . 39 H6
Seiland . . . 27 M1
Seiling . . . 101 B2
Seinäjoki . . . 27 M5
Seine . . . 37 F4
Sekondi . . . 79 D3
Selat Dampir . . . 63 (2)D3
Selat Karimata . . . 63 (1)D3
Selat Makassar . . . 63 (1)F3
Selat Mentawai . . . 63 (1)B3
Selat Sunda . . . 63 (1)D4
Selawik . . . 103 (1)F2
Selby . . . 97 G1
Selçuk . . . 47 K7
Selebi-Phikwe . . . 83 D4
Sélestat . . . 41 C2
Selfoss . . . 27 (1)C3
Selkirk . . . 95 G1
Selkirk Mountains . . . 95 C1
Sells . . . 103 D2
Selpele . . . 63 (2)D3
Selvas . . . 109 C5
Selwyn Mountains . . . 103 (1)L3
Semarang . . . 63 (1)E4
Sembé . . . 79 G4
Seminole . . . 103 F2
Semiozernoye . . . 53 L7
Semipalatinsk . . . 53 Q7
Semois . . . 33 H5
Sena Madureira . . . 109 D5
Senanga . . . 83 C3
Senatobia . . . 101 D3
Sendai . . . 59 L4
Senegal . . . 79 A2
Sénégal . . . 79 B1
Senftenberg . . . 31 J5
Senhor do Bonfim . . . 109 J6
Senica . . . 29 G9
Senigallia . . . 41 J7
Senj . . . 41 K6
Senja . . . 27 J2

Senlis . . . 33 E5
Sennar . . . 67 B7
Senneterre . . . 99 E1
Sens . . . 37 J5
Senta . . . 45 H4
Seoni . . . 65 C4
Seoul = Sŏul . . . 59 D5
Sept-Îles . . . 93 T6
Seraing . . . 33 H4
Seram . . . 63 (2)D3
Seram Sea . . . 63 (2)C3
Serang . . . 63 (1)D4
Serbia = Srbija . . . 45 H6
Serdobsk . . . 49 H4
Şereflikoçhisar . . . 47 R6
Seremban . . . 63 (1)C2
Serenje . . . 83 E2
Sergipe . . . 109 K6
Sergiyev Posad . . . 49 G3
Seria . . . 63 (1)E2
Serifos . . . 47 G7
Serik . . . 47 P8
Serov . . . 49 M3
Serowe . . . 83 D4
Serpa . . . 39 C7
Serpukhov . . . 49 G4
Serra do Cachimbo . . . 109 F5
Serra do Roncador . . . 109 G6
Serra dos Parecis . . . 109 E6
Serra Formosa . . . 109 F6
Serra Lombarda . . . 109 G3
Serra Pacaraima . . . 109 E3
Serra Tumucumaque . . . 109 F3
Serra da Estrela . . . 39 C4
Serres . . . 47 F3
Serrinha . . . 109 K6
Serui . . . 63 (2)E3
Sêrxü . . . 57 B4
Sesfontein . . . 83 A3
Sesheke . . . 83 C3
Sestri Levante . . . 41 E6
Sestroretsk . . . 27 Q6
Sestrunj . . . 41 K6
Sesvete . . . 41 M5
Sète . . . 37 J10
Setesdal . . . 27 D7
Sétif . . . 77 G1
Settat . . . 77 D2
Setúbal . . . 39 B6
Sŏul . . . 85 C2
Sevana Lich . . . 69 L3
Sevastopol' . . . 69 E1
Seven Lakes . . . 103 E1
Severn . . . 93 P5
Severnaya Dvina . . . 49 H2
Severnaya Osetiya . . . 69 L2
Severnaya Zemlya . . . 53 U1
Severn Estuary . . . 35 J10

Name	Pg	Grid
Severobaykal'sk	55	H5
Severodvinsk	49	G2
Severomorsk	27	S2
Sevier Lake	97	D3
Sevilla	39	E7
Seward Peninsula	103	(1)E2
Seychelles	83	(2)B2
Seychelles Islands	73	J6
Seydişehir	47	P7
Seydisfjöður	27	(1)G2
Seyhan	69	F5
Seymchan	55	S4
Seymour, *Australia*	87	J7
Seymour, *U.S.*	101	B3
Sézanne	37	J5
Sezze	43	H7
Sfakia	47	G9
Sfântu Gheorghe	45	N4
Sfax	77	H2
's-Gravenhage	33	G2
Shabunda	81	D4
Shabwah	67	E6
Shache	53	P10
Shag Rocks	111	N9
Shahdol	65	D4
Shah Fuladi	67	J3
Shahjahanpur	65	C3
Shahrak	67	H3
Shahr-e Bābāk	71	F1
Shakhty	49	H5
Shakhun'ya	49	J3
Shakotan-misaki	59	L2
Shamattawa	93	N5
Shamrock	103	F1
Shandong Bandao	57	G3
Shangdu	57	E2
Shanghai	57	G4
Shangqui	57	F2
Shangrao	57	F5
Shantarskiye Ostrova	55	P5
Shantou	57	F6
Shanyin	57	E3
Shaoguan	57	E6
Shaoxing	57	G5
Shaoyang	57	E5
Shaqrā'	71	A4
Sharjah = Ash Shāriqah	71	F4
Sharm el Sheikh	75	F2
Shashe	83	D4
Shashi	57	E4
Shatsk	49	H4
Shats'k	29	N6
Shaubak	70	C6
Shawano	99	C2
Shcherbakove	55	U3
Shchuchyn	27	N10
Sheberghān	67	J2
Sheboygan	99	C2
Sheffield, *New Zealand*	89	D6
Sheffield, *U.K.*	35	L8
Sheffield, *U.S.*	103	F2
Shelikof Strait	103	(1)F4
Shenandoah	99	A2
Shendam	79	F3
Shendi	75	F4
Shenkursk	49	H2
Shenyang	59	B3
Shenzhen	57	E6
Shepparton	87	J7
Sherbro Island	79	B3
Sherbrooke	99	F1
Sheridan	97	E2
Sherman	101	B3
's-Hertogenbosch	33	H3
Shetland Islands	35	M1
Sheykh Sho'eyb	71	E3
Shibata	59	K5
Shibetsu, *Japan*	59	M1
Shibetsu, *Japan*	59	N2
Shibotsu-jima	59	P2
Shihezi	53	R9
Shijiazhuang	57	E3
Shikarpur	67	J4
Shikoku	59	G7
Shikoku-sanchi	59	G7
Shikotan-tō	59	P2
Shiliguri	65	E3
Shilka	55	K6
Shilka	55	K6
Shillong	65	F3
Shimla	65	C2
Shimoda	59	K6
Shimoga	65	C6
Shimoni	81	F4
Shimonoseki	59	F7
Shīndan	67	H3
Shingū	59	H7
Shinjō	59	L4
Shinyanga	81	E4
Shiono-misaki	59	H7
Shirakawa	59	L5
Shīrāz	71	E2
Shiriya-zaki	59	L3
Shir Küh	67	F3
Shivpuri	65	C3
Shiyan	57	E4
Shizuishan	57	D3
Shizuoka	59	K6
Shkodër	45	G7
Shoshone, *Calif., U.S.*	97	C3
Shoshone, *Id., U.S.*	97	D2
Shoshoni	97	E2
Shostka	49	F4
Show Low	103	E2
Shoyna	49	H1
Shreveport	101	C3
Shrewsbury	35	K9
Shuangliao	59	B2
Shuangyashan	55	N7
Shubarkuduk	53	K8
Shulan	59	D1
Shumagin Islands	103	(1)E5
Shumen	45	P6
Shuryshkary	49	N1
Shwebo	61	B2
Shymkent	53	M9
Sialkot	67	K3
Sibay	49	L4
Šibenik	45	C6
Siberia = Sibir	51	N3
Siberut	63	(1)B3
Sibir	51	N3
Sibiu	45	M4
Sibolga	63	(1)B2
Sibu	63	(1)E2
Sibuco	61	G5
Sibut	81	B2
Sicilia	43	G11
Sicilian Channel	43	E10
Sicily = Sicilia	43	G11
Sidi Bel Abbès	77	E1
Sidirokastro	47	F3
Sidney	97	F2
Sidoan	63	(2)B2
Sidorovsk	53	Q4
Siedlce	29	M5
Siegen	33	L4
Siemiatycze	29	M5
Sierpc	29	J5
Sierra Blanca	103	E2
Sierra de Córdoba	111	H5
Sierra de Gata	39	D4
Sierra de Gúdar	39	K4
Sierra Grande	111	H7
Sierra Leone	79	B3
Sierra Madre del Sur	105	E5
Sierra Madre Occidental	95	E6
Sierra Madre Oriental	103	F3
Sierra Morena	39	D6
Sierra Nevada, *Spain*	39	G7
Sierra Nevada, *U.S.*	103	B1
Sierre	41	C4
Sifnos	47	G8
Sig	39	K9
Sighetu Marmaţiei	45	L2
Sighişoara	45	M3
Siglufjörður	27	(1)D1
Sigmaringen	41	E2
Siguiri	79	C2
Sihanoukville	61	C4
Siilinjärvi	27	P5
Siirt	69	J5
Sikar	65	C3
Sikasso	79	C2
Sikea	47	F4
Sikeston	99	C3
Sikhote Alin	59	H1
Sikinos	47	G8
Siktyakh	55	L3
Sil	39	C2
Šilalė	29	M2
Silandro	41	F4
Silba	41	K6
Silchar	65	F4
Šile	47	M3
Siliana	43	D12
Silifke	69	E5
Siling Co	65	E2
Silistra	45	Q5
Silivri	47	L3
Siljan	27	H6
Silvan	69	J4
Silver City	103	E2
Silver Lake	97	B2
Simanggang	63	(1)E2
Simao	57	C6
Simav	69	C4
Simeuluë	63	(1)A2
Simferopol'	69	F1
Şimleu Silvaniei	45	K2
Simpson Desert	87	G4
Sinabang	63	(1)B2
Sinai	75	F2
Sinaia	45	N4
Şinak	69	K5
Sinalunga	43	F5
Sinanju	59	C4
Sincelejo	109	B2
Sindelfingen	31	E8
Sines	39	B7
Singa	75	F5
Singapore	63	(1)C2
Singapore	63	(1)C2
Singaraja	63	(1)E4
Singen	41	D3
Singida	81	E4
Singkawang	63	(1)D2
Singkep	63	(1)C3
Sinj	45	D6
Sinjār	69	J5
Sinop	69	F2
Sinton	101	B4
Sinüiju	59	C3
Siófok	45	F3
Sion	41	C4
Sioux City	99	A2
Sioux Falls	99	A2
Sioux Lookout	95	H2
Siping	59	C2

Name	Page	Ref
Sipura	63	(1)B3
Siracusa	43	K11
Sir Banī 'Yās	71	E4
Siret	45	P2
Siret	45	Q3
Siri Kit Dam	61	B3
Sirk	71	G3
Sirohi	65	B4
Sirsa	65	C3
Sisak	45	D4
Sisŏphŏn	61	C4
Sisseton	97	G1
Sistema Central	39	E4
Sistema Iberico	39	E5
Sisteron	41	A6
Sitapur	65	D3
Siteia	47	J9
Sitges	39	M3
Sitka	93	D5
Sittard	33	H4
Sittwe	65	F4
Sivand	71	E1
Sivas	69	G4
Siverek	69	H5
Sivrihisar	47	P5
Siwa	75	E1
Siyäzän	69	N3
Sjælland	27	F9
Sjenica Jezero	45	G6
Skaerbaek	31	D1
Skagerrak	27	D8
Skardu	67	L2
Skawina	29	J8
Skegness	33	C1
Skellefteå	27	L4
Skiathos	47	F5
Skien	27	E7
Skikda	77	G1
Škofja Loka	41	K4
Skopelos	47	F5
Skopje	45	J7
Skövde	27	G7
Skowhegan	99	G2
Skuodas	27	L8
Skye	35	F4
Skyros	47	G6
Skyros	47	G6
Slagelse	31	G1
Slaney	35	F9
Slantsy	27	Q7
Slatina	45	M5
Slave Lake	93	J5
Slavonska Požega	45	E4
Slavonski Brod	45	F4
Slavyanka	59	F2
Sleaford	33	B1
Sligo	35	D7
Sliven	45	P7
Slobozia	45	Q5
Slonim	27	N10
Slough	33	B3
Slovakia	29	H9
Slovenia	41	K4
Słubice	29	D5
Slunj	41	L5
Słupca	29	G5
Słupsk	29	G3
Slyudyanka	55	G6
Smålandsfarvandet	31	G1
Smallwood Reservoir	93	U6
Smargon'	27	P9
Smederevo	45	H5
Smiths Falls	99	E2
Smoky	93	H6
Smoky Hills	101	B2
Smøla	27	D5
Smolensk	49	F4
Smolyan	47	G3
Smooth Rock Falls	99	D1
Smyrna	101	E3
Snæfell	27	(1)F2
Snake	97	C1
Snake River Plain	97	D2
Snåsavatnet	27	F4
Sneek	33	H1
Snežnik	41	K5
Snøhetta	27	E5
Snøtinden	27	G3
Snowdon	35	H8
Snowdrift	93	J4
Snowville	97	D2
Snyder	103	F2
Soalala	83	H3
Soanierana-Ivongo	83	H3
Soa-Siu	63	(2)C2
Sobral	109	J4
Sochi	69	H2
Socorro	103	E2
Socotra = Suquṭrā	67	F7
Sodankylä	27	P3
Söderhamn	27	J6
Södertälje	27	J7
Sodo	81	F2
Soest	33	L3
Sofia = Sofiya	45	L7
Sofiya	45	L7
Sofiysk	55	P6
Sõfu-gan	57	L5
Sognefjorden	27	C6
Sog Xian	65	F2
Sohåg	75	F2
Soignies	33	G4
Soissons	33	F5
Sokch'o	59	E4
Söke	47	K7
Sokhumi	69	J2
Sokode	79	E3
Sokol	49	H3
Sokolo	79	C2
Sokoto	79	F2
Sokoto	79	F2
Solander Island	89	A8
Solapur	65	C5
Solenzara	43	D7
Solikamsk	49	L3
Sol'-Iletsk	49	L4
Solingen	33	K3
Sollefteå	27	J5
Soller	39	N5
Solna	27	J7
Solomon Islands	85	F6
Solothurn	41	C3
Solov'yevsk	55	K6
Šolta	45	D6
Soltau	31	E4
Solway Firth	35	J7
Solwezi	83	D2
Soma	47	K5
Somalia	81	H2
Sombor	45	G4
Sombrerete	103	F4
Somerset	99	E2
Somerset Island	93	N2
Someş	45	K2
Somme	33	E4
Sömmerda	31	G5
Sømna	27	F4
Sondershausen	31	F5
Sondrio	41	E4
Songavatn	27	D7
Songea	81	F6
Song Hông	61	C2
Songhua	57	H1
Songhua	59	D1
Songhua Hu	59	D2
Songkhla	61	C5
Songnam	59	D5
Songnim	59	C4
Songo	83	E3
Songpan	57	C4
Sonid Yuoqi	57	E2
Sonid Zuoqi	57	E2
Son La	61	C2
Sonneberg	31	G6
Sonora	103	D3
Sonoyta	103	D2
Sonsorol Islands	63	(2)D1
Sopron	41	M3
Soracaba	111	M3
Sorel	99	F1
Sorgun	69	F4
Soria	39	H3
Sorø	31	G1
Soroca	45	R1
Sorong	63	(2)D3
Soroti	81	E3
Sørøya	27	L1
Sorrento	43	J8
Sortavala	27	R6
Sørvagen	27	G3
Sosnogorsk	53	J5
Sosnowiec	29	J7
Sos'va	49	M3
Sos'vinskaya	49	M2
Soto la Marina	103	G4
Soubré	79	C3
Sŏul	59	D5
Soulac-sur-Mer	37	D8
Soumussalmi	27	Q4
Soûr	70	C3
Sour el Ghozlane	39	P8
Souris	95	F2
Sousa	109	K5
Sousse	77	H1
South Africa	83	C6
South America	107	F5
Southampton	33	A4
Southampton Island	93	Q4
South Andaman	65	F6
South Atlantic Ocean	111	P6
South Australia	87	F5
South Bend	99	C2
South Carolina	101	E3
South Charleston	101	E2
South China Sea	61	E4
South Dakota	97	F2
South Downs	33	B4
South East Cape	87	J8
Southend-on-Sea	33	C3
Southern Alps	89	B6
Southern Cross	87	C6
Southern Indian Lake	93	M5
South Georgia	111	P9
South Harris	35	F4
South Hill	99	E3
South Island	89	B6
South Korea	59	D5
South Orkney Islands	112	(2)A3
South Pacific Ocean	111	P6
South Platte	97	F2
South Ronaldsay	35	K3
South Sandwich Islands	112	(2)C4
South Sandwich Trench	107	H9
South Saskatchewan	95	D1
South Shetland Islands	112	(2)MM4
South Taranaki Bight	89	D4
South Uist	35	E4
Southwest Cape	89	A8
South West Pacific Basin	85	L9
Southwold	33	D2
Sovetsk, *Russia*	27	L9

Name	Page	Grid
Sovetsk, *Russia*	49	J3
Soweto	83	D5
Sozopol	45	Q7
Spain	39	F5
Spalding	33	B2
Sparks	103	C1
Spartanburg	101	E3
Sparti	47	E7
Spassk-Dal'niy	59	G1
Spearfish	97	F2
Spencer	99	A2
Spencer Gulf	87	G6
Spey	35	J4
Speyer	33	L5
Spiekeroog	31	C3
Spišská Nová Ves	29	K9
Spitsbergen	112	(1)P2
Spittal	41	J4
Split	45	D6
Spokane	97	C1
Spoleto	43	G6
Sprague	97	C1
Spratly Islands	61	E4
Spremberg	31	K5
Spring	101	B3
Springbok	83	B5
Springe	31	E4
Springerville	103	E2
Springfield, *Colo., U.S.*	103	F1
Springfield, *Ill., U.S.*	99	C3
Springfield, *Mass., U.S.*	99	F2
Springfield, *Mo., U.S.*	99	B3
Springfield, *Oh., U.S.*	99	D3
Spring Hill	101	E4
Springs	83	D5
Springs Junction	89	D6
Springsure	87	J4
Springville	101	D3
Squamish	97	B1
Srbija	45	H6
Srbobran	45	G4
Sredenekolymsk	55	S3
Sredinnyy Khrebet	55	T6
Srednesibirskoye Ploskogor'ye	55	F3
Šrem	29	G5
Sretensk	55	K6
Sri Jayawardenapura-Kotte	65	D7
Srikakulam	65	D5
Sri Lanka	65	D7
Srinagar	65	B2
Stadlandet	27	C5
Staines	33	B3
Stalowa Wola	29	M7
Stamford, *U.K.*	33	B2
Stamford, *U.S.*	99	F2
Stanke Dimitrov	47	F2
Stanley, *Falkland Islands*	111	K9
Stanley, *U.S.*	97	F1
Stanovoye Nagor'ye	55	J5
Stanovoy Khrebet	55	L5
Starachowice	29	L6
Stara L'ubovňa	29	K8
Stara Pazova	45	H5
Stara Planina	47	F1
Staraya Russa	49	F3
Stara Zagora	45	N7
Starbuck Island	85	L6
Stargard Szczeciński	27	H10
Starnberg	41	G2
Starnberger See	41	G3
Start Point	37	B3
Staryy Oskol	49	G4
Statesboro	101	E3
Stavanger	27	C7
Stavropol'	69	J1
Stavropol'skaya Vovyshennost'	49	H5
Steens Mountains	97	C2
Stefansson Island	93	L2
Stein	31	G7
Steinach am Brenner	41	G3
Stendal	31	G4
Steno Antikythiro	47	F9
Sterling	97	F2
Sterlitamak	49	L4
Stevenage	33	B3
Stevens Point	99	C2
Stewart	93	F5
Stewart Island	89	A8
Steyr	41	K2
Stillwater	101	B2
Štip	47	E3
Stockerau	41	M2
Stockholm	27	K7
Stockton, *Calif., U.S.*	103	B1
Stockton, *Kans., U.S.*	103	G1
Stockton-on-Tees	35	L7
Stœng Trêng	61	D4
Stoke-on-Trent	35	K8
Stolac	45	F6
Stolberg	33	J4
Stollberg	31	H6
Stonehaven	35	K5
Stony Rapids	93	K5
Stora Lulevatten	27	K3
Stord	27	C7
Store Bælt	31	F1
Store Sotra	27	B6
Storlien	27	G5
Storm Lake	99	A2
Stornoway	35	F3
Storozhevsk	49	K2
Storsjön, *Sweden*	27	G5
Storsjön, *Sweden*	27	J6
Storuman	27	J4
Storuman	27	J4
Stour	33	C2
Stowmarket	33	D2
Stradella	41	E5
Strait of Bonifacio	43	D7
Strait of Dover	33	D4
Strait of Georgia	97	B1
Strait of Gibraltar	39	E9
Strait of Hormuz	71	G3
Strait of Juan de Fuca	97	B1
Strait of Malacca	63	(1)C2
Straits of Florida	101	E5
Strakonice	31	J7
Stralsund	27	G9
Stranraer	35	H7
Strasbourg	41	C2
Strasburg	99	D2
Stratford	99	D2
Stratford-upon-Avon	33	A2
Stratoni	47	F4
Straubing	41	H2
Straumnes	27	(1)B1
Strausberg	31	J4
Strehaia	45	L5
Strimonas	47	F4
Stromboli	43	K10
Strömsund	27	H5
Stronsay	35	K2
Struga	47	C3
Strumica	47	E3
Sturgeon Bay	99	C2
Sturt Stony Desert	87	G5
Stuttgart	41	E2
Suakin	75	G4
Subcule	75	H5
Subotica	45	G3
Suceava	45	P2
Sucre	109	D7
Sudan	75	E5
Sudan	79	D2
Suday	49	H3
Sudbury	99	D1
Sudd	81	E2
Sudová Vyshnya	29	N8
Suez = El Suweis	75	F2
Suez Canal	75	F1
Suḩār	71	G4
Suhl	31	F6
Suide	57	E3
Suifenhe	59	F1
Suihua	55	M7
Suir	35	E9
Suizhong	57	G2
Suizhou	57	E4
Sukabumi	63	(1)D4
Sukadana	63	(1)D3
Sukhona	49	H3
Sukkertoppen = Maniitsoq	93	W3
Sula	49	K1
Sulawesi	63	(2)A3
Sulgachi	55	N4
Sulingen	33	L2
Sullana	109	A4
Sulmona	43	H6
Sulphur Springs	101	B3
Sulu Archipelago	61	G5
Sulu Sea	61	F5
Sulzberger Bay	112	(2)CC2
Sumatera	63	(1)C2
Sumatra = Sumatera	63	(1)C2
Sumba	63	(2)A5
Sumbawa	63	(2)A4
Sumbawabesar	63	(2)A4
Sumbawanga	81	E5
Sumbe	83	A2
Šumen	69	B2
Sumenep	63	(1)E4
Sumisu-jima	59	L8
Summerville	101	E3
Šumperk	29	G8
Sumqayıt	69	N3
Sumter	101	E3
Sumy	49	F4
Sunch'ŏn	59	D6
Sun City	83	D5
Sundarbans	65	E4
Sunderland	35	L7
Sundsvall	27	J5
Sunnyvale	97	B3
Suntar	55	K4
Sunyani	79	D3
Suordakh	55	P3
Suoyarvi	49	F2
Superior	95	H2
Süphan Daği	69	K4
Suqian	57	F4
Suquţrā	67	F7
Sūr	67	G5
Surabaya	63	(1)E4
Surakarta	63	(1)E4
Surat	65	B4
Surat Thani	61	B5
Sûre	33	H5
Surgut	53	N5
Surgutikha	53	R5
Surigao	61	H5
Surin	61	C4
Surinam	109	F3
Surkhet	65	D3
Sürmaq	71	E1
Surt	77	J2
Surtsey	27	(1)C3
Susak	41	K6
Susanville	97	B2

Suşehri	69	H3	Syros	47	G7	Tajo = Tagus	39	G4
Susuman	55	R4	Syzran'	49	J4	Tak	61	B3
Sutherland	83	C6	Szamos	45	K1	Takaka	89	D5
Sutlej	65	B3	Szamotuły	29	F5	Takamatsu	59	H6
Suva	85	H7	Szczecin	29	D4	Takaoka	59	J5
Suwałki	29	M3	Szczecinek	29	F4	Takapuna	89	E3
Suweilih	70	C4	Szczytno	29	K4	Takasaki	59	K5
Suwŏn	59	D5	Szeged	45	H3	Takht	55	P6
Suzhou	57	G4	Székesfehérvár	45	F2	Takhta-Bazar	67	H2
Suzuka	59	J6	Szekszárd	45	F3	Takikawa	59	L2
Svalbard	112	(1)Q2	Szentes	45	H3	Takoradi	79	D4
Svalyava	45	L1	Szerencs	29	L9	Takum	79	G3
Sveg	27	H5	Szolnok	45	H2	Talak	77	F5
Svetac	45	C6	Szombathely	45	D2	Talara	109	A4
Svetlaya	55	P7				Talas	53	N9
Svetlogorsk	29	K3	**T**			Talavera de la Reina	39	F5
Svilengrad	47	J3				Talaya	55	S4
Svishtov	45	N6				Talca	111	G6
Svitovy	29	F8	Tab	45	F3	Talcahuano	111	G6
Svobodnyy	55	M6	Tabarka	43	C12	Taldykorgan	53	P9
Svratka	29	F8	Tábor	29	D8	Taliabu	63	(2)B3
Swain Reefs	87	K4	Tabor	55	R2	Talibon	61	G4
Swakopmund	83	A4	Tabora	81	E5	Talitsa	49	M3
Swan	107	C2	Tabou	79	C4	Tall 'Afar	69	K5
Swan Hill	87	H7	Tabrīz	69	M4	Tallahassee	101	E3
Swan Islands	105	H5	Tabūk	67	C4	Tall al Laḥm	71	B1
Swansea, *Australia*	87	J8	Tacheng	53	Q8	Tall Kalakh	70	D2
Swansea, *U.K.*	35	J10	Tachov	31	H7	Tallulah	95	H5
Swaziland	83	E5	Tacloban	61	H4	Tal'menka	53	Q7
Sweden	27	H6	Tacna	109	C7	Taloyoak	93	N3
Sweetwater	103	F2	Tacoma	95	B2	Talsi	27	M8
Świdnica	29	F7	Tacuarembó	111	K5	Taltal	111	G4
Świdnik	29	M6	Tadjoura	75	H5	Tamale	79	D3
Świdwin	29	E4	Tadmur	69	H6	Tamanrasset	77	G4
Świebodzin	29	E5	Tadoussac	99	G1	Tamanthi	65	G3
Swift Current	95	E1	Taech'ŏn	59	D5	Tambacounda	79	B2
Swindon	33	A3	Taegu	59	E6	Tambey	53	N3
Świnoujście	27	H10	Taejŏn	57	H3	Tambov	49	H4
Switzerland	41	C4	Tafalla	39	J2	Tambura	81	D2
Syalakh	55	L3	Tafila	70	C6	Tampa	101	E4
Sydney, *Australia*	87	K6	Taganrog	49	G5	Tampere	27	M6
Sydney, *Canada*	93	U7	Tagus	39	B5	Tampico	105	E4
Syke	33	L2	Tahiti	85	M7	Tamsagbulag	57	F1
Syktyvkar	49	K2	Tahoka	103	F2	Tamsweg	41	J3
Sylacauga	101	D3	Tahoua	79	F2	Tamworth	87	K6
Sylhet	65	F4	Tahrūd	71	G2	Tana, *Kenya*	81	G4
Sylt	27	E9	Tai'an	57	F3	Tana, *Norway*	27	P2
Sylvania	99	D2	T'ai-chung	57	G6	Tanacross	59	H7
Sym	53	R5	Taihape	89	E4	Tanacross	103	(1)J3
Sym	53	R5	T'ai-nan	57	G6	Tanaga Island	103	(3)C1
Symi	47	K8	T'ai-Pei	57	G6	T'ana Hāyk'	75	G5
Syracuse	99	E2	Taiping	63	(1)C1	Tanahjampea	63	(2)A4
Syrdar'ya	67	J1	T'ai-tung	61	G2	Tanami	87	E4
Syrdar'ya	53	L8	Taiwan	61	G2	Tanami Desert	87	F3
Syria	67	C3	Taiwan Strait	61	F2	Tandag	61	H5
Syrian Desert =			Taiyuan	57	E3	Tandil	111	K6
Bādiyat ash Shām	70	D4	Ta'izz	67	D7	Tanega-shima	59	F8
Syrna	47	J8	Tajikistan	67	J2			

Tanew	29	M7
Tanezrouft	77	E4
Tanga	81	F5
Tanger	77	D1
Tangmai	65	G2
Tangshan	57	F3
Tanimbar	85	D6
Tanjona Bobaomby	83	H2
Tanjona Vilanandro	83	G3
Tanjona Vohimena	83	H5
Tanjung	63	(1)F3
Tanjungbalai	63	(1)B2
Tanjung Datu	63	(1)D2
Tanjung d'Urville	63	(2)E3
Tanjungkarang =		
Telukbetung	63	(1)D4
Tanjungpandan	63	(1)D3
Tanjung Puting	63	(1)E3
Tanjungredeb	63	(1)F2
Tanjung Selatan	63	(1)E3
Tanjungselor	63	(1)F2
Tanjung Vals	63	(2)E4
Tankse	65	C2
Tanout	79	F2
Tanta	75	F1
Tan-Tan	77	C3
Tanzania	81	E5
Tao'an	57	G1
Taomasina	83	H3
Taormina	43	K11
Taos	103	E1
Taoudenni	77	E5
Tapachula	105	F6
Tapajós	109	F4
Tapsuy	49	M2
Tapuaenuku	89	D6
Tara	53	N6
Tarābulus	77	H2
Taracua	109	D3
Tarakan	61	F6
Taranaki =		
Mount Egmont	89	E4
Tarancón	39	H5
Taranto	43	M8
Tarapoto	109	B5
Tarare	37	K8
Tarawa	85	H5
Tarazona	39	J3
Tarbert	35	F4
Tarbes	37	F10
Tarcoola	87	F6
Taree	87	K6
Târgoviște	45	N5
Târgu Jiu	45	L4
Târgu Mureș	45	M3
Târgu-Neamț	45	P2
Târgu Ocna	45	P3
Tarif	71	E4

Name	Page	Grid
Tarija	111	J3
Tarim	53	Q9
Tarim Pendi	53	Q10
Taritatu	63	(2)E3
Tarko Sale	53	P5
Tarlac	61	G3
Tarn	37	H10
Tärnaby	27	H4
Tårnovo	47	K2
Tarnów	29	K7
Taro	41	E6
Taroudannt	77	D2
Tarquinia	43	F6
Tarragona	39	M3
Tarso Emissi	75	C3
Tarsus	69	F5
Tartagal	111	J3
Tartu	27	P7
Ţarţūs	70	C2
Tarvisio	41	J4
Tasbuget	49	N6
Tashkent	53	M9
Tash-Kömür	53	N9
Tashtagol	53	R7
Tasiilaq	93	Z3
Tasikmalaya	63	(1)D4
Tasman Bay	89	D5
Tasmania	87	H8
Tasmania	85	E10
Tasman Mountains	89	D5
Tasman Sea	89	B3
Tassili du Hoggar	77	F4
Tassili-n'-Ajjer	77	G3
Tasty	53	M9
Tata	45	F2
Tatabánya	45	F2
Tatarbunary	45	S4
Tatariya	49	J3
Tatarsk	53	P6
Tatarskiy Proliv	55	P7
Tateyama	59	K6
Tatvan	69	K4
Tauberbischofsheim	31	E7
Tauern	41	J4
Taumarunui	89	E4
Taungdwingyi	61	B2
Taungup	65	F5
Taunton	35	J10
Taunus	33	L4
Taupo	89	F4
Tauragė	29	M2
Tauranga	89	F3
Tauroa Point	89	D2
Tavda	49	N3
Tavda	49	N3
Tavoy	61	B4
Tawas City	99	D2
Tawau	63	(1)F2
Tawitawi	63	(1)F1
Taxkorgan	53	P10
Tay	35	J5
Tayga	53	R6
Taym	67	C4
Taymä'	75	G2
Taymylyr	55	L2
Tay Ninh	61	D4
Tayshet	55	F5
Taza	77	E2
Tazenakht	77	D2
Tāzirbū	75	D2
Tazovskiy	53	P4
Tazovskiy Poluostrov	53	N4
Tazungdam	61	B1
T'bilisi	69	L3
Tchibanga	79	G5
Tchin Tabaradene	77	G5
Tczew	29	H3
Te Anau	89	A7
Te Araroa	89	G3
Te Awamutu	89	E4
Teberda	69	J2
Tébessa	77	G1
Tebingtinggi	63	(1)B2
Tecuci	45	Q4
Tedzhen	67	H2
Tees	35	L7
Tegucigalpa	105	G6
Te Hapua	89	D2
Te Haroto	89	F4
Teheran = Tehrān	67	F2
Tehrān	67	F2
Teignmouth	35	J11
Tejo = Tagus	39	B5
Tekirda	47	K4
Tekirdağ	69	B3
Te Kuiti	89	E4
T'elavi	69	L3
Tel Aviv-Yafo	70	B4
Teles Pires	109	F5
Telford	35	K9
Telšiai	29	M2
Teltow	31	J4
Teluk Berau	63	(2)D3
Teluk Bone	63	(2)B3
Teluk Cenderawasih	63	(2)E3
Teluk Kumai	63	(1)E3
Teluk Tomini	63	(2)B2
Tema	79	D3
Temerloh	61	C6
Tempio Pausaria	43	D8
Temple	103	G2
Temryuk	69	G1
Temuco	111	G6
Ten Degree Channel	65	F7
Tendaho	75	H5
Ténéré	77	G5
Ténéré du Tafassasset	77	G4
Tenerife	77	B3
Ténès	77	F1
Tenkodogo	79	D2
Tennant Creek	87	F3
Tennessee	95	J4
Tennessee	91	K6
Tenojoki	27	P2
Teo	39	B2
Teófilo Otoni	109	J7
Tepic	95	F7
Teplice	29	C7
Terceira	77	(1)B2
Terek	69	L2
Teresina	109	J5
Tergnier	33	F5
Termez	67	J2
Termini Imerese	43	H11
Termirtau	53	N7
Termoli	45	C8
Ternate	63	(2)C2
Terneuzen	33	F3
Terni	43	G6
Ternitz	41	M3
Ternopil'	49	E5
Ternuka	89	C7
Terracina	43	H7
Terrassa	39	N3
Terre Haute	101	D2
Terry	97	E1
Terschelling	33	H1
Teruel	39	J4
Teseney	75	G4
Teshio	59	L1
Teslin	103	(1)L3
Tessalit	77	F4
Têt	37	H11
Tete	83	E3
Teterow	31	H3
Tétouan	77	D1
Tetovo	45	H8
Teulada	43	C10
Tevere	43	G6
Teverya	70	C4
Tevriz	49	P3
Te Waewae Bay	89	A8
Texarkana	101	C3
Texas	95	F5
Texel	33	G1
Thabazimbi	83	D4
Thailand	61	C4
Thai Nguyên	61	D2
Thames	35	L10
Thane	65	B5
Thanh Hoa	61	D3
Thar Desert	65	B3
Thasos	47	G4
Thasos	47	G4
Thaton	61	B3
The Bahamas	101	F4
The Dalles	97	B1
Thedford	97	F2
The Fens	33	B2
The Gambia	79	A2
Thelon	93	L4
The Minch	35	F3
The Naze	33	D3
Thenia	39	P8
Theniet el Had	39	N9
The Pas	93	L6
Thermaikos Kolpos	47	E4
Thermopolis	97	E2
The Solent	33	A4
Thessaloniki	47	E4
Thetford Mines	99	F1
The Wash	35	N9
The Weald	33	B3
The Whitsundays	87	J4
Thiers	37	J8
Thiès	79	A2
Thika	81	F4
Thimphu	65	E3
Þingvallavatn	27	(1)C2
Thionville	33	J5
Thira	47	H8
Thira	47	H8
Thiruvananthapuram	65	C7
Thisted	27	E8
Thiva	47	F6
Þjórsá	27	(1)D2
Thompson	93	M5
Thompson	93	H6
Thompson Falls	97	C1
Þorshöfn	27	(1)F1
Thouars	37	E7
Thrakiko Pelagos	47	H4
Three Forks	97	D1
Three Kings Island	89	C2
Thuin	33	G4
Thun	41	C4
Thunder Bay	99	C1
Thuner See	41	C4
Thüringer Wald	31	F6
Thurso	35	J3
Tīāb	71	G3
Tianjin	57	F3
Tianmen	57	E4
Tianqiaoling	59	E2
Tianshui	57	D4
Tianshuihai	67	L2
Tiaret	77	F1
Tibati	79	G3
Tibboburra	87	H5
Tibesti	75	C3
Tibet = Xizang	65	E2

Name		Page	Grid
Tichît	●	77	D5
Tichla	●	77	C4
Ticino	◪	41	D4
Ticul	●	105	G4
Tidjikdja	●	77	C5
Tieling	●	59	B2
Tielongtan	●	65	C1
Tien Shan	�	53	Q9
Tiétar	◪	39	E4
Tiflis = T'bilisi	■	73	H1
Tifton	●	101	E3
Tighina	●	45	S3
Tignère	●	79	G3
Tigris	◪	69	K6
Tijuana	●	95	C5
Tikanlik	●	53	R9
Tikhoretsk	●	49	H5
Tikhvin	●	49	F3
Tikrît	●	69	K6
Tiksi	●	55	M2
Tilburg	●	33	H3
Tilichiki	●	55	V4
Tillamook	●	97	B1
Tilos	🏝	47	K8
Timanskiy Kryazh	▲	49	K2
Timaru	●	89	C7
Timber Creek	●	87	F3
Timerloh	●	63	(1)C2
Timimoun	●	77	F3
Timişoara	●	45	J4
Timmins	●	99	D1
Timor	🏝	63	(2)C4
Timor Sea	◩	87	E2
Timor Timur	◪	63	(2)C4
Tinaca Point	◿	85	C5
Tindouf	●	77	D3
Tinglev	●	31	E2
Tingri	●	65	E3
Tingsryd	●	29	E1
Tinnsjø	◪	27	E7
Tinogasta	●	111	H4
Tinos	🏝	47	H7
Tinsukia	●	65	G3
Tipperary	●	35	D9
Tirana = Tiranë	■	47	B3
Tiranë	■	47	B3
Tiraspol	●	45	S3
Tire	●	47	K6
Tiree	🏝	35	F5
Tirschenreuth	●	31	H7
Tirso	◪	43	C9
Tiruchchirāppalli	●	65	C6
Tirunelveli	●	65	C7
Tirupati	●	65	C6
Tiruppur	●	65	C6
Tiruvannamalai	●	65	C6
Tisa	◪	45	H4
Tišnov	●	29	F8
Tisza	◪	29	M9
Tiszafüred	●	45	H2
Titu	●	45	N5
Tivoli	●	43	G7
Tiyās	●	70	E2
Tizi Ouzou	●	77	F1
Tiznit	●	77	D3
Tlemcen	●	77	E2
Tobago	🏝	105	M6
Tobelo	●	63	(2)C2
Tobermorey	●	87	G4
Tobermory	●	99	D1
Toboali	●	63	(1)D3
Tobol	●	49	M4
Tobol	◪	49	M4
Tobol'sk	●	49	N3
Tobseda	●	49	K1
Tocantins	◙	109	H5
Tocantins	◪	109	H5
Tocopilla	●	111	G3
Todi	●	43	G6
Tofino	●	97	A1
Togo	Ⓐ	79	E3
Tōjō	●	59	G6
Tokat	●	67	C1
Tokelau	🏝	85	J6
Tokmak	●	53	P9
Tokoroa	●	89	E4
Toktogul	●	53	N9
Tokushima	●	59	H6
Tokuyama	●	59	F6
Tōkyō	●	59	K6
Tolaga Bay	●	89	G4
Tôlañaro	●	83	H4
Tolbo	●	53	S8
Toledo, *Spain*	●	39	F5
Toledo, *U.S.*	●	99	D2
Toliara	●	83	G4
Tolitoli	●	63	(2)B2
Tol'ka	●	53	Q5
Tolmezzo	●	41	J4
Tolmin	●	41	J4
Tolosa	●	39	H1
Tol'yatti	●	49	J4
Tom'	◪	53	R6
Tomah	●	99	B2
Tomakomai	●	59	L2
Tomari	●	55	Q7
Tomaszów Lubelski	●	29	N7
Tomaszów Mazowiecki	●	29	K6
Tombouctou	●	77	E5
Tombua	●	83	A3
Tomelloso	●	39	H5
Tomini	●	63	(2)B2
Tomsk	●	53	Q6
Tonalá	●	105	F5
Tondano	●	63	(2)B2
Tønder	●	31	D2
Tonga	Ⓐ	85	J7
Tonga Islands	🏝	85	J8
Tongareva	🏝	85	K6
Tonga Trench	◎	85	J8
Tongchuan	●	57	D4
Tongeren	●	33	H4
Tonghae	●	59	E5
Tonghua	●	59	C3
Tongliao	●	57	G2
Tongling	●	57	F4
Tongyu	●	57	G2
Tónichi	●	95	E6
Tonk	●	65	C3
Tônlé Sab	◪	61	C4
Tönning	●	31	D2
Tonopah	●	97	C3
Toora-Khem	●	53	T7
Toowoomba	●	87	K5
Topeka	◻	95	G4
Topliţa	●	45	N3
Topock	●	103	D2
Topol'čany	●	29	H9
Torbali	●	47	K6
Torbat-e Heydarīyeh	●	67	G2
Torbat-e Jām	●	67	H2
Torells	●	39	N2
Torgau	●	31	H5
Torhout	●	33	F3
Torino	●	41	C5
Tori-shima	🏝	59	L8
Torneälven	◪	27	L3
Torneträsk	◪	27	K2
Tornio	●	27	N4
Toro	●	39	E3
Toronto	◻	99	E2
Toros Dağları	▲	69	E5
Torquay	●	35	J11
Torre de Moncorvo	●	39	C3
Torrelavega	●	39	F1
Torremolinos	●	39	F8
Torrent	●	39	K5
Torreón	●	103	F3
Torres Strait	◿	87	H2
Torres Vedras	●	39	A5
Torrington	●	97	F2
Tortolì	●	43	D9
Tortona	Ⓐ	41	D6
Tortosa	●	39	L4
Tosa-wan	◿	59	G7
Totaranui	●	89	D5
Tot'ma	●	49	H3
Tottori	●	59	H6
Touggourt	●	77	G2
Toul	●	37	L5
Toulon	●	37	L10
Toulouse	●	37	G10
Toummo	●	77	H4
Toungoo	●	61	B3
Tourcoing	●	33	F4
Tournai	●	33	F4
Tours	●	37	F6
Towanda	●	99	E2
Townsville	●	87	J3
Toyama	●	59	J5
Toyohashi	●	59	J6
Tozeur	●	77	G2
Trâblous	●	70	C2
Trabzon	●	69	H3
Tracy	●	99	A2
Trail	●	97	C1
Tralee	●	35	C9
Tralee Bay	◿	35	B9
Tramán Tepuí	▲	109	E2
Tranås	●	27	H7
Trang	●	61	B5
Trangan	🏝	63	(2)D4
Transantarctic Mountains	◎	112	(2)B1
Trapani	●	43	G11
Traun	●	41	K2
Traunreut	●	41	H3
Traversay Islands	🏝	107	H9
Traverse City	●	99	C2
Travnik	●	45	E5
Trbovlje	●	41	L4
Třebíč	●	29	E8
Trebinje	●	45	F7
Trebišov	●	45	J1
Trebon	●	41	K1
Tregosse Islets	🏝	87	K3
Trelew	●	111	H7
Trelleborg	●	27	G9
Tremp	●	39	L2
Trenčín	●	29	H9
Trent	◪	35	M8
Trento	●	41	G4
Trenton, *Canada*	●	99	E2
Trenton, *U.S.*	◻	99	F2
Tres Arroyos	●	111	J6
Três Corações	●	109	H8
Tres Esquinas	●	109	B3
Tres Lagos	●	111	G8
Treuchtlingen	●	41	F2
Treviglio	●	41	E5
Treviso	●	41	H5
Trichur	●	65	C6
Trier	●	33	J5
Trieste	●	41	J5
Triglav	▲	41	J4
Trikala	●	47	D5
Trikomon	●	70	A1
Trincomalee	●	65	D7
Trinidad	🏝	109	E1
Trinidad, *Bolivia*	●	109	E6
Trinidad, *U.S.*	●	103	F1

170

Name	Pg	Grid	Name	Pg	Grid	Name	Pg	Grid	Name	Pg	Grid
Trinidad and Tobago	109	E1	Tuktoyaktuk	103	(1)L2	Tutonchany	55	E4	Uh	45	K1
Tripoli, *Greece*	47	E7	Tula	49	G4	Tutuila	85	K7	Uherské Hradiště	29	G8
Tripoli = Trâblous, *Lebanon*	70	C2	Tulare	97	C3	Tuvalu	85	H6	Uiju	59	C3
Tripoli = Tarābulus, *Libya*	77	H2	Tulcea	45	R4	Tuxpan	95	G7	Uil	49	K5
Tristan da Cunha	73	B9	Tulsa	95	G4	Tuxtla Gutiérrez	105	F5	Uil	49	K5
Trivandrum = Thiruvananthapuram	65	C7	Tulun	55	G6	Tuy Hoa	61	D4	Uinta Mountains	97	D2
Trnava	45	E1	Tulung La	65	F3	Tuz Gölü	69	E4	Uitenhage	83	D6
Troisdorf	31	C6	Tulu Weiel	81	E2	Tuzla	45	F5	Ujiji	81	D4
Trois Rivières	99	F1	Tumaco	109	B3	Tver'	49	G3	Ujjain	65	C4
Troitsk	49	M4	Tumen	59	E2	Tweed	35	K6	Ujung Pandang	63	(2)A4
Troitsko-Pechorsk	49	L2	Tumkur	65	C6	Twin Falls	97	D2	Ukhta	53	J5
Trojan	47	G2	Tunceli	69	H4	Tylkhoy	55	U4	Ukiah	97	B3
Trollhättan	27	G7	Tunduru	83	F2	Tynda	55	L5	Ukkusissat	93	W2
Tromsø	27	K2	Tundzha	45	P8	Tyne	35	K6	Ukmergė	29	P2
Trondheim	27	F5	Tungir	55	L5	Tynemouth	35	L6	Ukraine	25	G3
Trondheimsfjörden	27	E5	Tungku	63	(1)F1	Tyra	53	S7	Ulaanbaatar	55	H7
Trotuş	45	P3	Tungusk	53	S5	Tyrnavos	47	E5	Ulaangom	53	S8
Troy, *Al., U.S.*	101	D3	Tunis	77	H1	Tyrrhenian Sea	43	F8	Ulan Bator = Ulaanbaatar	57	D1
Troy, *N.Y., U.S.*	99	F2	Tunisia	77	E2	Tysa	29	N9	Ulan-Ude	55	H6
Troyan	45	M7	Tunja	109	C2	Tyumen'	53	M6	Ulchin	59	E5
Troyes	37	K5	Tupelo	101	D3	Tyva	55	F6	Ulety	55	J6
Trujillo, *Peru*	109	B5	Tupper Lake	99	F2				Ulhasnagar	65	B5
Trujillo, *Spain*	39	E5	Tura, *India*	65	F3				Uliastay	53	T8
Truro	93	U7	Tura, *Russia*	55	G4	**U**			Ulindi	81	D4
Trutnov	29	E7	Turan	53	S7	Uaupés	109	D3	Ullapool	35	G4
Tryavana	47	H2	Turangi	89	E4	Ubá	109	J8	Ullŭng do	59	F5
Trzebnica	29	G6	Turayf	75	G1	Ubaitaba	109	K6	Ulm	41	F2
Tsetserleg	55	G7	Turbat	67	H4	Ubangi	81	B3	Ulongue	83	E2
Tshabong	83	C5	Turbo	109	B2	Ube	59	F7	Ulsan	59	E6
Tshane	83	C4	Turda	45	L3	Úbeda	39	G6	Ulu	55	M4
Tshikapa	81	C5	Turek	45	H5	Uberaba	109	H7	Ulubat Gölü	47	L4
Tshuapa	81	C4	Turgay	53	L8	Uberlândia	109	H7	Uluqqat	67	K2
Tsiafajavona	83	H3	Turgay	53	L8	Überlingen	41	E3	Ulukışla	69	F5
Tsimlyanskoy Vodokhranilishche	49	H5	Turgayskaya Stolovaya Strana	53	L7	Ubon Ratchathani	61	C3	Ulungur Hu	53	R8
Ts'khinvali	69	K2	Türgovishte	45	P6	Ubrique	39	E8	Uluru	87	F5
Tsugaru-kaikyō	59	L3	Turgutlu	47	K6	Ucayali	109	B5	Ul'yanovsk	49	J4
Tsumeb	83	B3	Turhal	69	G3	Ucharal	53	Q8	Umeå	27	L5
Tsumkwe	83	C3	Turin = Torino	41	C5	Uckermark	31	J3	Umeälven	27	J4
Tsuruga	59	J6	Turiy Rog	59	F1	Uda	55	F5	Umfolozi	83	E5
Tsuruoka	59	K4	Türkeli Adası	47	K4	Udachnyy	55	J3	Ummal Arānib	77	H3
Tsuyama	59	H6	Turkestan	53	M9	Udaipur	65	B4	Umm al Jamājim	71	A3
Tual	63	(2)D4	Turkey	69	D4	Uddevalla	27	F7	Umm Durman	75	F4
Tuapse	69	H1	Turkmenbashi	67	F1	Udine	41	J4	Umm Qaşr	71	B1
Tubarão	111	M4	Turkmenistan	67	G2	Udmurtiya	49	K3	Umm Ruwaba	75	F5
Tübingen	41	C4	Turks and Caicos Islands	105	K4	Udon Thani	61	C3	Umnak Island	103	(1)E5
Tubruq	75	D1	Turku	27	M6	Ueda	59	K5	Umtata	83	D6
Tubuai	85	M8	Turnhout	33	G3	Uele	81	C2	Unalakleet	103	(1)E3
Tubuai Islands	85	L8	Turnu Măgurele	45	M6	Uelen	55	AA3	Unalaska Island	103	(1)E5
Tucson	103	D2	Turpan	53	R9	Uel'kal	55	Y3	Ungava Bay	93	T5
Tucumcari	103	F1	Turpan Pendi	53	S9	Uelzen	31	F4	Ungheni	45	Q2
Tucuruí	109	H4	Turquino	107	D2	Ufa	49	L3	Unije	41	K6
Tudela	39	J2	Turugart Pass	53	P9	Ufa	49	L4	Unimak Island	103	(1)D5
Tuguegarao	61	G3	Turukhan	55	C3	Uganda	81	E3	Union	99	B3
Tugur	55	P6	Turukhansk	53	R4	Uglegorsk	55	Q7	United Arab Emirates	67	F5
Tui	39	B2	Tuscaloosa	101	D3	Uglich	49	G3	United Kingdom	35	G6
			Tuscola	101	D2	Ugljan	41	L6	United States	91	M5
			Tuticorin	65	C7	Ugol'nyye Kopi	55	X4	Unraven	103	E1
									Unst	35	M1

Unzha	49	H3
Upernavik	93	W2
Upernavik Kujalleq	93	V2
Upington	83	C5
Upolu	85	J7
Upper Hutt	89	E5
Upper Klamath Lake	97	B2
Upper Lough Erne	35	E7
Uppsala	27	J7
Urakawa	59	M2
Ural	49	K5
Ural Mountains =		
Ural'skiy Khrebet	25	L1
Ural'sk	49	K4
Ural'skiy Khrebet	25	L1
Urambo	81	E5
Uranium City	93	K5
Uray	49	M2
Urbana	99	D2
Urbino	41	H7
Urdzhar	53	Q8
Uren'	49	J3
Urgench	67	H1
Uritskiy	49	N4
Urla	47	J6
Uroševac	45	J7
Uro-teppa	67	J2
Urt	57	C2
Uruguaiana	111	K4
Uruguay	111	K5
Uruguay	111	K5
Ürümqi	53	R9
Uryupinsk	49	H4
Urziceni	45	P5
Usa	53	L4
Uşak	69	C4
Usedom	31	J3
Usingen	31	D6
Usk	35	J10
Usol'ye Sibirskoye	55	G6
Ussel	37	H8
Ussuriysk	57	J2
Ust'-Alekseyevo	49	J2
Ust'-Barguzin	55	H6
Ust' Chaun	55	W3
Ustica	43	H10
Ust'-Ilimsk	55	G5
Ústí nad Labem	29	D7
Ust'-Ishim	53	N6
Ust'-Kamchatsk	55	U5
Ust'-Kamenogorsk	53	Q8
Ust'-Khayryuzovo	55	T5
Ust'-Kulom	49	K2
Ust'-Kut	55	G5
Ust'-Kuyga	55	P3
Ust'-Labinsk	69	H1
Ust'-Maya	55	N4
Ust'-Nera	55	Q4
Ust'-Omchug	55	R4
Ust' Ozernoye	55	D5
Ust' Penzhino	55	V4
Ust'-Tatta	55	N4
Ust'-Tsil'ma	53	J4
Ust' Usa	49	L1
Ust'-Uyskoye	53	L7
Usu	53	Q9
Utah	95	D4
Utena	27	N9
Uthal	67	J4
Utica	99	E2
Utiel	39	J5
Utrecht	33	H2
Utrera	39	E7
Utsjoki	27	P2
Utsunomiya	59	K5
Uttaradit	61	C3
Uummannarsuaq	93	Y5
Uvat	49	N3
Uvinza	81	E5
Uvira	81	D4
Uvs Nuur	53	S7
Uy	53	M4
Uyar	53	S6
Uyuni	111	H3
Uzbekistan	53	L9
Uzhhorod	45	K1
Užice	45	G6

V

Vaal	83	D5
Vaasa	27	L5
Vác	45	G2
Vadodara	65	B4
Vadsø	27	Q1
Vaduz	41	E3
Vaganski Vhr	41	L6
Vakh	53	Q2
Valbonnais	41	A6
Valdagno	41	G5
Valdepeñas	39	G6
Valdivia	111	G6
Val-d'Or	99	E1
Valdosta	95	K5
Valdres	27	E6
Valence	37	K9
Valencia, Spain	39	K5
Valencia, Venezuela	109	D1
Valencia de Alcántara	39	C5
Valenciennes	33	F4
Vălenii de Munte	45	P4
Valentine	97	F2
Valenza	41	D5
Valjevo	45	G5
Valka	27	N8
Valkeakoski	27	N6
Valladolid	39	F3
Valledupar	109	C1
Vallejo	97	B3
Valletta	43	J13
Valley of the Kings	75	F2
Valli di Comacchio	41	H6
Valmiera	27	N8
Valparai	65	C6
Valparaíso, Chile	111	G5
Valparaíso, Mexico	103	F4
Val'tevo	49	H2
Valverde del Camino	39	D7
Van	69	K4
Vanadzor	69	L3
Vancouver, Canada	97	B1
Vancouver, U.S.	97	B1
Vancouver Island	93	F7
Vandalia	101	D2
Van Diemen Gulf	87	F2
Vänern	27	G7
Van Gölü	69	K4
Van Horn	103	F2
Vanimo	63	(2)F3
Vankarem	55	Y3
Vanna	27	K1
Vännäs	27	K5
Vannes	37	C6
Vanrhynsdorp	83	B6
Vantaa	27	N6
Vanua Levu	85	H7
Vanuatu	85	G7
Vanzevat	49	N2
Varanasi	65	D3
Varangerfjorden	27	R2
Varaždin	45	D3
Varazze	41	D6
Varberg	27	G8
Vardar	47	E3
Vardø	27	R1
Varel	31	D7
Varese	41	D5
Vârful Moldoveanu	45	M4
Vârfurile	45	K3
Varginha	111	M3
Varna	69	B2
Värnamo	27	H8
Vaslui	45	Q3
Västerås	27	J7
Västervik	27	J8
Vasvár	41	M3
Vathia	47	E8
Vatican City	43	F7
Vatnajökull	27	(1)E2
Vättern	27	H7
Vaughn	103	E2
Vawkavysk	29	P4
Växjö	27	H8
Vayuniya	65	D7
Vazhgort	49	J2
Vecht	33	J2
Vechta	33	L2
Veendam	33	J1
Vega	103	F1
Vega	27	F4
Vegreville	93	J6
Vejer de la Frontera	39	E8
Vela Luka	45	D7
Velenje	43	K2
Velenje	41	L4
Veles	47	D3
Vélez-Málaga	39	F8
Velikiye Luki	49	F3
Velikiy Ustyug	49	J2
Veliko Türnovo	45	N6
Velita Kladuša	41	L5
Velký Krtíš	29	J9
Velletri	43	G7
Vellore	65	C6
Vel'sk	49	H2
Velten	31	J4
Velva	97	F1
Venaria	41	C5
Vendôme	37	G6
Venezia	41	H5
Venezuela	109	D2
Veniaminof Volcano	103	(1)F4
Venice = Venézia	41	H5
Venice	101	D4
Venlo	33	J3
Venray	33	H3
Venta	49	D3
Ventimiglia	41	C7
Ventspils	27	L8
Vera	39	J7
Veracruz	105	E5
Veraval	65	B4
Verbania	41	D5
Vercelli	41	D5
Verdalsøra	27	F5
Verden	31	E4
Verdun	33	H5
Vereeniging	83	D5
Vereshchagino	55	D4
Verín	39	C3
Verkhneimbatsk	55	D4
Verkhnetulomskoe		
Vodokhranilishche	27	R2
Verkhniy Baskunchak	49	J5
Verkhnyaya Amga	55	M5
Verkhnyaya Toyma	49	J2
Verkhnyaya Tura	49	L3
Verkhovyna	45	M1
Verkhoyansk	55	N3
Verkhoyanskiy Khrebet	55	M3
Vermillion	97	G2

Name	Page	Ref
Vermont	95	M3
Vernal	97	E2
Vernon, *France*	33	D5
Vernon, *U.S.*	101	B3
Verona	41	F5
Versailles	33	E6
Verviers	33	H4
Veselí	41	N2
Vesoul	31	B9
Vesterålen	27	G2
Vestfjorden	27	G3
Vestmannaeyjar	27	(1)C3
Vestvagøy	27	G2
Vesuvio	43	J8
Veszprém	45	E2
Vetluga	49	J3
Vezirköprü	69	F3
Viana do Castelo	39	B3
Viangchan	61	C3
Viareggio	41	F7
Viborg	27	E8
Vibo Valentia	43	L10
Vic	39	N3
Vicenza	41	G5
Vichy	37	J7
Vicksburg	101	C3
Victor Harbor	87	G7
Victoria	87	H7
Victoria	111	G6
Victoria	51	J10
Victoria, *Canada*	97	B1
Victoria, *Malta*	43	J12
Victoria, *Seychelles*	83	(2)C1
Victoria, *U.S.*	101	B4
Victoria de las Tunas	105	J4
Victoria Falls	83	D3
Victoria Island	93	J2
Victoria Land	112	(2)W2
Victoria West	83	C6
Videle	45	N5
Vidin	45	K6
Viedma	111	J7
Vienna = Wien	41	M2
Vienne	37	K8
Vienne	37	F7
Vientiane = Viangchan	61	C3
Vierzon	37	H6
Vieste	43	L7
Vietnam	61	D3
Viêt Tri	61	D2
Vigan	61	G3
Vigevano	41	D5
Vigia	109	H4
Vigo	39	B2
Viho Valentia	43	L10
Vijayawada	65	D5
Vik	27	(1)D3
Vikna	27	E4
Vila Nova de Gaia	39	B3
Vilanova y la Geltru	39	M3
Vila Real	39	C3
Vila-real	39	K5
Vilhelmina	27	J4
Vilhena	109	E6
Viljandi	27	N7
Villablino	39	D2
Villacarrillo	39	G6
Villach	41	J4
Villacidro	43	C9
Villa Constitución	95	D7
Villafranca	41	F5
Villagarcia	39	B2
Villahermosa	105	F5
Villalba	39	C1
Villaldama	103	F3
Villaputzu	43	D9
Villarrobledo	39	H5
Villavicencio	109	C3
Villaviciosa	39	E1
Villefranche-sur-Saône	37	K8
Villeurbanne	37	K8
Villingen	41	D2
Vilnius	27	N9
Vilsbiburg	41	H2
Vilshofen	41	J2
Vilvoorde	33	G4
Vilyuy	55	L4
Vilyuysk	55	L4
Vimoutiers	33	C6
Vimperk	41	J1
Viña del Mar	111	G5
Vinaròs	39	L4
Vincennes	101	D2
Vinh	61	D3
Vinnytsya	49	E5
Vinson Massif	112	(2)JJ2
Vipiteno	41	G4
Vir	41	L6
Virac	61	G4
Virden	97	F1
Vire	33	B6
Virginia	95	L4
Virginia	99	B1
Virginia Beach	99	E3
Virgin Islands, *U.K.*	107	E2
Virgin Islands, *U.S.*	107	E2
Virovitica	45	E4
Virton	33	H5
Virtsu	27	M7
Vis	45	D6
Visalia	97	C3
Visby	27	K8
Viscount Melville Sound	93	J2
Viseu, *Brazil*	109	H4
Viseu, *Portugal*	39	C4
Vişeu de Sus	45	M2
Vishakhapatnam	65	D5
Visselhövede	31	E4
Vistula = Wisła	25	F2
Viterbo	43	G6
Viti Levu	85	H7
Vitim	55	J5
Vitolište	47	D3
Vitória	111	N3
Vitória da Conquista	109	J6
Vitoria-Gasteiz	39	H2
Vitry-le-François	33	G6
Vitsyebsk	49	F3
Vittel	41	A2
Vittorio Veneto	41	H5
Viveiro	39	C1
Vize	47	K3
Vizhas	49	J1
Vizianagaram	65	D5
Vizinga	53	H5
Vladikavkaz	69	L2
Vladimir	49	H3
Vladivostok	59	F2
Vlieland	33	G1
Vlissingen	33	F3
Vlorë	47	B4
Vltava	29	D8
Vöcklabruck	41	J2
Vogelsberg	31	E6
Voghera	41	D6
Vohipeno	83	H4
Voi	81	F4
Voinjama	79	C3
Voitsberg	41	L3
Vojens	31	E1
Vojvodina	45	G4
Volary	31	J8
Volcán Antofalla	111	H4
Volcán Barú	105	H7
Volcán Citlaltépetl	91	L7
Volcán Cotopaxi	109	B4
Volcán San Pedro	111	H3
Volcán Tajumulco	105	F5
Volgodonsk	49	H5
Volgograd	49	H5
Völkermarkt	41	K4
Volkhov	49	F3
Volksrust	83	D5
Volochanka	53	S3
Vologda	49	H3
Volos	47	E5
Volterra	41	F7
Volzhskiy	49	H5
Vorderrhein	41	E4
Vordingborg	31	G1
Voreios Evvoïkos Kolpos	47	E6
Voreria Pindos	47	C4
Vorkuta	49	M1
Vormsi	27	M7
Voronezh	49	G4
Vorstershoop	83	C5
Võru	27	P8
Vosges	41	C2
Voss	27	D6
Vostochno-Sibirskoye More	55	U2
Vostochnyy Sayan	53	T7
Vostok Island	85	L6
Votkinsk	53	J6
Vozhgora	49	J2
Vranje	45	J7
Vratsa	45	L6
Vrbas	45	G4
Vrbas	45	E5
Vrendenburg	83	B6
Vršac	45	J4
Vryburg	83	C5
Vsetín	29	G8
Vukovar	45	G4
Vuktyl'	49	L2
Vung Tau	61	D4
Vuotso	27	P2
Vyatka	49	K3
Vyborg	27	Q6
Vychegda	49	K2
Vyshniy Volochek	49	F3
Vytegra	49	G2

W

Name	Page	Ref
Wa	79	D3
Waal	33	H3
Wabē Shebelē Wenz	81	G2
Waco	101	B3
Wad Banda	75	E5
Waddān	75	C2
Waddeneilanden	33	G1
Waddenzee	33	H1
Wādī al Fārigh	75	C1
Wādī al Hamīm	75	D1
Wadi Halfa	75	F3
Wad Medani	75	F5
Wafangdian	57	G3
Wagga Wagga	87	J7
Wahiawa	103	(2)C2
Wahpeton	97	B1
Waiau	89	D6
Waidhofen	41	K3
Waigeo	63	(2)D3
Waiheke Island	89	E3
Waihi	89	E3
Waikabubak	63	(2)A4
Waikato	89	E4
Wailuku	103	(2)E3
Waimate	89	C7
Waingapu	87	B1

Name	Page	Grid
Wainwright	103	(1)F1
Waiouru	89	E4
Waipara	89	D6
Waipukurau	89	F5
Wairoa	89	F4
Waitakaruru	89	E3
Waitaki	89	C7
Waitangi	89	(1)B1
Waitara	89	E4
Waiuku	89	E3
Wajir	81	G3
Wakasa-wan	59	H6
Wakayama	59	H6
Wake Island	85	G4
Wakkanai	59	L1
Wałbrzych	29	F7
Walcheren	33	F3
Wałcz	29	F4
Wales	35	J9
Walgett	87	J6
Walkerville	87	J7
Walla Walla	97	C1
Wallis et Futuna	85	J7
Walpole	87	C6
Walsall	35	L9
Walsenburg	97	F3
Walsrode	31	E4
Walvis Bay	83	A4
Wamba	81	D3
Wanaka	89	B7
Wandel Sea	91	A1
Wandingzhen	61	B2
Wanganui	89	E4
Wanganui	89	E4
Wangerooge	31	C3
Wan Hsa-la	61	B2
Wanxian	57	D4
Wanyuan	57	D4
Warangal	65	C5
Warburg	31	D5
Ward	89	E5
Wardha	65	C4
Waremme	33	H4
Waren	31	H3
Warka	29	L6
Warmandi	63	(2)D3
Warm Springs	97	C3
Warren	99	D2
Warrensburg	99	B3
Warrenton	83	C5
Warri	79	F3
Warrington, U.K.	35	K8
Warrington, U.S.	101	D3
Warrnambool	87	H7
Warsaw = Warszawa	29	K5
Warszawa	29	K5
Warta	29	F5
Wasatch Range	103	D1
Wasco	103	C1
Washington	97	B1
Washington D.C.	91	J6
Watampone	63	(2)B3
Waterford	35	E9
Waterloo	99	B2
Watertown, N.Y., U.S.	99	E2
Watertown, S.D., U.S.	97	G1
Waterville	99	G2
Watford	33	B3
Watford City	97	F1
Watrous	93	K6
Watsa	81	D3
Watseka	101	D1
Watson Lake	103	(1)M3
Wau	81	D2
Waukegan	99	C2
Waukesha	99	C2
Waverly	99	C3
Wavre	33	G4
Wawa	99	D1
Wāw al Kabīr	75	C2
Waxxari	53	R10
Waycross	101	E3
Weaverville	97	B2
Weber	89	F5
Webi Shaabeelle	81	G3
Weddell Sea	112	(2)A2
Weed	97	B2
Weert	33	H3
Weiden	31	H7
Weifang	57	F3
Weihai	57	G3
Weilburg	31	D6
Weimar	31	G6
Weinan	57	D4
Weipa	87	H2
Weiser	97	C2
Wejherowo	29	H3
Welkom	83	D5
Welland	33	B2
Wellesley Islands	87	G3
Wellington	89	E5
Wells	97	C2
Wellsboro	99	E2
Wellsford	89	E3
Wels	41	K2
Wenatchee	97	B1
Wenchang	61	E3
Wenga	81	B3
Wenman	109	(1)A1
Wentworth	87	H6
Wenzhou	57	G5
Werder	81	H2
Wertheim	31	E7
Wesel	33	J3
Wesel Dorsten	31	B5
Weser	31	E4
Wessel Islands	87	G2
West Antarctica	112	(2)GG2
West Bank	70	C4
Western Australia	87	D5
Western Cape	83	B6
Western Ghats	65	B5
Western Sahara	77	C4
Westerschelde	33	F3
Westerstede	33	K1
Westerwald	33	K4
West Falkland	111	J9
West Glacier	97	D1
West Palm Beach	101	E4
West Plains	99	B3
Westport	89	C5
Westray	35	J2
West Siberian Plain = Zapadno-Sibirskaya Ravnina	51	L3
West Virginia	99	D3
West Wendover	97	D2
West Yellowstone	97	D2
Wetar	63	(2)C4
Wetaskiwin	93	J6
Wetumpka	101	D3
Wetzlar	31	D6
Wexford	35	F9
Weyburn	95	F2
Whakatane	89	F3
Whalsay	35	M1
Whangarei	89	E2
Wharfe	35	L7
Wheeler Peak	103	E1
Wheeling	101	E1
White Bay	93	V6
Whitefish Point	99	C1
Whitehorse	103	(1)L3
White Island	89	F3
Whitemark	87	J8
White Mountain Peak	97	C3
White Mountains	93	S8
White Nile = Bahr el Abiad	75	F5
White Sea = Beloye More	49	G1
White Sulphur Springs	97	D1
White Volta	79	D3
Whitney	89	E1
Whyalla	87	G6
Wichita	101	B2
Wichita Falls	101	B3
Wick	35	J3
Wickenburg	103	D2
Wicklow Mountains	35	F8
Wieluń	29	H6
Wien	41	M2
Wiener Neustadt	41	M3
Wieringermeer Polder	33	G2
Wiesbaden	31	D6
Wiesloch	31	D7
Wiesmoor	31	C3
Wigan	35	K8
Wilbur	97	C1
Wilcannia	87	H6
Wildeshausen	31	D4
Wilhelmshaven	31	D3
Wilkes Land	112	(2)U2
Willemstad	109	D1
Williams, Australia	87	C6
Williams, U.S.	97	B3
Williams Lake	93	G6
Williamson	101	E2
Williamsport	99	E2
Willis Group	87	K3
Williston	97	F1
Williston Lake	93	G5
Willow River	99	B1
Willow Springs	99	B3
Wilmington	101	F3
Wilson's Promontory	87	J7
Wiluna	87	D5
Winchester	35	L10
Windhoek	83	B4
Windorah	87	H5
Windsor, U.K.	33	B3
Windsor, U.S.	101	F2
Windward Islands	105	N6
Windward Passage	107	D2
Winfield, Al., U.S.	101	D3
Winfield, Kans., U.S.	103	G1
Winisk	93	P5
Winnemucca	97	C2
Winnipeg	93	M7
Winona	99	B2
Winsen	31	F3
Winslow	103	D1
Winston-Salem	99	D3
Winterberg	31	D5
Winterthur	41	D3
Winton, Australia	87	H4
Winton, New Zealand	89	B8
Wisconsin	95	H2
Wisconsin Rapids	99	C2
Wisła	29	H8
Wisła	29	H4
Wisłoka	29	L8
Wismar	31	G3
Wissembourg	31	C7
Witney	33	A3
Wittenberge	31	G3
Wittenoom	87	C4
Wittlich	33	J5
Wittmund	31	C3
Wittstock	31	H3
Witzenhausen	31	E5
Wkra	29	K5

Name	Page	Grid
Włocławek	29	J5
Włodawa	29	N6
Wokam	63	(2)D4
Wolf Creek	97	D1
Wolfenbüttel	31	F4
Wolf Point	97	E1
Wolfratshausen	41	G3
Wolfsberg	41	K4
Wolfsburg	31	F4
Wolgast	31	J2
Wollaston Lake	93	K5
Wollaston Peninsula	93	H3
Wollongong	87	K6
Wołomin	29	L5
Wolverhampton	35	K9
Wŏnju	59	D5
Wŏnsan	59	D4
Woodland	97	B3
Woodstock	99	G1
Woodville, *New Zealand*	89	E5
Woodville, *Miss., U.S.*	101	C3
Woodville, *Tex., U.S.*	101	C3
Woodward	97	G3
Worcester, *South Africa*	83	B6
Worcester, *U.K.*	35	K9
Workington	35	J7
Worland	97	E2
Worms	31	D7
Worthing	35	M11
Wosu	63	(2)B3
Wotu	63	(2)B3
Wowoni	63	(2)B3
Wrangell	93	E5
Wrangell Mountains	93	C4
Wrexham	35	K8
Wrigley	93	G4
Wrocław	29	G6
Wubu	57	E3
Wuchuan	57	E2
Wuday'ah	67	E6
Wudu	57	C4
Wuhai	57	D3
Wuhan	57	E4
Wuhu	57	F4
Wüjang	65	C2
Wukari	79	G4
Wuli	65	F2
Wunstorf	31	E4
Wuppertal	31	C5
Würzburg	31	E7
Wurzen	31	H5
Wusuli	57	J1
Wuwei	57	C3
Wuxi	57	F4
Wuxu	61	D2
Wuyuan	57	D2
Wuzhong	57	D3
Wuzhou	61	E2
Wye	35	J9
Wyndham	87	E3
Wyoming	95	E3
Wytheville	101	E2

X

Name	Page	Grid
Xaafuun	81	J1
Xaçmaz	69	N3
Xaidulla	53	P10
Xainza	65	E2
Xai-Xai	83	E4
Xam Nua	61	C2
Xankändi	69	M4
Xanten	33	J3
Xanthi	47	G3
Xapuri	109	D6
Xar Moron	55	K8
Xi	57	E6
Xiamen	61	F2
Xi'an	57	D4
Xiangcheng	57	E4
Xiangfan	57	E4
Xiangtan	57	E5
Xianyang	57	D4
Xichang	61	C1
Xigazê	65	E3
Xilinhot	57	F2
Xingtai	57	F3
Xingu	109	G5
Xingyi	61	C1
Xining	57	C3
Xinjin	57	G3
Xinmin	59	B2
Xintai	57	E3
Xinxiang	57	E3
Xinyang	57	E4
Xinyuan	53	Q9
Xique Xique	109	J6
Xiushu	57	E5
Xi Xiang	57	D4
Xizang	65	E2
Xizang Gaoyuan	65	D2
Xuanhua	57	E2
Xuchang	57	E4
Xun	61	E2
Xuwen	61	E2
Xuzhou	57	F4

Y

Name	Page	Grid
Ya'an	57	D3
Yabēlo	81	F3
Yablonovyy Khrebet	55	J6
Yabuli	59	E1
Yacuma	109	D6
Yadgir	65	D5
Yagodnyy	49	N3
Yakima	97	B1
Yako	79	D2
Yaksha	49	L2
Yaku-shima	59	F8
Yakutat	103	(1)K4
Yakutsk	55	M4
Yala	61	C5
Yalova	47	M4
Yalta	69	F1
Yalu	59	D3
Yalutorovsk	49	N3
Yamagata	59	L4
Yamaguchi	59	F6
Yamarovka	55	J6
Yambio	81	D3
Yambol	45	P7
Yamdena	63	(2)D4
Yamoussoukro	79	C3
Yampil'	45	R1
Yamsk	55	S5
Yan'an	57	D3
Yanbu'al Baḥr	67	C5
Yancheng	57	G4
Yandun	57	A2
Yangbajain	65	F2
Yangdok	59	D4
Yangjiang	61	E2
Yangon	57	B3
Yangquan	57	E3
Yangtze = Chang Jiang	57	D4
Yangzhou	57	F4
Yanhuqu	65	D2
Yanji	59	E2
Yankton	97	G2
Yano-Indigirskaya Nizmennost'	55	N2
Yanqi	53	R9
Yanqing	57	F2
Yanshan	61	C2
Yanskiy Zaliv	55	N2
Yantai	57	G3
Yaoundé	79	G4
Yap	85	D5
Yapen	63	(2)E3
Yaqui	95	E6
Yardımcı Burnu	47	E8
Yare	33	D2
Yaren	85	G6
Yarensk	49	J2
Yarlung Zangbo	65	F3
Yarmouth	93	T8
Yaroslavl'	49	G3
Yar Sale	49	P1
Yashkul'	49	J5
Yāsūj	71	D1
Yatağan	47	L7
Yatsushiro	59	F7
Yavari	109	C5
Yawatongguzlangar	53	Q10
Yaya	53	R6
Yazd	67	F3
Yazoo City	101	C3
Ydra	47	F7
Ye	61	B3
Yecheng	67	L2
Yefremov	49	G4
Yei	81	E3
Yekaterinburg	49	M3
Yelets	49	G4
Yell	35	L1
Yellowknife	93	J4
Yellow River = Huang He	57	C3
Yellow Sea	57	G3
Yellowstone	97	E1
Yellowstone Lake	97	D2
Yelwa	79	E2
Yemen	67	D7
Yemetsk	49	H2
Yengisar	67	L2
Yenisey	53	S6
Yeniseyskiy Kryazh	53	S5
Yerbogachen	55	H4
Yerevan	69	L3
Yermak	53	P7
Yermitsa	49	K1
Yershov	49	J4
Yerupaja	109	B6
Yerushalayim	70	C5
Yesil'	49	N4
Yeşilköy	47	L4
Yessey	53	U4
Yevlax	69	M3
Yevpatoriya	49	F5
Yeysk	49	G5
Yibin	57	C5
Yichang	57	E4
Yichun, *China*	57	E5
Yichun, *China*	57	H1
Yilan	57	H1
Yıldız Dağları	47	K2
Yinchuan	57	D3
Yingkou	57	G2
Yining	53	Q9
Yirga Alem	81	F2
Yitulihe	55	L6
Yiyang	57	E5
Yli-Kitka	27	Q3
Ylivieska	27	N4
Yoakum	101	B4
Yogyakarta	63	(1)E4
Yokadouma	79	G4
Yokohama	59	K6

Yokosuka . . . . ● 59 K6
Yokote . . . . ● 59 L4
Yola . . . . ● 79 G3
Yonago . . . . ● 59 G6
Yonezawa . . . . ● 59 L5
Yongxiu . . . . ● 57 F5
York, *U.K.* . . . . ● 35 L8
York, *U.S.* . . . . ● 97 G2
Yorkton . . . . ● 93 L6
Yoshkar Ola . . . . ▣ 49 J3
Yōsu . . . . ● 59 D6
Youngstown . . . . ● 99 D2
Yozgat . . . . ● 69 F4
Yreka . . . . ● 97 B2
Ystad . . . . ● 29 C2
Ysyk-Köl . . . . ● 53 P9
Yuan 61 C2
Yuanmou . . . . ● 61 C1
Yuanping . . . . ● 57 E3
Yucatán . . . . ●105 F5
Yucatan Channel 105 G4
Yudoma 55 Q4
Yuendumu . . . . ● 87 F4
Yueyang . . . . ● 57 E5
Yugoslavia . . . . △ 45 H6
Yukagirskoye
   Ploskogor'ye . . . . . . ● 55 S3
Yukon . . . . 103 (1)E3
Yukon Territory . . . . ▣ 103 (1)K2
Yukorskiy Poluostrov . . . ● 53 L4
Yukta . . . . ● 55 H4
Yulin, *China* . . . . ● 61 E2
Yulin, *China* . . . . ● 57 D3
Yuma . . . . ●103 C2
Yumen . . . . ● 57 B3
Yuogi Feng . . . . ▲ 53 R8
Yurga . . . . ● 53 Q6
Yurimaguas . . . . ●109 B5
Yuroma . . . . ● 49 J1
Yu Shan . . . . ▲ 61 G2
Yushkozero . . . . ● 27 S4
Yushu, *China* . . . . ● 57 B4
Yushu, *China* . . . . ● 57 H2
Yutian . . . . ● 53 Q10
Yuyao . . . . ● 57 G4
Yuzhno Kuril'sk . . . . ● 59 N1
Yuzhno-Sakhalinsk . . . . . ● 55 Q7
Yuzhno-Sukhokumsk . . . . ● 69 L1
Yverdon-les-Bains . . . . . . ● 41 B4

Yvetot . . . . ● 33 C5

Z

Zaanstad . . . . ● 33 G2
Ząbkowice Śląskie . . . . . ● 29 F7
Zabok . . . . ● 41 L4
Zābol . . . . ● 67 H3
Zacatecas . . . . ●103 F4
Zadar . . . . ● 41 L6
Zafra . . . . ● 39 D6
Zagora . . . . ● 77 D2
Zagreb . . . . ■ 41 L5
Zāhedān . . . . ● 67 H4
Zahirabad . . . . ● 65 C5
Zahlé . . . . ● 70 C3
Zahrān . . . . ● 67 D6
Zaječar . . . . ● 45 K6
Zakamensk . . . . ● 55 G6
Zākhō . . . . ● 69 K5
Zakynthos . . . . ● 47 C7
Zakynthos . . . . ● 47 C7
Zalaegerszeg . . . . ● 41 M4
Zalău . . . . ● 45 L2
Zalim . . . . ● 67 D5
Zaliv Aniva 55 Q7
Zaliv Kara-Bogaz Gol . . . 67 F1
Zaliv Paskevicha 49 L5
Zaliv Shelikhova 55 T5
Zambezi . . . . ● 83 C2
Zambezi 83 E3
Zambia . . . . △ 83 D2
Zamboanga . . . . ● 61 G5
Zamora . . . . ● 39 E3
Zamość . . . . ● 29 N7
Zanjān . . . . ● 69 N5
Zanzibar . . . . ● 81 F5
Zanzibar Island 81 F5
Zapadnaya Dvina 49 E3
Zapadno-Sibirskaya
   Ravnina . . . . ● 53 L5
Zapadnyy Sayan . . . . . . ▲ 53 S7
Zapata . . . . ●103 G3
Zaporizhzhya . . . . ● 49 G5
Zaprešić . . . . ● 41 L5
Zaqatala . . . . ● 69 M3
Zara . . . . ● 69 G4
Zarafshan . . . . ● 53 L9

Zaragoza . . . . ● 39 K3
Zarand . . . . ● 71 G1
Zaranj . . . . ● 67 H3
Zarasai . . . . ● 27 P9
Zaria . . . . ● 79 F2
Zarqā' . . . . ● 70 D4
Zarqān . . . . ● 71 E2
Żary . . . . ● 29 E6
Zarzadilla de Totana . . . . . ● 39 J7
Žatec . . . . ● 29 C7
Zavidovići . . . . ● 45 F5
Zavitinsk . . . . ● 55 M6
Zēḇāk . . . . ● 67 K2
Zeebrugge . . . . ● 33 F3
Zefat . . . . ● 70 C4
Zeilona Góra . . . . ● 29 E6
Zeitz . . . . ● 31 H5
Zelenoborskiy . . . . ● 27 S3
Zelenogradsk . . . . ● 29 K3
Zelenokumsk . . . . ● 69 K1
Zell am See . . . . ● 41 H3
Zémio . . . . ● 81 D2
Zemlya Alexsandry 53 G1
Zemlya Frantsa-Iosifa . . . 53 J2
Zemlya Vil'cheka 53 L1
Zenica . . . . ● 45 E5
Zermatt . . . . ● 41 C4
Zeven . . . . ● 31 E3
Zeya . . . . ● 55 M6
Zeyskoye
   Vodokhranilishche . . . 55 M5
Zgierz . . . . ● 29 J6
Zgorzelec . . . . ● 29 E6
Zhaltyr . . . . ● 49 N4
Zhambyl . . . . ● 53 N9
Zhanatas . . . . ● 53 M9
Zhangguangcai Ling . . . 57 H2
Zhangjiakou . . . . ● 57 E2
Zhangling . . . . ● 55 L6
Zhangwu . . . . ● 57 G2
Zhangye . . . . ● 57 B3
Zhangzhou . . . . ● 61 F2
Zhanjiang . . . . ● 61 E2
Zhaoqing . . . . ● 61 E2
Zharkamys . . . . ● 53 K8
Zharma . . . . ● 53 Q8
Zhaxigang . . . . ● 65 C2
Zheleznogorsk . . . . ● 49 G4
Zhengzhou . . . . ● 57 E4

Zhenjiang . . . . ● 57 F4
Zherdevka . . . . ● 49 H4
Zhezkazgan . . . . ● 53 M8
Zhigansk . . . . ● 55 L3
Zhob . . . . ● 67 J3
Zholymbet . . . . ● 53 N7
Zhongba . . . . ● 65 D3
Zhongdian . . . . ● 57 B5
Zhongshan . . . . ● 61 E2
Zhucheng . . . . ● 57 F3
Zhumadian . . . . ● 57 E4
Zhuo Xian . . . . ● 57 F3
Zhytomyr . . . . ● 49 E4
Zibo . . . . ● 57 F3
Zigong . . . . ● 57 C5
Ziguinchor . . . . ● 77 B6
Žilina . . . . ● 29 H8
Zillah . . . . ● 75 C2
Zima . . . . ● 55 G6
Zimbabwe . . . . △ 83 D3
Zinder . . . . ● 79 F2
Zittau . . . . ● 31 K6
Ziway Hāyk' 81 F2
Zlatoust . . . . ● 49 L3
Zlín . . . . ● 29 G8
Złotów . . . . ● 29 G4
Zomba . . . . ● 83 F3
Zonguldak . . . . ● 47 P3
Žovka . . . . ● 29 N7
Zrenjanin . . . . ● 45 H4
Zug . . . . ● 41 D3
Zugdidi . . . . ● 69 J2
Zugspitze . . . . ▲ 31 F9
Zunyi . . . . ● 57 D5
Županja . . . . ● 45 F4
Zürich . . . . ● 41 D3
Zvishavane . . . . ● 83 E4
Zvolen . . . . ● 29 J9
Zvornik . . . . ● 45 G5
Zwedru . . . . ● 79 C3
Zweibrücken . . . . ● 33 K5
Zwettl . . . . ● 41 L2
Zwickau . . . . ● 31 H6
Zwiesel . . . . ● 31 J7
Zwolle . . . . ● 33 J2
Zyryanka . . . . ● 55 S3
Zyryanovsk . . . . ● 53 Q8